D0078259

THE DIALECT OF THE TRIBE

THE DIALECT
OF
THE TRIBE

*Speech and Community
in Modern Fiction*

Margery Sabin

New York   Oxford
OXFORD UNIVERSITY PRESS
1987

Oxford University Press

Oxford   New York   Toronto
Delhi   Bombay   Calcutta   Madras   Karachi
Petaling Jaya   Singapore   Hong Kong   Tokyo
Nairobi   Dar es Salaam   Cape Town
Melbourne   Auckland

and associated companies in
Beirut   Berlin   Ibadan   Nicosia

Library of Congress Cataloging-in-Publication Data
Sabin, Margery, 1940-
The dialect of the tribe.
Includes index.
1. English fiction—20th century—History and criticism.
2. Speech in literature. 3. James, Henry, 1843–1916. Golden bowl.
4. Joyce, James, 1882–1941. Ulysses. 5. Lawrence, D. H. (David Herbert),
1885–1930—Criticism and interpretation. 6. Beckett, Samuel, 1906-
Criticism and interpretation. 7. Literature, Comparative—English
and French. 8. Literature, Comparative—French and English. I. Title.
PR888.S64S23   1987   823'.912'09   86-8431
ISBN 0-19-504153-4 (alk. paper)

10 8 6 4 2 1 3 5 7 9
Printed in the United States of America on acid-free paper

For my mother
Syd Feldstein Mauser

ACKNOWLEDGMENTS

Robert Garis has been an invaluable friend to this book throughout; I have benefited enormously from his deep and detailed engagement with all the novelists discussed here. I am grateful also to Richard Poirier and Thomas E. Edwards, editors of *Raritan Quarterly,* and to James Maddox, each of whom gave generous encouragement and editorial help at crucial stages in the work. My several points of contention with Leo Bersani will, I trust, in no way blur the extent of my long-standing debt to his provocative mind and work.

Other friends and colleagues have also helped me by their responses and suggestions: William Cain, Adele Dalsimer, Anne Davidson Ferry, David Ferry, Philip Finkelpearl, Arthur Gold, Marie-Hélène Gold, Eugene Goodheart, Timothy Peltason, William Pritchard, Patricia Meyer Spacks, L. Terryll Tyler, William Youngren. My family has steadily kept me in mind of what this book is about: my husband, James E. Sabin, by his subtle psychological understanding—both general and personal—and our sons, Michael Sabin and Paul Sabin, by their relish for story and talk and their willingness to put up with so much of both from me.

A fellowship from the Bunting Institute in 1978–79 supported the initial work for this book; a grant from the National Endowment for the Humanities in the fall of 1985 gave me time to complete it. I am grateful to Wellesley

College for providing sabbatical leaves in 1980–81 and in the fall of 1985—and, in addition, for making a Mellon grant available for a released unit from teaching in the fall of 1983. Mary-Ann Winkelmes devoted many careful and patient hours to early preparation of the manuscript.

Earlier versions of chapters 1 and 2 appeared in *Raritan Quarterly* (Fall 1981; Winter 1982; Winter 1985) and are reprinted by permission. Part of Chapter 6 first appeared, in an earlier version, in *Prose Studies* (Spring 1982) and is reprinted by permission.

CONTENTS

THE DIALECT OF THE TRIBE

Introduction

I could give all to Time except—except
What I myself have held. But why declare
The things forbidden that while the Customs slept
I have crossed to Safety with? For I am There,
And what I would not part with I have kept.

—ROBERT FROST

Robert Frost likes to display his power to evade impassive authorities bent on leveling the world—even the authority of Time. He can keep what he wants to save by his way of declaring, or rather *not* declaring, his most precious possessions. The witty figuring of Time's servant as a kind of dull-witted customs official is resonant not only for Frost's bravado generally but perhaps even more for the English-language fiction that is the subject of this book. One or another kind of smuggling past the barrier of customs may be detected in all the novels I discuss, and the image even elucidates certain practices of literary criticism in this century, including perhaps my own. Certainly for F. R. Leavis, Frost's pun on "Customs" has resonance in suggesting how mere conventions— old or new—present more of an obstacle than a protection for personally cherished things. Leavis, like Frost, saw himself crossing over into an inhospitable era where those things most valued by him were being discarded by the customs of the time. The one salvageable possession might be language itself—expressive, dramatic, personal language, as Frost in his poem does so craftily manage to save it, if only by avoiding any outright declaration of what he is up to.[1]

3

The novelists grouped together in this book—Henry James, D. H. Lawrence, James Joyce, and Samuel Beckett—were all significantly more intrepid crossers of boundaries than Robert Frost—or F. R. Leavis. In relation to the fiction of this century, Leavis himself sometimes plays the inglorious role of a kind of customs official, examining and sorting out what foreign products should or should not be allowed into English fiction. All four novelists, by contrast, were famous venturers into foreign territories. Not content to stay at home—wherever home initially was—they also never completely crossed over into the safety of any other place where they became fully at home. For them, the activity of smuggling, in relation to language and culture, becomes an even more complex two-way traffic, crossing national as well as temporal boundaries. Some novels by Lawrence and Joyce were, in actuality, contraband for a long time in England and Ireland and America; less literally, all these novelists bring into English fiction alien things, imports from France and elsewhere. At the same time, and no less importantly, they stealthily take certain things with them out of situations willingly and even willfully left behind. And for them, too, the drama is centered intensely in language. They were all, in their separate ways, masters of that dramatic, expressive, idiomatic English so variously "kept," in Frost's word, by writers and readers in English since Shakespeare. If their novels present even more elusive dramas than Frost's poetry, that is partly because they are even more indirect than he in not declaring exactly which qualities of the English tradition they have chosen to keep and which to discard—what, after all, they may in effect save, even in the midst of radical gestures of repudiation.

At our late date, the repudiations of these great modern novelists may need less new attention than their strong, if also often ambivalent, actions of holding on to what they present themselves as giving up. Their experimentation includes, even thrives on, intense, unresolved dramas of affiliation and withdrawal, especially in relation to inherited values of language. By now, modernist experimentation has passed so fully into our literary consciousness that the survival rather than the subversion of speech values in literature is what requires demonstration. Literary theory imported from France has now made a whole generation of English-language readers and critics entirely at home in decoding apparently expressive language according to the patterns of self-deception or conformity that French authorities have declared to be lurking everywhere behind the appearances of all kinds of language. The systematic "deconstruction" of verbal designs in literature flattens out the kind of ambivalence I want to identify in James, Lawrence, Joyce, and Beckett. Even words like "ambivalence" must now be smuggled back into the language of criticism.

For James, Lawrence, Joyce, and Beckett, however, the speech forms of language now given up so impassively by critical theory escape systematic rejection because they are associated with such personal and even dangerously uncontrollable forces of life, and with forms of knowing and acting not readily contained in any system. I will argue that this association is itself handed down through identifiable habits and tendencies in the English tradition, where French-style intellectual disdain for the familiar and the illogical never entirely cancels out responsiveness to quite diverse signs in language of human energy, resourcefulness, and sheer physical vitality. Without ascribing to the expectation that language works primarily as an instrument for absolute self-manifestation or thoroughly rational knowledge, this English tradition endorses the constitutive force of language as it serves desires for self-assertion and the forging of relationship: between past and present, self and world, and even between the depths and surfaces of the individual personality. In focusing on four writers who so vigorously sought freedom from all conventional and settled wisdom, I will be dealing with this tradition in radically disrupted form—shaken up and broken down, reappropriated only after, or in the midst of, loud rejections—but present in striking form nonetheless.

The fact that James, Lawrence, Joyce, and Beckett—a good slate for the greatest modern novelists in English—cannot even be securely classified as English novelists gives an initial measure of their elusiveness. "English," as an inherited language, still more as a culture or social community, is very far from a clearly declared value for them.

To start with, Beckett: the last and in certain obvious ways the most radical. With the composition of *Molloy* in the late 1940s, Beckett transposed himself into a French novelist; the English versions of Beckett's trilogy, completed in the late fifties, are works of self-translation from French into English. They are the work, moreover, of an Irish writer who, by the very fact of his Irishness, had an eccentric relationship to his "native" English language all along. In Beckett's case, the estrangement from English culture endemic to Irish writers was further intensified by the odd intersection of his literary career with that of Joyce, his Irish predecessor in Paris and a sufficiently disorienting case in his own right. Although at the time of *Ulysses* Joyce's established distance from both Irish and English voices paradoxically freed him to allow every version of the English language to circulate in his prose without his earlier, more rigid, irony, Joyce's development after *Ulysses* took another line. The "revolution of the word" in *Finnegans Wake* all but broke the connection with English and any other single vernacular. For Beckett, it was Joyce's last, most artificial stylistic phase which first exerted the most influence. The Paris of 1928–30 was for Beckett mainly the circle gathered in deferential service to Joyce's *Work in Progress,* later entitled *Finnegans Wake.* Beckett's expatriation thus had the doubly peculiar effect of distancing him from the ordinary voices of his English-speaking home-land, while also enclosing him in a circle of worship around the most extraordinarily denaturalized writing in English of the time. In the early thirties, whether back in Ireland or wandering in England, Germany, or again in France, the only English-language writer Beckett evidently carried with him was Joyce—except for Samuel Johnson, about whom he began a never-to-be-finished play.

Beckett got his biggest help toward a radically un-Joycean style from his reading in French—for example, from Jules Renard's long, often colloquial, and intimate journal and from Céline's *Voyage au bout de la nuit* (which he declared in 1937 to be "the greatest novel in both French and English literature").[2] Still, it was not until the mid-forties, with Joyce dead and Beckett himself established in an independent Parisian life, that Beckett began to grapple with his own dark truths of style. And it was only five years later that he began to translate this original achievement back into a strangely intimate, colloquial English, as if he had kept certain voices in his head all the time, along with certain models of English-Irish speech from the Joyce of *Ulysses.*

Moving from Beckett's trilogy back to *Ulysses,* however, presents but another linguistic and cultural tangle, for it is hardly more accurate—and perhaps even more politically offensive—to call Joyce's great book an *English* novel. While the language of *Ulysses* is entirely accessible, and even pleasurably familiar in idiom to any English-language reader (with a bit of help from the annotators), Joyce's language and content are also steeped in Irish (which is to say specifically anti-English) coloring. Of course Joyce is hardly less aggressive in *Ulysses* toward Irish verbal, social, and religious institutions. The systematic parodic experiments in the second half of the novel stop just short of repudiating all versions of English as instruments for any expressive purpose. Yet the humor and vitality of the book are impossible to separate from its saving as well as damning representations of familiar English speech forms.

Common English, abused and abusive as Joyce felt it to be, was still valuable enough to be among the chief possessions from home that he took with him to the Continent. Indeed, far more than Beckett, Joyce almost superstitiously carried around a considerable collection of souvenirs as reminders of home. One of the most curious was the large portrait of his father which he took from one flat to another in Paris. More significantly, he carried in his mind very exact sound images of his father's voice. But in contrast to his fictional character, Stephen Dedalus, who is merely haunted, if not actually possessed, by hostile voices, Joyce succeeded in taking powerful possession himself. He liked to tell people how he had appropriated his father's jokes, stories, songs, and turns of phrase, distributing them among more than one character in his fictions. Richard Ellmann reports Joyce remarking in 1931, the year his father died, "The humour of *Ulysses* is his; its people are his friends. The book is his spittin' image."[3] Ellmann also helps us to see how Joyce transposed whole anecdotes from his family memories into *Finnegans Wake,* where John Joyce's witty voice is not entirely suppressed even by the artificially fabricated language. By 1931 there is something excessive in Joyce's elaborate mourning for the father he had refused to visit through all the intervening years, just as there is an unnerving willfulness of performance in the extraordinary deformations of English in the style of *Finnegans Wake.* But earlier, with his father alive in Dublin and himself at a safe distance in Trieste, Rome, Zurich, and Paris, Joyce managed a delicate equilibrium which allowed him to release, in all its living indignity, the English-language voice of his father, along with the voices of his father's friends, enemies, neighbors—indeed, the whole repudiated Dublin community. Although this language is never altogether liberated from Joyce's ironic control in *Ulysses,* the authorial rein is so much looser than in his earlier (and later) fiction that we are never forced, or even allowed, to stop short in final judgments. Flight from possessive, intrusive, oppressive voices might have been a prerequisite for Joyce's personal and artistic independence, but his writing also discloses the value to him of a continuing connection to those voices: to declare absolute separation, even if it were possible, would be to risk the independence only of sterility or even death.

D. H. Lawrence, at first glance, seems a much simpler case: a genuine *English* novelist, right down to an intimacy with local dialect that affiliates him with a whole line of earlier English fiction. Indeed, as a novelist of the lesser ranks of English society, his working-class origins make him even better, more "natural," than middle-class predecessors like George Eliot. Lawrence's provincial and working-class background, however, dislocated him in relation to the English literary culture of his day almost as much as if he had been a colonial. Alienated from his original home, never at home in London, he eventually left England altogether. Moreover, Lawrence nurtured rather than minimized his aggrieved sense of separateness even while in England. In the end, his extreme marginality was half-chosen, half-imposed by such circumstances as the banning of *The Rainbow,* tuberculosis, and the official distrust he suffered during World War I for his marriage to Frieda, a German. However the multiple reasons are sorted, the outcome is the famous Laurentian saga of self-exile, intensified (as in the case of Joyce) by brutal official acts of censorship that cut him off for most of his life from any natural relationship with an English reading public. And in Lawrence's case, too, the biographic facts of dislocation matter because they underlie bold, even violent, repudiations of conventional English language in the novels. Lawrence's aggressive physico-mystical jargon, even his wrenchings of diction and syntax, violate the norms of English prose with hardly less audacity than Joyce's pseudonarrative styles in *Ulysses.* The early British reviewers of *The Rainbow* recognized this violence in Lawrence's language and cried out against it as much as against the supposed sexual indecency.[4] Yet Lawrence's style, even in *The Rainbow* and *Women in Love,* also returns for crucial infusions of strength to common forms of spoken English, devised with as much dramatic and expressive force by him as by any English novelist of any period. Lawrence often goes so far as to tie the destiny of his characters to their powers of vital speech; like his characters, Lawrence both strains against the confines of common English and relies on it as a resource for sanity and survival. His fiction cannot part with English speech forms, at least not without becoming hysterical or, more simply, inert.

Finally, though chronologically first, there is Henry James, considered here in the major, last phase of his career, when the ambiguities of his relationship to the larger community of English language and culture become most acute. As an American (also a "colonial"), James's expatriation in some respects resembles that of Joyce and Beckett, except that James (and his American circle) had an entirely different cordiality toward everything English. By the time of the late novels, James was at home in England and famous both there and in America. He had attained eminence with an English-language reading public whose standards of decency he not only respected but refined almost past comprehension. It is, of course, this very push in the late James toward the outermost boundary of intelligibility that so oddly raises the question for him, too, of exactly what he wishes either to preserve or reject. Like Lawrence, Joyce, and Beckett, James radically and, in a sense, willfully disrupted his community of understanding with both English and American readers by strange and elaborate de-formations of familiar English style. And even certain members of his own intimate circle were dismayed by this extravagance, beginning with his brother William, who complained about the obscurity of *The Golden Bowl,*[5] and continuing through a succession of critics who "draw the line" if not before *The Golden Bowl* then between Volumes One and Two (as other, and sometimes the same, critics draw the line of acceptability down the middle of *Ulysses* or in between *Malone Dies* and *The Unnamable*).

In sum, I have gathered here a most trouble-making group of novelists—writers who went to considerable lengths to make many kinds of trouble both for themselves and for readers and critics. As a linguistic instrument for their modern fiction, the English language demonstrates its flexibility for the most varied individual dramas, involving all those psychological and social, as well as artistic, structures in which language participates as both substance and sign. The single choice between conformity and alienation, so often seen in the formulations of the French avant-garde since Flaubert, does not at all exhaust the possibilities that these writers enact. The very differences of verbal texture and design in the novels by James, Lawrence, Joyce, and Beckett show an astonishing variety of imaginative movements away from and also back into common English. Nostalgia for a more settled allegiance to English traditions has made conservative Anglo-American criticism balk at the extravagant inventiveness of the boldest modern writers in the language. But the equally settled categories of subversion imported from the French modernist tradition are just as inadequate to these verbal and human dramas.[6]

My selection of books and writers thus delineates a tensely charged but nevertheless free zone between competing customs: traditional Anglo-American values are subjected to sharpest skepticism in this writing, but the dramatic expressiveness so important to the English tradition is very far from entirely being given up. The terms of French modernism do partially address the revulsion against common language and life that led these writers to their strange departures, but French theoretical categories do not entirely hold them in place either. The play of forces in the language of these novelists, seen in relation to more fixed alternatives, points to their extraordinary independence of spirit, an exciting but very precarious accomplishment that can and sometimes does collapse, suggesting the difficulty of such freedom for the modern writer—and for the reader as well.

1

The Life of English Idiom, the Laws of French Cliché

English and French Traditions

It is fitting that the French contributed *cliché* to our modern repertoire of pejoratives, for it was in France, in the mid-nineteenth century, that the literary avant-garde first seized upon banality as an object of major contempt. At the start of the nineteenth century, the clatter of new typesetting machines had generated the onomatopoetic verb *clicher* for the copying process, and the noun *cliché* for the metal plate from which reproductions of print or design could be made in unending quantity. *Cliché* was a neutral technical term for this achievement of modern technology, like the English "stereotype" for the same device. Only toward the middle of the century did both English "stereotype" and French *cliché* begin to be transferred for purposes of derision to other kinds of (figuratively) mechanical molds, especially of verbal expression. *Cliché* as a derisive term entered *Larousse* in the 1860s, approximately a decade after Flaubert had launched his definitive compendium, *Le Dictionnaire des idées reçues*. After reading the *Diction-*

naire, Flaubert predicted with satisfaction that "one would be afraid to talk, for fear of using one of the phrases in it."[1]

Flaubert sardonically exposed a loss of distinction between printed commonplace and so-called natural speech. The technology of copying had added to the age-old vices of the trite and the hackneyed the new features of automatic fixity and limitless reproduction. The term *cliché* gave doleful recognition to the power of machinery to press more and more language into common currency and then to make hackneyed language, like other commodities, available to an ever larger public. For the self-consciously alienated writers of mid-nineteenth century France, it was only a short step from seeing cliché as the general doom of language in bourgeois society to seeking private refuge in irony or idiosyncrasy. Hence the strong link of antipathy between cliché and the stylistic experiments of early French modernism, and the nonaccidental circumstance that the two greatest French connoisseurs of cliché—Flaubert and Proust—achieved distinction, respectively, as the most thoroughly ironic and the most elaborately idiosyncratic of French novelists. In recent years the "distrust of the stereotype" insisted upon, for example, by Roland Barthes, has attained so much official intellectual prestige that it threatens to become itself a cliché, the pivot of an ideology set against the banality of all other ideology. As Barthes asserts in *The Pleasure of the Text,* "all official institutions of language are repeating machines: schools, sports, advertising, popular songs, news, all continually repeat the same structure, the same meaning, often the same words: the stereotype is a political fact, the major figure of ideology . . . Whence the present configuration of forces: on the one hand, a mass banalization (linked to the repetition of language) . . . and on the other, a (marginal, eccentric) impulse toward the New."[2]

Barthes's own far-from-marginal position in the "new New Criticism" has supported the authority of French imprecations against "the stereotype" on both sides of the Atlantic. Barthes does not locate his "configuration of forces" in relation to a specifically French tradition, nor do American *comparatistes* like Geoffrey Hartman, so quick to decry Anglo-American provinciality, bother much with the possibly embarrassing fact that such general theoretical pronouncements as those of Barthes depend on a very limited canon of French texts. In his recent *Criticism in the Wilderness,* Hartman berates the "prissy and defensive" Anglo-American "resistance to imported ideas" and, in his scolding condescensions, refuses to acknowledge the legitimacy of opposition based on ideas no less compelling because domestically produced.[3] Barthes's antithesis between "the stereotype" and "new" or authentic expression *ought* to meet with Anglo-American resistance, not out of groundless chauvinism but because the specific terms of the antithesis are too reductive for the complexities and ambiguities found in the Anglo-American tradition of language and judgment.

The *Oxford English Dictionary* shows that the figurative "stereotype," for example, appears in nineteenth-century English most often as an adjective—"stereotyped smile," "stereotyped epithets"—a construction which allows for discriminations of value between things equally commonplace in themselves. The degree to which there is more than redundancy in the phrase "stereotyped commonplaces" (attributed by the *OED* to Mrs. Gaskell) marks a confusing but characteristically English distinction between the contemptible and the possibly valuable, even in commonplaces. The French nouns *stéréotype* and *cliché* more sweepingly dismiss in a stroke all fixed forms of expression. Barthes gives the point aphoristic finality: "every old language is immediately compromised, and every language becomes old once it is repeated."[4] In English, a continuing ambivalent attachment to the old and familiar—in language as in sex and politics—has kept even the most notably defiant of modernists from enlisting in the French avant-garde. The French slogan of *le Nouveau,* repeated (paradoxically) from Baudelaire to Barthes, becomes complicated, if not compromised, in the English modern tradition by deeply rooted yearnings toward the common, and by anxious intimations that to repudiate old language is to risk repudiating the life of language itself.

In current criticism this risk, for anyone in the Anglo-American tradition, is masked by the intimidating assurance with which Continental theory presents itself as no less universal than philosophy or nature or science. A good example is the determinedly objective study of cliché offered by the structuralist critic Michael Riffaterre in his *Essais de stylistique structurale.* The method of "structuralist stylistics" rests its claim to novelty on its scientific neutrality; it pretends not to evaluate style, but only to describe how elements of style function in different verbal contexts. Thus in his well-known essay "Fonction du cliché dans la prose littéraire," Riffaterre proposes to move beyond modernist prejudice by reestablishing cliché as a neutral technical term. Yet in practice, his wrenching of cliché from the derisive associations of common usage does not so much neutralize the term as cut conspicuously against the grain of ordinary language, like some of the stylistic experiments of modernism itself. Riffaterre does not discover new value in language that has previously been disdained; he only re-presents the familiar, despised object in a new, technically striking form. The method does not so much redeem the mediocre object as reveal the merit of the analytic technique itself, part of that merit being its supposed indifference to the value of the object exhibited.

Riffaterre detaches cliché from its nineteenth-century milieu, extending it to refer to any group of words which convention has solidified into a linguistic unity. His category of cliché thus includes the formulae of neoclassical prose as well as the banalities spoken by the likes of Flaubert's Homais. In accord with his programmatic neutrality, Riffaterre observes the sheer variety rather than the varying value of the functions that fixed locutions perform in different literary styles. His taxonomy gives the name "constitutive cliché," for example, to the presence of fixed formulae within a writer's own style, a device which creates the "literariness" of the text, rather like the effect of meter in poetry.[5] The idea of a function performed by "constitutive cliché" thereby rescues, in a very limited way, the conventional formulae of neoclassical prose from modern scorn, without claiming any interesting expressiveness for the locutions themselves. At the same time, a few examples of "constitutive cliché" from other periods contribute to the impression of a metahistorical taxonomy of stylistic functions for cliché in general.

As Riffaterre's argument unfolds, however, his structuralist analysis conforms ever more closely to postromantic French literary assumptions. Indeed, he does not try very hard to remove the structural category of "constitutive cliché" from more familiar (and dismissive) historical classifications, for he observes that formulaic language eventually all but disappears as a legitimate constitutive element of style in the nineteenth century, a decline which coincides with "la mort d'une esthétique."[6]

The typically French allegiances of Riffaterre's own *esthétique* appear most strikingly in the way his main category of cliché for prose since the mid-nineteenth century endorses without question the orthodox postromantic French antithesis between the commonplace and the authentic or original in language, especially in the language of social speech. His crucial category for the modern period is *cliché mimétique,* by which he means what I began by describing: the deliberate presentation of fixed verbal locutions in a way that underscores and mocks their banality, as in the satiric characterizations of Flaubert and Proust, two of his own leading examples.

According to Riffaterre's analysis of *cliché mimétique,* fixed verbal locutions always degrade character because they inevitably signify the character's loss of self in one or another kind of conformity, "in the social or mental postures through which he abdicates his personality."[7] Without arguing the point, Riffaterre assumes that personality is strongest when it is most singular; unself-conscious conformity to common social and mental categories signifies loss of power and authority in personality—an abdication. Supported by the ample evidence in Flaubert's *Dictionnaire,* Riffaterre formulates a seemingly unequivocal law of *cliché mimétique* according to which conventional language in fictional characters points the text inevitably in the direction of satire: "All realism of style which rests on the equation verbal stereotype = mental or moral ankylosis results in satire."[8]

Riffaterre's terms for the law of *cliché mimétique* oddly skirt, however, the issues that most call for scrutiny. The point that satire results from an equation between stereotyped language and mental or moral stiffness (ankylosis) seems almost too obvious to warrant restatement, even with a fancy Greek term. But what about the status of the equation itself? Its very terminology blocks speculation about the effect of conventionality in speech, because it evades the question of whether all fixed expressions in spoken language should be placed under the scarcely neutral label of "verbal stereotype" or "cliché." In other words, Riffaterre's equation allows no room for the existence of *un*stereotyped commonplaces. And it makes no provision for the ambiguous and complex relationship between conventional speech and personality that has been a subject of more than satiric interest in the English novel from its beginnings even to Joyce, the greatest English master of *cliché mimétique,* whose irony, at least in *Ulysses,* has such a strange capacity to hover between mockery and appreciation.

Relationships between conventional language and individual expressiveness are relatively simple in any structuralist account of them, but they are revealed to be more complex just as soon as the derisive concept of cliché yields to a more genuinely neutral recognition that all speech, and especially speech in novels, conforms in some degree to recognizable conventions. Novelistic dialogue artfully intensifies the patterns which may be all but imperceptible in the disorder of actual speech, as Norman Page observes in *Speech in the English Novel.*[9] In reading novels, Page demonstrates, we more or less consciously identify and respond to "the kind and degree of convention adopted." "Dialect" and "idiolect," the two poles of speech in Page's analysis, offer a telling countermodel to Riffaterre's structuralist taxonomy of cliché, first, because these conceptual opposites are not in practice mutually exclusive, and second, because their stylistic effects are as much a matter of verbal texture as of structure.[10] "Idiolect" refers to the speech characteristics which distinguish one character from others. At its extreme, as in the great creations of Dickens, the master of idiolect in the English novel, the individualizing marks of speech serve comic characterization, as personality shows itself caught in the machinery of its own idiosyncrasy.

For Dickens, the tics of individual speech can be said to constitute a realm of private cliché, creating the impression of individual personality rigidified as well as intensified by seemingly automatic repetitions. The fixed phrases of idiolect usually appropriate material from the public domain, but so colored by private eccentricity that the speech comes to signify not the conformity of personality but the positive resistance of certain personalities to the elementary flexibility of common discourse. Thus in *Great Expectations* Wemmick's invocations of "portable property" and "the Aged P." are, like the paraphernalia of his little castle-home, "mechanical appliances" of language that only ambiguously serve character in what he calls its "private and personal capacities."

The relationship between fixed speech and personality is problematic in idiolect, at the private extreme of language, but the equally ambiguous expressiveness of dialect, at the other end, cuts even closer to the phenomenon of cliché. For dialect, in its broadest sense, refers to all the characteristics of speech which identify the individual with some recognizable social or regional grouping beyond the self. Dialect, then, represents that force in language which locates the individual within a community, as idiolect sets him apart. What I shall later call "idiom" is closely related to dialect in that both terms can mean, simply, the "vernacular," and thus refer to the entire system of language native to a particular place. Dialect, however, more usually signifies the totality of a deviant sublanguage, while idiom, among its many meanings, identifies smaller, often fixed units of expression. Idioms appear with high frequency in dialect, contributing to the traditional, conventional, and ritualistic character of regional speech. But idiomatic phrases also pass by custom into the mainstream of the vernacular, often hardly noticeable, but sometimes standing out as conspicuously as clichés— indeed, sometimes indistinguishable from the class of cliché known as "vulgarisms."

It is the complex working of vulgar (or popular) idiom in otherwise standard English that I want to distinguish as having value beyond cliché in postromantic English fiction and in Anglo-American culture more generally. The route to that distinction requires, however, a bit more attention to the literary history of dialect, since the uses of dialect by the great masters of English realism show, sometimes inadvertently, the same ambivalent social allegiances more subtly represented by later writers through the play of idiomatic speech.

For the most part, the conspicuous vulgarity of dialect—even its funny look on the printed page—disqualified it as a serious language for the representation of personality in the nineteenth-century English novel. Dialect could provide humor or local color, but fluency in standard English was a necessary credential for a central serious character in the novels of George Eliot, Dickens, and even Hardy. In *The Country and the City,* Raymond Williams has observed the sometimes awkward conventions of bilingualism by which Victorian novelists could, at significant moments, raise certain of their regional and humble characters to the linguistic competence presumed necessary for serious personal experience.[11] Variants of this bilingualism appear in the narrative representation of meditation or inner speech in standard English, another example of the assumption that serious private as well as social gestures of personality can be enacted only through language free of the fixed colorings of region or class.

The strength of this convention in English fiction provides the base for such exuberant and defiant American experiments in dialect as *Huckleberry Finn,* as it later supports D. H. Lawrence's more heavy-handed social protest in *Lady Chatterley's Lover.* Lawrence makes a rather dreary show of reversing the bilingual conventions of nineteenth-century fiction; his gamekeeper hero switches back and forth from dialect to standard English, depending upon his somewhat willfully alternating moods of personal ease or social constraint. Dialect becomes a paradoxically aggressive language of tenderness, the verbal weapon of Mellors (and Lawrence) against the sterile, hypocritical, and repressive formulae of "correct" society. Mellors's dialect is meant to oppose and discredit the entire language of standard English as nothing but bourgeois cliché. Yet since Mellors is the only major character who commands this privileged verbal resource, the dialect has an oddly artificial effect, more like a pastoral costume which the hero can don at will than a natural verbal medium of personal expression.

Although Lawrence's polemical subversion of novelistic speech conventions in *Lady Chatterley's Lover* only dubiously succeeds, it interestingly points back to less assertive but still conspicuous conflicts of value in earlier English fiction, conflicts noticeable often in unintended failures of style. The frequently stiff or dreary standard English of

Scott, Dickens, and Hardy can weaken the emotional crises in their novels, and inadvertently affirm the greater interest of lesser figures and events. The idea that expressive vigor appears most naturally in the special dialects that the mature personality must nevertheless transcend, figures thematically in *Great Expectations,* for example, but it is precisely this intimation that also confuses the moral design and weakens the last portion of the book.

The novelist's dilemma has a distinguished precedent, of course, in Wordsworth's division of allegiance between the "real" language of men ("purified indeed of all lasting and rational causes of dislike or disgust") and the elevated variants of standard English that the poet sought for heroic and visionary expression.[12] The English novelistic tradition draws on Wordsworth's ambivalent attachment to the idea of "common" language as the means of access to "elementary" passion and to the values of the historical and personal past. Norman Page notes, for example, Scott's use of dialect for heroic and tragic effects, while remarking also that Scott fails to make of standard English a spoken language equal in vigor to his dialect speech.[13] Later examples of more or less deliberate contrasts between vigorous dialect and comparatively stilted or bland standard English appear in Emily Brontë, Robert Louis Stevenson, Dickens, Hardy, and early Lawrence himself. This list constitutes a substantial tradition throughout the great period of English realism in which there is a tension, not always acknowledged, between the conviction that serious personality must express itself within the flexible medium of standard English, and the suspicion that this medium is somehow thinner than the inherited language of the tribe—the language associated with childhood, home, and family, and with those traditional unlettered communities which the writer eagerly, necessarily, leaves behind for his great expectations of literary renown.

There is an absence in the greatest of French nineteenth-century novelists of any comparable tension between dialect and standard French. Although nineteenth-century French heroes jeopardize many virtues when they leave the provinces for Paris, the loss of vigorous and expressive speech is not one of their main risks. Indeed, for Balzac as well as for Flaubert, to enter the larger culture of standard French is in effect to acquire speech itself, with all the resources of charm, wit, desire, disappointment, sincerity, hypocrisy—and banality—that constitute the articulate personality. It is true that peasants and servants, especially in Flaubert, sometimes exemplify almost superhuman virtue and passion: there is the peasant who wins a prize for fifty years of service in *Madame Bovary,* for example, and Félicité in *Un coeur simple.* But the sign, perhaps even the substance, of their virtue is their positively heroic silence. The sincerity and the stoicism which are the strengths of Flaubert's illiterate poor show forth as an almost inhuman muteness. To become verbal in Flaubert's fiction, as in other French literature of the nineteenth century, is to become bourgeois—and thereby exposed to all the contagion of cliché represented in the *Dictionnaire des idées reçues.*

The shift of interest within the English tradition from dialect to idiom in the twentieth century, and the intensified consciousness of vitality in popular speech, show vividly in a somewhat neglected book of the 1920s called *Words and Idioms* by Logan Pearsall Smith. Smith's work impressed F. R. Leavis, who cites it in his *Scrutiny* essay on Joyce of 1933, the essay where (with some reservations) he praises *Ulysses* but excoriates the Parisian cult of Joyce for bowing before the destruction of the English language in *Work in Progress.*[14] Leavis invokes *Words and Idioms* because he recognizes that Smith, though an American with a Frenchified taste for Flaubert, Proust, and late Henry James, had a definite enough allegiance to the distinctive character of the English language to give support to Leavis in his own heated attack on the Parisian avant-garde.

In *Words and Idioms* Smith lovingly gathered many hundreds of common English expressions, accompanying his lists with short essays of commentary. Smith's method is unsystematic, his tone enthusiastic, except for an elegiac and nostalgic worry that idiom, the most durable species of language, may at last be seriously endangered. For him, however, the threat to expressive language is not cliché in the French sense of mechanical repetition. Indeed, he grants idiomatic phrases an almost magical "radioactive quality," the "power to give out life and never lose it."[15] The danger to living language for him, as for Leavis, is to be found not in popular commonplace, but in something nearly its opposite—in standardized education and the jargon that accompanies specialized modern knowledge.

For Smith, idiom rather than cliché offers the natural approach to the subject of conventionality in the English language. He mentions clichés, but only to observe that no rigorous technical distinction between cliché and idiom can be sustained. Cliché is the failure of language on particular occasions and thus represents a possible though not necessary outcome of speech in every form. But Smith has no French impulse to brood over the sinister threat to personality posed by speech when it evokes familiar social categories. He wants instead to acclaim the more than natural energy held in potential by language, especially by language seasoned through long associations with commonplace social activities. In accounting for the expressiveness of idiom, Smith emphasizes its power to connect the individual to other men and women, both present and past. It is this Wordsworthian affirmation of shared experience that he regards as the social and psychological effect of common idiom in writing as well as in talk.

> A writer cannot create his own language; he must take what society provides him, and in his search for sensuous and pictured speech he naturally has recourse to the rich and living material created by generations of popular and unconscious artists. Here he finds an energetic and picturesque language, rich in images and irony, and full of zest, a joy in life, which are of priceless value to him.[16]

Though writing in the 1920s, Smith enjoys a sense of comfortable continuity with the past that undoubtedly distances him from the struggles as well as from the innovations of his more famous literary contemporaries. Remarkable neither as an imaginative artist nor as a critic, he fails to assess the possibly ruinous cost of simply taking what society provides, nor does he sympathize with the excitement of English as well as French modernists in their experiments with new and strange creations of language. In a stunningly obtuse essay of 1927, "The Prospects of Literature," Smith pronounces (like Arnold before him) that the age is not conducive to literary greatness. The very state of the language is unpropitious, he argues, for the moderns lack "the unhackneyed freshness of an unexploited idiom" which blessed the Elizabethans, and they cannot achieve "the vigour borrowed from popular speech" which renovated the language of the Romantics.[17] Smith was too old and too fixed in his tastes in the twenties to respond to the complex literary experimentation going on all around him. He stuck to the position of elegiac regret that modern social forces were undermining the strength of the language he loved. This social nostalgia starts early and runs deep in the English literary tradition, as Raymond Williams has observed, and as almost any issue of *Scrutiny* will illustrate.[18] James, Lawrence, Joyce, and Beckett became great, innovative writers partly because of their eccentric relation to that tradition; they gave much less rein than a Logan Pearsall Smith to the elegiac, and they corrected nostalgia by fiercer and tougher social judgments.

The continuing value of Smith's work rests on his capacity to locate idioms still so active in the language that their appeal goes well beyond nostalgia. What is mainly at stake for Smith is the strengthening of expressiveness available through the social inheritance of speech, and the impoverishment of language when this inheritance is neglected, whether from snobbery, fastidiousness, or simply lack of vital spirits. This view has a corollary in Lawrence, who suggests in "Daughters of the Vicar," for example, that the "balanced, abstract" speech of the dwarfish rector is as far from lively talk as his body is from manly grace or force: "There was no spontaneous exclamation, no violent assertion or expression of personal conviction, but all cold, reasonable assertion."[19] Smith offers the verbal material for "spontaneous exclamation" and "personal" if not "violent" assertion in English through lists of idioms organized according to various principles, like the grammatical principles of the phrases or their social origins. Although common usage mainly ignores these origins, Smith enjoys displaying the range of social experience from which English idiom historically derives: hunting, agricultural labor, fishing, weather, houses, furniture, eating. He especially likes idioms which derive from the sea, but his list traceable to the kitchen is even richer in ingredients for cheerfully malicious, shrewd, or wry responses to the human scene: "to boil over," "to butter up," "to have other fish to fry," "to cook someone's goose," "to make hash of," "to put the lid on," "to make mincemeat of," "to have a finger in every pie," "to go to pot," "to skim off," "to be in a stew," "to stew in one's own juice," "to be half-baked," "to be in hot water."[20]

Among the common grammatical (or ungrammatical) patterns, the most interesting is the form he calls "phrasal verbs": "to keep up," "to pull through," "to put up with." Schoolmasters, Smith explains, always want to press the particles back into earlier parts of the sentence, priggishly indifferent to how the very life of idiomatic English goes on in the phrasal combinations of abstract and simple verbs followed by particles of motion. These common and fixed phrases have the capacity, he observes, to evoke the entire range of human actions and relationships. We can take to people, take them up, take them down, take them off, take them on, or take them in! There is, he tells us, "hardly any action or attitude of one human being to another which cannot be expressed by means of these phrasal verbs."[21]

Smith's lists and commentary offer a salutary experience of the conventional character of language altogether different from anything in French writers like Flaubert, Proust, Barthes, or even Riffaterre. His compendium posits a kind of personal expressiveness not vitiated by fixed verbal configurations, but positively reliant on them for power, wit, and even subtlety of connotation.

To move from *Words and Idioms* back to Flaubert's *Dictionnaire des idées reçues* is to cross a very murky channel between cultural as well as linguistic traditions. For it is not immediately apparent why such common coinage as "rotten to the core" or "dull as ditchwater" should retain "radioactive" power, while more or less equally common locutions in Flaubert's collection persuasively exemplify language in full rigor mortis. In the *Dictionnaire* under "BRAS," for example: "Pour gouverner la France, il faut un bras de fer" (p. 958) ("To govern France, one needs an arm of iron").

Elusive discriminations of verbal structure may be at stake, though they hardly require systematic linguistic analysis. *Bras de fer* as a phrase may seem flatter than English idioms involving the arm, because the first to come to mind in English are not substantives, but prepositional phrases evoking actions and relationships: "at arm's length," "up to the elbow," "head and shoulders above." Does *bras de fer* represent some linguistic inertness more common in French than in English idiom? It would be hard to prove such a contention, though Smith hints in that direction when, in citing pairs of related English and French idioms, he notes the greater vividness of the English versions.[22] And Hugh Kenner, who sees Joyce partly as an ironist in the tradition of Flaubert, is nevertheless quick to notice an irrepressible "racy" life in Joyce's Dublin clichés missing from the language of his French predecessor.[23] Similarly Christopher Ricks, stressing the greater vitality of cliché in the English as compared to the French versions of Beckett's writing, has suggested the mysterious interplay between the individual imagination and characteristic linguistic structures within a particular vernacular.[24]

Flaubert's antipathy to clichés like *bras de fer* is best understood, however, in relation to an even broader interplay between language and culture. Some of the clichés in the *Dictionnaire* fall flat because of their intrinsic verbal weakness, but that weakness is itself underlined by expectations of language embodied in the design of Flaubert's book. The very conception of an *idée reçue* focuses the problem of cliché not on linguistic form alone but on the discrepancy between a verbal formula and the intellectual purpose of language construed as the statement of *idées*. *Bras de fer,* for example, carries the burden of articulating a political idea, nothing less than a philosophy of government!

The locutions in Flaubert's *Dictionnaire* often fail mainly because they so grossly disappoint the intellectual expectations set up by their content and even by the grammatical form of the sentences. The discrepancy between the insight promised by the syntax—"Pour gouverner la France, il faut . . ."—and the letdown of the cliché—"un bras de fer"—is the kind of contextual incongruity that Riffaterre's structuralist approach to *cliché mimétique* is so well suited to discern. The French, of course, have no monopoly on this form of cliché, neither on its practice nor on its exposure. It was precisely the steady incongruity between intellectual pretension and banality of phrase in C. P. Snow's lecture on "The Two Cultures" which led F. R. Leavis to call the whole Snow performance "a document for the study of cliché."[25] Leavis disliked Flaubert, but not because he was himself any more tolerant of bourgeois *idées reçues.*

Common English speech may escape the sorry fate of *idées reçues* only when it manages to stay clear of ideas altogether. It is not necessary to say that idiomatic phrases may seem most appealing in meaningless lists like those in *Words and Idioms,* in order to observe that their quality shines most brightly when they appear, as they so often do, detached from elaborate grammatical structures and therefore from any of the complex intellectual responsibilities of language. "Spontaneous exclamation" and "violent assertion," to return to Lawrence's terms, leave language almost free of intellectual burden. In his *Dictionnaire,* by contrast, Flaubert puts the most taxing intellectual demand on common language. Every entry, by the very form of the book, carries some responsibility to work as a definition of other words, ideas, or things.

Only the most brilliant aphorism or maxim could survive Flaubert's method: a successful maxim is precisely a detached sentence which, through perfection of phrasing, transforms a commonplace into a memorable definition. As Barthes remarks: "The language of the maxim always has a definitional and not a transitive activity; a collection of maxims is always more or less . . . a dictionary."[26] In Flaubert's *Dictionnaire,* an implicit standard of aphorism and maxim governs the entire satiric attack on *idées reçues.* He leads us to understand cliché as failed aphorism, and it is perhaps only in the light of French pride in its brilliant tradition of aphorism that the demand on language made by this implicit standard does not seem more arbitrary and limited than it does. It is likewise the oppressive authority of this same tradition that gives force to political protests like Barthes's against "the Sentence" and "the agents of the Sentence" in control of French culture since the seventeenth century. Flaubert anticipates Barthes's attack on the pretension to intellectual completeness embodied in the very institutions of grammar. He also anticipates Barthes's inability, or refusal, to envision more freely expressive forms of language in either speech or writing. Although Barthes laments the absence in French of a "locutive grammar," that is, "a grammar of what is spoken and not of what is written," his own example of language liberated from the tyranny of the sentence is not spoken expostulation but the stereophonic effect of many simultaneous auditory sensations, as in a bar where, half-asleep, he at the same time hears music, conversation, noises of chairs, glasses; the sole alternative to the oppressiveness of grammatical completeness is "a definitive discontinuity."[27] Flaubert likewise sustains the sovereignty of the very forms of language that he discredits. His satire in the *Dictionnaire* eventually becomes tedious, however, from the ease of mockery guaranteed by the very organization of the book into self-destructing sentences. Flaubert has no difficulty exposing the intellectual inadequacy of common language, but he seems willful in his own determination to restrict language to definition, and to abstract it from the more disorderly social and personal interchanges which give force to common speech in actual life.

But, of course, the organization of the *Dictionnaire* also and in itself represents Flaubert's interpretation of speech in a social community. It is the bourgeoisie which lacks the finesse for aphorism, yet reduces language to the self-important pronouncement of sentences—true or false—on every subject. Many of Flaubert's entries create miniature social occasions, so that there is no doubt about the kind of people who say these banalities and in what situations: "CHEMINS DE FER . . . —S'extasier sur l'invention et dire: 'Moi, monsieur, qui vous parle, j'étais ce matin à X; je suis parti par le train de X; là-bas, j'ai fait mes affaires, etc., et à X heures, j'étais revenu!' " (p. 959) ("RAIL-ROADS . . . —Enthuse over the invention and say: 'I, sir, who am speaking to you now, this morning I was at X; I left by the X train; I did my business there, etc., and at X o' clock I was back!' ").

Flaubert's *homme d'affaires* or *père de famille* sounds clichéd, even when his language contains no fixed configurations of words. Indeed, dull correctness is often the most notable feature of Flaubert's version of the bourgeois sentence. When casual metaphor appears, one is left to wonder whether the bourgeois speakers take their own dead metaphors literally, especially when those metaphors convey their favorite philistine prejudices: "ARTISTES . . . —Gagnent des sommes folles, mais les jettent par les fenêtres" (p. 956) ("ARTISTS . . . —Earn fantastic sums but throw them out the window"). For the most part, Flaubert's prototypical bourgeois speaker articulates nothing so vivid as throwing money out the window. His platitudes are drearily empty of the detail that constitutes color and action in idiomatic speech.

The abstract regularity of bourgeois cliché derives, at least in part, from the privileges and pretensions of the social class celebrated in the clichés themselves. In Flaubert's France a complacent bourgeoisie disdains the vulgarity of popular idiom. It identifies itself with enlightened knowledge, progress, and science, allowing itself only the most patronizing regard for the unlettered masses: "LABOUREURS. Que serions nous sans eux?" (p. 971) ("FARM HANDS. What would we be without them?"). Although Flaubert satirizes this blandly crude snobbery, I have already noted that, in matters of language at least, his own fiction is hardly more receptive to signs of life from below. Most of the concreteness of idiomatic language, however, refers back to humble occupations: in some distant past this language arose naturally in relation to familiar things on the farm or at sea or in the kitchen. That is why dialect is characteristically rich in idiomatic phrasing. Although the specific origins fade as the phrases move into standard speech, idiomatic language still has the effect, and sometimes the implicit purpose, of evoking connection to those origins, both downward in social class and backward in historical time.

There may be social complacency in deliberate commonness of language, too, but it is different in kind from bourgeois pleasure in prosperity. Idiomatic speech offers a means of affiliating the self with the larger mass of the social body, an affiliation that has been a long-standing political and social ideal, if not reality, in the English cultural tradition. That tradition is accustomed to locate certain human virtues—not just stoicism, but resilience and practical energy—in the common, even illiterate population. A person in full command of standard English who can nevertheless tap this resource increases rather than abdicates authority. Thus Shakespeare shows it to be both good politics and a sign of natural spirit in the future Henry V that, as Prince Hal, he has learned to "drink with any tinker in his own language."

Flaubert's bourgeoisie finds neither spontaneous pleasure nor calculated advantage in such verbal promiscuity. Insofar as bourgeois language reaches out socially, the direction is up, toward the aristocracy. While kneeling in worship only to their own idols—money and domesticity—the bourgeois in Flaubert's *Dictionnaire* also lean upward. This awkward combination of postures further drains vitality from speech, for it requires a habit of hypocrisy ruinous to any spontaneity of expression: "CHASSE. Excellent exercice que l'on doit feindre d'adorer" (p. 959)

("HUNT. Excellent exercise which one ought to pretend to love"); "CHAM-
PAGNE. Caractérise le dîner de cérémonie.—Faire semblant de le détester
en disant que 'ce n'est pas un vin' " (p. 959) ("CHAMPAGNE. Characterizes
the ceremonial dinner.—Pretend to despise it by saying that 'it is not a
wine' "). Even more than the inevitable decline of all spoken language to
cliché, or the wearing out of a particular culture's speech, Flaubert shows
the ruination of language when it is habitually dedicated to affectations of
experience and feeling.

Flaubert exposes bourgeois cliché as hypocritical even on its own
sacred domestic terrain: "ENFANTS. Affecter pour eux une tendresse
lyrique, quand il y a du monde" (p. 964) ("CHILDREN. Show a lyric
tenderness for them, when there is company"). *Tendresse lyrique* is a
verbal cliché, and tenderness for children is a banal sentiment; but the
worst vice that Flaubert's sentence evokes is the mere affectation of
feeling. From a certain angle, the *Dictionnaire* and *Madame Bovary*
may be seen as two forms of Flaubert's consistent, even obsessive
perception of how conventional language may be seized upon to hide
the disturbing emptiness within the character of individuals or even the
whole community. The clichés in the *Dictionnaire* show how easily
mere convention can masquerade as thought and feeling, but the special horror in Flaubert's version of this perception is not so much the
deforming power of conventional language as the absence of genuine
life which the habit of cliché both covers and reveals. It is Joyce's
knowledge of this same social and psychological horror which makes
Dubliners the most Flaubertian of his works.

The Life of Idiom in Joyce and Lawrence

Of the four novelists in this study, James Joyce and D. H. Lawrence
make the best (if also the most unlikely) pairing to demonstrate the
force of English cultural values in language. For if these two very
different writers can be paired at all—most schemes of criticism fix
them at opposite poles—the most obvious link is the shared intensity
of their estrangement from the English culture of their time.[28] Joyce
was estranged, first, by the very condition of his Irishness, and second,
by his scorn for that class of the Dublin literati who strained, like
Gabriel Conroy in "The Dead," for affiliation with English habits of
speech and taste. Joyce's Flaubertian revulsion from Irish as well as
English forms of cliché, moreover, eventually made him at home in
Paris and amid the polyglot contrivances of *Finnegans Wake*. Lawrence

ended his wandering career almost equally far from contemporary standard English, castigating its sterilities through his visionary jargon as well as through the idealized rural dialect of *Lady Chatterley's Lover.*

Yet these most defiant of expatriates are also remarkable—in their best work—for their continuing if intensely ambivalent absorption in the common English-speaking voices they left behind. For Joyce, the crucial text is *Ulysses;* for Lawrence, the dialogue portions of *Sons and Lovers, The Rainbow,* and *Women in Love,* and also the colloquial authorial voice in many short stories, in the nonfictional prose, and in the best of the late works, *St. Mawr.* In all these books the distance of exile allowed the voices of home more generous play and presence by diminishing the immediate threat of constraint so undiluted in Flaubert and Proust, settled firmly as they were within calling distance of the voices they most resented. It is the ambiguous value of remembered common English speech amid a tangle of cultural rejection that matters for the distinction between cliché and idiom in Lawrence and Joyce, writers for whom any simple nostalgia was obviously out of the question from the start.

Joyce's early hostility to common language is well-documented; he documented it himself through the severe ironies of *Dubliners* and, in more open autobiographical terms, through the story of Stephen Dedalus, the artist as a young man, preparing himself for a career as exile and ironist by his arrogant, almost paranoid alienation from the voices of home and community. Early in *Stephen Hero* the narrator records, with more admiration than criticism, the moments for Stephen when "life on any common terms" seemed "an intolerable offense."[29]

> He read Skeat's *Etymological Dictionary* by the hour and his mind, which had from the first been only too submissive to the infant sense of wonder, was often hypnotized by the most commonplace conversation. People seemed to him strangely ignorant of the value of the words they used so glibly. And pace by pace as this indignity of life forced itself upon him he became enamoured of an idealizing, a more veritably human tradition . . . and he began to see that people had leagued themselves together in a conspiracy of ignobility and that Destiny had scornfully reduced her prices for them. He desired no such reduction for himself and preferred to serve her on the ancient terms.[30]

Stephen's obsession with the "conspiracy of ignobility" in common speech undergoes many transformations from *Stephen Hero* to *Ulysses,* perhaps the most significant being his diminishing conviction of an alternate "more veritably human tradition" of language. In *Ulysses,* moreover, the ever greater reach of Joyce's ironic and parodic skills intensifies the impression, already intimated in the early works, that all traditions of language may rigidify into system and fade into cliché.

Although Flaubert's irony becomes similarly inclusive in *Bouvard et Pécuchet,* the effect on common idiom of this larger irony in *Ulysses* is not at all the same as in Flaubert's nihilistic satire. For one thing, Joyce's inventive energy makes every parodied style oddly more alive than the stereotype it parodies, a frequent but by no means inevitable concomitant of parody. Flaubert's cold ironies demonstrate the contrary phenomenon of fascination devoid of love. Common idiom, moreover, has special status among the parodied styles of *Ulysses,* both because it creates a more various and interesting social reality than appears in any of Flaubert's novels and because, even more significantly, it is the distinguishing stylistic mark of Bloom's interior monologues which, set off against the quite different styles of Stephen and Buck Mulligan, create the stylistic norm of the first half of the novel.[31] The commonness of Bloom's consciousness has an elusive value that *Ulysses* mocks but never repudiates, just as the experimental styles in the novel strain but do not repudiate our powerful sense of engagement with the personality of a character called "Bloom."

Before reflecting further on how Joyce locates value (as well as limitation) in the style of common English idiom, it is useful to hear directly how it sounds. The first speaking voice heard in *Ulysses* is Buck Mulligan's, goading Stephen Dedalus for being so moodily bothered by everything, especially by the memory of his mother's death and by Mulligan himself.

—Then what is it? Buck Mulligan asked impatiently. Cough it up. I'm quite frank with you. What have you against me now? (1.179–80 / 7)[32]

—And what is death, he asked, your mother's or yours or my own? You saw only your mother die. I see them pop off every day in the Mater and Richmond and cut up into tripes in the dissectingroom. It's a beastly thing and nothing else. It simply doesn't matter. (1.204–7 / 8)

—Look at the sea. What does it care about offences? Chuck Loyola, Kinch, and come on down. The Sassenach wants his morning rashers.
   His head halted again for a moment at the top of the staircase, level with the roof.
—Don't mope over it all day, he said. I'm inconsequent. Give up the moody brooding. (1.231–36 / 9)

In "Calypso," idiomatic language in a milder key belongs to Bloom, not spoken aloud but in the form of interior monologue. After his notably uncommunicative conversation with Molly in the morning, Bloom leaves the house, still thinking about her.

—You don't want anything for breakfast?
    A sleepy soft grunt answered:
—Mn.
    No. She didn't want anything. He heard then a warm heavy sigh, softer, as she turned over and the loose brass quoits of the bedstead jingled. Must get those settled really. Pity. All the way from Gibraltar. Forgotten any little Spanish she knew. Wonder what her father gave for it. Old style. Ah yes! of course. Bought it at the governor's auction. Got a short knock. Hard as nails at a bargain, old Tweedy. Yes, sir. At Plevna that was. I rose from the ranks, sir, and I'm proud of it. Still he had brains enough to make that corner in stamps. Now that was farseeing. (4.55–65 / 56)

On his way to the butcher, Bloom notes to himself how the country bumpkins who come to Dublin as bartenders get enough money to set themselves up as publicans.

Where do they get the money? Coming up redheaded curates from the county Leitrim, rinsing empties and old man in the cellar. Then, lo and behold, they blossom out as Adam Findlaters or Dan Tallons. Then think of the competition. General thirst. Good puzzle would be cross Dublin without passing a pub. Save it they can't. Off the drunks perhaps. Put down three and carry five. What is that, a bob here and there, dribs and drabs. On the wholesale orders perhaps. Doing a double shuffle with the town travellers. Square it you with the boss and we'll split the job, see? (4.126–33 / 58)

One of the most significant events in Bloom's day is the funeral of his acquaintance, Paddy Dignam. Toward the end of the long interior monologue of the episode, we get Bloom's response to the sight of a rat in the cemetery.

Tail gone now.
    One of those chaps would make short work of a fellow. Pick the bones clean no matter who it was. Ordinary meat for them. A corpse is meat gone bad. Well and what's cheese? Corpse of milk. I read in that *Voyages in China* that the Chinese say a white man smells like a corpse. Cremation better. Priests dead against it. Devilling for the other firm. Wholesale burners and Dutch oven dealers . . . Wonder does the news go about whenever a fresh one is let down. Underground communication. We learned that from them. Wouldn't be surprised. Regular square

feed for them. Flies come before he's well dead. Got wind of Dignam. They wouldn't care about the smell of it. Saltwhite crumbling mush of corpse: smell, taste like raw white turnips.

The gates glimmered in front: still open. Back to the world again. Enough of this place. Brings you a bit nearer every time. (6.979–96 / 114)

The irreverent energy given to style by the presence of common idiom is what first strikes the ear, created by the broken syntax and brisk rhythms of the phrasing as much as by particular fixed expressions: "cough it up," "pop off," "hard as nails," "blossom out," "doing a double shuffle," "square it," "make short work," "dead against it," "got wind of." Further specimens from the talk of Simon Dedalus or from the narrator of "Cyclops" offer unlimited material for structural and other kinds of analysis of how Joyce sets fixed phrases of common speech in the midst of his other styles, making us hear both their conventionality and also a range of tones: from quite nasty aggressiveness to bluster to tolerant humor. Joyce perfectly illustrates, in these displays of common language, the satiric procedure of *cliché mimétique* described by Riffaterre, for he means to mock many varieties of impotent self-assertion in his representation of the Dublin social world. Mulligan, Simon Dedalus, and the Cyclops narrator are bullies whose power of speech has no corresponding political, social, or moral authority. Bloom in his interior monologues is less bullying, though he is the least powerful figure of all, daring his assertions only to himself.

Yet Joyce's brilliant satiric powers notwithstanding, idiomatic language in *Ulysses* is allowed enough vitality to confound the law of *cliché mimétique,* whereby conventional language signifies the abdication of personality. For it is precisely through their colloquial verve that figures like Mulligan (in speech) and Bloom (in thought) impress us with their force of personality. Their easy access to common resources of language is part—far from the least appealing part—of their characters. At the start of *Ulysses,* for example, Mulligan's energetic reproaches to Stephen articulate what is likely to be the irritated impatience of the reader, too, at Stephen's "moody brooding" and pretentious formality. Joyce combines Mulligan's appeal with intimations of something less savory in his liveliness, a persistent bullying undertone that tends to justify Stephen's resentment. The crudity of a phrase like "cough it up," in its callous indifference to all delicacies of grief and anxiety, more or less cancels out Mulligan's bid for intimacy. His offensiveness, however, remains a rather subtle matter at the start, since the novel does not encourage too prissy a response to such brash exuberance. Judgment hesitates before a standard still emerging from within the book, a standard that has to assimilate both Stephen's high melancholy and Bloom's idiomatic lovableness.

Bloom's unillusioned observations of the human scene—his taking mental note of Major Tweedy's acumen (and pomposity) or of the shady deals of Dublin business life—have a tolerance not heard in young Mulligan, even though it is soon apparent that the generous mildness of Bloom's skepticism has as its condition almost total social isolation. Through the technique of the interior monologue, Joyce develops the interesting paradox that Bloom, though master of a kind of language that in its very essence is sociable, exercises this skill exclusively alone, in thought, not in conversation. When Bloom actually speaks to other people, his voice loses the idiomatic verve of the interior monologues. This conspicuous split makes Bloom's flexible vitality seem proportionate to the distance he keeps from direct social business. He does not deploy his idiomatic speech in the social fray as Mulligan does, and his avoidance of any kind of open parrying limits his authority as a standard for judging the articulated speech of others.

Joyce makes Bloom's interior style very appealing, however, even while he insists on its limiting conditions. Like Mulligan's tough remarks about death at the start of the book, Bloom's idiom during the funeral conveys an impressive commonsense courage. In the context of the Irish funeral, so self-protectively enclosed in euphemisms of speech and ritual, the plain terms of common language for the physical realities of death have a particularly bracing clarity. Bloom's power to keep hold of these realities during a funeral partakes of a larger power to confront the common physical truths of human existence with admirable directness, as Hamlet manages to do after his encounter with the gravediggers. Bloom's version of graveyard strength is more impressive than Mulligan's toughness, which approaches mere bravado. Death may be a beastly thing and nothing else, but Bloom, without flinching from the beastly realities, includes among his perceptions the equally powerful reality of the human desire to survive. His inner speech is flexible enough to evoke not only the full physical reality of death, but also the common and profound human urge to get out and back to the living world again.

In the cemetery scene, moreover, Bloom seems to go beyond the customary relation of the idiomatic talker to his own speech. Without sacrificing the characteristically loose and noninsistent movement of his inner speech, Joyce makes Bloom seem more conscious here than elsewhere of the buried metaphors in his idioms. He makes macabre jokes out of their implications, as when he says that the flies "got wind of" Dignam even before he was well dead. The jokes convey the poise that Bloom brings to the grotesque unsociability of death. He confronts and is yet not overwhelmed by the mockery it makes of ordinary human business.

The unusual range allowed to Bloom's interior style makes its limitation correspondingly harder to articulate, which is perhaps why Joyce must rely on the multiple devices of language in *Ulysses* in order fully to place Bloom. His limitation, beginning in the monologues, is deeply connected to his habits of language—to the habit, I would say, of idiom, rather than, as some critics would have it, of cliché—and it has much to do with what can be said summarily about the spirit of English idiom. Generally speaking, idiomatic speech is a kind of language that draws on the common experience of the community in its resistance to airs of special wisdom, mystery, and otherworldliness. In that spirit Bloom in the cemetery resists, very circumspectly, the ritual of the Catholic funeral service. Yet the painful specters of death that plague Bloom himself, as well as Stephen, throughout the book suggest a more haunting mystery than Bloom's language, or idiomatic language generally, is equipped to contemplate. Idiomatic language holds mystery and terror at bay, but it does not finally dispel the terrible truths that are supposedly accounted for by religious or philosophic doctrine. In its deflating concreteness, idiom thereby enacts human energies of resilience and fortitude, but it also tends to cut off reflectiveness, to fracture the activity of contemplation by its characteristic broken rhythms and short, conclusive phrasing. The decisive quality of idiom is also its limitation: it contributes to effectiveness in dispute, or to quick give-and-take in conversation generally, and yet as an interior language, as the language of thought, it breaks subjects off before any sustained encounter with mystery.

Idiom in this sense can leave the mind receptive to *idées reçues,* a vulnerability from which Bloom is protected only by his comical tendency to get received ideas always slightly askew. Even more pertinent to Bloom's limitation of thought is a digressive habit also related to his reliance on brief idiomatic locutions. The brevity of idiomatic phrasings in conversation allows openings for another speaker's reply, but has the effect, if one is alone, of leaving gaps for the entrance of almost any tangential association. While the very absence of full sentences in the interior monologues allows for one kind of free expressiveness, it also suggests a capacity to evade the suffering or endurance required of orderly sequence and depth in thought. Without any commitment to logical or grammatical structure, a mind like Bloom's can wander off to *Voyages in China* even while thinking about death in a Dublin graveyard. In the interior monologues Joyce shows Bloom's inner language to be by turns pathetically and ludicrously inadequate as a medium for sustained, consequential contemplation. In *Ulysses,* it must be said, Joyce equally refuses allegiance to any of the traditional literary styles which presume to offer such a medium. Nevertheless, he does aspire to induce in the reader some version of a sustained contemplative state. That is why he eventually disengages us from the appealing rhythm of idiomatic language in which a character like Bloom habitually lives. And yet among those things he would have us contemplate (not merely satirically but appreciatively, too) is the attractive, sociable, sane resourcefulness of his hero, a resourcefulness that draws strength from common idiom, as Joyce did himself, especially in this, his greatest book.

Lawrence, in his own way, also fled the oppression of common voices while trying to sustain connection with the values he heard in them. In 1912 he wrote from Austria to beg for some English books: "I've not read a thing in English for 5 months, except *Under Western Eyes* which bored me."[33] The first of the books sent, however, Arnold Bennett's *Anna of the Five Towns,* provoked an outburst of revulsion: "I don't know where I am. I am so used to the people going by outside, talking or singing some foreign language, always Italian now: but today, to be in Henley, and to read almost my own dialect, makes me feel quite ill. I hate England and its hopelessness . . . I hate it. I want to wash again, quick, wash off England, the oldness and grubbiness and despair."[34] Yet this time of vigorous cleansing for Lawrence— other letters to England brag of how he and Frieda bathe naked in the waters of Austria and Italy—was also the time of his thorough absorption in English "grubbiness" through the massive revision of *Sons and Lovers.* The force of idiom within dialect is heard in that novel mainly through the voice of the father, Morel. Lawrence wrote the portrait out of what he thought was unequivocal hatred of his father, but Morel's voice, it has been noted before, does not stay put within this intended design.[35]

One particularly suggestive passage occurs late in the novel where Morel is shown, interestingly enough, doing his own washing off, removing the grubbiness of his miner's life.

Presently he came running out of the scullery, with the soapy water dripping from him, dithering with cold.

"Oh, my sirs!" he said. "Wheer's my towel?"

It was hung on a chair to warm before the fire, otherwise he would have bullied and blustered. He squatted on his heels before the hot baking-fire to dry himself.

"F-ff-f!" he went, pretending to shudder with cold.

"Goodness, man, don't be such a kid!" said Mrs. Morel. "It's *not* cold."

"Thee strip thysen stark nak'd to wesh thy flesh i' that scullery," said the miner, as he rubbed his hair; "now't b'r a ice-'ouse!"

"And I shouldn't make that fuss," replied his wife.

"No, tha'd drop down stiff, as dead as a door-knob, wi' thy nesh sides."

"Why is a door-knob deader than anything else?" asked Paul, curious.

"Eh, I dunno; that's what they say," replied his father. "But there's that much draught i' yon scullery, as it blows through your ribs like through a five-barred gate."

"It would have some difficulty in blowing through yours," said Mrs. Morel.

Morel looked down ruefully at his sides.

"Me!" he exclaimed. "I'm now't b'r a skinned rabbit. My bones fair juts out on me."

"I should like to know where," retorted his wife.

"Iv'ry-wheer! I'm nobbut a sack o' faggots."

Mrs. Morel laughed. He had still a wonderfully young body, muscular, without any fat. His skin was smooth and clear. It might have been the body of a man of twenty-eight, except that there were, perhaps, too many blue scars, like tattoo-marks, where the coal-dust remained under the skin, and that his chest was too hairy. But he put his hand on his sides ruefully. It was his fixed belief that, because he did not get fat, he was as thin as a starved rat.

Paul looked at his father's thick, brownish hands all scarred, with broken nails, rubbing the fine smoothness of his sides, and the incongruity struck him. It seemed strange they were the same flesh.[36]

Like Joyce in more than one episode of *A Portrait of the Artist,* Lawrence here allows the idiom of a wiseacre father to express human impulses that repel but also provoke and disturb a sensitive adolescent son. In part, Morel's talk is mere bluster. There is no use in Paul's asking for the logical sense of his father's expressions—not only "dead as a door-knob," but also "five-barred gate," "skinned rabbit," "sack o' faggots," and "thin as a starved rat." The miner neither knows nor cares to satisfy philological curiosity in his adolescent son. His offhand reply ("Eh, I dunno; that's what they say") instinctively resists what may, anyway, sound less like genuine curiosity than like a sullen challenge to the very spirit of the father's palaver. Mrs. Morel, though she habitually speaks correct English, responds more warmly than Paul to Morel's vulgar speech, at least on this occasion. Without quite descending into dialect, she pleasurably banters with her husband in common terms.

The tones of companionable talk in the Morel household differ from their Irish counterparts in parlor or pub. Though Joyce's versions of Irish speech have a broad range, his most sociable talk occurs among men, and its motive as well as effect is the boosting of friendship. That is why Stephen feels so scarily isolated as well as superior when he listens to his father and cronies in the Cork pub in *A Portrait of the Artist* or when, in *Ulysses,* he rejects Mulligan's bid for cameraderie in the Martello tower. It explains, too, why the interiority of Bloom's idiom underlines, by incongruity, his lack of actual social connections. Lawrence is master of a different kind of common talk, more sexually charged and teasing, verging even on quarrel. Insult and reproach can become so loud in this banter between men and women that audible laughter is often necessary to differentiate benign from nasty occasions. In *Sons and Lovers,* Lawrence is delicate and touching in the way he shows how Mrs. Morel, even at a late date in the ruined marriage, can sometimes still respond with humor and sexual pleasure to the swaggering of her husband's voice, as if she felt in his idiom the verbal counterpart of his still intact physical attractiveness: " 'You've had a constitution like iron,' she said; 'and never a man had a better start, if it was body that counted. You should have seen him as a young man,' she cried suddenly to Paul, drawing herself up to imitate her husband's once handsome bearing."

Walter Morel's sex appeal is very like the appeal of popular idiom itself, and idiomatic talk is a good measure for both the force and the limit of reawakened (or remembered) passion in the Morel marriage. What charm Morel possesses derives less from any distinctive qualities of mind or sensibility than from his ability, at moments, to embody a common and durable type of human attractiveness. He's "had a constitution like iron." At his best, Morel represents the strength of the common life handed down through popular idiom, as well as through silent physical gesture. He stands (or squats) firmly in his house, still rich in physical vigor and sustained by pleasure in his body, speaking with an ease that comes from his natural sense of affiliation with a group beyond the self, be it sexual or social. In the washing-up scene he uses common idioms the way he uses his body, with the instinctive confidence of one who knows what these common instruments are for, what they can do to elicit a response. Mrs. Morel does indeed respond, but there is also a sad weight to her qualification: "if it was body that counted." Even Morel knows that his failures in other ways that count make this blaze of good feeling with his wife only transitory. Lawrence makes the glow of passion here a temporary and isolated occurrence, beset as it is by misfortunes and disappointments too complex to be resolved in a mere lively exchange of banter.

Lawrence enlarges the moral and psychological significance of dialect speech in *The Rainbow* through the figure of the farmer Tom Brangwen, specifically in the way he domesticates through talk his foreign stepdaughter, Anna. To be sure, in *The Rainbow* the value of common talk is from the start firmly limited and placed in relation to the mysteries of Tom's feelings in courtship and marriage, mysteries which require the invention of the famous Laurentian "deep" narrative style. But the scenes of intimate, playful talk between father and child are not devalued by Lawrence's more daring and innovative narrative style elsewhere in the book. Indeed, Lawrence quite explicitly shows how Tom *needs* the ballast of his sociable affection with Anna to keep his balance in the oceanic turbulences of his marriage. Moreover, the fading away of dialect speech through the three generations of Brangwens in *The Rainbow* marks the only ambiguously valuable progress toward bourgeois culture that earlier English novelists had also represented with similarly divided feelings. The farmer Tom has the most vivid idiom, and the strongest, clearest, most resilient emotional life as well. The novel ends with the modern young teacher Ursula, whose more standardized speech is flatter and drearier than her grandfather's to the same degree that her inner experience is more confused and socially displaced.

Lawrence's perception of a historical deterioration in the vitality of common speech is considerably complicated, however, by his primary interest in the rub of strong individual personalities against the tight press of history. The difference between Ursula's voice in *The Rainbow* and her voice in *Women in Love* illustrates a kind of personal freedom within history that Lawrence increasingly wanted to allow certain gifted temperaments. In the later novel Ursula continues to speak the correct standard English appropriate to her training and position of schoolteacher, and she continues to suffer the confusion and helplessness associated in the earlier novel with that anomalous social role. But instead of being merely stuck in the impasse of a historical breakup, as in *The Rainbow,* the Ursula of *Women in Love* also gives signs of exceptional latent powers of personality. One such sign, interestingly enough, is her lively access to common idiom, especially when she is moved to anger or protest.

In one of the famous courtship scenes, for example, Birkin has taken the opportunity to lecture Ursula about the mating laws of cats and also of men and women. The voice of protest is Ursula's:

> "Oh, it makes me so cross, the assumption of male superiority! And it is such a lie! One wouldn't mind if there were any justification for it."
>
> "The wild cat," said Birkin, "doesn't mind. She perceives that it is justified."
>
> "Does she!" cried Ursula. "And tell it to the Horse Marines."
>
> "To them also."
>
> "It is just like Gerald Crich with his horse—a lust for bullying—a real Wille zur Macht—so base, so petty."
>
> "I agree that the Wille zur Macht is a base and petty thing. But with the Mino, it is the desire to bring this female cat into a pure stable equilibrium, a transcendent and abiding *rapport* with the single male. Whereas without him, as you see, she is a mere stray, a fluffy sporadic bit of chaos. It is a volonté de pouvoir, if you like, a will to ability, taking pouvoir as a verb."
>
> "Ah—! Sophistries! It's the old Adam."
>
> "Oh yes, Adam kept Eve in the indestructible paradise, when he kept her single with himself, like a star in its orbit."
>
> "Yes—yes," cried Ursula, pointing her finger at him.
>
> "There you are—a star in its orbit! A satellite—a satellite of Mars— that's what she is to be! There—there—you've given yourself away! You want a satellite, Mars and his satellite! You've said it—you've said it— you've dished yourself!"
>
> He stood smiling in frustration and amusement and irritation and admiration and love. She was so quick, and so lambent, like discernible fire, and so vindictive, and so rich in her dangerous flamy sensitiveness.
>
> "I've not said it at all," he replied, "if you will give me a chance to speak."
>
> "No, no!" she cried. "I won't let you speak. You've said it, a satellite, you're not going to wriggle out of it. You've said it." (p. 142)[37]

As elsewhere in Lawrence, the best talk hovers somewhere between quarrel and flirtation. When Ursula exclaims to Birkin, "And tell it to the Horse Marines," she vigorously resists his bullying imagery of love. Common idiom seems especially well-suited to Ursula's protest here, for the very reason that it comes out of the accumulated knowingness of the social community. The conventionality of idiom, from this perspective, strengthens rather than dilutes expressiveness; originality is not only unnecessary but out of place in speech that aims to deflate pretentiousness by evoking common truths of experience. Ursula implicitly backs up her resistance to Birkin's planetary sophistries by calling on the authority of a larger tradition of tough-minded skepticism. The idiom is a quick way for her to evoke a social tradition in support of her individual feeling. Though Birkin, stubbornly (or desperately) committed to his theories, reacts irritably to Ursula's outburst, Lawrence also shows that he is enormously attracted by the vibrant energy in her speech. He falls in love with her because of her talk, not in spite of it. Whether or not his doctrines of love account for it, Birkin knows his need for Ursula's vitality. And he knows what she offers, as well as what he needs, by hearing her, by listening to her speech.

The weightier counterforce in the Ursula-Birkin courtship comes, of course, from Ursula's own intuition that her practical energy has only limited efficacy. She yearns for a release from her tedious social world and also from the limited common sense on which she relies in argument. She thus responds with wary hope to the boldness and mystery of Birkin's visions even while protesting against them. The story of Ursula and Birkin in *Women in Love* dramatizes the conflicts and attractions between personalities which transcend the resources of the surrounding culture at a particularly dismal moment in history. Significantly, Lawrence shows the couple leaving England, presumably for good, to carry on their tense but invigorating private quarrels in exile.

It should be clear from my examples that there is no idealization of common language in either Lawrence or Joyce; nor does either writer turn away from the constriction of personal and intellectual power that the social conventions of language both embody and perpetuate. The important point is that idiomatic language carries enough value in these writers to support more than satiric dramas of conflict and attraction between the high-toned and the idiomatic characters and between the values that different modes of speech convey, sometimes even within the personality of a single individual.

The power of idiomatic speech to criticize other, more intellectual or visionary styles has been astutely examined by Richard Poirier in relation to Robert Frost. Poirier follows, in Frost's poetry and statements about poetry, the lively tensions between language "presumably taken fresh from talk" and other, more obviously "poetic" voices.[38] For Poirier, this tension identifies Frost as distinctively American (in the tradition of Thoreau) and distinctively apart from other modern (and modernist) responses to the legacy of romanticism. He persuasively separates Frost's work not only from poets like Pound, Eliot, Stevens, and Yeats, but also from Joyce and Lawrence, by the richness and constancy of the dialectic Frost creates through the play of colloquial against more literary language.

Yet Frost is less remote from the English-language novelists than Poirier implies when he defines Frost's "unique difficulty" to be his demand that "we be common and literary all at once."[39] Even the rich thematic connections in Frost between the dialectic of different voices and the tension between "home" and "extravagance" has its counterpart in the fiction of Lawrence and Joyce, for whom the literal experience of foreign exile gave such full social and cultural meaning to the choice of being "at home" in language or not. In a sense, the bold flights away from home of both Lawrence and Joyce gave the lead to extravagance in their lives and work, in contrast to what Poirier calls Frost's "congenital circumspection."[40] But the different weighting of terms occurs within the same dialectic. Although both Lawrence and Joyce left their homes and homelands with a vengeance, neither of them simply left familiar idiom behind. For both Lawrence and Joyce, the very extremity of living as a writer surrounded by foreign voices had the effect of intensifying idiomatic English as a distinct object of consciousness and as a repository of values and associations to be neither accepted nor rejected as a matter of course.

Within the French tradition, by contrast, the investigation of cliché in Flaubert's *Dictionnaire* is extended by Proust in the direction of an ever more profound rejection of common speech. The bourgeois figures in Proust's novel include artists and other delicate sensibilities with no lack of inner life. They suffer from the different horror that their essential life—the *moi profond*—is verbally incommunicable to one another and, over time, even to themselves. The composer Vinteuil and the painter Elstir escape this predicament through the nonverbal forms of their art. But it is the narrator whom we know to suffer this plight most acutely, and it is also he who transcends it superbly, through the discovery that his mind can privately liberate language from bondage to conversational norms.

Marcel's disillusion with spoken language is shown to begin in childhood, on a splendid autumn morning at Combray when he failed to elicit more than a surly grunt from a passing peasant he had greeted: "Beautiful day, isn't it? Fine weather for walking."[41] Marcel, middle-aged, recalls and elaborately re-creates the intense and delicate joy he had felt in every detail of the scene, in the reflection, for example, of tiled roofs in a pond. But Marcel also recalls the bad mood of the peasant, not improved by the fact that the child in his ecstasy had just barely missed hitting him with his umbrella. Proust gives just enough detail to suggest a satiric social reading of the scene. We may wonder what a peasant might wish to reply in such a situation, or why he should answer at all. The strains of social class in the provinces may account for the awkward encounter: the vacationing Parisian child seems almost imperiously to expect regard from a peasant neighbor with whom he shares no enterprise, no local dialect, no common experience—nothing, indeed, but the platitudinous fine day. Proust can display the tension of social class on such an occasion, but that is not his main interest, despite his suggestive detail. He endorses the narrator's placing of blame on the inadequacy of ordinary speech itself.

Later in the novel, just before he subjects Albertine to a *petit discours* on the nature of style in art, Marcel again recalls—and this time generalizes—the significance of his boyhood disappointment. He argues for the superiority of music to speech for re-creating *l'inflexion de l'être* ("the inflection of the thing itself"), "that interior and extreme point of our sensation which is the part that gives us that peculiar exhilaration which we recapture from time to time and which when we say, 'What a fine day! What glorious sunshine!' we do not in the least communicate to our neighbor, in whom the same sun and the same weather arouse wholly different vibrations."[42] Through Marcel, Proust invites us to lament the inevitable failure of common speech to convey to any other person (not just a peasant) the uniqueness of sensation—in childhood, in nature, in love. This uniqueness constitutes our "real life": private, secret, anterior to language, and which only the radically uncommon language and structure of art can hope to make manifest.

The influence of the Proustian generalization on more recent theoretical approaches to verbal conventionality in the novel can be seen in Gabriel Josipovici's study of modern fiction, *The World and the Book*. With considerably less interest than Proust in the social determinants of speech, Josipovici uses Marcel's boyhood encounter with the peasant to exemplify his own general point about the prison of convention constituted by even the simplest forms of normal discourse. He insists on the general importance and validity of the Proustian lesson "that words are mere labels, generalizers, and thus unable to convey anything except the tired life of habit, the progression of instants devoid of any meaning."[43]

English idiomatic language rebukes an impulse like Josipovici's—to extend the domain of cliché into the entire structure of ordinary language—by reminding us that the motive of self-manifestation does not exhaust the play of personality in speech. Marcel's disillusionment rests on the premise that what a speaker mainly and always wants to convey refers back to the unique vibrations of experience within his sole self. This narrowly egotistical conception of speech (and of personality) seems mocked in advance by Flaubert's analysis of the myriad forms of bourgeois self-love. Even the man in the *Dictionnaire* who has taken a train from X behaves as though he has a unique adventure to report. The conviction of unique experience does not, however, guarantee that it is other than banal, even when the figure is a sensitive boy enraptured by his vision of the morning. The vain insistence on uniqueness may paradoxically unite the bourgeois *homme d'affaires* and the self-consciously artistic sensibility in the same romantic cliché of the *moi profond*.

My differentiation of idiom from cliché depends fundamentally on a more diverse conception of the motives of speech and of the variable directions in spoken gestures. English "speech act theory," as in John Austin's *How to Do Things with Words,* has elaborately codified this diversity of social speech, but for the crucial point about common idiom, L. P. Smith's informal perception in *Words and Idioms* may suffice: "In idiomatic speech, the person or persons spoken to are more important than the speaker."[44] Conventional phrases can hardly be turned to the expression of a unique self because they are by nature communal and tend, often insistently, to affirm the shared character of human experience. Idiom implicitly, and often explicitly, asserts that we are, in one of Leopold Bloom's favorite expressions, all in the same boat! That sometimes compassionate, often deflating recognition is precisely what idiomatic language offers; it most effectively goes to work when a speaker wants to get that point across to a hearer, drawing the other person into a relationship, often through exhortation or reproof. Thus L. P. Smith summarizes the spirit and subject matter of idiom as "prudent and foolish conduct, success and failure, and above all, human relations—the vivid attitudes and feelings of people intensely interested in each other and their mutual dealings—approval, but far more largely disapproval, friendly, but more often hostile feelings, fallings out and makings up, rivalries and over-reachings, reprobation, chastisement, and abuse."[45]

Idiomatic speech may thus appear even more aggressively hostile to individual genius than cliché; it may seem to express the community's demand that the individual shape up and fit in to its regular order. Yet a more complex relationship between the conventional and the regular also emerges from the study of idiom, for idiomatic language in itself, almost by definition, is irregular: ungrammatical, illogical, made of untranslatable archaisms and combinations of words that are nonsensical apart from their conventional meaning. The appeal of idiom, Smith nicely explains, partly depends on its irregularity, as it provides for "a certain irrelevance in the human mind, a love for the illogical and absurd, a reluctance to submit itself to reason."[46] One English philologist, noting that "idiom" comes from the Greek for "peculiarity," observes that grammar is its natural enemy, since grammar serves the "faculty which promotes regularity and logical order in the economy of language."[47]

The resistance of idiom to the regulations of grammar and logic reflects virtues ordinarily associated with individuality. But in idiom these virtues are spread and shared through a community and across generations. If cliché is the emblem of personality abdicating its authority to convention, idiom is the emblem of the subversive life possible, and even strengthened, within and through convention. Idiomatic speech is a form of expression through which the individual may call on the knowingness of generations to support his resistance to the rulings of institutionalized society.

Socially nostalgic lovers of English idiom imagine stable social communities in the past where the vitality of popular speech corresponded to other kinds of human freedom and energy. Both Lawrence and Joyce were protected from this nostalgia by their actual social origins. The English coal town in the one case, and the depressed Irish city in the other, offered the more dissonant experience of communities where more than ordinarily vigorous speech was being preserved directly in proportion to the absence of most other kinds of power, and even stability. The adolescent autobiographical protagonists, Stephen Dedalus and Paul Morel, both righteously and rightly resent the impotent disorder in their misruled homes and communities. In *Sons and Lovers, Stephen Hero, A Portrait of the Artist as a Young Man,* and even *Ulysses,* adolescent rebellion in part takes the form of disgusted impatience with the disorder of family and familiar speech. Joyce, especially, insists on his young hero's yearning for an order as logical as grammar (or Catholic theology), and it is this deep longing for order which separates the future artist from other dexterous Dublin talkers. Joyce's own leaving home to be an artist can likewise be interpreted as the very opposite of conventional bohemianism, for what Joyce, like Stephen, most intensely distrusted was the often lively but almost always futile disorder conspicuous through the voices of song, story, and barroom chat. Art offered the promise of order, yet Joyce also feared (and knew, from his struggle with the Church) the threat of deadness carried by all established forms of order. Lawrence equally held himself apart from all the high structures of order offered by his culture, even as he recoiled from the empty bluster and grim resignation so oppressively audible in the voices of common life. The struggle to be free of the constraints embodied in the language of the community, yet still not to relinquish the life associated with that idiom, creates uncommon depth and unresolvable tension in the work of both of these English-speaking novelists. Their sensitivity to the vitality of common idiom disrupts any systematic laws of cliché, preserving in their greatest work an irreducible ambiguity about the relationship of both literature and personality to the common terms of life.

2

The Community of Intelligence and the Avant-Garde

"Chaque jour j'attache moins de prix à l'intelligence" ("Every day I attach less value to intelligence").[1] With this opening to *Contre Sainte-Beuve,* Proust may seem to challenge a whole configuration of values in the English even more than in the French critical tradition. F. R. Leavis's notorious distaste for Proust suggests a clear-cut division in modern literary culture: Leavis and kindred Anglo-American spirits clinging to the provincial banner of "intelligence," versus Proust in the vanguard of the Continental modernist opposition. Although such a formulation has a degree of truth, comparison of French and English concepts of intelligence in criticism curiously blurs any such neat boundaries. While Leavis does reject, in the name of intelligence, the way Proust dissociates art from all other kinds of human interchange, it must be understood that *l'intelligence* so thoroughly scorned by Proust is significantly different from the quality championed in modern English usage of the term. Indeed, one reason why avant-garde French criticism, with its large debt to Proust, can seem so alien to the Anglo-American mind is that the very vocabulary of this criticism intersects only erratically with English meanings of even the same words.

As with the distinction between idiom and cliché, the divergence between French and English conceptions of intelligence can be traced back to the seventeenth century, even though the cultural contrasts become more conspicuous later. In the Renaissance, as can be seen from Littré's *Dictionnaire, l'intelligence* carried the same range of political, social, and semiphilosophic meanings in French as "intelligence" does in English, and it appears in a similar variety of contexts. In Latin the verb *intellego* gives both *intellegentia* (in the philosophical essays of Cicero) and later *intellectus* (for example, in Seneca and Tacitus) as names for mental understanding.[2] Enough of this ancient overlap survives in sixteenth-century vernacular to make Sir Thomas Elyot, searching for an English word to translate the Latin *intellectus,* consider "intelligence" as the most plausible candidate. (Curiously, he does not propose "intellect.") But Elyot disqualifies "intelligence" because, he explains, current political usage has been fashioning it into an "elegant word where there is mutuall treaties or appoyntements."[3] The specific association of "intelligence" with the information needed for war and peace does not appear in Latin; it probably enters English diplomacy in the sixteenth century from French. In both languages, political and social meanings connected to this usage come to dominate the word between the sixteenth and seventeenth centuries. Diverse other connotations of "intelligence" also survive in both languages during this period. The eighteenth-century French *Encyclopédie,* however, suggests the elusive cultural phenomenon of a word that has not so much shifted as simply gone dead.

What is most striking in the *Encyclopédie* is the sheer dreariness of the whole entry for "L'intelligence." Compared to the ten double-columned pages on "L'imagination," or the intricate logical discussion for "Impossible," the brief paragraph on "L'intelligence" shows a concept that has become uninteresting because it is too vague or too unstable to analyze: "this word has a great number of different accepted meanings which we are going to define by as many examples," says the *Encyclopédie.*[4] However, the examples offer only a series of remarkably perfunctory sentences manufactured for the sole purpose of definition. The word remains without literary or social or colloquial vitality, in striking contrast not only to other French words in the *Encyclopédie,* but also to Johnson's handling of the English equivalent in his *Dictionary.*

Although in his own writing Johnson, like his contemporaries, uses "reason" when discussing human understanding, in the *Dictionary* he registers and also preserves the vitality of the word "intelligence" and its variants through his interesting examples from such writers as Spenser, Sidney, Shakespeare, Bacon, Hooker, Denham, and Addison:

> It was perceived there had not been in the catholicks so much foresight as to provide that true *intelligence* might pass between them of what was done. (HOOKER)

> Let all the passages
> Be well secured, that no *intelligence*
> May pass between the princes and them. (DENHAM)

> . . . whereupon commonly ensueth that ill *intelligence* that we see between great personages. (BACON)

> He lived rather in a fair *intelligence* than any friendship with the favourites. (CLARENDON)

> Heaps of huge words, up hoarded hideously,
> They think to be chief praise of poetry;
> And thereby wanting due *intelligence,*
> Have marred the face of goodly poesie. (SPENSER)[5]

Johnson's examples show that while "intelligence," like "reason," kept the general meaning of "understanding" all through the Renaissance, actual usage gave the word to political and social rather than philosophic discourse. Other words, specifically "reason" and to a lesser extent "intellect," acquired technical prestige in official Renaissance analyses of mental faculties and their hierarchical structure. "Intelligence" was a more disorderly word, both conceptually and grammatically, as can be seen in Johnson's evocative but not very precise definitions: "Intelligence: 1. Commerce of information; notice; mutual communication; account of things distant or secret . . . 2. Commerce of acquaintance; terms on which men live with one another." Johnson relegates the meaning of "intelligence" as a faculty of individual understanding to a lowly fourth place in his list of definitions. Emphasis falls instead on the object or the account of what is to be known and on the process of communicating knowledge in society. "Intelligence," as it survives in eighteenth-century English, connotes a kind of understanding that pertains to communication and human relationship—knowledge as it lives in one or another form of discovered or reported news.

Grammatical variants show the evaluative responsibilities connected with this worldly usage. Johnson defines the adjective "intelligent" as "knowing, instructed, skillful." He cites Bacon: "It is . . . in the order of nature for him to govern that is the more intelligent" (1626). The "intelligent" ruler needs to be properly "intelligenced"; and he needs skillful "intelligencers," not only spies but all bringers of messages and instructions.

Drawing on many of the same Renaissance sources as Johnson, the *Oxford English Dictionary* gives an even fuller historical picture of what might be called the communicative dimension of knowing attached to the English word "intelligence" from Renaissance usage. Examples come from plays and narrative poems, but even more from chronicles, histories, court letters, personal gossip, and travelers' reports. It is true that one reach of the word (for example, in Donne and Milton) does specify the very purest form of knowing—angels are called "intelligences"; but in its full life it regularly participates in the comings and goings of the less pure world of court, town, and battlefield. In the sixteenth and seventeenth centuries, it referred mainly to a worldly kind of knowing and to the human business, however practiced, of exchanging knowledge about the world.

Many faculties of body as well as mind could function as agents of understanding in this Renaissance conception of knowing. In Sidney's *Arcadia,* eyes are "diligent intelligencers." One seventeenth-century commentator remarked, perhaps wittily, "Oliver's Nose was no doubt a wonderful intelligencer" (1687). For worldly purposes, it mattered little whether intelligence operated through the eye, ear, mind, nose, or all faculties together. What mattered was getting the feel of some situation accurately, and also being able to communicate that knowledge to others.

In Renaissance English one may have true intelligence *of* the seasons or *between* friends or even *with* the enemy. The frequent prepositions reinforce the sense of a knowledge which connects the mind to the physical world and also to other people. In the absence of systematic regulation or even a fixed decorum for these connections, all the urgency focuses on somehow knowing how to get it right.

In English as well as French, the looseness of the term "intelligence" no doubt contributed to its decline in the eighteenth century and to its availability for appropriation by new fields of natural philosophy and psychology in the nineteenth. Less fixed than "intellect" or "reason" in older conceptual schemes, the word "intelligence" could more easily be adjusted to serve a science which itself wished to display a drama of interaction between living creatures and their environment. Thus Darwin (1881): "If worms have the power of acquiring some notion, however rude, of the shape of an object and of their burrows, as seems to be the case, they deserve to be called intelligent."

In English, however, an older tradition of worldly, social usage sur-vived into the nineteenth century to create continuing tension with new scientific theories of intelligence, whether in worms or children or men. This tradition allowed "intelligence" to be turned as a pointed instrument precisely *against* the claims of theory and system in all branches of psychology, philosophy, and the arts. The argument that French rationalism of the seventeenth century artificially narrowed our self-understanding is a key point in Gilbert Ryle's *The Concept of Mind*. Sustaining in terms of "ordinary language" his anti-Cartesian argument, Ryle protests the abstraction of "knowing" from practical skills, social relationships, or even such nearly physical aptitudes as having "a good nose for arguments or jokes." In his chapter entitled "Knowing How and Knowing That," Ryle explains that "there are many activities which directly display qualities of mind, yet are neither themselves intellectual operations nor yet effects of intellectual opera-tions. Intelligent practice is not a step-child of theory. On the contrary, theorizing is one practice amongst others and is itself intelligently or stupidly conducted."[6]

In literary criticism, F. R. Leavis similarly insists on the centrality for literature, even more than for philosophy, of what Ryle calls "intel-ligent practice," and his meaning too draws on the continuity of "ordi-nary language" with Renaissance distinctions. Even when defending tough exertions of mind in relation to poetry, Leavis relishes any op-portunity for the polemical paradox of playing "intelligence" off against "intellect" as well as against more obvious contraries. He espe-cially enjoys turning the standard of intelligence against presumed in-tellectual authorities, even against T. S. Eliot, who had been such an authority in his own education. He obviously likes the incongruity of defending D. H. Lawrence against Eliot on the grounds of Lawrence's "intelligence," a quality generally as absent from the rare praise as from the common blame of Lawrence's work at the time Leavis took up his defense in 1930. Leavis similarly likes the incongruity of calling Eliot's contempt for Lawrence "a failure of intelligence" in Eliot himself.[7] With rather less complication of personal allegiance for Lea-vis, the standard of intelligence is also turned against the Parisian cult of *Finnegans Wake,* and against other avant-garde esthetes, especially French ones, and their intellectual masters, Flaubert and Proust: "Flaubert is supposed to be pre-eminently the intelligent artist, but what we have here . . . is essentially a failure of intelligence."[8]

Against the new intellectual claims of scientific system on the one hand and esoteric modernism on the other, the English standard of intelligence tries to revive the unsystematic knowingness associated with the literature and society of the English Renaissance. Indeed, as explicit terms of value, "intelligence" and "intelligent" become more important in modern English criticism than they ever were before, because they name the quality that was not so much conceptualized as enacted in the language of the golden past. In the England of Shakespeare, Arnold nostalgically affirms, "society was, in the fullest measure, permeated by fresh thought, intelligent and alive."[9]

L'intelligence enters the vocabulary of nineteenth-century French natural and social science without comparable competition from an older speech idiom. As in Taine's two-volume treatise on psychology, *De l'intelligence* (1870), the modern French term picks up and even extends old connotations of diversity in the pursuit of knowledge, but this meaning encounters much less tension and is likewise subject to much less ambiguity than in English. The diversity of mental activity gathered under the rubric of French *intelligence* comes to be more simply associated with a judicious, if not positively stolid disinterestedness; *l'intelligence* comes to represent the very spirit of the scientific mind, methodically gathering all kinds of information to bear upon its investigations of the objective world.

It is this aura of natural science that Proust so much dislikes in Sainte-Beuve's recommendation of intelligence in literary criticism. To Sainte-Beuve, intelligent critical method meant the gathering around the literary work of as many kinds of information as possible—social, biographical, economic—as one collects varied information about any object of investigation. This accumulative conception of literary intelligence stands out clearly in the passage from *Nouveaux Lundis* selected for particular scorn by Proust:

> One cannot have too many methods and too many means if one is to know a man, that is to say, something other than a pure spirit. So long as one has not asked oneself a certain number of questions about an author, and answered them, if only silently and for oneself, one cannot be sure of having a complete grasp of him, even if these questions seem to have nothing to do with his writings. How did he view religion? How was he affected by the spectacle of nature? Where did he stand on the issue of women? on the issue of money? Was he rich, poor; what rules did he live by, what was his daily way of life? . . . None of the answers to these questions is irrelevant in judging the author of a book and the book itself, if the book is not a treatise of pure geometry, above all, if it is a work of literature, that is, where everything plays a part.[10]

Proust observes with distaste the model of descriptive natural science which underlies Sainte-Beuve's critical method, a model which Taine was to make more systematic, to Proust's even greater disgust.[11] For Proust, the nineteenth-century French idea of intelligence in literary matters made of criticism only a kind of "literary botany." The critical intelligence gathers observations and then classifies authors as if they were not unlike pure or hybrid plants. Proust scorns the superficial labeling which passes for literary judgement in Sainte-Beuve's method, as when Sainte-Beuve is pleased to conclude that Chateaubriand was "an epicurean with a Catholic imagination."[12]

Although the pleasure of turning a phrase remains available to the critic as taxonomist, as does the possibility of particular astute judgments, this activity as a *method* has virtually nothing in common with the firsthand responsiveness to the life in language so insisted upon in the English conception of literary intelligence in the twentieth and even the nineteenth century. On the contrary, Sainte-Beuve wants to circumscribe the role of what he calls "rhetoric" in criticism as a way of surmounting the dangers of subjectivity. Although style has its value, he concedes, in creating "immediate and lively impressions," an impartial criticism must learn to discipline personal impressions by fuller knowledge of surrounding circumstances.[13] Nothing could be further from Leavisite (or Arnoldian or Jamesian) intelligence than this deliberate subordination of direct personal response. Whereas in English criticism the judgments of intelligence are most valuable precisely when they are most direct and personal, for Sainte-Beuve the knowledge that ought to control the unreliable feel of a literary work is to be collected specifically by intelligence.

The later development of French criticism has been profoundly shaped, not to say hollowed out, by the academic establishment of critical method according to the model of Sainte-Beuve. Roland Barthes cites this legacy when he protests the iron grip of Gustave Lanson and "Lansonism" on academic French criticism for fifty years, an oppression still felt in the objections of Raymond Picard to Barthes's own "new" structuralist critique of Racine.[14] Lanson's explicit derivation of academic literary method from Sainte-Beuve plainly demonstrates the long-entrenched power of the old criticism which Barthes and his French contemporaries undertake to combat.

Lanson's program for the study of literary history is virtually the same as Sainte-Beuve's, but hardened into institutional fiat through endless repetition down the ranks of an entire nation's educational system. Lanson reiterates the same principles again and again, from the turn of the century to his death in 1934. Here, for example, is Lanson in a 1904 pronouncement of "Méthodes" republished in 1925 for the enlightenment of French educators abroad: "What is the writer? biography, psychology, esthetic or social tendencies. What is the work? its place in a genre, a group, a movement, its special nuance or character."[15] The impassivity of Lanson's questions (and of his style) is not inadvertent. For him, both the intellectual and the moral value of formal literary study involves the regulation—by which he means the subordination—of subjective, personal response. Proper literary methods, he sternly pronounces, constitute "procedures of control, of reduction, and of interpretation whose value is to mark out our path so well that it will become impossible for us to go astray, in spite of all internal impulses."[16] While for Leavis the "discipline" of intelligence enables richer and deeper personal responses to literature, the very idea of discipline in Lanson works to enforce the straight and narrow of objective knowledge: "All our methods are instituted in order to neutralize the misleading influences within us and to preserve us from the tyrannical seduction of the misleading influences which come from within other men."[17] Lanson does bow toward Sainte-Beuve, in allowing the effects of literary style their (limited) due. Style, Sainte-Beuve taught, identifies the individuality of an author and makes a direct impression on our "esthetic sentiment." But neither the moral nor the intellectual core of literary study is constituted by what Lanson calls this "individual caprice." Lanson categorically separates the personal from the objective, which is also a way of separating knowledge from feeling, and the content of thought from the concrete and particular effects of style.

Roland Barthes assimilates Lansonism (and thereby French academic criticism in general) to a "classical" tradition whose ideology is at once rationalistic, bourgeois, and authoritarian, and his analysis quite accurately identifies the intellectual, moral, and social constriction of the ostensibly impartial activity of French literary intelligence. The act of judgment, in this criticism, tends inevitably to be conformist, because the method programmatically encourages distrust of individual personal response. Moreover, the issues at stake in literary judgment are structured in accord with the most conventional moral categories of bourgeois society at large. Did Racine, in spite of his apparent probity, harbor "the spirit of a courtier"? Do details of Molière's private love affairs damage the moral shape of his comedies? These are questions to be clarified by research outside the literary work, rather than through contested perceptions of its language or organization. The classical authors of the French tradition come up for moral interrogation, so to speak, but not primarily on the grounds of their literary expression.

Perhaps even more disappointing, or at least more tedious, than the form of moral trial in this criticism is the predictability of judicious acquittal. Even though, in the name of truth, moral lapses may need to be acknowledged here and there in the classic canonical authors, they all ultimately manage to pass the moral test. For, true to the spirit of other projects of national rapprochement in the Third Republic, Lansonist literary research has as a quite explicit goal the healing of long-standing ideological wounds. Instead of the strenuous English sport of pitting, say, the "line of wit" against the Miltonic influence, or of searching the tradition for particular forebears to sponsor controversial new talents, a contrary desire to put to rest the all-too-bitter schisms of old and recent history sounds through Lanson's grandly conciliatory rhetoric. The great French writers of the past all together constitute "the permanent possibility of intellectual and emotional stimulation for civilized humanity."[18] The rhetoric of affirmation is general enough to include everyone, as the very ordering of names joins in amicable pairing the great historical rivalries of the French tradition. The resources of civilization are "in Montaigne and Pascal, in Bossuet and Rousseau, in Voltaire and Chateaubriand." Lansonism works to neutralize not only individual sentiment but the destructive passions of the nation's entire past: "For the acceptance of the same discipline establishes a communion between the men of every party and of every faith . . . monarchist or republican, Catholic or socialist."

To Roland Barthes, only a simple inversion is necessary to repudiate the entire ritual of this ecumenical "communion." For him as for Proust, the morality of bourgeois intelligence is as superficial as its rhetoric is banal. The conception of life which the academic intelligence extracts from virtually every classic text, Barthes asserts in *S/Z*, is nothing but "a nauseating mixture of common opinions, a smothering layer of received ideas."[19] All classic texts, read conventionally, are boringly alike; they can become interesting again only by a critical activity directed to subverting the cultural myths which orthodox opinion has used them to sustain.

In his contempt for the myths of French bourgeois culture, Barthes identifies as a malady for "ethno-psychiatry" the French compulsion to expunge disorder, even from the language, and to maintain enclosure by ritual obeisance to the idols of logic and clarity.[20] What Barthes does not as readily diagnose is his own participation in the very culture which he is contesting. What he calls *la critique,* for example, perpetuates as much as it challenges the Lansonist separation between knowledge and feeling. *La critique* is an activity of intellectual analysis, and in this way sharply distinct from the private emotions aroused by reading. Barthes eroticizes certain experiences of reading by celebrating them under the sexually provocative label of *la jouissance.* Yet for all its unorthodoxy, his *jouissance* is only a sexually liberated version of what an earlier generation called *sentiment,* still distinct from knowledge, and still an irrational temptation, a seduction, however voluptuously treasured. *La critique,* by contrast, is a discipline of interrogating, distinguishing, and classifying the constructions of meanings in a text, and as such it remains separate from the intensely personal activity of "reading": "to read is to desire the work, it is to want to be the work, it is to refuse to duplicate the work in any language other than the very language of the book."[21] The dichotomy between reading and criticism—in other words, between feeling and thought—remains intact in Barthes's *nouvelle critique,* which is why his productions can seem so unnervingly hot and cold alternately, or even at the same time.

Although Barthes and his colleagues are quick to expose the false pretensions to objectivity of the old academic criticism, the prestige of science continues to haunt their new methodologies. The difference is only that science itself has become more sophisticated, more self-critical. Yet such new sciences as linguistics, psychoanalysis, or anthropology reduce the margin of freedom for individual expression or response even more than did the looser sciences of the past. Barthes explains that the very progress of the "human sciences" reduces the authority, if not the freedom, of literature to say anything significant at all about the human experience, for the sciences have now partitioned the "human" into a plurality of specialized constructions. The arrogance (or naiveté) of the classical writer's pretension to speak for and to Man in a normative, natural language is exposed by "scientific" demonstration to the effect that no language is normative and natural, and that there is no integrated figure to be called "Man": there are psychoanalytic or anthropological or Marxist or capitalist constructions of human experience, but no possibility of any whole vision not controlled by one or another limited and specialized code. The pretension of classical French rhetoric to a voice of universal truth represents, from this perspective, only the bad faith of a narrow and exclusionary social class. The "universal" of French classicism, Barthes protests, is only "a universal of petty landlords"[22]; French literary history between 1650 and 1848 must therefore be re-viewed (and unmasked) as the ritual of a social class confirming its power through the rhetorical costumes of logic, clarity, and truth. The present moment of liberating crisis begins in 1848, when such writers as Flaubert began to seek ways of subverting the "community of stereotypes."[23] Revulsion from the received ideas of academic criticism is closely linked, rhetorically and ideologically, to modern French protest against the rule of the stereotype in all aspects of bourgeois culture.

As with the distinction between *cliché* or *stéréotype* in French and "idiom" in English, the separate evolution of "intelligence" in the two cultures shows the power of national traditions in which a few key values have extraordinary persistence through many changes of terminology and taste. The pivotal figures for the English development of intelligence as a critical concept are Matthew Arnold and Henry James, Arnold because he was himself rather confusedly trying to straddle two cultures, and James because he elaborated such a full argument for intelligence as the central qualification specifically for the novelist—as well as for the readers and the main characters of fiction. In view of the English chauvinism later associated with Leavis's standard of intelligence, it is interesting to note that these two nineteenth-century figures, themselves so important to Leavis, write self-consciously as cosmopolitans acquainted with French as well as English literature, and that they recommend intelligence as a value likely to be underrated by their English audiences.

Arnold admires Sainte-Beuve, and he takes the term "intelligence" directly from him to use as a foreign corrective to English provinciality. In a common nineteenth-century division of national virtues, Arnold grants "genius" to the English, and to the French, "intelligence," by which he means "the prosaic virtue of a free play of mind on all subjects which it touches."[24] Arnold so admires Sainte-Beuve's idea of controlling personal impression by the more impartial exercise of intelligence, that he imagines the benefit of institutionalizing this disinterestedness in some English equivalent of the French Academy, where standards of "tone and taste" could be authoritatively established and promoted.

Yet what makes Arnold so pivotal is the way he cannot help but Anglicize the very ideas he imports in order to correct what he deplores as English provinciality. No sooner does he take the word "intelligence" from the French than he assimilates it into the very tradition of "genius" which he intended it to counterbalance. In both principle and practice, Arnold does not imitate Sainte-Beuve's excursions into the biographical, social, and historical environs of the literary work. He continues to hold, with such provincial English "geniuses" as Wordsworth and Coleridge, that the highest quality of literature is "inseparable from the superiority of diction and movement marking its style and manner."[25] Rather than consigning style to a separate, legitimate, but subordinate "esthetic" sphere, Arnold continues the English Romantic centering of criticism in rhetoric. Moreover, he goes on to explain that the best approach to the superiority of artistic language is not through acquiring information or rules about it but through direct and intimate acquaintance with particular examples.

Literary intelligence, for Arnold, thus remains a matter of direct, personal perception, even while he tries to integrate into his idea of judgment some more general standards which could raise perception beyond mere prejudice. His model clearly draws on an ideal of moral training in other areas of life. Sufficient acquaintance with the best examples of language, Arnold optimistically proposes, can create an internal standard, a version of conscience in matters of taste. Arnold thus transfers to esthetic experience the central tension of Protestant ethics: conscience must be personal and yet also a discipline of personality: "We like to be suffered to lie comfortably in the old straw of our habits, especially of our intellectual habits, even though this straw may not be very clean and fine."[26] The tension between the piggish and the fine in literary response ultimately constitutes for Arnold an internal drama, not a conflict between feeling and knowledge or between the personal and the objective, but between the better and worse parts of one's own sensibility.

As Arnold internalizes the drama of literary judgment, "intelligence" loses most of the objective impartiality it was imported from France to establish. Arnoldian judgment defers not to extraliterary evidence (as Sainte-Beuve and later Lanson recommend), but to an ideal that needs to become part of one's own sensibility: "Those whose intelligence is quickest, openest, most sensitive, are readiest with this deference; those whose intelligence is less delicate and sensitive are less disposed to it."[27] Through words like "sensitive" and "delicate," and repeated phrases like "sensitiveness of intelligence," Arnold evokes a natural, almost physical gift of mind that is also a gift of feeling, a version (moved only a few degrees toward the worldly and the intellectual) of what Wordsworth had earlier in the century called "organic sensibility" when identifying the qualifications of the poet. Thus Arnold's sensitive intelligence ceases to pose opposition, or even serious correction, to English ideas of genius. Sensitiveness of intelligence, as Leavis will go on to insist with provocative emphasis, is itself a form of genius, in literature as well as life.

Before Leavis, however, Henry James had already gone further than Arnold to elaborate the activity of intelligence, not as an adjunct or supplement or corrective to other creative or critical activities, but as the very center of the artistic process itself. Writing criticism as a novelist trying to promote better understanding of his own fiction, James appeals to the reader's intelligence to respond to the intelligence of the artist with a receptivity that will be an act of both understanding and appreciation. The reader's response must be direct and individual, James explains, as he goes on to endow directness of perception with intense moral significance for both reader and artist. This moral position has a liberating, nonconformist motive in James; there are no intrinsically "moral" or "immoral" subjects, he asserts in the preface to *The Portrait of a Lady*. The moral quality of a subject must be assessed by more personal measures of individual intensity of engagement with whatever subject: "is it valid, in a word, is it genuine, is it sincere, the result of some direct impression or perception of life."[28]

James's questions, unlike those of Sainte-Beuve and Lanson, cannot be answered by evidence gathered from the environs of the literary work. The quality of direct impression or perception exists only as the amount of "felt life" communicated through language and form to the reader. "Felt life," the Jamesian phrase adopted almost as a slogan by a later generation of "intelligent" English critics, is synonomous with "experience," which will become another slogan. James himself is at some pains to define quite specifically what he means by "felt life" and "experience." The muddle of what ordinarily passes for life—what simply *happens*—does not become experience, in James's sense, until it has been perceived, individually apprehended, with some "mark" made on "the intelligence." The capacity for experience, in this specific sense, is what enables the novelist to shape a subject out of the inchoate material of mere life, and it is also the indispensable quality that enables a reader to have an experience of this art. And it is this same capacity to see feelingly and to feel perceptively that makes the characters in art interesting to us. In the preface to *The Princess Casamassima*, James names Hamlet and Lear as the "really sentient" characters in English literature.[29] On a less grand scale, the "intense perceivers" at the center of George Eliot's novels also capture our interest for their adventures of consciousness. Emma Bovary, on the other hand, lacks sufficient intelligence in this sense, and she is therefore finally "too small an affair" for James, despite the perfection of rendering that he recognizes in Flaubert's masterpiece.[30] His own fiction, he explains in virtually every preface, is about nothing but "intelligence": Isabel Archer, Hyacinth Robinson, Maisie, Fleda, Strether, Millie, Merton, Maggie—all his main characters are interesting because they are "intense perceivers," and thus what happens to them is not lost in the muddle of circumstance but seen, apprehended, interpreted in passionate actions of feeling and thought.

The experience of the Jamesian character, like that of the novelist and reader, too, is of course not objective. James's famous image of the windows of consciousness, all of dissimilar shape and size, expresses the particular and necessarily partial focusing of perception, as well as the crucial contact through "vision" between the eye of consciousness and some object distinct enough to be seen.[31] Elements of Wordsworthian imagination thus enter this Jamesian idea of creative perception, except that, by his preference for the word "intelligence," James sets lucidity rather than mystery as the goal of the creative process. What he calls "the bewildered state" is the normal, vulgar condition of life; intelligence transforms confusion into "intelligibility." Less enthralled with mystery than the Romantics, and yet more insistently personal than the classical French spokesmen for universal *clarté,* James finds in the term "intelligence" a way of identifying a richly distinctive mode of knowing in both life and art.

As a value for the genre of the novel, specifically, older connotations of the social and the communicative give support to James's wish to make intelligence a normative standard, personal but not finally eccentric. "Experience, as I see it," he explains in the preface to *The Princess Casamassima,* "is our apprehension and our measure of what happens to us as social creatures—any intelligent report of which has to be based on that apprehension."[32] The adventure of the intelligent character will presumably become intelligible in the novel's report of it. The intelligent reader completes the circuit by responding with full perception to that report and thus appreciating, in turn, the full value of the character's experience. Jamesian intelligence thus includes the meanings stated by Johnson: mutual communication; account of things distant or secret; commerce of acquaintance; terms on which men live with one another. James elaborates these meanings into an art focused on dramas of individual consciousness, but he holds consciousness responsible for specific and personal knowledge of what "happens to us as social creatures." "What he wrote about was always present in somebody's specific knowledge of it," remarks R. P. Blackmur: "By insisting on intelligence and lucidity something like an ideal vision was secured; not an ideal in the air but an ideal in the informed imagination."[33]

Yet it is, of course, James's very promise of intelligibility that has led especially those admirers most influenced by his principles to react with bewilderment to certain of his own remarkable "reports." Even Blackmur, one of James's most appreciative readers, has to acknowledge the obscurity, the mysterious idiosyncrasy of the late fiction where, he observes, both subject and style are so "difficult to coordinate with the reader's own experience" as to seem perverse, if not positively unintelligible. The normative connotations of intelligence and intelligibility seem to promise more open coordination. Blackmur somewhat awkwardly works his way out of the problem by making it quantitative, the mere excess of a virtue: James's late style, he says, shows a tendency to "an excess of intelligence" and an "excessive effort to communicate it."[34] Yet the evaluative force of the very word "intelligence" makes paradoxical the idea of such an excess: one may be judged too obscurely intellectual by the standard of intelligence, but intelligence itself is almost by definition not excessive, not incommunicative. This standard is at the heart of Leavis's turning of James's own critical vocabulary against the writings of the late phase, where Leavis sees not an excess of intelligence but, more simply, its failure.

Leavis objects that the technical elaborations of the late James style lack dramatic intensity and focus, weaknesses that reveal a loss of that close touch with experience for which the earlier James is himself one of the touchstones.[35] The standard of intelligence does not require a "plain style" of either narration or dialogue. Leavis's own examples of dramatic language, from James as well as from Shakespeare and other writers, are meant to show how the densest, most complex uses of English can work to express the richest visions of human experience.[36] At the same time, it is evident that Leavis most clearly hears the actions of intelligence in the English language when he can identify elements of speech idiom pressing on whatever other styles may be present. In Leavis's criticism, the connection between literary intelligence and the tradition of living English idiom becomes an explicit and fully developed principle of critical judgment.

Not only do what he calls "the sinew and the living nerve of English" show most powerfully in masterful uses of speech forms but, equally important, speech idiom exerts a critical pressure on other kinds of style—a pressure which is crucial to the effect of drama and therefore to the impression of vital intelligence. The "wearying dead-

ness" of Milton's Grand Style, to Leavis's taste, is a reaction based on
this fundamentally Shakespearean standard. "To the ear trained on
Shakespeare," Leavis argues in *Revaluation,* any style totally drained
of "the life of idiom, the pressure of speech" will seem finally dead.[37]
Likewise, it is the absence of palpable critical pressure behind the
"monotony" of Lawrence's style in *The Plumed Serpent* which makes
Leavis suspect a falsity and a forcing of belief in that novel, in comparison to other writings by Lawrence that are admirable precisely
because their language does enact "a sustained, tense and living relation with the concrete, with the particulars of experience."[38] To look
for tension in literary language is to look not only for verbal complexity in itself, but for the pressure of other, extraliterary kinds of complexity on the texture of language. That is the standard by which
Leavis (for the most part) admires *Ulysses,* but denies *Finnegans Wake*
the Shakespearean stature claimed for it by some commentators. In
what he perceives as the "external and mechanical" multiplication of
linguistic complication in Joyce's last book, Leavis detects something
spurious as well as boring. "It is not that one objects to conscious
management, which is inevitable. But conscious management in the
Work in Progress is not the agent of a deeply serious purpose; it serves
in general an inveterate solemn ingenuity, and it is often the very
willing pimp to a poor wit."[39] In its outspoken impatience with all
kinds of singlemindedness, whether grand like Milton or ingenious like
the late Joyce, "intelligent" English criticism tends toward a consistent
if not inflexible standard of judgment: worldly and dramatic; sociable
but also suspicious, on the lookout for impostors and spurious reports.

It is by this standard that Leavis attacks certain extravagances in
James's last novels; but critical dispute about James exposes more
ambivalence in James's entire work than Leavis would be happy to
acknowledge. There are points within all the prefaces where the intelligibility of experience, in its highest sense, seems delicately called into
question. Emphasis on the "free spirit" of Fleda Vetch, for example,
especially when set against the "vulgar" stupidity of life, shows James's
attraction to a more reckless breaking of the sociable circuit of intelligence than he openly admits.[40] We shall see in Chapter 3 that even in
the earlier fiction James displays considerable ambivalence toward
common, normative versions of intelligence. The uncommon arrangements of language in all his fiction correspond to a consistent insinuation that consciousness may act most richly when it positively displaces
rather than merely apprehends the vulgar stuff of life, including common speech.

Similar ambivalences toward common language on the part of Lawrence, Joyce, and Beckett correspond also to a more unsettled commitment in their writing to the normative and sociable standard of intelligence that English critics like Leavis want to find confirmed by them. The fact that James and Lawrence have themselves so strongly influenced this critical standard only makes the unease provoked by their work more unsettling. Just as Leavis simultaneously relies on James for his "great tradition" and largely rejects James's later career, he both celebrates Lawrence as the very embodiment of "intelligence" and turns the knife of this standard against large portions of Lawrence's own fiction. Paragraphs of "jargon" and even whole novels must be put aside to secure Lawrence's stature. Joyce has given even more trouble. S. L. Goldberg, extending Leavis's qualified praise for *Ulysses,* undertakes to bring Joyce's novel forward as the very greatest of modern novels, but he ends by rejecting (also on grounds of excessive technical preoccupation) what amounts to almost half of it.[41] Although Beckett has come too late (or from too far) to be subjected to these rigors of English critical discrimination, his combination of brilliant concrete verbal life and obsessive repudiation of ordinary language presents the same provocations to judgment.

While "intelligent" Anglo-American critics have been proud of their openness to the boldest, most original modern talents in English fiction, they tend to be stopped short by the very challenge of these extravagant imaginations to cherished communal values. The exercise of critical discrimination, especially in the form of boundaries outside of which a writer is judged to have "lost touch" or gone "too far," preserves an exciting freedom for the individual critic (one can admire without abject worship), yet this solution also tends to be suspiciously self-protective. In practice, intelligent discrimination in English criticism has moved to assimilate the new without suffering the full violence to social and dramatic intelligibility which that originality has entailed for the modern novelist, even in English.

Sharper French dichotomies in the early modern period between conformist academic criticism and the literary avant-garde make for more coherent if also more reductive demarcations. Since the most influential established critic in nineteenth-century France, Sainte-Beuve, combines social complacency with rhetorical naiveté, a simple dialectic defines the shape of the radical opposition. The very simplicity of the would-be scientific conception of literary intelligence, which includes an uncritical respect for social authority, has the effect of releasing the esthetic opposition from confusing English standards of accountability. Thus Proust pronounces the sacred isolation of art from all social responsibilities. His antisocial intensity takes its cue from Baudelaire and Flaubert, who were significant also for reintroducing serious attention to language into modern French critical thought. In nineteenth-century France rhetorical self-consciousness appeared at the same time as and tightly linked to a sharply antisocial estheticism. In *Contre Sainte-Beuve,* Proust shows the continuing French dialectic in which social alienation is almost a precondition for serious critical understanding of language in art.

Thus Proust denounces any intermingling by the critic of ideas about art and ordinary experience, about the artist as person in society and as creator, and even about the language of art and the language of ordinary life. In his fiction, of course, Proust gives one of the richest records to be found in any novelist about precisely all these interminglings. But what the fiction records is the comic or tragic menace of the ordinary, not its enlivening power. Consequently, although speech idiom pervades Proust's novel, forms of speech do not exert "pressure," in Leavis's sense. All the critical pressure is in the opposite direction, as Barthes notes with admiration when he praises Proust as the first novelist in French to represent fully the imprisoning codes of all social talk.[42] There is no conflict of evaluation between the rich social panorama of Proust's fiction and his critical dicta that the artist must disentangle both his life and his language from the social world.

In *Contre Sainte-Beuve* Proust describes literary form as a hermetically closed structure, "this unique world, closed, without communication with the outside."[43] His image of linguistic self-enclosure rejects not only Sainte-Beuve's excursions into the writer's milieu but also the rhetorically focused English conception of a continuous life of language circulating with enlivening effect between literature and the world of social experience. In the process of arguing against Sainte-Beuve's distracting attention to social trivia, Proust offers a radical vision of the true artist's alienation from any life other than that of his own deep and solitary creative self. The happiness of the artist, in Proust's vision, comes only in that utterly private moment when all human interchange has ceased and the only voice heard is that of the *moi profond:*

> the deep self which one can regain only by excluding others and the self that knows others; the deep self which waited while one was with others, which one knows to be the sole real self, and for which artists end up by living exclusively, as for a god whom they leave less and less and to

whom they have sacrificed a life which has no purpose other than to honor him.[44]

The English tradition of intelligence resists this Proustian worship of the deep self, a conception in a way as pure as that of intellect in that it excludes other people and even the other, more ordinary parts of the artist's own being. It is the combination of this exclusion and this reverential hush in Proust that Leavis finds so boring and that D. H. Lawrence regards as suffocation.

Protest against the alleged failure of intelligence in the advanced modern novel gets its most indignant statement from D. H. Lawrence, whose critical prose exemplifies both the vitality and the rash prejudice of a certain characteristically English cast of mind.

> So there you have the "serious" novel, dying in a very long-drawn-out fourteen-volume death-agony, and absorbedly, childishly interested in the phonomenon. "Did I feel a twinge in my little toe, or didn't I?" asks every character of Mr. Joyce or of Miss Richardson or M. Proust. Is my aura a blend of frankincense and orange pekoe and boot-blacking, or is it myrrh and bacon-fat and Shetland tweed? The audience round the death-bed gapes for the answer. And when, in a sepulchral tone, the answer comes at length, after hundreds of pages: "It is none of these, it is abysmal chloro-coryambasis," the audience quivers all over, and murmurs: "That's just how I feel myself."
>
> Which is the dismal, long-drawn-out comedy of the death-bed of the serious novel. It is self-consciousness picked into such fine bits that the bits are most of them invisible, and you have to go by smell. Through thousands and thousands of pages Mr. Joyce and Miss Richardson tear themselves to pieces, strip their smallest emotions to the finest threads, till you feel you are sewed inside a wool mattress that is being slowly shaken up, and you are turning to wool along with the rest of the woolliness.
>
> It's awful. And it's childish. It really is childish, after a certain age, to be absorbedly self-conscious. One has to be self-conscious at seventeen: still a little self-conscious at twenty-seven; but if we are still going it strong at thirty-seven, then it is a sign of arrested development, nothing else. And if it is still continuing at forty-seven, it is obvious senile precocity.[45]

However outrageous, Lawrence's own language here does not sew one into a wool mattress. What we can identify as strength in this passage from "Surgery for the Novel—or a Bomb" is the sheer polemical verve of Lawrence's style, his lively trust in his own direct responses, and his appeal to the reader on the ground of human values that govern or should govern life as well as art. The force of this colloquial and sociable prose is indeed enough to blow away the pretensions of more sepulchral tones in criticism, if not in fiction. Lawrence makes us feel that the solemn worship of self by the novelist or reader is worthy only of satire. The "serious" novelist may strike the posture of profundity, but Lawrence, going by his intelligent nose, can smell the essential difference between life and death.

But can he? The unfairness of Lawrence's judgment appears in his offhanded lumping together of Joyce and Proust, and in the superficial understanding of both shown in the very terms of the ridicule. There is a real failure by Lawrence to recognize the complex and original achievements of these novelists. This failure, moreover, is not dismissible merely as personal crankiness; it exposes the more general limitations of intelligence itself as a standard of literary judgment—in relation to Lawrence's own daring fiction as well as that of others. For in its very reliance on direct and immediate responses, intelligence always runs the danger of being disabled in the face of any radical innovations or experiments in style. Joyce's narrative systems, the sentences of Proust or the later James, even the specialized language of feeling in Lawrence's own novels, assault the faculty of recognition. They seem and indeed are private contrivances set against, if not hermetically sealed off from, the common norms of speech and literary convention. Such departures from intelligible language feel like and indeed are defiant rejections of the community. Lawrence calls upon shared recognitions for the comic force of his caricatures in "Surgery for the Novel—or a Bomb." Yet even within this same essay he also suggests how his own serious ambitions as a novelist assault communal structures just as violently as the experiments of Proust or Joyce.

> The novel has a future. It's got to have the courage to tackle new propositions without using abstractions; it's got to present us with new, really new feelings, a whole line of new emotion, which will get us out of the emotional rut. Instead of snivelling about what has been, or inventing new sensations in the old line, it's got to break a way through, like a hole in the wall. And the public will scream and say, it is sacrilege: because, of course, when you've been jammed for a long time in a tight corner, and you get really used to its stuffiness and its tightness, till you find it suffocatingly cosy; then, of course you're horrified when you see a new glaring hole in what was your cosy wall. You're horrified. You back away from the cold stream of fresh air as if it were killing you. But

gradually, first one and then another of the sheep filters through the gap and finds a new world outside.[46]

Although Lawrence sees and even dramatically insists that any really new creation must be felt by the community as violence, he cannot bear to accept isolation as the consequence of the artist's deviance. He imagines instead a religious mission for the novelist as prophet and apostle, somewhere between a shepherd-pastor and a Noah, prodding the enervated beasts out of the Ark. Like Leavis, Lawrence was deeply reluctant to accept the extremity of social isolation that the French avant-garde had become accustomed to associate with artistic value. With a characteristically English mixture of social outrage and reformist zeal, Lawrence labors to sustain faith that the most discriminating passion for art will contribute to more general social liberation. The English standard of intelligence rests on this faith, though only disappointment can account for the frequent shrillness of its insistence.

The intelligent English reader expects the language of literature to be fresh and alive and yet directly accessible. He wants, in the words of Marvin Mudrick, to trust to "the feel of it."[47] Yet every reader sensitive to the textures of language has to feel assaulted by the very strangeness which is inseparable from the large ambitions of novels like *The Golden Bowl, Women in Love, Ulysses,* and the Beckett trilogy. At many points in these novels James, Lawrence, Joyce, and Beckett make our familiar world all but disappear, and they strangely manipulate and distort the common terms of our language. At such points, Proust's sharp antithesis between art and social communication may seem more adequate to the case than the tortuous English straining for reconciliation and communicative expression. Considering how public screams of sacrilege hounded Lawrence to seek his "new world" ever more apart from the social community he had wanted to inspire, the sociable standard of intelligence comes to seem perhaps more a nostalgic and tragic yearning than a clear-sighted perception of contemporary possibilities.

I deliberately hold to the note of uncertainty, however, regarding Lawrence as well as James, Joyce, and Beckett. For all their experiences of disappointment, their alienation from the world of social intelligence never hardens into a closed structure of irony. As in their intense ambivalence toward common idiom, their relation to the unsystematic knowingness of ordinary life remains permanently unsettled. And in this double pull—toward privacy, abstraction, and isolation on the one hand, and back to the shared and shareable understanding of a community on the other—these four writers are closer to each other than any of them is to Proust or to the French esthetic tradition more generally. It is commonplace to see Joyce as more steadily detached than Lawrence from all English values; hence his appeal to critics in the French mode, and the distrust he has aroused among "intelligent" English critics like Lawrence and Leavis. But even as Lawrence is more alienated from English intelligence than Lawrence himself, or an admirer of his like Leavis, wants to admit, Joyce, especially in the great work, *Ulysses,* owes more to that configuration of values than has been commonly granted. Similar tensions appear in the fiction of James and Beckett. For all these writers, intelligence is a menaced and at times shallow or even corrupt standard of judgment. But the language of intelligence—concrete, particular, socially intelligible language—retains the power to criticize the artist's contrary impulses toward abstraction, system, and self-deification.

3

Competition of Intelligence in
The Golden Bowl

Charlotte's Risk

No happy ending in literature has been more provoking to intelligent readers than Maggie's victory at the end of *The Golden Bowl*. Maggie succeeds in saving her marriage (and that of her father, too). Yet rarely have the claims of marriage appeared so at odds with intelligent judgment of human character and values. At the center of the problem is James's own ambiguous contribution to judgment in fiction by the standard of intelligence. As observed in Chapter 2, James's critical authority rests on the large appeal of his principles to normative values. When he defines experience as "our apprehension and our measure of what happens to us as social creatures," the "we" and "our" in his critical language imply a bond of community between reader and character. The intelligent character, James explains in the preface to *The Princess Casamassima*, is one we can "count on not to betray, to cheapen, or, as we say, give away the value and the beauty of the thing."[1] In *The Golden Bowl*, however, it is precisely our sense of betrayed values that alienates us from Maggie, and also from the strange elaborations of diction and metaphor that James devises to register her consciousness.

As we move back and forth between James's criticism and his fiction, suspicion grows that he is using familiar terminology to mask certain of his peculiar, special commitments, or at least to submerge his deep ambivalence toward normative values, including the very measure of what to value most. For James's language implicitly identifies the main threat to value as some kind of cheapening, some sacrifice of beauty, an emphasis which measures the worth of different kinds of apprehension by esthetic criteria alien to the largest meaning of intelligent judgment in our culture. In English, as observed in Chapter 2, "intelligence" has long been allied with the widest, most inclusive possibilities of understanding, without too fastidious an allegiance to beauty or other abstractions. That is precisely why Maggie's drive for a beautiful solution in *The Golden Bowl* seems so perverse, so unreliable, despite all the success that James gives her in his fictional design. For Maggie, anything but a beautiful resolution to life's entanglements is intolerably vulgar, and her will to avert unseemly "terrors and shames and ruins" (II, 236) feels like a version of James's own artistic will dressed out, for the other characters and for the reader, in deceptively normative terms.[2]

Although eminent English precedents—Shakespeare, for example, or George Eliot—support James's desire to transcend tragedy at the end of his career, his willed refusal of the tragic in *The Golden Bowl* involves more arbitrary shifts of judgment, more tortuous manipulations of perspective than in either Shakespeare or Eliot. James makes transcendence feel like pressure rather than release, if only because he forces the transcendent meaning to inhere in the secular, social world known to us from realistic fiction—the world of sex, marriage, furniture, money, daily walks and talks. No magical restorations from death or incredible, wondrous reunions help us to submerge worldly judgment in awe and faith. Because experience in *The Golden Bowl* does refer to "our measure of what happens to us as social creatures," the common psychological and moral discriminations of intelligent judgment are never firmly displaced. The social context of the novel makes such vulgar, even ugly possibilities as shame and ruin less unthinkable to us than to the strangely pure and limited character of Maggie.

Through the design of *The Golden Bowl*, however, we can feel James working to suppress our dissent, so that we as well as the characters will count on Maggie's high apprehensions. The second half of the novel quite simply silences dissenting voices within the book. Amerigo, Maggie's husband, repudiates his own earlier, separate perceptions. Even the skeptical Colonel Assingham converts to Maggie in Volume Two. The only remaining nonbeliever, we may suppose, is Charlotte, the lover of Maggie's husband and the wife of her father. And Charlotte is so outcast by the end, so doomed and yet so oddly "saved" by Maggie's design, that any independent point of view she might harbor counts for naught.

Yet if James were as thoroughly identified with Maggie's will as I have so far been implying, *The Golden Bowl* might be more or less persuasive, more or less oppressive, but hardly the disturbing and fascinating ordeal for the reader that it is. The enormous tension aroused by the book, and the very strength of the resistance that it provokes, are perhaps the key facts about its effect, more striking even than its manifest coerciveness. Furthermore, this tension arises from within the book as well as from the reader's struggle with it. For while Maggie avoids open conflict, James allows the impression of radical division to survive his own as well as Maggie's will to cohesion.

The bipartite form of the novel sharpens this effect of tension, for the feelings and judgments which Amerigo so thoroughly repudiates in Volume Two retain their presence in the novel as a whole. James's unforgettable art in Volume One establishes ineradicably in our minds the complex, ambiguous, even vulgar texture of these characters' social experience. Although Volume Two adheres systematically, even obsessively, to quite another conception of art, associated with Maggie's vision, the first half of the book survives, too strong to be altogether converted by Maggie's power at the end.

The power of Volume Two is beyond question, I think, if power means intensity of pressure. The powerful operation of an ambitious artistic will is what Leo Bersani, among others, has described in calling attention to the radically exclusionary character of James's art.[3] Yet Bersani takes the will too much for the deed in *The Golden Bowl*. Distinct from Maggie's uncontested triumph within the plot, there is an ineradicable vitality in the writing of Volume One, especially associated with Charlotte, which remains as the challenge, if not the menace, that the high plan of Volume Two cannot fully control. The relationship of Volume Two to Volume One is therefore hauntingly unsettled. Volume Two transforms and transcends the meanings of Volume One, yet not altogether. Insofar as Volume One remains *there*, unrevised, Volume Two may overpower what came before, without replacing it for the reader. Nor is it clear that Maggie is either willing or able to understand what James has so vividly shown us in Volume One. Even when she awakens to knowledge, her learning proceeds in strict and specialized channels. Moreover, once Maggie begins to force changes in the behavior and even the feelings of the other characters, what she did not understand earlier in a sense ceases to exist—except for the reader, who remains free to refer back to how things were before Maggie began to change them.

In Volume One, before all the surprising conversions, James does offer in the figure of Charlotte, and in his style of representing her, a compelling image of intelligence richly in accord with normative English values. Blackmur makes the point in the terms of his praise for Charlotte: "full of intelligent good and, equally because necessary, intelligent evil. The only force she cannot cope with is the good which has grown, from her point of view, fanatic, inhuman, a pure creation out of human losses."[4] Blackmur articulates the refusal of many unregenerate readers to allow Maggie's virtue transcendent inclusiveness; from certain points of view, Maggie's "good" is as humanly destructive as it is creative. Against redemptive interpretation (including his own of the previous year), Blackmur acknowledges the disturbing impression that competing conceptions of love, morality, and knowledge are harshly pitted against each other in the novel, with Maggie's victory exacting the painful defeat of other precious values.[5] Blackmur reserves the praise "intelligent" for Charlotte, but, we shall see, James more peculiarly splits the very concept of intelligence into opposed meanings in a rivalry which precludes reconciliation and even mutual understanding. Single terms—"love," "knowledge," "experience"—partially mask this conflict in James's language. But the doubleness of his usage also focuses struggle with special intensity on competing forms of human understanding, interpretation, and expression. Volume Two gives victory to Maggie's way of knowing and using knowledge. Volumes One and Two together show the conditions which ultimately favor her success, but also its huge cost in terms of other cherished possibilities.

The intelligence of Charlotte Stant in Volume One belongs to a full-blooded personality rarely shown with such attractiveness in James's fiction. Charlotte demonstrates, more vividly than just about any character in any novel, the appeal of a rich and integrated personality—body, mind, will; perception, imagination, speech—all working in harmony, and the whole human figure wonderfully ready to act in the given world.

" 'Don't you think too much of 'cracks,' and aren't you too afraid of them? I risk the cracks,' said Charlotte" (I, 359). This brave remark comes just before her risky expedition with Amerigo from Matcham to Gloucester, the occasion which will culminate the lovers' adulterous passion and complete their full (if possibly cracked) "cup of happiness." Charlotte's imagery shows her witty boldness in turning clichés—the "cup of happiness" had been the Prince's phrase—into opportunities for self-assertion and argument. The relative importance of "cracks" has been an unsettled matter between Charlotte and Amerigo since the beginning of the book, when Charlotte was ready to buy the golden bowl in the antiquario shop even after learning that it was flawed. " 'Thank goodness then that if there *be* a crack we know it! But if we may perish by cracks in things we don't know—!' And she smiled with the sadness of it. 'We can never then give each other anything' " (I, 119–20).

Charlotte is intelligent, in the specifically English sense of understanding how judgment and action in the world cannot always conform to either abstract or conventional moral law. Intelligence of this sort shows itself in supple grasp of the particular, whether in politics, art, friendship, or love. Intelligence adapts rule to circumstance and uses experience to feel a way through situations as they evolve. Charlotte's combination of courage and skill in such inevitably risky maneuvers gives her a reputation for great intelligence in her social world, especially since she manifests her qualities so dramatically, so expressively. Charlotte likes to show others the particular perceptions which shape her judgments, and this communicativeness also belongs to the common identification of intelligence with intelligibility, palpable and comprehensible ways of enacting knowledge in a world of specific, interpretable detail.

In Volume One James's own art seems wonderfully congruent with Charlotte's most impressive qualities. Her tall and strong figure, her wit and boldness, are presented dramatically so as to elicit the most admiring responses from the reader as well as from Amerigo. As soon as she appears at the Assinghams, all bright with the look of her "adventurous situation," her capacity to make an opportunity of almost anything quickens the spirit of the novel. With an ease at least as free as in his earlier, supposedly more dramatic fictions, James sets Charlotte expressively before us—physically, audibly. He makes us take pleasure in the way Charlotte's personality looks boldly outward and tolerates the gaze of others. Neither reckless nor timid, she moves on the energy of her personality, guided by her "extremely personal, always amusing taste" (I, 45).

Charlotte likes to show, through gesture and talk, who she is and how she thinks. She is always showing herself, showing some genuine version of her interesting self. Charlotte is an unusually intelligible character in the satisfying way that certain expressive people in life seem knowable to us when we have enough occasion to watch them. Intelligibility here does not mean simple transparency. Charlotte's motives are not at all clear, in part because she seems to invent them as she goes along. Nor can we ever simply take her word for her thoughts or feelings at any particular moment.[6] The romantic ideal of self-expression as the making known of a deep, true self needs to be put aside if one is to define Charlotte's social and dramatic expressiveness. As Richard Poirier has explained about a whole line of James's heroines, they do not simply reveal themselves, partly because they are always still in the process of inventing themselves, discovering new possibilities for themselves in response to their opportunities.[7] As with Eugenia of *The Europeans,* Charlotte's accomplished social style arouses distrust of what she may secretly have up her sleeve in the way of motive. Yet, also like Eugenia, she is less fixed in motive than one might suspect, less precisely calculating and more experimental in her readiness to test out the latent opportunities of situations and relationships.

Charlotte, moreover, is better than her type, better at least than Eugenia. It is true, as Poirier (and more recently Leo Bersani) observe, that the absence of fixed character in Eugenia makes questions about her relative honesty irrelevant, for to lie or not to lie presumes a truth to be violated, and Eugenia's character lacks fixed truth, even what one may call a real identity.[8] This indeterminateness, however, also lightens Eugenia's value, even as it allows her to be so enjoyably unpredictable, so full of entertaining surprises in word and deed. As a figure in a comic action, Eugenia seems just right, but the interest of watching her is limited by the sense of make-believe which Acton is not wrong to suspect in her.

By the time of the late characters, Kate Croy and especially Charlotte Stant, James had deepened his conception of the intelligent worldly personality. While constrained (and stimulated) by the same need to invent their own opportunities in the social world, Kate and Charlotte do have real—that is, rich and continuing—emotional attachments. For that reason, and also perhaps because they are younger, better-looking, and living in the more responsive environment of Europe, they seem less in need than Eugenia of props and scripts, costumes and ornaments. The tragedy of Kate Croy is that, for all her genuine attachment to Densher and all her justified self-confidence, she is caught by Britannia's overestimation of the ornaments money can buy. This conventionality compromises her judgment, her freedom, and her love. Charlotte seems less corruptible because, in spite of all her Europeanizing experience, she has not lost what in James seems a distinctively American quality of confidence in her unadorned self. It is this deeper and larger personal independence in Charlotte's intelligence which affiliates her, as Jean Kimball has suggested, with Isabel Archer (before her marriage) and even more with James's beloved memory of Minnie Temple, with her "free range of observation," her "felt interest in life," and her taste, "superlatively personal and . . . independent."[9] When Charlotte tells Adam Verver, for example, that she will be ready to take off with him for Brighton with only "a toothbrush and sponge," we feel that she knows how adequate she is to any occasion without further baggage.

"I might get what I want for less" (I, 220), Charlotte bluntly points out to Adam Verver, when he proposes marriage. She is trying to explain to this millionaire why marrying him would be, for her, a great—perhaps too great—venture. Her cool perception of all relationships as a kind of commerce—payment for a purchased good—reflects the worldliness which she has in common with a Kate Croy. But Charlotte's plain statement to Adam also shows her less conventional insistence on measuring value given and received according to her own personal standards. Moreover, her genuinely limited social ambition shows an independence of judgment missing in other worldly characters in James. As so clearly demonstrated in the shopping expedition, Charlotte likes to buy what appeals to her personally, however its value may be assessed by others. And what costs too much she can do without, though she does not in the end turn down Adam's offer.

The individual personal force of Charlotte's intelligence makes her more substantial than Eugenia in *The Europeans* and freer and franker than Kate Croy in *The Wings of the Dove*. Conscious of social values and of her own social performance, Charlotte nevertheless rarely seems trapped in false or merely conventional scripts in Volume One. Bent on her own personal satisfaction, she expresses her intelligence not so much in performance as in bold personal "demonstration," a significantly different thing.

The distinction between performance and demonstration is important to understand in Volume One, because its disappearance in Volume Two marks one of the big sacrifices exacted by Maggie's rising power. Pressed by Maggie to ever greater feats of concealment and artifice, in Volume Two all the characters become performers, not in a free and suggestive way, but cautiously, anxiously, so as not to mistake a cue. These performances are also called "demonstrations" by James because they are calculated tests or moves, conducted as precisely as in a mathematical or logical proof. But the very precision of the calculations involved, and the systematically duplicitous relationship between intention and expression, make these careful demonstrations as different as possible from Charlotte's earlier kind of expressiveness.

In Volume One James shows how Charlotte demonstrates, in the largest and most easily recognizable senses of the word. She likes to demonstrate in what one may call the argumentative sense: that is, she likes to *make her point,* and she becomes positively radiant when she thinks she has made it thoroughly. Although she is more elegant in her wit than the "idiomatic" talkers I discussed earlier, Charlotte's speech comes as close as any talk in James to the assertive vitality of English idiom at its best. Even in the midst of the ornate conversations characteristic of the later James, Charlotte is given the gift of energetic plain speech. She punctuates elaborate conversational maneuvers with straight-sounding common expressions which create that sense of the "directly and immediately real" (I, 201)) so refreshing to the fatigued sensibilities of men like Colonel Assingham and Adam Verver. That same note of personal energy alarms Fanny and alternately soothes and unnerves Amerigo: "Oh you don't need me!" (I, 52)) she exclaims, in response to Amerigo's artificial cordiality at their first meeting. " 'Enough,' she had smiled, 'is as good as a feast!' " (I, 92), in response to his careful show of concern for her lack of money to spend on a gift. "You may cry it on the housetops—anything I ever do" (I, 120). That briskly ends her tense sparring with the Prince about conditions of secrecy between them. As with the other energetic speakers already remarked, the point of Charlotte's talk is usually some form of self-assertion. Her speech makes points about herself to particular listeners, and speech for her is an action directly intended to shape the terms of personal relationship. The same particularity and the same expressiveness appear in Charlotte's unspoken demonstrations. She can be regal, as at the embassy party, but she can also expressively snub style, as when her dull dress and "Bowdlerized hat" make a point of cheerful indifference to decorum on the dreary wet day of her private visit to Amerigo at Portland Place. Judged as pure argument, by strictly logical (or esthetic or moral) criteria, Charlotte's points are hardly flawless. Their power depends less on their logical or moral beauty than on the richness of passionate and personal suggestiveness that she creates.

Performance—in a more narrowly theatrical sense—may also serve and suggest personal passion, but the referentiality is limited, indeed often disguised, by the structure of a role or script. Bersani emphasizes that the self-composing performances of Jamesian characters break the expected circuits of reference between intention and expression, so that the analysis of psychological or historical motives customary in response to realistic fiction becomes impossible and irrelevant, especially to the reading of his late novels.[10] In the figure of Charlotte, however, James quite explicitly shows his continuing interest in the possibility and value of "referentiality," in the normative sense which current criticism is often so quick to dismiss.

"*I* refer," Charlotte provocatively argues to the Prince in the antiquario shop, by way of explaining why a gift from her to him on the eve of his marriage to Maggie might be a significant *ricordo,* while a gift from him to her "is a *ricordo* of nothing. It has no reference" (I, 108). In Charlotte's terms, meaningful reference is both psychological and historical, connecting deeds to motives and also the present to the past in an affirmation of continuous personal identity. To give a gift to a cast-off mistress has no reference for Charlotte because it is merely the conventional gesture of a *galantuomo*; the entire convention seems indeed designed to break off personal continuity in finished love affairs. This negation of personal reference is precisely what the Prince wants at this hour, as he tries to avoid any personal complications for his fresh start as loving bridegroom and decent son-in-law. The convenience to this Italian Prince of using English—"even for his relation with himself" (I, 5)—is the linguistic sign of his more general readiness to relinquish the most intimate personal references (so unprofitable in his case), and to embark on the adventure of a new identity in the role invented for him by the Ververs.

Charlotte, in contrast to the Prince, is a demonstrative rather than a performing character, which is to say that she eagerly seeks out the multiplication of personal references. To the Prince's continuing surprise, she can do so in Italian as well as in English, because both languages richly figure in her intimate history. Charlotte shows a greater fondness for her motley past than other homeless, stateless, and moneyless characters in James. In relation to the Prince, she affirms a rich shared past, however futile its outcome.

From the moment she arrives, Charlotte intends to make the point to Amerigo of how their past survives in the form of both memory and continuing desire. Bersani misses the importance of this insistence by Charlotte when he argues that her prior love affair with Amerigo has no importance to the new liaison which they devise within the odd

arrangement of their marriages.[11] Charlotte's talent for evoking the
personal past is a major source of her sensuous and witty charm for the
reader and, more uneasily, for Amerigo, too. We see this charm in
operation from the moment of her first provocative greeting to the
Prince: "You see, you're not rid of me. How is dear Maggie?" (I, 47).
Her reminders later become more insistent, but she also keeps up a
light note, as when she recalls to Amerigo the great little bargains he
used to help her find in Rome (she has them all still). In the great
scene at Portland Place, her emphasis is on the connection between
memory and personal taste, as she suggestively connects her present
rainy-day adventure in London to the remembered freedom of her
single life: "It makes me feel as I used to—when I could do as I liked"
(I, 299). The Assinghams had underrated Charlotte's attractive quality
of connectedness to her personal past when they argued whether she
would choose to "cover her tracks" or, alternately, make "new tracks
altogether" (I, 87). Both alternatives fail to take account of Charlotte's
pleasure in keeping open the highly personal tracks she has already
made.

Charlotte's power to revive the feelings of the personal past is visible
whenever she is alone with the Prince; the very rhythm of her speech
with him infuses the revival of past feeling with sensuality. The effect
reaches its climax in the Portland Place scene. " 'It's the charm, at any
rate,' she said from her place at the fire, 'of trying again the old
feelings. They come back—they come back. Everything,' she went on,
'comes back. Besides,' she wound up, 'you know for yourself' " (I,
300). The Prince, although still protesting himself unequal to what he
calls Charlotte's "courage," does indeed know this feeling for himself;
he has already yielded to her suggestiveness the moment before.

> The sense of the past revived for him nevertheless as it hadn't yet done:
> it made that other time somehow meet the future close, interlocking with
> it, before his watching eyes, as in a long embrace of arms and lips, and
> so handling and hustling the present that this poor quantity scarce re-
> tained substance enough, scarce remained sufficiently *there,* to be
> wounded or shocked. (I, 298)

Amerigo's "sense of the past" is sensuous primarily, no doubt, because it refers specifically (and more narrowly than for Charlotte) to
past sexual pleasures. But in the setting of his empty dreary day and
life, there is also the suggestion that the return of memory for the
Prince signifies a larger reawakening of personality. Charlotte not only
goes far in the direction of seducing the Prince at Portland Place; she

also makes her seduction appear to serve a richer, more integrated version of personality than the "poor quantity" of Amerigo's present role as ornamental Prince in the Verver ménage.

Fullness of reference also defines for Charlotte, as for other intelligent people, a moral standard. Maggie and her father are not only incomprehensible to her, but reprehensible by their conspicuous exclusions. As they play house together, they seem oblivious to any reminders of how they have managed to achieve this position, what powers of manipulation and suppression (and sheer bribery) they have used, and who else they have implicated in their arrangement. At Portland Place Charlotte is the temptress, but she also is the voice of intelligent outrage.

> "What do they really suppose," she asked, "becomes of one?—not so much sentimentally or morally, so to call it, and since that doesn't matter; but even just physically, materially, as a mere wandering woman: as a decent harmless wife, after all; as the best stepmother, after all, that really ever was; or at the least simply as a *maîtresse de maison* not quite without a conscience. They must even in their odd way," she declared, "have *some* idea!" (I, 305–6)

In her wittily indignant run-through of all the unelevated roles that she knows she has been "brought in" by the Ververs to perform, Charlotte asserts her superiority to the artificial and closed domestic circle of Maggie and her father. It is true that their intimacy may be defended as only the counterpart on their side of a continuity with the past at least as natural as that which Charlotte cherishes. Yet the Ververs' continuing intense mutual absorption also reflects almost insolent denial of their complicated situation of remarried father and married daughter. Charlotte's three reappearances at Eaton Square on the rainy day in question conspicuously demonstrate her physical, material reality as a complication that has entered their history, but the demonstration fails to penetrate the Ververs' closed circle.

Although James allows us to see how intently Charlotte presses her self-justifying points in her conversations with the Prince, his writing in the whole marvelous Portland Place episode also goes far to endorse her arguments. Her tangible truths are given such fullness of life in the writing, that the Prince's fully awakened desire for her seems to signify not so much the betrayal as the recovery of his own more precarious sense of self.

Illicit intimacy can carry such positive promise in *The Golden Bowl* partly because the "decency" of the Prince's initial resistance to Charlotte so thinly masks his essentially ignoble social and sexual conventionality. The return of his former mistress would not be a threat, Amerigo first reasoned, because it showed her helplessness, her characteristic female "abjection"—the Prince's term for any exposure of feeling by women. Interpreting Charlotte's reappearance through a grid of male vanity, the Prince reduces her bravura to the stereotyped helplessness of the cast-off woman: "She always dressed her act up, of course, she muffled and disguised and arranged it, showing in these dissimulations a cleverness equal to but one thing in the world, equal to her abjection: she would let it be known for anything, for everything, but the truth of which it was made" (I, 50).

Although Amerigo's easy, conventional contempt for open female passion will justify the practical wisdom of Maggie's sexual resistance to him in Volume Two, in Volume One James allows Charlotte to confound the Prince's clichés. Her willingness, even eagerness, to let the truth of her feelings be known to Amerigo constitutes an important part of Charlotte's stature and has the effect of rebuking his banal categories for women. At the least, his simplistic distinction between "disguise" and "truth" seems inadequate for Charlotte in particular. At Portland Place his full response to her includes acknowledgment that her expressiveness has nothing abject about it. On the contrary, her open pursuit of desire suggests the individual richness that can be wrested out of even conventionally abject conditions, and this is why Charlotte has the power to revive Amerigo's own faltering sense of individual personality, too. Still later, at Matcham, Amerigo realizes that only in his time alone with Charlotte does he come to a sense of himself as a "congruous whole," the one luxury not provided for in his otherwise so well-furnished married life.

During the climactic country-house weekend at Matcham, Charlotte's confidence in the worth of her relationship with Amerigo seems finally justified by their astonishing harmony of desire: "They had these identities of impulse—they had had them repeatedly before; and if such unarranged but unerring encounters gave the measure of the degree in which people were, in the common phrase, meant for each other, no union in the world had ever been more sweetened with rightness" (I, 356). Set against the thin and childlike exclusions of Maggie and Adam, the adulterous love affair thus comes to stand for the possibility of intelligent, personal love, the closest approximation in the book to a "decent passion," as F. R. Leavis has argued.[12]

Of course Leavis and other admirers of Charlotte must work to resist the ever stronger ironic insinuations in James's language that our "common" idea of passionate love may be commonly overvalued. Although Volume One gives Charlotte's claims full space, James also tests them in ways that show their flaws, even before he sets rival powers in motion. There is a heavy atmosphere of test for Charlotte and Amerigo in all the scenes at Matcham. The strain shows from the start in the impoverished quality of their talk by comparison to the great earlier scenes. Charlotte's voice has a new dryness; there is a "slightly hard ring" in her overemphatic way of dismissing the relevance of others (especially the helpless Fanny) to their special case. The freedom offered by Matcham seems, moreover, tainted by being so little a personal accomplishment. In this decadent social setting every voice is "a call to the ingenuities and impunities of pleasure." It matters to Charlotte and Amerigo that they be special lovers, and especially justified in their love by the peculiarities of their "arrangement." What they have not had to measure, before Matcham, is how much their very sense of specialness is yet another luxury paid for by Verver money. At Matcham a general rule of license replaces this privileged freedom; no individual line seems more than "funny" there. This general air of acceptance cheapens as much as it protects Charlotte and Amerigo, for their difference from other irregular couples—Lady Castledean and Mr. Blint are the unelevating parallel—would not be striking to an observer. Charlotte maintains a light disdain for Lady Castledean, in accord with her characteristic acceptance of the world as setting the conditions but not the measure of her private actions. But the perfect "match" between Lady Castledean's need for an arrangement to cover her own affair, and the need of Charlotte and Amerigo, taints the lovers with a vulgarity avoided up to that point in the privileged privacy of their marriages.

The house party at Matcham shows how society threatens, even while it licenses, the freedom of private passion. When Charlotte had Amerigo alone at Portland Place, she could evoke a rich private atmosphere of intimacy, continuous with their personal past. At Matcham there is no time or space for such evocations. Charlotte and Amerigo enjoy only strained, snatched moments, which makes for an urgency and falsity audible in their talk and also in James's narrative comments about it. At Matcham the lovers are constrained to artful imitations of the unpremeditated; the very intensity of their shared strain becomes, paradoxically, their main form of intimacy, and it is only a "workable substitute for contact" (I, 339). The need for continual arrangements has the effect, moreover, of turning what little talk they have almost exclusively to strategy, as if the social conditions of their freedom reduced the very faculty of intelligence to its narrowest political function. Charlotte ventures the expression "safe" to name the happiness of their opportunity at Matcham, but her very consciousness of some baseness in all their conspiring, and her sensitivity to the Prince's wincing at it, acknowledge that Matcham is the very opposite of safe for their kind of love. In a social world which in no way supports the private and the personal, even these special lovers begin to look like merely conventional adventurers.

That the Matcham episode ends thrillingly, in spite of all the strains, is James's highest tribute to the power of Charlotte's intelligence. Against all odds, she does make the country-house weekend into a persuasively romantic opportunity. Her success, as before, comes not from denying the abject elements in her situation, but from managing, through wit and taste, to turn them to the service of her own personality. We shall see how Maggie's later conversions of reality differ from this open personal manipulation of the "common" by Charlotte. Here it suffices to note how James allows Charlotte to glow amid the dull structures of the scene. In accord with the dramatic quality of her character, she exerts her power in what may be called a scenic style. Throwing down a white rosebud from the balcony of the country-house, and answering the Prince's Italian by her own light "Vengo, vengo!" Charlotte turns the conventional house into an Italian opera set, but so lightly, so playfully, that the performance refers less to any conventional theatricality than to her own charm and to the promise of romance in their special afternoon. Her idea of visiting Gloucester (it was vaguely the Prince's idea, too), her readiness to go at just the right moment, her almost breathstopping efficiency about trains and schedules and alibis, turn the merely "funny" situation of Matcham into a triumph of romance. But the details of the episode also show what dangers the social world poses to the very possibility of personal romance. Charlotte successfully shapes an opportunity for passion out of the decadent and conventional social setting, but we feel it to be a rare tour de force sustained against the deforming power of the surrounding social structure and offering no enduring structure of its own.

The weakness of Charlotte's kind of love can be identified as a flaw both in the very center of her faith in her own intelligence, and in the power of intelligence more generally. The flaw breaks two ways. First, there is in Charlotte, as in other intelligent people, too quick a dismissiveness toward what she cannot refer in some way to her own experience. As an unusually free and responsive observer, Charlotte has an exceptionally large range of reference: the swindling machinations of shopkeepers fall within her range, as do the Semitic family rituals of the Gutermann-Seuss clan in Brighton. But Maggie in childlike contentment sipping tea with her father is an incomprehensible oddity: "I can't put myself into Maggie's skin—I can't, as I say. It's not my fit—I shouldn't be able, as I see it, to breathe in it" (I, 311). Charlotte's contempt for what is not her "fit" eventually makes her helpless in relation to it. By contrast, in Volume Two James will make the reader breathe through Maggie's skin—whether liking the fit or not. And through this experience of Maggie (in all her strangeness), we learn to know, if not to like, forces which are inaccessible to ordinary intelligent recognition.

Charlotte's overrating of intelligent recognition shows even more ominously in her opposite mistake of placing too much trust in what she thinks she does perceive. When the Prince complains that he cannot understand the Ververs because, as Americans, they are not of the "same general tradition," Charlotte rejects the seemingly abstract bond of race and tradition by reiterating her personal sense of closeness to him: " 'Yet you're not'—Charlotte made the important point— 'too different from *me*' " (I, 311). Charlotte presumes to make the foundation of all relationships personal and particular, based on her direct impressions and perceptions. In contrast to Maggie, who cheerily acknowledges at the start that she loves the Prince precisely not for his "particular self," but for his princely identity, Charlotte's love is all for that "personal quantity" in Amerigo that he half-jokingly accused Maggie of knowing nothing about. Charlotte believes that she can and does know the Prince through her direct perceptions of him, and this pride makes her misjudgments especially dangerous.

One trouble with the common idea of intelligent love—lovers "meant for each other"—is that it is based on individual perceptions which may not be—indeed, may never imaginably be—accurate enough apprehensions of reality outside the self. Thus James goes beyond what Charlotte perceives to qualify her impression of perfect mutuality: "What in fact most often happened was that her rightness went, as who should say, even further than his own; they were conscious of the same necessity at the same moment, only it was she who as a general thing most clearly saw her way to it" (I, 356). This slight disequilibrium between the lovers reinforces the worrying intimation all along that Charlotte counts too much on signs of responsiveness in the Prince that are not so much autonomous expressions of his character as reflections of her own vitality. By the time she utters her passionate faith—"I go but by one thing . . . I go by *you*" (I, 360)—

her self-abandon seems more foolhardly than intelligent. Or, put another way, her kind of intelligence—what I have been defining as normative English intelligence—trusts even to the point of foolhardiness in the evidence of what often turn out to be unreliable personal perceptions. When Charlotte says to Amerigo, "I go by you," she means, "I go by my own experience of you; I take that experience, that impression, as reality, without superstitious fear of hidden cracks and flaws." Since this trust in direct perception and response lies at the very heart of intelligent passion and judgment, we feel the risk taken by Charlotte as heroic, while her error seems tragic, a flaw in our own most optimistic ideas about both love and knowledge.

Recognizing the social and psychological risks in Charlotte's adventure of passion underscores the point that it is not simply Charlotte's eventual failure to hold Amerigo which baffles our own intelligence as readers. Volume One ends with vivid indications of both the excitement and the danger of a love based exclusively on personal perception and expressive response. The doom of Charlotte's adventure is intimated just strongly enough so that the stages of her eventual failure can be predicted and understood without further step-by-step representation. By showing, in the very midst of his admiring presentation of Charlotte, the limit of what she can do in and with the world as she finds it, James satisfies his own dictum that the novelist should love his characters enough to allow them a "long rope" for acting themselves out. The point is made in the famous essay "The Lesson of Balzac," where James, agreeing with Taine, criticizes Thackeray's meddlesome and moralistic interference with Becky's liberty as a character, in contrast to Balzac's "love of each seized identity, and of the sharpest and liveliest identities most."[13]

In "The Lesson of Balzac" James admires in the character of the "fatal" courtesan, Mme. Marneffe of *Les Parents pauvres,* the way Balzac allows her to be exposed by the working-out of the situation itself: "We do not feel, very irritatedly, very lecturedly, in other words with superfluous edification, that she has been sacrificed."[14] Although this may seem the very lesson violated by the coercive narrative structure of *The Golden Bowl,* James does sufficiently dramatize in Volume One the social and sexual risks of Charlotte's passionate adventure to make her failure entirely intelligible, while his turning away from the scene of doomed passion may seem a delicate stroke of artistic tact. He has shown us all we need to see. He does not have to trace each step in the sequence to demonstrate the proof of Fanny's dismal sociology about the outcome of such affairs in "nine cases out of ten." Nor do we need to see the wages of sin in the form of grotesque bodily punishment, such as Balzac metes out to Mme. Marneffe through an exotic South American toxin. The Matcham episode is so brilliantly conclusive because James fully shows us all Charlotte's individual power—he gives her "all her value" (*la faire valoir* in the language quoted from Taine in "The Lesson of Balzac"), while representing also the social reality that encloses her, after all, in a common majority. At Portland Place Charlotte could almost seem the tenth out of ten. But at Matcham the social logic of the scene, along with the unredeemed sexual conventionality of Amerigo's character, presses Charlotte back into more common probabilities.

If, by the end of Volume Two, James does nevertheless seem to sacrifice Charlotte brutally, the problem comes not in the mere fact of her failure, but in the way the novel manipulates our understanding of that fact. Anna Karenina also fails in her adulterous adventure, without seeming to be sacrificed by Tolstoy. To be sure, novelists in the realistic tradition—as D. H. Lawrence complained in relation to Tolstoy (and Hardy)—punish adultery with a regularity that reveals them to be among the most orthodox servants of official domestic order.[15] Yet this imaginative support to an essentially conservative vision of the conflict between passion and marriage also creates the great tragic dramas of nineteenth-century fiction. Since James in his own way is no more satisfied than Lawrence with tragedy, he is similarly drawn to break certain kinds of communal understanding with the English fiction audience (and even certain connections to parts of his own imagination) in order to reach beyond the intelligible tragedy of passion. The further sense of sacrifice in *The Golden Bowl* cannot therefore be separated from its great and daring originality. What feels radical in the novel is not the plausible enough turn of events, but the powerful, even violent overturnings of our familiar structures for understanding and evaluating such a development. And it is only appropriate that such an overturning should produce enormous tension. The novel creates a state of crisis in which only extreme and special conditions can avert tragedy. It will take not only an astonishing move to power by the naive and passive American girl, but also a willingness on the part of everyone to break with the very meanings of character and event that the novel itself has proposed, in more familiar normative terms, in its own first part. James of course preserves rather than represses this tension for the reader by ensuring, through the very presence of Volume One, our continuing possession of what the characters themselves so strangely give up.

Maggie's Method

Although all of *The Golden Bowl* comes in the manner of the later
James, the two halves also in a sense reenact the most conspicuous
divisions in James's entire career, the second half being related to the
first as all of the later James is related to the earlier fiction which both
generates what follows and yet seems severely violated by it. The suppression of expressive speech in Volume Two, the deflection away from
any open shows of feeling or intention, the substitution of bizarre unuttered messages for either dialogue or more conventional narration—
all belong to the conversions of style that accompany Maggie's rise to
power. Our very intensity of involvement in Maggie's point of view is a
contrast to the flexibility of judgment encouraged as a value by the
dramatic openness of Volume One. Officially, Volume One belongs to
the Prince, as Volume Two to Maggie, but the characters in Volume
One make their impressions not only on the Prince but directly on each
other and on us. There is a freedom of motion and of judgment in
Volume One which James allows, perhaps partly because it corresponds
to the Prince's own mildness. Amerigo reacts to the various impressions
made on him, but he does not try very hard to apprehend, much less
control his experience through consciousness. It is this intellectual and
moral passivity which allows Charlotte so much freedom to make her
points prevail, with us as well as with him. Once pressed into Maggie's
"skin" of consciousness, by contrast, we are as uncomfortably deprived
as Charlotte of our own freedom, both of perception and of judgment.
Compelled to accept not only the fact of Maggie's success but also the
peculiarly elaborate and rigid terms of interpretation given her by
James, our resistance is fed mainly by acts of reference back to the
world of the book as it existed anterior to her awakening. At the same
time, as we go the length of the book with Maggie, that resistance
becomes progressively more insecure, for James succeeds in imposing
upon us the conviction that it is the very peculiarity of Maggie's method
that exactly constitutes her strength. And memory—open reference
back to what came before—is one of the chief normative values her
method discards.

It takes some time in Volume Two for the specialness of Maggie's
procedure to make its full strangeness felt. Despite the extreme mood
of agitation from the start, Maggie's move into action begins intelligibly enough as a self-conscious awakening in her of faculties which have
thus far been almost unaccountably dormant. Since her innocence has
seemed so immature in Volume One, this initial movement seems no

stranger than the similarly delayed development of other naive girls in English fiction—Dorothea Brooke, say, or Isabel Archer. Maggie's maturing is belated, but she (and her father) turn out to be less constitutionally inaccessible to knowledge than the Prince and Charlotte had so derisively concluded at Matcham, where (in the Prince's terms) the Verver duo would "be a little less trying if they would only once for all peacefully admit that knowledge wasn't one of their needs" (I, 334). As if in response to a gauntlet thrown down in the face of her ignorance, Maggie's desire to know awakens on the very day of the Prince's return from Matcham. The consciousness of a want stirs in Maggie a need for knowledge that her husband and friends did not expect her to have. And the merest whiff of knowledge excites her almost immediately to a vast plan of investigation and strategic action.

Once Maggie embarks on her adventure of learning, her progress is so engrossing that we can forget for a while to question the strangeness of the excitement that we are drawn to share. Yet at some point—no doubt different for different readers—the very agitation of her activity becomes a peculiarity to notice. Maggie herself makes knowledge a more dangerous and thrilling adventure than Charlotte, or we, ever supposed. Once she begins to glimpse the extent and also the chaos of what she does not know—wonderfully figured as a "roomful of confused objects" into which she has been tossing fresh contributions and then locking the door (II, 14)—knowledge becomes for Maggie not only a need but an obsession: "Knowledge, knowledge, was a fascination as well as a fear" (II, 140).

Looking back to Volume One, we recall that knowledge for Charlotte had never seemed such a fascinating object; it was hardly an object for her at all. Likewise, Charlotte was not obsessed with knowing as an exclusive, competitive activity. Her pleasure in "making her point" led her to publicize her perceptions, with Amerigo certainly, and even with Adam and Fanny. Maggie, by contrast, nervously guards what she knows, as if to share knowledge were either to relinquish power or else to unleash it with the utmost destructive consequences.

The first lesson Maggie learns is about the connection between knowledge and power in her social world. She discovers, simultaneously, the power of the others based on what they have known and the potential retaliatory power of her own capacity to know. Through careful processes of observation and inference she reaches a full measurement of the "quantity of earnest intention" at work in the others, including the intention of keeping her happily and helplessly ignorant

in a "gilded cage." She can open the door of her cage, as she understands it, only through further knowledge of these forms of power.
Specifically, she needs to find out the hidden motive of the others'
scheme. Yet Maggie is more devoted than anyone to secrecy, most
obviously in order to protect her father's serenity, but also to protect
the conditions of her own freedom of action in this increasingly covert
battle of subtle and silent wills. Although Maggie has reasons for proceeding through what she herself calls "humbuggery," the method of
covert investigation also perfectly fits her own taste. She not only sees
humbuggery as the rule of the ongoing social game, she also infuses
this rule with altogether new excitement and rigor.

The combination of nervous excitement and infinitely subtle logical
scheming sets the atmosphere in Volume Two for what knowledge is
and how it works in human relationships. Under Maggie's pressure,
both Charlotte and Amerigo themselves seem to become more narrowly scheming in their every move, and this shift in their manner is
made further conspicuous by the intensity of Maggie's covert observation of them. Her experimental pressure on them makes them warier,
more carefully duplicitous, and meanwhile Maggie observes their increasingly false demonstrations with an unnerving blend of pain and
satisfaction. Viewed now through Maggie's skin, and changed already
by her subtle touch, both Charlotte and Amerigo come to seem more
basely false than before. Eventually they also become more helpless,
as Maggie increases her power to disarrange their arrangements and
baffle their grasp of her position.

Thus Maggie imposes on the other characters (and on us) an intensely competitive drama of knowledge. At stake is a potent secret,
possession of which determines power more rigidly than we have earlier in the book been led to believe. Although this new drama of
knowledge is thrilling, infusing every moment of daily experience with
the suspense of a detective or pirate adventure, the atmosphere of
tension and secrecy divorces the entire idea of knowing in Volume
Two from social communicativeness. In her anxiety, in her agitated
concealments and calculations, Maggie rejects (or rather never even
entertains) the idea of knowledge as shareable wisdom or as an open
ground on which people might meet each other, whether for agree-
ment or dispute. Likewise, although Maggie's learning is based on the
most subtle perception of appearances, the very activity of perception
as she performs it altogether loses its more normative associations with
free-ranging observation and response. Maggie displaces Charlotte's
virtue of intelligent perception by a new and different activity of mind

and eye—covert, private, and systematic. She improvises, but not on the impulses of taste so much as according to the dictates of her "method." Or, put another way, her strongest taste is for a method in which both observation and response are bound by the terms of a fixed and inflexible inquiry.

One of the most troubling redefinitions of value accomplished by Maggie's new method of learning concerns the relationship between knowledge and freedom. In Volume One Charlotte seemed free because she dared to act according to her personal perceptions and desires. The very word "free" in that volume registers this palpable quality of expressive individuality in Charlotte, so impressive even to Adam Verver—at Brighton, for example, where he enjoys "this free range of observation in her" (I, 213) and her "free response" (I, 216) to the novel opportunities for experience that he provides. Such meanings of freedom recall the happy openness affirmed on so many occasions in the early James, as in the character of Felix in *The Europeans,* for example, or Isabel as appreciated by Ralph. Charlotte's freedom, to be sure, is conspicuously contingent from the start on flawed circumstances. The limitations of her purse constrain her, as do the social regulations of a decorous society with its limiting rules for her behavior, first as an unmarried woman and then as a wife. Charlotte's freedom is contingent on her "place," a situation which she accepts with the understanding that place, like other social conventions, is open to considerable argumentative interpretation.

Maggie never contemplates the possibility for herself of Charlotte's individual, openly assertive mode of freedom. Once her old freedom of simple intimacy with her father is lost, she moves directly to envision another kind of freedom that requires the very opposite of Charlotte's qualities. Maggie's new freedom necessitates constant self-suppression and the rigorous narrowing of observation. For her, moreover, freedom now involves not merely interpreting her place in personal terms, but positively transforming the essential structure of her situation by changing the places of all the others. Her conception of freedom is therefore more ambitious than Charlotte's but, like her conception of knowledge and perception, it is also more covert and competitive. Once she learns that Charlotte and Amerigo have made a freedom for themselves in response to her ignorance, she can conceive of herself as free only by seeing them helpless in her place: "They're paralysed, they're paralysed!" (II, 52), she inwardly exclaims triumphantly, on the occasion of the Castledean dinner at Eaton Square. The retaliatory nature of Maggie's idea of freedom is audible through the aggressive tones of her unspoken inner language in Volume Two, and through her fierce imagery of paralysis, bondage, imprisonment, and escape. Her unuttered speech evokes a shockingly brutal condition of warfare and hunt beneath the gilded surface of the social scene. Knowledge and freedom, according to this vision, cannot be shared, nor can they be negotiated on the surface of social arrangements. Knowing one's place can become a basis for freedom only if it rigorously progresses to the further action of knowing how to place others, that is, how to displace them from their positions of attack.

Under the pressure of Maggie's vision, the novel thus comes to offer a new, more strictly polarized image of social drama than in Volume One, a double drama performed now on a clearly split stage, the outer action of social life having all but lost connection to private intention. Maggie's method, which also becomes James's method as novelist in Volume Two, even deliberately hardens the false surface of social behavior by so overscrupulously refusing to disrupt it. What had earlier seemed a loosely organized scene of conventional social occasions and rituals, in which individual motives are partially hidden but partially discernible to ordinary observation, darkens into a virtual Elsinore of hypocrisy. The absolute artifice of the social surface is a mere cover for horrible crimes, while it is also newly fascinating as the stage on which secret struggles of appetite and will are enacted in disguise. Questions of knowledge and freedom cannot enter directly into social discourse in a world of Elsinore. There is nothing to negotiate and no terms for compromise. Action must be arranged privately, strategically, according to plans elaborated under cover of a surface even more impenetrable than that of the opposition.

Compared to Hamlet, who is disabled for effective action in Elsinore by superfluities of knowledge, Maggie is naturally suited to the role of avenger by her positive drive to reduce the range of her knowledge to the limited requirements of the action she wants. The progressively narrower character of the knowledge Maggie needs, or even desires, must be considered along with the special and limited character of the freedom which is the goal of knowledge for her. Ruth Yeazell, one of the critics who attributes Maggie's final victory to her superior intelligence, does uneasily notice that, in relation to her father at the end, Maggie's power is more impressive than her knowledge, and her will more conspicuously at work than her understanding.[16] But Yeazell oddly confines this problem to the very end, where Maggie closes off curiosity about the details of her father's thought and feeling. This final refusal of inquiry on Maggie's part, however, is not in the least exceptional; it is entirely consistent with her willed restrictions of interest all along. Adam Verver's inner state is only one among many items which prove untouchable in the closet of Maggie's ignorance. Of the vast "accumulations of the unanswered" jumbled together there, Maggie picks out only a very few questions to investigate, and her inquiries are governed throughout as much as by her impulse to avoid as to approach fuller understanding.

James gives Maggie a dazzling capacity to handle the confused contents of her mental closet by every method except direct airing. Quite early in Volume Two she begins to organize her general state of mystification into the relatively simple and clear question of how Charlotte and Amerigo have betrayed the Verver trust. For all the subtlety of Maggie's speculations on this subject, the novel itself at this point takes on the simpler organization of a detective story. James makes Maggie's progressive detection of betrayal exciting, partly by convincing us of her own state of tension, and partly by giving her such extraordinary genius as an investigator. Maggie is indefatigably ingenious at the staging of events and at the converting of every occasion into opportunity for further silent interrogation and disclosure. Finally, she has the luck of the successful detective in that she accidentally comes into possession of the evidence which confirms her suspicions.

All this excitement of detection, however, does not quite submerge the crude point that the object of Maggie's investigation—the special relationship between Charlotte and Amerigo—in a sense has been perfectly manifest. There is a bizarre excess, almost a lunatic waste of mental energy, in Maggie's total concentration for many weeks on the single activity of finding out what any reasonably observant person—even Colonel Assingham—has hardly been able to avoid seeing. It is true that Maggie began from deepest innocence, and also that any puncture in her great trust—that faith she had so extravagantly compared at the start to a watertight ship—threatens to sink the entire enterprise of her character. And it is further true that her need to conceal her growing mistrust from her father may slow her down. Nevertheless, there seems an excessive multiplication of mystery in Maggie's pursuit of a motive for the scheming of others. What else but adulterous passion could it be?

The superfluity of mystery in Maggie's question is the reverse side of an extraordinary simplicity in the terms of the answer she comes to call "truth." For her, mystery is painfully but decisively resolved when she comes into possession of the bowl and of the antiquario's story. She accepts both as the equivalent of documentary proof; the bowl becomes for her a witness to the crime of betrayal. As she tells Fanny in the climactic scene before Fanny smashes the bowl, it embodies and represents the sheer and entire "fact" of her betrayed condition.

If Fanny imagines that she can eradicate Maggie's new knowledge by simply smashing the bowl on the floor, the peculiar objectification of knowledge in this fantasy quite accurately corresponds to Maggie's own mode of interpreting the bowl. The contrast to Charlotte earlier is again conspicuous. For Charlotte the bowl resembled other ambiguous objects—the Prince's telegram, for example, or Adam's strangely worded proposal—all worth remembering for their puzzling suggestiveness and as literal and metaphoric "evidence" in future arguments. Charlotte also collects and interprets evidence, partly in the form of suggestive metaphor. Indeed, in Volume One James gives her the privilege of initiating metaphoric thinking about the novel's central image of the golden bowl. But Charlotte is only moderately, not obsessively or rigidly committed to metaphor. Like other intelligent and expressive people, she makes metaphors, as she makes other arguments, on the spot, when occasion suggests or requires them. Maggie, by contrast, hardens the bowl into a definite symbolic object and into the fixed representation of a definite and objective truth.

The bowl as what we might call a symbol had not previously been so rigidly settled in the novel. In Volume One James's own dramatic art was more in accord with Charlotte's style, as he allowed different interpretations of the bowl to suggest, for example, contrasts between the characters of Charlotte and Amerigo. Reference back to this dramatic understanding of metaphor in relation to character has in part the effect of distancing us from Maggie's interpretation. We can see the very method of her symbol-making as symptomatic of her character, as it competes with rival interpretive styles.[17] For Maggie, the bowl does not simply *refer,* in the flexible sense that I earlier explained in regard to Charlotte's pleasure in reference; for Maggie, the bowl *represents.* Placed on the mantelshelf for Fanny or her husband to see, or equally definite in pieces on the floor, it represents both betrayal and Maggie's new condition of knowing her betrayed state. Both the object of knowledge and the condition of knowing are thus stabilized through Maggie's interpretation of the bowl and her identification of it with what she now calls "real knowledge" (II, 201).

By the standard of the earlier narrative presentation of events, Maggie's method of interpretation simplifies; indeed it may seem reductive to the point of untruth. The details, the essential substance of narrative truth, are askew in Maggie's version, for she goes by the antiquario's story, which differs in detail, and thus in texture and shape, from the story that James has presented dramatically in Volume One. Although the antiquario understood the shoppers' Italian, his conclusion that their main motive was to exchange gifts with each other eliminates the complex play of other motives perhaps only partially heard by him and necessarily only partially understood from his vantage point.

By funneling Maggie's evidence through the report of an only partially competent onlooker, James positively underlines the increasing separation for Maggie between truth and direct perception. Maggie's extrapolations from the antiquario's already skewed story move even further from the dramatic particulars of the incident as presented earlier. For Amerigo, though confused, had not chosen to be unfaithful to Maggie that morning, nor had Charlotte at that time proposed that their old love affair could be continued. In the narrative of Volume One the shopping expedition, including the nonpurchase of the bowl, seems first to "refer" to the flawed relationship between the former lovers (which the Prince determinedly rejects), while it also "refers" to the brave desire of Charlotte to risk action in an unpredictably imperfect world. Of course the secrecy of the shopping expedition, tensely remarked by both the Prince and Charlotte at the time, adds further and darker ambiguity to the scene. James's rich presentation in Volume One creates the sense that Charlotte and Amerigo may not fully know exactly what they are doing.

Maggie's subsequent reductive interpretation can then be taken as a moral clarification of the murky bad faith in which Charlotte and Amerigo have drifted toward their eventual acts of betrayal. What earlier English fiction has taught us to think of as moral complexity may be a dressing-up of simple squalor through superficially intricate detail. There is a certain penetrating rigor to Maggie's interpretation which I do not wish to controvert. My point is more simply to underscore the conflict between that firmness of moral interpretation and the more complex, ambiguous quality of the evidence understood in relation to what we ordinarily call dramatic narrative. Maggie's conversion of the bowl into a symbol of Betrayal radically turns away from a whole kind of narrative truth brilliantly presented earlier in this novel. By reducing the bowl to a "damnatory piece" which "demonstrates" the bad faith both of Amerigo in marrying her and then of Charlotte in marrying her father, Maggie stabilizes the unformulated, mixed motives dramatized earlier, as she also conflates events separated by years in time.

Her very vocabulary of damnation, faith, and betrayal moves the meanings of events into a timeless spiritual realm where the specific texture of day-to-day experience ceases to count as important truth.

Maggie's increasingly simplified yet also more vaguely inclusive speech is the outward linguistic sign of her reconstruction of meaning. In her tête-à-tête with Fanny over the golden bowl, vagueness of reference gives every supposed explanation a grandly simple but also mystifying generality: " 'It was *on* the whole thing that Amerigo married me.' With which her eyes had their turn again at her damnatory piece. 'And it was on that—it was on that!' But they came back to her visitor. 'And it was on it all that father married *her*' " (II, 170). Perhaps one reason that Maggie undertakes so few explanatory arguments in Volume Two is that, unlike Charlotte's "points," Maggie's truths virtually defy the distinctions of ordinary, intelligible speech. "It" and "that" in her language refer to nothing specific and to everything, "the whole thing," the namable references having lost even clear syntactic relationship. Maggie's agitated but flat spoken voice in Volume Two shows how ordinary language becomes strangely empty when the meanings of events are understood as single, whole, and absolute.

Fanny's inability to correct Maggie except by smashing her evidence on the floor contributes greatly to our sense of the power held by Maggie's kind of truth. For Fanny has been a close enough observer of events to complicate Maggie's simplifications, if she would. Yet although she feebly tries a bit—drawing Maggie along into speculations on who knew what when—in the end Fanny lacks the moral confidence to rely on a reconstructed narrative for any clarifying or reassuring corrective. In her earlier scene of crisis with her husband, directly after Matcham, we see in Fanny an almost hysterical split in consciousness between historical specificity and moral abstraction. On the other hand, Fanny has the most vivid imagining of the step-by-step evolution of this situation, as it has developed through the mixture of good and bad faith in everyone, including Maggie and herself: "the queerness has been, exactly, in the detail," she tells her husband (I, 398). But this particularized vision is like deep, dangerous water: escape requires more than skillful navigation; it calls for flight above the dangerous element altogether. Thus through an "effort of wing" Fanny rises to an altogether different, more sublime story, a prophecy of Maggie's awakening-to-come: "To what's called Evil—with a very big E" (I, 385). And then, still flying high, she envisions how Maggie will save them all out of the "beautiful" motive of serving and sparing her all but divinely beneficent father. Fanny, however, is too nervous to sustain high vision under the pressure of the queer specificity of things in her consciousness. In the scene with her husband, she can ultimately escape from the intolerable burden of her own responsibility only by a radical and almost unintelligible denial that anticipates her later smashing of the bowl: "Nothing—in spite of everything—*will* happen. Nothing *has* happened. Nothing *is* happening" (I, 400). It will take Maggie's stronger, if also more rigid, powers of abstraction to sustain a conception that *something* has happened, and yet to act on that something as a coherent moral whole, without sinking into the dangerous waters of detail—the treacherous and dirty "specific," as Maggie later explicitly calls her greatest danger (II, 84).

In the relatively brief meditative time immediately following the Matcham incident, Maggie herself went through a narrative reconstruction of experience not unlike Fanny's account to her husband. She recalled, for example, how ready she had been to bring Charlotte "in" as a partner for her father and as a kind of Verver ambassador to society. She saw herself, in other specific ways too, as a chief contributor to the disorder of the family's superficially beautiful arrangement. But Maggie's retrospection is very brief, lasting only long enough to stimulate her new and "lucid little plan" for a recuperative strategy of action. Within the terms of that strategy, Maggie's sense of responsibility shifts its focus—away from her intricate, tangled, ambiguous complicity in the disorder to a clearer, more abstract projection of a new role to play in the future of the group. Whatever her role in the past, Maggie sees herself recast in the future as both scapegoat and savior. Her plan for action requires the conversion of the entire situation into a moral and spiritual allegory in which her own role can be clearly abstracted from temporal particulars. Like Fanny's narrow escape from reconstructed narrative to prophecy, Maggie's more sustained shift from past to future and from memory to new action has the effect of displacing retrospective meditation as the climax of moral experience, in the sense familiar to us from certain great scenes of nineteenth-century English fiction, including James's own.

Contrast to the famous meditative climax in Chapter 42 of *The Portrait of a Lady* is illuminating here, because James so emphatically constructs the dignity of Isabel as heroine on her capacity for sustained retrospection. Isabel's willingness to "live it over again" sets the standard of self-critical introspection for critics like Philip Weinstein when they praise earlier Jamesian heroines over Maggie.[18] There is a steadiness of self-interrogation in Isabel's meditation that wins our admiration, especially if we have been trained by English fiction to admire such accomplishments of lucidity in young women: Emma Woodhouse, Dorothea Brooke, and Margaret Hale, to name a few. In direct line of descent from these English heroines, Isabel reviews the history of her courtship with Osmond in a way which recognizes her own contribution to moral confusion. She understands how her deliberate self-effacement amounted even to a kind of deception of Osmond, however innocent by comparison to his cruder deceptions of her. Isabel accepts her connection to her own past. Her meditation also strengthens the reader's sense of connection to her, because her new vision so intelligibly matches and even elucidates the narrative version of events presented earlier in the book. Of course, Isabel's retrospective vision is also an interpretation of her history, governed by her newly self-acknowledged personal standards of, for example, the truly personal as distinct from the merely snobbish, the civilized as distinct from the merely conventional. In reconstructing her history, Isabel assigns moral meanings, differentiates greater from lesser blame; we feel the force of her intelligence in her effort toward fairness of judgment. The long meditation of Chapter 42 is justly admired—James himself later called it the best thing in the book—because it so powerfully records the strength of a free intelligence, for whom even deep personal disappointment is "a passion of thought, of speculation, of response to every pressure."[19]

Yet even in *The Portrait of a Lady,* the high watermark of Jamesian meditation, Isabel's enlightened intelligence leads her only to a nightmarish vision of her permanent, ineradicable doom. If Isabel seems strong because of her power of thought, that is not because her recognitions yield strength for new action. History in the novel (both personal and public) does not in the end provide energy but only consolation. Thus Isabel later feels comforted in her sorrow by the history of Rome, and by the sense it gives her of the "continuity of the human lot." But lucid recognition has only the strength of tragedy in *The Portrait of a Lady,* and James's drawing back from the decisiveness of tragedy, even in this early book, may account for the peculiarly anticlimactic, even incoherent movement of the novel's last part. Isabel's brilliant meditation leaves her in the end strangely adrift. Moreover, the impression of strength, even in the meditation scene itself, comes in no small part from the fact that what she chiefly recognizes in the scene is her already real personal strength, that "mind of her own" which she had hidden from Osmond. James does not suggest that Isabel becomes strong through the activity of reconstructing her history. Rather he shows her seeing more clearly the strengths she had had in reserve all along. And even with this new openness of strength, she can reach no new plan of action, no new sense of responsible freedom, except the rather feeble duty of tending Pansy and the single, final act of saying good-bye to Ralph at Gardencourt.

Intelligent retrospective meditation elsewhere in the earlier James also leads only to resignation, if not to actual collapse, even when meditative lucidity constitutes the moral climax of the novel. In *The Bostonians* Olive Chancellor's retrospective lucidity in regard to Verena Tarrant results in her literal, physical prostration in the house at Cape Cod; she recovers her energy for action only when she reenters the delusion of her hope to keep Verena to herself. And in the case of Olive also, it is clear that intelligent self-recognition reflects strengths of character and mind already part of her identity earlier. Although less coherent a personality than Isabel, Olive too can find some solace in meditation, because memory brings recognition that she is more substantial than the person who has hurt her. The pain of lucid insight has at least the dignity of confirming individual identity, even at the very moment of greatest loss.

In the figure of Maggie, James departs from the patterns of moral experience in nineteenth-century English fiction by turning attention to a heroine for whom retrospective, self-critical meditation can promise no self-confirming satisfactions. The past which awaits Maggie's contemplation includes not only the responsibility of her own pernicious meddling but, more scarily, her own virtual nonexistence in the past as a thinking, feeling, reactive individual. Maggie was not holding herself in reserve in Volume One. On the contrary, her doll-like character seemed devoid of a self substantial enough either to give or to hold back. Charlotte, we have seen, can and does draw largely on her sense of the past for personal satisfaction, but in Charlotte James suggests the decline of memory from a faculty of moral investigation into an instrument of seduction. Perhaps because James's faith in the value of intelligent retrospection had been precarious all along, in this last book he seems fascinated by possibilities of consciousness quite different from, and even antagonistic to, the self-critical reviewing of the past so central to the moral dramas of English realistic fiction. In *The Golden Bowl* it is only by turning thought away from the details of the past that the heroine can create in herself an identity which she did not have earlier. If that action compromises the identities of the other characters in her world, the sacrifice is justified by Maggie's further boldness in envisioning new and better versions of them, too.

Maggie resembles one or another kind of artist throughout Volume Two, partly because she accepts responsibility for re-creating the reality of her world. The art that she enacts, however, breaks the alliance between story and history fundamental to so much English realistic fiction. Out of her strange combination of weakness and strength, the American heroine—perhaps like Americans generally—chooses to shake off history as an alien and demeaning constraint. Re-creation of the self and of the world becomes redemptive through more radically new conceptions of a fresh start than the English novel in the nineteenth century typically envisioned.

Although the Prince too had already sought a fresh start in his alliance with the Ververs, he does not begin to understand the demands of the "new" until Maggie silently demonstrates them to him. In the scene where they stand together in the presence of the broken bowl, Maggie says nothing until she has in a sense already demonstrated her position through a dumb show. Her careful pantomime of cleaning up, first carrying two pieces back to the mantel, then the third, then slowly showing how the pieces can be held together only by her own hand, is designed to catch the conscience of the Prince, but not in any direct outburst of guilt. She wishes only to make him watch her act out her interpretation of what has occurred and also her chosen method of dealing with it. The method, in fact, rejects open expressiveness on either side. Maggie wishes neither to show her feelings of hurt, anxiety, or anger, nor to elicit a response of feeling—whatever it might be—from him. Yet her gestures make a point very loudly and the point they make allows for no ambiguity: "He should have no doubt of it whatever: she *knew,* and her broken bowl was proof that she knew" (II, 183). Maggie reduces the point to be made down to the elements of what she calls her "simple certainty." The Prince's protest that he does not understand the meaning she has connected to the bowl ruffles her composure not at all. For she is hardly involved in the immediate, temporal experience of this encounter with her husband. When she silently directs him to "see" ("Only *see,* see that *I* see"), she is absorbed in a drama of moral vision that transcends the immediate scene of marital discord and also the detailed past scene of betrayal.

Amerigo can neither withstand nor compete with Maggie's method of producing meaning. Without faith in any autonomous organizing power of his own consciousness, Amerigo simply turns from his earlier reliance on Charlotte to dependence on Maggie. In many ways Maggie's method suits him better, for from the beginning it is clear that Amerigo abhors broken and flawed things as much as Maggie does.

His very decision to marry was a move to escape the broken past; he needs only to be more carefully instructed in the requirements of the "new," admittedly mystifying to him all along. What is required, he now begins to learn, is a more radical repudiation of the "old" than he had realized. He must repudiate not only his current liaison with Charlotte, but also the entire history of his attachment to her—and even the old personal self which was entangled in that history. These are very large requirements, but the Prince understands and complies.

The difficulties of such compliance, however, remain conspicuous, not to say horrifying, especially as they obstruct any free expressiveness of speech. In one of the last conversations, about the possibility of Maggie's spending a final evening with her father before the Ververs depart for America, Maggie has a strange "inspiration" of speech, the narrator tells us, that leaves her husband (as well as the reader) silent in dismay.

> After which while Amerigo watched her, and in fact quite because of it, she had an inspiration to which she presently yielded. If he was wondering what she would say next she had found exactly the thing. "In that case he'll leave you Charlotte to take care of in our absence. You'll have to carry *her* off somewhere for your last evening; unless you may prefer to spend it with her here. I shall then see that you dine, that you have everything, quite beautifully. You'll be able to do as you like." (II, 343)

By any normative standard, Maggie's speech here is certainly chilling. Amerigo, by this time so "converted," or at least so thoroughly mystified, hardly knows how to respond, except to show by his serious look that he takes it "for no cheap extravagance either of irony or oblivion." While it is easy to see the extravagance of taking Maggie to be oblivious of allusions to the "old" affair at this point, ironic interpretation of her speech seems hardly farfetched. Heard ironically, Maggie would be brutally rubbing in the fact of her new power by a parody of her old naiveté, as if to say: Amerigo had *thought* he could do as he liked, even to carrying Charlotte off somewhere, because Maggie was otherwise engaged with her father. But now he must see that he cannot have that autonomy. They may pretend together that he is independent, but in fact what he prefers must depend on her arrangements, her provisions. Insofar as he wishes to remain connected with the Verver enterprise, that must become what he likes. She is neither as stupid nor as undemanding as he used to think.

Such a display of power through irony would be unnerving, from loving wife to husband, but hardly unintelligible. James, however, guides us to agree with Amerigo's avoidance of ironic interpretation as "cheap," even though the noncheap—that is, the high and beautiful—meaning of such a speech is harder to decipher. Maggie's references to the past are manifestly there, yet not modulated into any of the familiar tonalities of personal speech. In ironic self-assertion (as we have heard it, for example, from Charlotte), references are twisted and turned to make argumentative points. Maggie is inspired, however, to the different feat of loading her speech with apparent personal charge, while breaking the circuit of reference. Leo Bersani's dismissal of referential meaning in James, cited earlier as inadequate to Charlotte's value in the book, does seem illuminating for James's conception of Maggie's speech at the end. She devises a mode of what may be called negative referentiality, as she evokes the details of the past with a blankness so powerful as to deny that past continuing reality as an object of reference. Maggie's superficial tone of perfect trust is thus somehow to be accepted whole—a rectified version of the oblivious trust of earlier times, as the reconstituted marriages are redeemed versions of the earlier arrangement: "the bowl without a crack." Maggie speaks from inspiration, in the specifically religious sense that she demonstrates how the past may be transcended. Under Maggie's new dispensation the past is canceled as a subject of reference in this marriage.

Or at the least, Maggie takes absolute responsibility for controlling the quality and quantity of reference in her world. She sets the allowable degree of specificity; she names or does not name situations. She even distributes the right amounts of admiration, sorrow, and pity all around. Amerigo humbly relies on Maggie's strict ordering of appreciation. He counts on her, as James said we always count on the most intelligent character, "not to betray, to cheapen, or give away the value and the beauty of the thing."

As readers, our sense of both the grandeur and the perversity of Maggie's accomplishment comes to sharpest focus in the terms of her new appreciation of Charlotte. As noted by Amerigo, Maggie proves better than Charlotte because she does make the effort to "live in her skin," as Charlotte had been unable to do in reverse. As she "hears" the unuttered cries of Charlotte's anguish and "sees" the silken halter of her bondage, Maggie envisions the Charlotte whom she has defeated as a magnificent tragic and heroic figure. Maggie therefore "saves" Charlotte, not only by allowing her to preserve her outward dignity (and her Verver prosperity), but also by appreciating her value in the face of what might be construed as mere abject defeat. Maggie's vision of Charlotte transcends the mere social figure discernible to ordinary perception. By "appreciating" Charlotte, Maggie raises her value. Through Maggie's consciousness of her, Charlotte again becomes special, indeed more special than she ever aspired to be—a grandly proud and suffering representation of Woman and therefore the splendidly worthy Wife of the magnificent Adam.

James in a sense revises George Eliot's famous ideal of the "sympathetic" imagination by showing us the subtly different and more unnerving accomplishment of what might be called the "appreciative" imagination.[20] Whereas sympathetic imagination enables Eliot's best characters to reach what we, as readers, have already perceived through the narrative as the reality of particular other people, by the end of *The Golden Bowl* Maggie appreciates the Charlotte earlier known to the reader virtually out of existence. In true Verver fashion, Maggie appreciates through acts of possessiveness and appropriation. Thus, in the last parting scene with her father, Maggie invites that connoisseur to join her in tribute to Charlotte as another precious object of art in the Verver collection: " 'Father, father—Charlotte's great!' . . . They could close upon it—such a basis as they might immediately feel it make; and so they stood together over it, quite gratefully, each recording to the other's eyes that it was firm under their feet" (II, 364). James's narrative language baffles judgment here because he seems so clearly to acknowledge Maggie's will to steady the ground beneath her, even if she must flatten other people into the ground she stands on. Yet we are also urged to see this "great" Charlotte through Maggie's eyes and in the light of Maggie's satisfaction that she has preserved her valuable splendor from any mere worldly waste.

Maggie's same use of "appreciating" Charlotte in order to steady herself becomes even more disturbing on the very last page of the book where, still forestalling her husband's long-awaited embrace, she again invokes Charlotte's grandeur: " 'Isn't she too splendid,' she simply said, offering it to explain and to finish" (II, 368). Maggie's ostensible motive here is to obviate once and for all any vulgar confessions from Amerigo that would mar their new intimacy. But the odd effect of Maggie's bringing Charlotte in yet again, at the very moment when she is finally gone, suggests some more peculiar need on Maggie's part to keep exorcising the ghosts of the past by converting them, over and over again, into more controllable images. To place Charlotte so insistently as a figure of splendor in effect removes the less controllable Charlotte of the past. Only by being appreciated as an object of high but fixed value, can the old Charlotte be expelled from the mind as well as from the house.

Maggie's conversion of Charlotte from figure to image is very like what James elsewhere describes as the saving activity of art itself in relation to mere vulgar life.[21] For Maggie's most daring creative venture in the novel, James uses the metaphor of "translation," a form of art whose presumptuousness is somewhat masked by a surface of humility. In a remarkable passage Maggie imagines herself in the role of humble messenger to Amerigo of Charlotte's unuttered anguish. In accord with Maggie's own strict separation of inner from outer speech, she invents a voice for Charlotte quite different from any either of them might conceivably use in actual social speech. What Maggie hears is the sound of Charlotte's anguished bewilderment tapping all but inaudibly against the glass of her cage. It is this tap that Maggie "translates" into an imagination of speech, presented by James in the same peculiar mode of internal quotation used earlier for Maggie's own unspoken soliloquies:

> She could thus have translated Mrs. Verver's tap against the glass, as I have called it, into fifty forms; could perhaps have translated it most into the form of a reminder that would pierce deep. 'You don't know what it is to have been loved and broken with. You haven't been broken with, because in *your* relation what can there have been worth speaking of to break? Ours was everything a relation could be, filled to the brim with the wine of consciousness; and if it was to have no meaning, no better meaning than that such a creature as you could breathe upon it, at your hour, for blight, why was I myself dealt with all for deception? Why condemned after a couple of short years to find the golden flame—oh, the golden flame!—a mere handful of black ashes?' (II, 229–30)

As a translation of Charlotte's feelings, Maggie's imaginary speech raises serious problems of judgment, because the projected voice is at once more pathetic and more sublime than any we have previously associated with the character of Charlotte herself. The artificial "poetic" quality makes us miss the directly dramatized tones of Charlotte's actual speech in Volume One. *That* Charlotte did not go in for beautiful tragic speeches, even under the severest stress. When, for example, the Prince crudely referred to her poverty in relation to the purchase of a wedding gift, Charlotte's reproach was distinctive for its light and easy touch: " 'There's always something to be done. Besides, Prince,' she had gone on, 'I'm not, if you come to that, absolutely a pauper. I'm too poor for some things,' she had said—yet, strange as she was, lightly enough, 'but I'm not too poor for others' " (I, 93).

Perhaps we are to believe that Charlotte's earlier lightness has been destroyed, or perhaps that her social voice has always covered up her deeper pain, in the same way that her wit and grace have masked the more brutal dimensions of her ambition. In the dramatic confrontation scene on the terrace at Fawns, the menace of Charlotte's power becomes visible to Maggie as she sees her advancing across the terrace like a supple, dangerous creature escaped from a cage. Like Maggie's lurid imagery for Charlotte's motions and gestures, her later hearing of the beaten creature's voice may signify the depth and sensitivity of her imagination. Perhaps she alone sees and hears the inner voice of Charlotte, like the novelist who has traditionally assumed the power to know and then to translate the inner life of character. In that case, Maggie in relation to Charlotte is no more presumptuous, no more falsifying, and no more bound to the tonality of social speech and appearance than any novelist who ventures to give voice to the inaudible "taps" of a character's deepest feeling.

Yet insofar as we hold on to the earlier impressive sound of Charlotte's social voice in the book, we become aware of two distinct novelistic modes of rendering the voice of character, with the translation of Volume Two coming as a substitution for, rather than an extension of, the earlier figure. James allows Maggie to translate Charlotte's voice into the key of high anguish. But the lighter note of her assertive wit has also had a value in James's rendering of it, and that tone is nowhere to be heard through the medium of Maggie's imagination. At the end, the Prince seems closest to that earlier worldly note in his one down-to-earth demurral from Maggie's high vision: " 'She's making her life,' he said. 'She'll make it' " (II, 349). The Prince, of course, callously dismisses Charlotte at the end, while Maggie saves her high value through appreciative imagination. And yet Amerigo's image of capable energy making a life, even in the flawed conditions of American City, may seem to acknowledge the kind of strength carried by Charlotte's social voice in Volume One better than Maggie's artistic translation of her pain into high metaphors of flame and ash.

The end of *The Golden Bowl* thus leaves the reader suspended in uncertainty about exactly what has been saved and what sacrificed by James's endorsement of Maggie's artistic visions and revisions. Maggie's own sharpest sense of sacrifice involves the separation from her father required by her new commitment to marriage. From another perspective, however, Maggie's intimacy with her father remains the least damaged relationship in the book, especially for readers of James who are used to his identifying the fullest intimacy with the most irrevocable separations. That such separations always include sorrow-

ful loss contributes pathos to James's imagining of love, without subverting the integrity of the emotion. We can thus believe in Maggie's
pain of parting from her father, without necessarily interpreting the
separation as a sacrifice of the love between them.

Yet the splitting of values that I have been observing in relation to
knowledge, freedom, and expression extends, finally, even to the
meaning of Maggie's love for her father. Earlier James novels, and
even so late a book as *The Wings of the Dove,* substantiate the ideal of
loving in absence by affiliating the highest experience of love with
memory. Thus Kate charges Merton Densher with being in love with
the memory of Milly, and the brooding Venetian and London scenes at
the end of that novel confirm Kate's charge by showing Merton's withdrawal to the absorbing inward contemplation of Milly and his relation
to her. Kate simplifies, of course, because her understanding of love
cannot cover the mysterious expanse of what Merton remembers with
an inexpressible mixture of pain, wonder, and moral relief. Since there
have been virtually no scenes of intimacy between Milly and Merton
for him to remember, he is left largely with an imaginative creation of
his own conscience and faith, and the novel ends by leaving the boundaries between memory and other forms of consciousness open for
contemplation. Earlier, in *The Portrait of a Lady,* James assured more
direct satisfaction by establishing clearer continuities between actual
scenes of intimacy and the idea of a love that can transcend even the
absolute separation of death. Ralph Touchett makes this connection
explicit in his deathbed scene with Isabel: "You won't lose me—you'll
keep me," Ralph reassures her. "Keep me in your heart; I shall be
nearer to you than I've ever been."[22]

As I have suggested before in relation to retrospective meditation,
the relatively clear values affirmed by *The Portrait of a Lady* underline, by contrast, James's stranger ambiguities in *The Golden Bowl.*
Ralph's valedictory forbidding mourning provides emotional satisfaction, to the reader as well as to Isabel, because the deathbed scene
itself affirms the possibility of direct, living, spoken intimacy, even as it
projects the scene of love into a future of solitary inward feeling. In
The Portrait of a Lady James offers a palpable and moving image of
experience to give content to what Isabel's memory will preserve. It is
not simply that we imagine Isabel lingering in memory over the
deathbed scene, rich in emotion as it is. More significantly, the realiza-
tion of love in that dramatic scene gives final substantiality to the
entire relationship of love between Ralph and Isabel, ambiguous as it
has been earlier.

James exploits religious as well as secular conventions of final part-
ings to heighten the emotional intensity of the farewell between Ralph
and Isabel: "for nothing mattered now but the only knowledge that
was not pure anguish—the knowledge that they were looking at the
truth together." "She wished to say everything; she was afraid he
might die before she had done so."[23] Love, memory, knowledge,
truth—all the key terms of value can be named on the threshold of
death. The final sense of ultimate communion between Ralph and
Isabel comes from the impression that these key terms have the same
meanings for them both. Speech between them at the end is fully
intelligible; feelings are spoken and mutually understood.

Of course Ralph and Isabel do not in fact say everything. The actual
quantity of dialogue in the scene is quite small. There is not much time
for talk; also, Ralph is weak with illness. Most significantly, both Isabel and Ralph continue to speak, even at this last moment, through the
masks of character that keep human speech from ever becoming totally
expressive, absolutely transparent. Thus Ralph's continuing gestures
toward wit and protective courtesy belong to the mysterious diffidence
which he—and the book itself—never fully explains. And on Isabel's
side, the ambiguity of her final cry ("Oh, my brother") strangely denies sexuality even as she affirms her highest reach of passion. However, our sense that considerably less than everything is being said in
the scene increases rather than diminishes its emotional intensity.
James can go perilously close to melodramatic emotionality in the
dialogue because he preserves just enough opacity to keep even this
truest of speech within the boundaries of psychological and social realism. What is important is how much can nevertheless be said. Ralph
confesses his anguish in possibly ruining Isabel by his gift of money,
and Isabel acknowledges her shame that she had fallen in love with a
man who married her only for that money. And together they articulate the more subtle point that Osmond had indeed been in love with
her—and yet would not have married her but for the money. Without
long elaboration, these truths—which are also the truths of the narrative as we have witnessed it—are understood by Ralph and Isabel
together: " 'I only want you to understand. I always tried to keep you
from understanding, but that's all over.' 'I always understood,' said
Ralph. 'I thought you did, and I didn't like it. But now I like it.' 'You
don't hurt me—you make me very happy.' And as Ralph said this
there was an extraordinary gladness in his voice."[24] The openness of
this mutual understanding of the past constitutes the foundation of the
love which Isabel will keep as memory in her heart.

James never again indulged his readers with such rich gladness of direct emotional communion. Perhaps the point is only that, once he had done such a scene in *The Portrait of a Lady,* its interest faded as an artistic enterprise for him. Or perhaps the truth articulated in these charged sentences came to seem less interesting than the unspoken shadows of feeling that here mark the outer boundaries of expressiveness. However explained, articulated intimacy becomes ever less frequent and ever more suspect in James's later fiction. In *The Golden Bowl* the rupture between expressiveness and intimacy goes so far as to assault intelligent faith in any possibility of open mutual understanding in love, even as a basis for memory. The satisfaction so richly provided by the deathbed scene of Ralph and Isabel is not simply missing from *The Golden Bowl;* its possibility as an experience seems positively denied.

The communion of Maggie and Adam in their last big talk at Fawns proceeds on terms virtually opposite to those of Ralph and Isabel at Gardencourt. The Ververs float in a high, mysterious element of "the unsaid" (II, 265). They are most together in their joint obedience to the rule of "avoiding the serious, standing off anxiously from the real" (II, 257). At the same time, the content of their long, even excessively abundant talk consists entirely of their relationship, the marriages, the meaning of love, jealousy, and privilege, and finally, their past as father and daughter that is now about to end. The systematic avoidance of serious truth in the conversation is therefore no crude matter of skirting real subjects. The scene is so baffling, so disturbing (in all the ways that the scene between Isabel and Ralph is reassuring) precisely because Maggie and her father do indeed talk about everything while saying nothing, at least nothing that we or even they can see as truth. To Maggie's consciousness, there are many truths to be silent about—most inclusively, the truth that something dreadful has occurred: "for if something dreadful hadn't happened there wouldn't for either of them be these dreadful things to do" (II, 269). But the very possibility of redeeming the dreadful in their history seems to depend exactly on their *not* naming it for what it has been. Instead, they devote their entire scene to a joint pretense that nothing dreadful has happened or is happening. The very setting of a walk at Fawns imitates the crucial scene in Volume One where Maggie so naively "proposed" marriage for her father. Now their intimacy paradoxically leads them to perfect joint understanding that they can indulge in no direct, open closeness. They can only imitate what they had, deliberately and consciously imitate it, as if in ritual tribute to a possibility of experience forever lost.

Talk about the past, under these conditions, becomes the very opposite of Isabel's and Ralph's "looking at the truth together." Looking back in conversation becomes instead the most daring kind of performance, a dizzying acrobatic feat at the very edge of the abyss of memory. "Don't you remember," Maggie ventures at the start of the conversation, going back in memory to the earlier time at Fawns when Fanny had "put them onto" Charlotte to improve their social situation. Maggie positively insists that Adam go over these events again, remounting with her "the stream of time." But the past she offers up in talk is only, in her own image, a "contracted basin"; it is not the dark, vast water where one might sink and drown, as Fanny almost had in her crisis scene with the Colonel. Fanny got to safe ground by substituting prophecy for the queer and dangerous details of history. Maggie, as part of her method for fulfilling that prophecy, now skillfully reconstructs the past as "story," a story game in which she and her father can pretend to play safely again. Thus she brings back Kitty and Dotty, the ridiculous Rance sisters, and she and Adam oddly recite together how one step after another led to their brilliant "arrangement": " 'That was the way—that was the way. And you asked me,' Maggie added, 'if I didn't think we ought to tell them. Tell Mrs. Rance in particular I mean that we had been entertaining her up to then under false pretences.' 'Precisely—but you said she wouldn't have understood.' 'To which you replied that in that case you were like her. *You* didn't understand' " (II, 259).

This stupendously empty conversation gives Maggie's face a "kindled brightness," as she enjoys this sign that they could "thus, in talk . . . live again together" (II, 260). But of course their pleasure in shared memory depends on their clear and conspicuous distance from the real details of pretense, understanding, and possible misunderstanding between them in the past and now. When the conversation approaches those shoals, Maggie's speech rises to a vague generality which escapes the charge of falsity only by her acknowledgment that she hardly knows herself what she is talking about or where she is: " 'I do *feel* however beyond everything—and as a consequence of that, I dare say,' she added with a turn to gaiety, 'seem often not to know quite *where* I am' " (II, 263). The pages of conversation that follow—all about jealousy and sacrifice and trust—tantalize for the very reason that they so closely approach the strange high place where Maggie *is* (the habit of italicization in Maggie's speech is contagious), without once clearly identifying it. In Maggie's own vision, a "thin wall" protects her equilibrium with her father by separating them both from any actual touch of their situation. The imagery of light and vibration in the scene carries Maggie's conviction that tacitly they both know the same truths in the same way, and also that they know why they must not name them. This sense of communion is ultimately confirmed for Maggie in the perfect embrace with her father at the end. The embrace signifies a farewell—Maggie has sacrificed her father to her marriage, and he has generously offered himself as sacrifice out of his perfect love and trust of her. Yet our sense in the whole scene of how little this performance of transcendent intimacy allows of any actual, openly intelligible contact calls into question the entire meaning of this parting as either fulfillment or sacrifice. Perhaps something more and different has been lost than Maggie—or James—will measure. In Volume One Maggie and her father innocently enjoyed the "free" (if by some standards boring and perverse) pleasure of each other's company. All versions of that experience have been lost. Also in Volume One, Charlotte and Amerigo not so innocently enjoyed their freedom of private converse. That more exciting possibility of experience has also been lost. Perfect intimacy now is one or another version of a love that remains unblighted only insofar as it preserves a safe distance from the menacing, uncontrollable specificities of the real.

James's manifestly religious language of communion and faith has rightly governed interpretation of the love between Maggie and her father at the end of the novel.[25] Having demonstrated the corruption and also the ephemerality of personal, worldly love, James endows Maggie with a new strength supported by her higher belief in the father who is the generative source and object of her deepest love. Intelligence figures as a value in this drama of transcendence only in the specialized poetic sense used by Milton and other Renaissance poets to refer to the supranatural understanding of angels in relation to each other and to God. The worldly meaning of intelligence has no place in Maggie's final relationship to her father. Such intelligence— the knowing in detail of the textures, sequences, and palpable substance of lived human experience—can hardly be admitted into their relationship at all. In his writing of the novel James leaves us, however, uneasily burdened with an image of the sublime that seems as much an act of willed repudiation as of transcendence. And the activity of will is never-ending. For Maggie to keep up the "thin wall" of falsity with her father is a "beating against the wind." Charlotte, even caged and exiled, must be ever freshly exorcised, as in Maggie's final private scene of union with her husband. And this pressure of the expelled, felt even at the very end of Volume Two, may keep us, as readers, bafflingly tied to our own memories of Volume One. Even while giving himself to the highest apprehensions of his highest character, James keeps hinting at what is not fully erasable in the lower regions of experience, not even for her. And we are considerably less driven toward erasure than Maggie.

A further reason why the reader of *The Golden Bowl* may resist Maggie's transcendent vision is that James gives her no adequate language to distinguish sublime from commonplace goals. At the end of the scene with her father, Maggie wants only certainty that she (and he) have been and are "decent and competent": "It swelled in her fairly; it raised her higher, higher: she wasn't in that case a failure either—hadn't been, but the contrary; his strength was her strength, her pride was his, and they were decent and competent together. This was all in the answer she finally made him. 'I believe in you more than anyone' " (II, 274–75).

Although Maggie flies, throughout Volume Two, "higher and higher" above the world as we know it by ordinary intelligent perception, "decency" and "competence" name accomplishments associated precisely with that mundane world. They are the untranscendent virtues of the middling character in fiction and in life. Perhaps James again splits the meanings of our common language, offering a new and higher vision of decency and competence through Maggie's apprehension, as he has already empowered her to redefine the meaning of knowledge, truth and love. But the common meaning of words do not disappear in James's writing. Instead, we are left with a palpable substitution of meanings in an action directed to warding off painful feelings of loss and anxiety. Like intelligence, the virtues of decency and competence normally belong to the social community, but no such community is in evidence in the world of this book. In the air of the actual social world, the book seems to argue, ordinary human values, along with ordinary language, are threatened and cheapened. Only isolated acts of mind and language can save human values from the vulgarity, incoherence, and terror of the real. Yet this special artistic salvation also renders our precious common values hardly recognizable; they all but disappear in these strange conversions of artistic vision. James coerces us in Volume Two to see only Maggie, to count only on her apprehensions of experience. At the very end, however, he also records in Maggie's own buried gaze of pity and dread, the look of that tragic sense of experience which she (and the book itself) have so brilliantly and so oddly strained to transcend.

4

Constructing Character: Speech and Will in *Women in Love*

The novels of D. H. Lawrence can almost tediously accommodate the current move in criticism against the idea of character in realistic fiction: that is, the idea (now called "ideology") of coherent personalities enacting their identities through such social activities as speech, thought, and deed.[1] Thus Leo Bersani, who admires in principle Lawrence's deconstruction of "the old stable *ego* of the character" (the phrase comes from Lawrence's famous letter of 1914 to Garnett), finds the very thoroughness of the job as done in *Women in Love* rather monotonous: "The variety of social encounters and the richness of psychological textures are constantly being dismissed by unrelentingly repetitious references to those currents of life and death energies which underlie both social history and the nuances of individual psychology."[2]

The dissolution of common social reality as the effect of Lawrence's deliberate excavations "a stratum deeper" than other novelists right away struck the early reviewers of *The Rainbow*. They too found Lawrence's deep currents monotonous—though in their case, tedium did not preclude outrage against this violence to the very structure of sane human identity: "These people are not human beings," pro-claimed the journalist James Douglas.[3] "They are creatures who are immeasurably lower than the lowest animal in the Zoo." Douglas (whose condemnation was read as evidence at the public hearing in which the novel was banned) charged Lawrence with using language "to express the unspeakable and to hint at the unutterable. The mor-bidly perverted ingenuity of style is made the vehicle for saying things that ought to be left unthought, let alone unsaid."[4]

The English journalists' severe prohibitions of speech and thought go so far as to recall Maggie's coercive censorship in *The Golden Bowl,* but without any Jamesian ambivalence about the costs of civilization. "Why open all the doors that the wisdom of man has shut and bolted and double-locked?" Douglas asks rhetorically, imagining no answer except the dismal possibility (proposed by another reviewer) that this author is "under the spell of German psychologists."[5] In *The Rainbow,* and then again in *Women in Love,* Lawrence sounded to the English reading public like some foreign magician, calling up mad spirits from the vasty deep: "we cry for relief from such madness and long to turn to a world infinitely varied and bracingly sane."[6]

Although quite beyond provincial English taste for the "bracingly sane," a current cosmopolitan critic like Bersani oddly repeats the early reviewers' impatience with Lawrence's insistent puncturing of worldly surfaces—not, from Bersani's point of view, because those surfaces should be preserved, but rather because Lawrence's depths overwhelm the critic's interpretive role: "Now the impulse to live and the impulse to die are not exactly attributes of personality; rather, they are attempts to enlarge on or to obliterate the very field in which the anecdotes of personality are possible. Personality must therefore be read as a system of signs or of choices which can be deciphered back to a primary choice of life or of death. And the deciphering takes almost no time at all in Lawrence. Interpretation is immediate, and tends to bypass the mediating and distorting vehicle of language. There are flashes of recognition instead of an interpretive process."[7] Bersani solves the problem of the unspeakable and the unutterable in Law-rence's style in *Women in Love* by casting the entire language of the novel into a single rather too obviously crackable code.

The deciphering of signs, initiated by structuralist criticism as the liberating alternative to naive "anecdotes of personality," can turn into an oppressive exercise with *Women in Love* because of the very zeal with which Lawrence commands, and even preempts, this critical activ-ity. "His own voice is so loud," as Gudrun and Ursula complain at one point about Birkin (p. 255). Lawrence thus fails to offer what post-structuralist criticism so relishes in the novels of, say, Flaubert or even James: a coherent surface whose "edges of intelligibility," in Culler's phrase, are just visible enough so that the surface can be deconstructed (can indeed be exposed as mere surface) by the critic's detection of more problematic depths.[8] *Women in Love* benumbs the contemporary critic almost as much as it did the early English reviewers, though for different reasons: the early reviewers were stupefied by the savage violence of the life and death energies displayed by Lawrence beneath the surface of civilized social life, whereas critics like Bersani are just a bit bored by Lawrence's display of depths, and irritated as well by his loud rhetorical directives for navigating them.

To be sure, critics (including Bersani) have already plunged to deeper depths where the currents charted by Lawrence himself are more confused than his schematic oppositions may at first disclose. Thus Bersani discovers a deathly stillness paradoxically at the heart of Lawrence's supposedly life-renewing ideal of sexuality, and Colin Clarke (pressing on the same Laurentian rhetoric from a somewhat different angle) discovers in *Women in Love* (as in English Romantic poetry) an ambiguous promise of regeneration bound to the antithetical concept of "dissolution" as menace.[9]

What remains oddly the same, however, in both old-style scorn (or reverence) for Lawrence's map of the depths and new-style forays beneath and behind it, is the impression of a relatively dismissible and unproblematic social surface in Lawrence's fiction that unambiguously endorses the subordination of surface to depth. Even Julian Moynahan, one of the main defenders of Lawrence as a reviver rather than a destroyer of novelistic character, explains Lawrence's originality as a "moving *down* from ego or will, a movement downward toward essential substance."[10] In both social and psychological terms, the Laurentian surface is associated with ego or will, concepts as little admired in the literary criticism that has become dominant in recent years as they were by Lawrence in his own theoretical writing.

Women in Love becomes a newly interesting book, however, when the almost automatic strategies of current criticism, and of long-standing Lawrence criticism, are resisted if not reversed: instead of further and predictably demonstrating that problematic depths subvert surfaces, in this instance it is more illuminating to notice how the particularities of the surface display actions designed both to create and to defend character against the dangers of depth. The details of psychological and social experience in the novel have their own texture and their own way of intimating distinctions between life and death energies, in particular calling into question the doctrinaire anthipathy toward ego and will so famously associated with Lawrence's ideology.

The move from depth back up to surface is called for, moreover, by the organization of plot, theme, and language in the second, if not also the first, of Lawrence's great mature novels. Already in the account of Ursula's ordeal as schoolteacher in *The Rainbow,* and then through the subsequent ordeals of all the characters in *Women in Love,* Lawrence offers more social encounters, more incident, and more occasions of talk than one might expect from his remark to Garnett in 1914 that he no longer cared to write the "vivid scenes" of conventional English fiction.[11]

The 1914 disclaimer makes sense in relation to the first two thirds of *The Rainbow,* which is most startling for Lawrence's daring to write in a new way about depths of feeling and impulse beneath the most commonplace social surfaces. Yet even here, it may be argued, the emotional turbulence of characters like Tom Brangwen or Will and Anna acquires such disturbing power precisely because of Lawrence's periodic return to a social surface even more commonplace than that in other novels. Lawrence's style in *The Rainbow* moves, sometimes smoothly, sometimes with astonishing leaps, from surface to depth and back again, while the characters themselves move hardly at all from their provincial English locale. They travel no foreign river into the heart of darkness; they merely live out their experience in a circumscribed local world where they work, marry, have children, shift jobs or social position a bit. In drawing us almost hypnotically into the strange intensities of feeling submerged under commonplace surfaces, Lawrence forces recognition in *The Rainbow* of the powerful deep currents that flow, not only in distant savage lands or in the pathological space of dreams or delirium, but beneath and even within the waking consciousness of "sane" English people.

The more episodic design of *Women in Love* makes the relationship between surface and depth matter from the start even more than in *The Rainbow,* and in rather different ways. In the later novel the social surface is itself more unsettled; energies from the depths erupt more dangerously, leaving their mark in the form of strange fissures and ugly debris. This destabilized modern setting calls for even greater attention to the ambiguous interplay between surface and depth. Whereas *The Rainbow* dared to excavate beneath what the English accepted as the stable ego of character, *Women in Love* starts from a manifest condition of instability and investigates a variety of human efforts to shape coherent forms of life out of fragmentary and damaged materials. While much of what happens in *Women in Love* may seem thrust upon the characters by mysterious and deep fatalities, they are hardly represented as passive. Lawrence shows them in different ways actively trying to construct their lives, using as best they can the materials of the depths, as the town of Beldover makes its living, not very attractively, from the subterranean mine. Lawrence changes our understanding of social and psychological surfaces by insistently pointing to what is underneath, but such conscious acts as arguing, courting (or breaking up courtship), and seeking friendship (or abandoning it) dominate the action and, intermittently, even the language of the book. In Lawrence's presentation these are at least in part acts of ego or will, and it is the form of these acts that differentiates the destinies of the characters as much as the contrasts between impulses at work in one depth and another. Under the dark water, Gerald grimly remarks after diving for his drowned sister, there is room for thousands, and one drowning hardly differs from another: "you're as helpless as if your head was cut off" (p. 176). Individuality, and in a sense life itself, is a feature of the surface in *Women in Love,* as in more traditional novels.

The urgency of Lawrence's movement from depth back to surface is signaled thematically in *Women in Love* by the haunting image of the Crich daughter's drowning in the early chapter "Water-party." The danger of death by drowning has some of the same connotations in Lawrence as in James, but the danger is greater in Lawrence (as it also is in Joyce, as seen in Chapter 6). James's characters can save themselves decisively: Isabel, for example, darts free from the "rushing torrent" of Goodwood's embrace at the end of *The Portrait of a Lady,* and Fanny Assingham prefigures Maggie's power to control floods of dangerous feeling by willed acts of denial in *The Golden Bowl.* Lawrence's characters habitually live in more intimate relation to the real and figurative dangers of drowning. Will Brangwen in *The Rainbow* suffers his dependency in marriage with the desperation of a helpless drowning man, and this agony continues for a long time; even the stable farmer Tom Brangwen meets his death in an actual flood on the farm. In *Women in Love* the accidental drowning of a minor character emphatically radiates the threat of death and dissolution to all the surrounding characters and events. The accident occurs just after the first waves of desire begin to carry the two couples—Ursula and Birkin, Gerald and Gudrun—into the current of passion. Just as the frantic cry for the drowning girl—"Di—Di"—destroys the festive drifting of the couples in the rowboats, so the whole incident of the drowning disrupts the courtships with its nightmarish image of the young girl clutching her would-be rescuer to death under the dark water.

The chapters following the drowning give dramatic consequence to the symbolic dangers of depth by recording the struggles of all the characters to keep hold of some lifeline to the surface of consciousness. Activities of speech and thought, in this context, become versions of such lifelines, complicating any schematic opposition between energies toward death or life. The last illness and agony of the all-but-indomitable Crich father, for example, stands in the very center of the novel, its poignant intensity defying reduction into schematic terms. It is the drowning that sends Crich to his final sickbed, where he tenaciously holds to his shrinking "unit of self" by keeping up the surface of domestic and social life through talk. Although, in part, Crich's rigid denials during his last weeks of illness merely extend what Lawrence analyzes as the destructive pattern of his entire work and family life, the psycho-logic of illness and survival never quite settles into a clear scheme. On the very pages where Crich's illness can be deciphered as the "sign," the physical correlative of his lifelong destructive impulses, Lawrence also presents the disease as a literal menace to life that the sick man is simply doing his pitiable best to resist. At the same time as Crich is made to seem destroyed by his denials, Lawrence also makes his persistence in the structure of his character the very condition of his survival. For Crich to relinquish his "armour" would be a form of "breaking down."

Lawrence's brilliant portrait of Crich's work, marriage, and illness, together with the interesting metaphor of "armour," anticipate psychoanalytic studies of neurotic character such as those in Wilhelm Reich's *Character-Analysis*.[12] Crich's history reads like a case study in what some psychoanalysts after Freud came to identify as "character," in the sense of a stable structure supported by a variety of resistances and defences.[13] The rigidity of this psychic dynamic in Crich alienates him from other people as well as from parts of his own emotional reality. Yet his capacity to persist "constant to his lights" is also a last resource of character that does hold death back until the last physical inevitability: "Day by day the tissue of the sick man was further and further reduced, nearer and nearer the process came, toward the last knot which held the human being in its unity. But this knot was hard and unrelaxed, the will of the dying man never gave way. He might be dead in nine-tenths, yet the remaining tenth remained unchanged, till it too was torn apart" (p. 275).

In this battle of will against impending dissolution, speech bears a paradoxical relationship to the living self. Crich grasps at talk as at a lifeline but it is only, Lawrence says, a "catching at straws." Still, he has nothing else to catch at: "To adhere to life, he must adhere to human relationships, and he caught at every straw" (p. 275). Most passionately with his daughter Winifred, and also with Gudrun, who is engaged as her art teacher, Crich uses commonplace social talk to adhere to others and blot out consciousness of his coming end.

> "I would love some curaçao—" said Gudrun, looking at the sick man confidingly.
> "You would. Well then, Thomas, curaçao—and a little cake or a biscuit?"
> "A biscuit," said Gudrun. She did not want anything but she was wise.
> "Yes."
> He waited till she was settled with her little glass and her biscuit. Then he was satisfied.
> "You have heard the plan," he said with some excitement, "for a studio for Winifred over the stables?"
> "No!" exclaimed Gudrun, in mock wonder. (p. 274)

Gudrun can "play" at this talk, but it is horrible to her and virtually intolerable to everyone else, because of its illusory surface of participation in life. Yet it is also through the motions of such conversation that Crich asserts and indeed sustains the remnant of his connection to life. In Lawrence there is no image of ultimate release into death, such as illuminates the end of Tolstoy's *The Death of Ivan Ilyitch*. With the same immediacy as in the vivid death scenes of the mother in *Sons and Lovers*, Lawrence registers the unending struggle of the human will against death, and against even the idea of death. Even while making us recognize denial as part of a deep, destructive pattern in human character, Lawrence also honors the painful manifestation of human character in forms of extraordinary tenacity. It cannot be said of Crich's will, as it is said of Lawrence's idea of the will in general, that it simply represents a "death impulse." At the end Crich's tenacity, his unyielding demand to "catch into connection with the living world," is the only possible expression of his impulse to life.

Since some form of dissolution threatens every one of the characters in *Women in Love*, Crich's terrible tenacity has the most direct import for them all. His desperate "catching at straws" brings vividly to mind how many of the gestures of ordinary life may also be but willed denials of an ongoing process of dissolution. Gudrun's wishful relief that, despite the nightmare of Crich's slow dying, "the everyday world held good," suggests her own version of resistance to the deathly chill that Crich's disease throws on all everyday reachings toward life. In the social world of Lawrence's vision, Crich exemplifies not only the destructiveness of the will, but also the virtual equivalence of willed persistence to continuing life itself. And although Birkin, like Lawrence himself at certain moments, toys with the imaginative and moral glamour of embracing death as both natural and purifying, strenuous resistance to death characterizes Birkin's behavior throughout, as it so famously characterized Lawrence in his actual life as in his art. At many points in the novel, not yielding to death becomes—perhaps most of all for Birkin—a matter of sheer tenacity, however supported by illusion, denial, or whatever other psychological or ideological "straws" the character can catch at. Weaving through the novel's polarities between the forces for life and the forces for death is a single dark thread of intimation that only persistence sustains the one life so precariously granted to the individual. Yet the sources of persistence themselves remain mysterious and only uncertainly available for the seeking. And perversions of the will may direct persistence into the very current of the destruction that needs to be resisted. Set against the broad theoretical opposition between the generative, spontaneous forces for life on the one hand, and the sinister mechanical will which leads to death on the other, the action of speech and thought in Lawrence's world shows distinctions between survival and doom that operate more ambiguously and within a much narrower spectrum.

Social speech constitutes the principle arena in *Women in Love* for the ambiguous interplay between deliberate will and spontaneous impulse. As the most consciously governed of human gestures, talk offers the main opportunity for the novel's characters to assert their individual "unit of self" and seek connection with others. The very act of arguing about children or marriage or friendship, even about life and death, presumes and enacts a sense of liberty to direct one's fate and to accept or reject the adherence asked for by others. At the same time, the gestures of conversation reveal, sometimes even to the speakers themselves, uncontrollable deep forces which call into doubt the very meaning of verbal choice and persuasion: "Ah!" says Gudrun, closing her first earnest probing of the subject of marriage with Ursula, "What is it all but words!" (p. 4). "What was the good of talking, anyway?" Birkin thinks during a quarrel with Ursula. "It must happen beyond the sound of words" (p. 242). All the main characters in *Women in Love* recognize that words are not equivalent to the experiences they want. They recognize also that their actions and reactions are shaped (or misshaped) by forces inaccessible to their verbal probing. Yet they continue to talk a great deal—rather too much for some readers—and they listen to each other with strange attentiveness, too, registering more than the ideological content of speech, and yet not merely ignoring the content either.

Listening, in *Women in Love,* is the crucial counterpart of talking, and in Lawrence it is just as complex an activity: both combine will and impulse in mysterious, often confusing ways. Lawrence describes Ursula's way of listening to Birkin in one crucial conversation as if he had an eye on the reader's activity of response, too: "She listened, making out what he said. She knew, as well as he knew, that words themselves do not convey meaning, that they are but a gesture we make, a dumb show like any other. And she seemed to feel his gesture through her blood, and she drew back, even though her desire sent her forward" (p. 178). As a listener, Ursula is often mixed-up, principally because she is open to the full expressiveness of speech, neither naively literal-minded nor programmatically cynical. Although she recognizes, as do virtually all the characters in the novel, that words are no more absolutely communicative than other gestures in the dumb show of human interchange, she does not therefore dismiss speech as insignificant. She feels the gestures of speech "through her blood"; she also tries to make out what is being said and responds in her own words, not always agreeably, to that articulated meaning also.

Ursula's capacity for wary but earnest attentiveness makes her the best listener in the novel, the one most in accord with Lawrence's distinctive conception of speech as expressive gesture. The reader too is being asked to be such a listener, making out meanings while also feeling them in an intuitive, almost physical way, even when such response means confusion. Clearer, more decisive responses to what people say are a temptation endorsed by the habits of talk among "advanced" people. But the air of finality characteristic of so much intellectual social speech is itself, as Ursula recognizes, only another kind of gesture, with its own repellent as well as seductive qualities. Thus, after first assenting, she gradually revolts against Gudrun's glib dismissal of Birkin. Gudrun's style of response to Birkin is as bullying as what she objects to in him:

> "He cries you down," repeated Gudrun. "And by mere force of violence. It makes talking to him impossible—and living with him I should think would be more than impossible."
> "You don't think one could live with him?" asked Ursula.
> "I think it would be too wearing, too exhausting. One would be

shouted down every time, and rushed into his way without any choice. He would want to control you entirely. He cannot allow that there is any other mind than his own. And then the real clumsiness of his mind is its lack of self-criticism. No, I think it would be perfectly intolerable."

"Yes," assented Ursula vaguely. She only half agreed with Gudrun . . .

Then there started [in Ursula] a revulsion from Gudrun. She finished off life so thoroughly, she made things so ugly and so final. As a matter of fact, even if it were as Gudrun said, about Birkin, other things were true as well. But Gudrun would draw two lines under him and cross him out like an account that is settled. There he was, summed up, paid for, settled, done with. And it was such a lie. This finality of Gudrun's, this dispatching of people and things in a sentence, it was all such a lie! Ursula began to revolt from her sister. (p. 256)

Like so many of the conversations in *Women in Love,* the subject of talk here is talk itself—ways of talking and ways of feeling in response. By the speechlike rhythms and phrasing of narrative style, Lawrence increases the sense of a conversational exchange on this subject between Ursula and Gudrun, even though it is Gudrun who does most of the talking here. Ursula articulates her fullest response only to herself, mentally resisting the pressure of Gudrun's emphatic judgment. Lawrence gives Ursula's mental protest here the vitality I observed in Chapter 1 in her spoken rebuttals to Birkin's theorizing. It is significant, we shall further see, that Ursula tends to speak out openly against Birkin, while revolting only by inward speech against Gudrun. Whether openly or to herself, however, she is aroused to strong language by the need to press back against the aggressively "final" pronouncements of others. Birkin can arouse her revolt at least as much as Gudrun: " 'Oh, it makes me so cross, the assumption of male superiority,' " she protested in the chapter "Mino" after Birkin dispatched the subject of male / female relations in a high-handed sentence or two about the cats. " 'And it is such a lie!' " (p. 141). Ursula was initially drawn into Gudrun's derision of Birkin because it spoke to qualities in his speech oppressive to her also. There is truth, Ursula knows, in Gudrun's way of hearing Birkin. What she revolts against as lying—in the speech of both Birkin and Gudrun—is the rush to settle the accounts of interpretation, to reach a single, final sum, to cross out the intermediate detail and the qualifying, contrary truths—such as the truth that Birkin's insistence is also a gesture of hope. Even while Ursula resists Birkin's violence of emphasis, she also hears and responds to the gestures of hope in his speech; even while she acknowledges the (partial) truth of Gudrun's judgment, she draws back from her sister's finality, and also from her aggressive meddling in the still unsettled matter of her own feelings.

The lying that comes from converting partial truths to final ones is the worst vice and the greatest temptation presented in *Women in Love*. Final truths—whether about society, sexuality, or individual motive—are what speakers, listeners, readers, and even writers want to achieve in a world menaced by dissolution. Lawrence's own notorious finality of pronouncement at many points in the novel implicates him in the temptations of his characters, making him, like Birkin, vulnerable to the charge of lacking self-criticism. Yet there is also a resistant intelligence manifest in the whole procedure of the novel's adversarial conversations on every key Laurentian theme. While no doubt too fitful to satisfy an "orthodox" standard of self-criticism, like that imposed so condescendingly against Lawrence by T. S. Eliot,[14] this action of resistance in *Women in Love* saves the book from the lying of false closure, including the closure of knowing critics like Gudrun (or for that matter, T. S. Eliot). Particular paragraphs in the narrative, like particular conversations among the characters, may end or break off in the partial truths which are lies, but the effect of a continuing reach toward other things that are true as well remains through the novel's last conversation on the last page.

Without being naive, Lawrence's commitment to the counterpressures of conversation is still strikingly more optimistic than other famous postromantic models of talk, those to be found, say, in Flaubert or Proust or (among English novelists) Virginia Woolf. These writers all dictate, by the varieties of emptiness they devise for speech, correspondingly different stances of listening in other characters and different stances of interpretation in the reader as well.

Speech in *Madame Bovary,* for example, is an altogether debased coin of exchange which the characters trade in with varying degrees of self-delusion or cynicism. Flaubert is romantic in that he intimates a vague but authentic yearning beneath or behind Emma Bovary's banalities, but the novel concentrates in its irony on exposing the *dumb* show of false feeling in every actual form of expression that desire takes.

Virginia Woolf's pessimism about speech is different but no less systematic than Flaubert's. In *To the Lighthouse* spoken language is vapid enough to make a Flaubertian compendium of cliché, but Woolf dedicates her narrative language to the evocation of the turbulent emotional undercurrents held down beneath the dull surface of talk. The radical incongruity between speech and feeling in the novel is partly the consequence of a social decorum which seems to require rigid conventionality of speech. But even more stringently, it is the consequence of the psychological decorum which sustains the social forms. The feelings of Woolf's characters are presented as far too dangerous to be integrated into their acknowledged social relationships. These feelings—from parricidal rage to regressive infantile longings—never really subside in the consciousness of the characters, but neither do they erupt into speech. Woolf makes us aware of the fabric of banal talk as a kind of lifeboat in which the characters manage, however uncomfortably, to keep afloat.

The conversation of Crich on his deathbed shows that Lawrence understands the shaky lifeboat of banal social speech. But he does not confine his social vision to this conception. The main characters in *Women in Love,* whether from bravery or desperation, are always leaping overboard or at least perilously rocking the boat. "I get no feeling whatever from the thought of bearing children" (p. 3), asserts Gudrun to Ursula in the first conversation of the novel. Lawrence indicates further, half-buried emotions of fear and hostility in Gudrun that are more complex than the bravura of her words taken by themselves. Yet Gudrun's words do not merely avoid the dangerous waters of her emotions, and we can believe that the rather shocking indifference she states is indeed part of her confused feeling. Moreover, her very assertion of indifference constitutes an expressive gesture in itself. There is a willful hardness in Gudrun's remark by which she seems to want to startle Ursula, though at the same time perhaps elicit some reassurance from her. Ursula, absorbed in her own uncertainties, draws back from Gudrun's demand, even while she likes the freedom of talk that her sister's return home allows. In the richest conversational scenes in *Women in Love*—and there are many—it is disastrous to Lawrence's art to proceed according to Bersani's dictum that the truest interpretation of Laurentian character "is immediate and tends to bypass the mediating and distorting vehicle of language." To bypass Gudrun's talk is to settle the account of her character in just the way Ursula criticizes Gudrun for doing about Birkin. It is true that Lawrence's narrative at times sounds as though the fate of these people were fixed from the start. Yet other things are true as well. Recognition of deep impulses mediated through their talk touches some parts of the truth, but not the final truth, partly because Lawrence gives us characters who have not yet settled into their final choices. Against the impression of settled fatalities in the novel, Lawrence sets up an equally strong, contrary mood of open choice, confusion, and even incoherence. In a sense, these figures of his have not yet even made themselves into characters—at least not in the fixed and stable sense that old Crich is a character—and that is why they seem both more and less vividly alive than he.

What I have been observing about speech in *Women in Love* so far only in part reaffirms the conventions that govern interpretations of character in everyday life and in earlier realistic novels. Insofar as Lawrence dramatizes the play of human relationship through speech, he does maintain the normative stance that I have associated in earlier chapters with intelligent English understanding of such matters. Intelligent listening is customarily alert to expressiveness more complex than what is conveyed by the meanings of words alone; intelligent judgment of character regularly identifies speech as but one among the expressive gestures in human behavior. In *Women in Love,* however, these habits of attention become radically upset as well as sustained by the extraordinary instability of the human figures Lawrence represents. While earlier social novelists use speech to show characters shifting from one moral or psychological condition to another, Lawrence goes further to make speech bear the burden of a more rudimentary struggle to make the self into a character of any coherent sort. Thus Gudrun tries to stabilize her confused impulses by shaping sentences which define a stance toward marriage and children—and even toward Birkin. Ursula, Gerald, and Birkin do similarly. If such sentences by the main characters so often sound "insistent rather than confident" (as Gerald says at one point about Birkin), that is because the action of speech seems directed as persuasion toward the self as much as toward the listener. If sometimes odd cross-echoes baffle efforts to keep these voices distinct in any stable configuration, that is because their distinctness is so provisional, so dependent on how the dynamic of a particular conversational situation brings to the fore one impulse or another. Put in slightly different terms, one hears Lawrence's main characters insistently pressing for response to a self they construct through speech, as if to confirm in the context of human relationship a coherence of character that otherwise eludes them.

Birkin is the most insistent speaker in *Women in Love,* and Lawrence also shows in him the most unstable, even self-contradictory character. The two qualities go together, for it is through his insistences that Birkin works to organize confusing and conflicting impulses. Because this at least partially self-directed activity most often takes the exasperating form of exposing the conflicts and confusion in others, the issue of how to respond to Birkin, how to interpret him, is paramount to everyone else in the book. Much of the others' talk indeed comes out as resentment against the liberties he takes and the kind of attention he claims. "You don't expect me to take you seriously, do you?" Gerald asks Birkin many times, beginning with their conversation at the Crich wedding, when Birkin asserts his hatred of all general standards of behavior in favor of spontaneity and each person's fidelity to "the purely individual thing in themselves." Here as elsewhere, Lawrence allows Birkin the privilege of affirming in conversation key Laurentian values, but in a way which implicates every ideological formulation in ambiguous social and psychological drama. Birkin's stated ideas about spontaneity and individuality, like his other ideas, may correspond to Lawrence's own ideological biases in the book, but in the scenes of talk, attention is also drawn to the very promulgating of such ideas as an activity in itself, with only oblique and sometimes paradoxical connection to the ideological content of statement.

Gerald's question of how seriously to take Birkin pervades the book, keeping the reader as well as the other characters permanently off balance, close to Gerald's own state of mixed ridicule, bewilderment, and agitation. In the wedding scene, to stay with that early example, Birkin himself makes questions about seriousness an explicit issue, as he chides Gerald for excessive solemnity about the indecorous behavior of the wedding couple.

"But why do you look so cross? Does it hurt your sense of the family dignity?"

"It does, rather," said Gerald. "If you're doing a thing, do it properly, and if you're not going to do it properly, leave it alone."

"Very nice aphorism," said Birkin.

"Don't you agree?" asked Gerald.

"Quite," said Birkin. "Only it bores me rather, when you become aphoristic."

"Damn you, Rupert, you want all the aphorisms your own way," said Gerald.

"No, I want them out of the way, and you're always shoving them in it."

Gerald smiled grimly at this humourism. Then he made a little gesture of dismissal with his eyebrows.

"You don't believe in having any standard of behavior at all, do you?" he challenged Birkin, censoriously.

"Standard—no. I hate standards. But they're necessary for the common ruck. Anybody who is anything can just be himself and do as he likes."

"But what do you mean by being himself?" said Gerald. "Is that an aphorism or a cliché?"

"I mean just doing what you want to do. I think it was perfect good form in Laura to bolt from Lupton to the church door. It was almost a masterpiece in good form. It's the hardest thing in the world to act spontaneously on one's impulses—and it's the only really gentlemanly thing to do—provided you're fit to do it."

"You don't expect me to take you seriously, do you? asked Gerald.

"Yes, Gerald, you're one of the very few people I do expect that of." (pp. 26–27)

As is usual in the sparring conversations between the two men, Birkin gains the upper hand, not mainly because his ideas are so much more persuasive, but because he shifts the rules of conversation more recklessly to secure his dominance. He seems to believe in standards of decorum no more for talk than for weddings, and he acts out in speech the rebellious freedom from propriety that he advocates. He will say whatever he feels like saying and will change the ground as he likes. If Gerald speaks solemnly, as responsible host of the Crich wedding, Birkin mocks him for stodgy "aphorism." But if Gerald in turn ridicules Birkin's maxims about individuality, Birkin suddenly turns disconcertingly earnest. Sometimes Gerald tries to challenge Birkin's theorizing by general social terms of his own, as when he pictures the cutthroat anarchy that would follow from Birkin's ideal of spontaneity. At such moments Birkin is likely to shift suddenly back to the intensely personal: "That means *you* would like to be cutting everybody's throat." Then he outrageously generalizes: "No man," says Birkin, "cuts another man's throat unless he wants to cut it, and unless the other man wants its cutting. This is a complete truth." Gerald is characteristically left helpless and exasperated by Birkin's exercises of power in these exchanges, being on the one hand confirmed in his distrust by what he reasonably sees as Birkin's "nonsense," and on the other hand agitated and exposed by his friend's power to touch him with wounding accuracy.

As readers of such dialogue, we are hardly more inclined than Gerald to accept Birkin's statements as "complete truth." Here is an example of what Gudrun later means about Birkin crying one down, making talk impossible. And here is an example, too, of that dispatching of things and people in a sentence that Ursula so resents in both Gudrun and Birkin. His proposition about murderers and victims is perhaps interesting, certainly startling, but Birkin has no foundation for a complete truth about murder. His very extravagance of generalization on such a subject would seem ridiculous, if it were not even more striking for its aggressive arrogance.

At the same time, the partial truths in Birkin's most outrageous talk make what he says in a particular circumstance hard to dismiss entirely. Gerald's stiffness about the wedding, and about social decorum generally, does seem to be warding off anxiety about what forces in himself as well as in others might be unleashed, if the rules of propriety were lifted. Both the anxiety and the defensive posture against it are audible in the way Gerald talks. "How do you make that out?" Gerald asks about Birkin's interpretation of him. " 'From you,' said Birkin." His power in conversation draws support from a certain kind of intelligence in him, an intuitive quickness in making out the self-exposing gestures in others' speech; this is one of the qualities that joins him to Lawrence as narrator. In addition, Birkin is bold in confronting people with his provocative interpretations, and the narrative backs this virtue of daring also. In the wedding scene Birkin presents himself to Gerald in the character of confident social and psychological diagnostician. He works to dazzle his friend by his ready analysis of everything, including the friend's deepest conflicts, and he caps this show of power by a special, flattering bid for intimate, serious attention.

The common, not always enthusiastic, identification of this aspect of Birkin's character with Lawrence tends, however, to overlook how much both dialogue and narrative also endorse resistance to Birkin and skepticism about the solidity of the character he offers to others. In the wedding scene Birkin's speech is indeed conspicuously aphoristic, so that we hear for ourselves the truth of Gerald's point that Birkin wants the aphorisms his own way, rather than out of the way, as he wittily claims. Going beyond Gerald's objections, we see further how aphorism serves a bid for power in conversation and how the distinction between truth and aphorism, or between aphorism and cliché, may depend on contests of power whose outcome has relatively little to do with content or even verbal form. The power of Birkin's talk—aphoristic or otherwise—comes from the very quickness of his approaches and shifts. By changing ground so fast, he never gets dully caught even in what he himself proposes as complete truth. This quickness is exciting to others, but it also calls into question the relationship of his ideas to his beliefs, and even to what may be called his character. While demanding serious hearing, he hardly seems to believe half of what he says, or at least he believes it only in the immediate moment of saying, the moment of making his bid in the relationship constituted by speech. He throws out statements recklessly, on impulse, in accord with his ideal of spontaneity, perhaps, but often with the paradoxical opposite effect of falsity. Thus Gerald observes: "It seemed almost like hypocrisy and lying, sometimes, oh, often, on Birkin's part, to talk so deeply and importantly" (p. 198).

The impression of Birkin's lying, especially to Gerald but to others also, is a view partially created by the narrator's intimations that all the verbal parries and thrusts between the two men are but the distorted surface of their unacknowledgeable man-to-man love. There is a perceptible evasiveness on both sides in these conversations that may be deciphered as the sign of their mutual refusal of greater intimacy. Lawrence offers this "deep" interpretation in the narrative commentary on the wedding scene: "They burned with each other, inwardly. This they would never admit. They intended to keep their relationship a casual free-and-easy friendship. They were not going to be so unmanly and unnatural as to allow any heartburning between them" (p. 28).

Seen as a manifestation of the will to deny deep "heartburning," the ideological content of these conversations may seem hardly worth assessing, as does even the manifest vitality of Birkin's manner: for all his "complete truth" and all his spontaneity of manner, Birkin is as busy as Gerald in warding off impulses toward heartburning for the sake of general standards, in this case standards of the manly and the natural. However, if one too systematically follows the narrative lead down into some inward, more essential space of erotic impulse, one loses the equally interesting impression of how Birkin harnesses the sexual tension of the encounter to his urgent need to articulate (for himself as much as for anyone else) a position, a stance as social rebel and gadfly. Birkin needs and wants Gerald to acknowledge him in the guise of this social character, and this form of his desire is no less real than the more primitive impulses which feed into it. Indeed Birkin's social identity, his character, depends on winning acknowledgment of his position as rebel and gadfly from others, women as well as men. Thus, while heartburning between the men may not be overt in their conversation, neither is it fully buried. It animates the tone of manipulative flirtation, with Birkin boldly pushing Gerald off balance, presuming the liberty to handle his most private fears, in a sense stripping away his social costume to force a closer contact.

It is hard, of course, to separate the vital from the destructive force of such action of speech. In his aggressive intrusiveness, his blindness to the full range of his motives, his complacency in weakly founded ideas, Birkin's insistent making of himself into a character at Gerald's expense hardly shows a choice of life on his part in any normally attractive way. At the same time, it is the energy which Birkin's dubious impulses infuse into the talk that makes for its compelling vitality. Birkin in speech has a heightened presence which stimulates Gerald, as it will excite Ursula, even when what he says is offensive or dismissible. "It was the quick-changing warmth and vitality and brilliant warm utterance he loved in his friend. It was the rich play of words and quick interchange of feelings he enjoyed" (p. 51). Whether to the man or the woman, Birkin's sexual appeal cannot be separated from his exasperating activity of speech. With him, language is not merely a "sign" in the sense of either a pointer or a substitute for deeper impulse. Birkin's talk is the living form that his consciousness gives to impulse, and his gestures of talk offer an experience that comes very close in quality to an actual physical contact—warm and rich and quick.

Birkin's talk comes very close to a physical contact but, of course, it is also the gesture through which he keeps his distance from those with whom closer union feels dangerous. The sexual energy of Birkin's talk differs from, say, Charlotte Stant's, in that James's fully sexual character carries through on what her language offers, whereas Birkin (as both Gerald and Ursula observe) is a kind of tease. Charlotte's voice belongs to her body, and her actions make good on her suggestiveness. Birkin, by comparison, is an incoherent character: his powerful voice comes out of a frail and sickly body; he proclaims spontaneity with willful insistence; he glorifies individuality while darting away from his own individual feelings. He contradicts, in both word and deed, almost every one of his own ideas. One good reason to bypass the social surface of Birkin's character in the novel is that it is too problematic to fit any simple scheme, especially a scheme which neatly opposes the forces of life to those of death. Birkin can securely represent the choice of life in the book, only if many particularities and nuances of his character are dismissed.

In terms of the novel's polarities, Ursula is the other character on the side of life, while Gerald and Gudrun are given over to death. Yet Ursula's vitality often appears in forms no less disconcerting than Birkin's. After the Crich daughter's drowning, Ursula, like the other characters, struggles to reassert some unit of living self against a mysterious pull toward dissolution. Interrupted by the drowning in her newly felt love for Birkin, Ursula spends the rest of that bleak Sunday sitting alone and depressed, almost drugged into longing for death. The main interest of the chapter "Sunday Evening," however, comes not in the rather overlong death reverie itself as much as in the dazzling recovery from despondency that Ursula experiences through her articulation of rage at Birkin's eventual visit—as he comes, pale, sick-looking, and much later than she had expected. She speaks to him (and he responds) coldly, even brutally, and the visit ends nastily with his abrupt departure. The act of angry speech does not exactly express Ursula's commitment to life; it is rather an action through which she reconstitutes that commitment for herself. She recovers from her inert depression through a violent and negative activity of speech.

"Don't you feel well?" she asked, in indefinable repulsion.

"I hadn't thought about it."

"But don't you know without thinking about it?"

He looked at her, his eyes dark and swift, and he saw her revulsion. He did not answer her question.

"Don't you know whether you are unwell or not, without thinking about it?" she persisted.

"Not always," he said coldly.

"But don't you think that's very wicked?"

"Wicked?"

"Yes. I think it's *criminal* to have so little connection with your own body that you don't even know when you are ill."

He looked at her darkly.

"Yes," he said.

"Why don't you stay in bed when you are seedy? You look perfectly ghastly."

"Offensively so?" he asked, ironically.

"Yes, quite offensive. Quite repelling."

"Ah!! Well, that's unfortunate."

"And it's raining, and it's a horrible night. Really, you shouldn't be forgiven for treating your body like it—you ought to suffer, a man who takes as little notice of his body as that."

"—takes as little notice of his body as that," he echoed mechanically. This cut her short, and there was silence. (pp. 188–89)

Some impulse twists Ursula's solicitude into nasty scolding. In part, her opposition seems strangely unmotivated, elemental, almost like a nightmare demonstration of the impersonal grammatical principle with which she had just bewildered her little brother: " 'Well, what is *whom?*' 'It's the accusative of *who*' " (p. 188). The speech of Ursula to Birkin (and his to her) often has a sharp accusative (and accusatory) structure, every "I" and "you" distinctly focused. In this scene the pronoun "you" is filled with a violence shocking to Ursula even as she feels it. The narrative language registers this mystery in the portentous Laurentian style of ultimate depths: "When he was gone Ursula felt such a poignant hatred of him, that all her brain seemed turned into a sharp crystal of fine hatred. Her whole nature seemed sharpened and intensified into a pure dart of hate. She could not imagine what it was. It merely took hold of her, the most poignant and ultimate hatred, pure and clear and beyond thought" (pp. 189–90). The conversation of "Sunday Evening," however, gives wonderful psychological texture and nuance to Ursula's anger, so that "ultimate" hatred diminishes to a distinct mood and and active gesture, rather than a final condition. Birkin has come like a dumb-show figure of need and helplessness, as Gerald will later come to Gudrun during his father's illness and, most dramatically, after the death. But unlike Gudrun, Ursula draws back in revulsion from the claim made on her. Her nasty speech sends Birkin away to take care of himself as at the same time, through her anger, she revives her attachment to her own autonomous existence. For it was her disappointment in Birkin's failure to come, just after she inwardly acknowledged her deep love of him, that began her lapse into despair. In rebuffing him, she rejects her own need of him as well as his need of her. She does not understand the complex impulses which go into her sudden hate, and as readers we can only guess at them. In any case, the deep origin of her anger seems to matter less in the scene than her vivid way of joining conscious will to the energy of mysterious impulse. Ursula persists in lashing out at Birkin until he leaves, and she persists in her violent feeling long after he goes home to bed.

Lawrence's account of Ursula and Birkin in the scenes following the drowning is in a way the most disturbing part of the novel, because they are both shown to rely for recovery so much less on attractive surges of natural vitality than on violent gestures of resistance and assertion. When Ursula and Birkin revive from their bouts of sickness and depression, there is a quality of fight to the recuperation, some fierce, even ugly opposition that seems necessary to their recovery of strength.

Thus Birkin in bed, after Ursula has turned him out: "He lay sick and unmoved, in pure opposition to everything. He knew how near to breaking was the vessel that held his life. He knew also how strong and durable it was. And he did not care. Better a thousand times take one's chance with death, than accept a life one did not want. But best of all to persist and persist and persist for ever, till one were satisfied in life" (p. 191). During his bedsickness Birkin "persists" mainly through rebellious thoughts that have much the same insistent quality as his speech. He starts in furious hostility to the demand for conventional union that he feels from Ursula (and from all women): "What it was in him he did not know, but the thought of love, marriage, and children,

and a life lived together in the horrible privacy of domestic and connubial satisfaction, was repulsive" (p. 191). Although Birkin's disgust
seems pathological (if not slightly comic as it rises to the awkward
rhetoric of "domestic and connubial"), Birkin himself accepts without
analytic curiosity the unaccountable "something in himself" that feeds
his frenzy of revulsion.[15] Instead of probing the deep sources of his
emotion, he turns the energy of revulsion to animate his yearning
vision of another kind of love: "There is now to come the new day,
when we are beings each of us, fulfilled in difference" (p. 193). Birkin
does not repress his disgust, but neither does he fully confront it.
Lawrence shows in him the more complex activity of a consciousness
that recasts obscure anxieties into self-affirming expressions of hope
and belief. Birkin harnesses his rage into a force that transforms the
chaotic sick feeling with which he began into a self-cheering prophetic
vision, the fullest statement of his ideal of love in the novel. By the
end of the meditation, he feels very much better indeed: "So Birkin
meditated when he was ill. He liked sometimes to be ill enough to take
to his bed. For then he got better very quickly, and things came to him
clear and sure" (p. 193).

The self-cheering dynamic of Birkin's sickbed theorizing is very like
his movement from feeling to ideology in conversation, and it is this
dynamic, so loudly displayed in the scene of the meditation, that
makes critics blame Lawrence (as well as Birkin) for ideas obviously
rooted in self-justifying and defensive motives.[16] In other writings
Lawrence himself criticizes ideology, or what he calls "metaphysics,"
because it serves the psychological function of self-justification: "And
the danger is, that a man shall make himself a metaphysic to excuse or
cover his own faults or failure. Indeed, a sense of fault or failure is the
usual cause of a man's making himself a metaphysic, to justify
himself."[17]

While Birkin in part dramatizes this danger, Lawrence in the novel
also invites admiration for the recuperative powers of self-justifying
energies. Whatever the deep impulses generating Birkin's revulsions,
the movement of his consciousness from inert rage to prophetic vision
is shown as a coming back to life, the counterpart in consciousness to
that sudden "gay motion" of his solo dancing at Breadalby, so enviable
and irritating to the others watching.

Gerald's incapacity for this kind of self-transforming motion angers
and bores Birkin, even while for the reader Gerald often has a poignant and also dignified emotional honesty missing from Birkin's habitual flights into ideas. "I only feel what I feel," Gerald protests to

Birkin's charge that he is "a born unbeliever" (p. 51). Against Gerald's honorable but hopeless acceptance of fault and failure, Lawrence sets the exasperating consciousness of Birkin, always flitting away from what he feels: denying, obscuring, transforming deep feeling through leaps and flights of speech and thought.

Solitary thought, however, is to Lawrence an inferior and even dangerous activity in comparison to conversation. Here Lawrence interestingly differs from James's vision of very similar human and artistic possibilities. Maggie's strength in *The Golden Bowl* derives precisely from her silent and solitary reconstruction of reality. It is Maggie's extraordinary autonomy of imagination that enables her to dominate the other characters, and James lends her vision the backing of his own elaborate style and design. As observed in Chapter 3, it is only by resisting the coerciveness of the writing in the second half of the novel that we feel the perverseness of her operation. Lawrence, for all his notorious infatuation with ideas, distrusts the speculative faculties of consciousness more than James does and gives them less free rein.[18] Like James, Lawrence is not mainly concerned about the absolute truth or falsity of his character's theories, since no theory for either writer has claim to absolute truth. As with James, the value to Lawrence of any theory is to be measured by where it leads.[19] From Lawrence's perspective, however, the danger of Birkin's meditation is that it occurs in solitude and thus may lead to a fixity in emotional falseness. According to Lawrence's psychology, the individual mind lacks self-corrective power, orthodox exhortations to self-criticism notwithstanding; liberation from the falsity of metaphysics (which can become an enclosing "armour" of consciousness as rigid as any neurosis) comes only from resistance to the self by the unyielding world outside. Hence the precious sanity that in Lawrence's view belongs to the novelist (over the philosopher), if he remains open to a "living sense" of all that will not succumb to his metaphysic.[20] The importance of spoken struggle in *Women in Love* applies the same logic to the characters. Although when he is on his sickbed Birkin needs to marshall his theories to strengthen himself, Lawrence dramatizes through the events of the novel as a whole how Birkin's sanity depends on the very assertiveness in Ursula that he is so strongly driven to oppose. That is why the mutually accusative form of their speech sometimes seems to be the best promise of life in their relationship.

Yet too sanguine a view of Ursula and Birkin in the middle of the novel is certainly wrong. They avoid the fate of the drowned couple, clutching each other under the water, but they are in the opposite danger of hardening into mere separate instruments of antagonism. It is the relationship itself that Ursula and Birkin most clearly endanger in their mutual self-assertion. Ursula's final alienation from her father illustrates the end point of another such combat, where the forces of mutual resistance have absorbed all the energy of feeling. "And I *have* loved him," weeps Ursula in angry hurt at her father's brutal bullying. "It's been a love of opposition, then," Birkin explains to comfort her (p. 359). But such comfort is double-edged. By the time of this scene in the chapter "Flitting," Ursula has broken away from her father to join Birkin in a presumably better kind of love. Yet for the first half of the novel, at least, the dialogue portions of the book represent a "love of opposition" between Ursula and Birkin hardly less shattering than her conflict with her father.

The "love of opposition," as it occurs within and across generations, is the great Laurentian domestic drama from *Sons and Lovers* to *The Rainbow* and then *Women in Love*. In expository form, in the essay *Psychoanalysis and the Unconscious* (1920), Lawrence develops the theme into a provocative model of psychological development that gives primacy to the human capacity for self-assertion. Replacing the Freudian "incest-motive" with his own generic myth, Lawrence identifies as the crucial moment of development that occasion when the infant first discovers the satisfaction of screaming as well as sucking. Significantly, the first gesture of individual freedom to Lawrence is a primitive form of speech, an audible action of opposition, discovered even while still cleaving to the mother:

> The child stiffens itself and holds back. What is it, wind? Stomach-ache? Not at all. Listen to some of the screams. The ears can hear deeper than eyes can see. The first screams of the ego. The screams of asserted isolation. The scream of revolt from connection, the revolt from union. There is a violent anti-maternal motion, anti-everything. There is a refractory, bad-tempered negation of everything, a hurricane of temper. What then? After such tremendous union as the womb implies, no wonder there are storms of rage and separation. The child is screaming itself rid of the old womb, kicking itself in a blind paroxysm into freedom, into separate, negative independence.
>
> So be it, there must be paroxysms, since there must be independence. Then the mother gets angry too. It affects her, though perhaps not as badly as it affects outsiders.[21]

Tolerance for the intimate storms of family life connects the best writing in *Psychoanalysis and the Unconscious* to the memorable scenes of childish revolt in Lawrence's fiction, especially in *The Rainbow*. But the essay goes further to make this uneasy, inherently unstable mixture of cleaving and kicking into another version of the ideal given to Birkin of a balance between union and separateness in all human love: "A soul cannot come into its own through that love alone which is unison. If it stress the one mode, the sympathetic mode, beyond a certain point, it breaks its own integrity, and corruption sets in in the living organism."[22] Lawrence's ideal of love in *Psychoanalysis and the Unconscious,* like Birkin's ideology in *Women in Love,* proposes a balance between sympathy and separateness. Yet Lawrence's model of infant development makes the kick and the scream into the progressive forces, whereas the urge to union is regressive and dangerous. Setting himself against both Victorian idealization of "sympathy" and psychoanalytic diagnoses of revulsion as psychopathology, Lawrence sets forth a human history in which "hurricanes" of loud negation represent the strongest force for life itself. Although willful in its violence, the impulse to self-assertion signifies for Lawrence the natural and spontaneous origins of the life-preserving human will in all its later manifestations. The language of quarrel is the expression, on the surface of adult human relationship, of the kick and scream vital to individual human life.

Yet one cannot merely adopt the theory put forth in *Psychoanalysis and the Unconscious* as a new map to the Laurentian depths, because the model in the theoretical essay does not confront the question that becomes so dire midway through *Women in Love* in relation to Ursula and Birkin: what force shall keep these assertive individualities from simply kicking each other into permanent separation, into nothing but "separate, negative independence"? Lawrence exposes this danger of his own metaphysic more daringly in the novel than in his theoretical exposition, where he somewhat shiftily covers the ominous fact that in his model of infancy the appropriate movement is toward eventual separation, while the adult ideal of love has somehow to transform this natural progression into a stable balance of attraction and separateness. The first half of *Women in Love* does show Ursula and Birkin in effect resisting each other into virtual nonrelationship. An indeterminate time of actual separation follows Birkin's illness. Upon his return in the crucial chapter "Moony," his continuing ferocity of opposition shows in the violence of his throwing stones against the reflection of the moon. Ursula has meanwhile solidified her sharp hatred into a steady bitterness.

Lawrence begins the movement of the second half of the novel by showing Ursula and Birkin groping awkwardly back into relationship again, mainly through further conversation. But the subdued tenderness of their reunion in "Moony" lasts hardly a moment before the mutual self-assertion between them begins again. Significantly, their quarrel has to do with the very nature of the character each is offering to the other:

> A shiver of rage went over his veins, at this repeated: "You don't want to serve me." All the paradisal disappeared from him.
> "No," he said, irritated, "I don't want to serve you, because there is nothing there to serve. What you want me to serve is nothing, mere nothing. It isn't even you, it is your mere female quality. And I wouldn't give a straw for your female ego—it's a mere rag doll."
> "Ha!" she laughed in mockery. "That's all you think of me, is it? And then you have the impudence to say you love me!"
> She rose in anger, to go home. (pp. 242–43)

Every time Ursula and Birkin begin to speak, and they always do so before long, the same accusatory structure reappears, until the battering rhythms of their opposition threaten to become merely mechanical. The forces of repulsion that act through their gestures of speech seem to overwhelm choice and absorb all the energies that might be directed to create harmony or accord.

This perilously repetitive rhythm of discord breaks significantly only after the climactic quarrel in the chapter "Excurse," when the couple comes together in the big reconciliation scenes: first on the road, then at the inn, and finally during the joyful night together in Sherwood Forest. Lawrence needs some such big scenes of harmony for his surviving couple so that their union seems more than mere mechanical endurance in strife. He also needs a language to convey, even if just for the space of a scene or two, a state of peaceful erotic union: "It was peace at last. The old, detestable world of tension had passed away at last" (p. 302). But the peculiar problem of language (and of imagination, too) in these scenes comes from Lawrence's lack of any vocabulary for silent harmony that is not either inert jargon (as Leavis called it[23]) or deadly in its associations with the book's earlier imagery of death, as for example in the word "dissolved" and the image of the broken "knot" for Birkin's relaxation of will: "There was a darkness over his mind. The terrible knot of consciousness that had persisted there like an obsession was broken, gone, his life was dissolved in darkness over his limbs and his body" (p. 301).

The main reason why the scene at the inn does not altogether give Ursula and Birkin over either to mere theory or to the vivid but dangerous forces of dissolution is that Lawrence does not actually eliminate the "detestable" but animating sound of tension from the scene for very long. In a way that seems more fortunate than not, even in "Excurse" the knot of self draws together again, to disrupt but also reenliven the dissolving calm. In the bits of conversation we see, almost with relief, that though the tension has been eased for the moment, it has not really been dissipated. Ursula is still insisting on the word "love," and Birkin, however lovingly, still resists her: " 'We love each other,' she said in delight. 'More than that,' he answered, looking down at her with his glimmering, easy face" (p. 305). She is in a mood to make the feeling between them a full and final event; he barely pauses before pressing on to his bold though vague plans for getting out of their responsibilities: " 'What responsibilities?' she asked, wondering" (p.307). Ursula's questions here are more genuinely interrogative than the aggressive challenges of earlier scenes, but Lawrence nicely registers the restrained yet still undissolved unit of separate self audible through her seeming docility.

"Excurse" shows Lawrence (like Ursula and Birkin) almost irresistibly drawn to interrupt the stillness of union with the assertive sounds of speech. The total effect, however, seems not really under artistic control. The elevated rhetoric of "mystically-physically satisfying" feeling (so often explicated, and so little relished by most readers) suggests that Lawrence did want, at least in part, to endorse Birkin's thought that his union with Ursula "must happen beyond the sound of words." The most significant event that has to happen, of course, is sexual union. The narrative peculiarly celebrates this event, without anything very clear yet having happened, while the couple wait, fully clothed, for tea in the parlor of the inn. When the sexual union finally occurs, in the night scene of Sherwood Forest, the narrative gives a remarkably brief account in an abstract rhetoric which is much less sexually evocative than the language for Gerald's night visit to Gudrun or even for the wrestling scene between the two men. Lawrence wants the successful sexual union of Ursula and Birkin to constitute a sustaining bond that will carry them through all their subsequent quarrels and discords, and he does succeed in creating the sense of a bond between them in the more intimate, softened tones of their later interchanges. But, for whatever reason, he cannot effectively render the supposedly perfect and silent equilibrium of the sexual event itself.

Lawrence makes the union between Ursula and Birkin vivid for us only in the sexually charged but finally not quite sexual terms of their continuing gestures of speech. Even with new tones of tenderness, the conversations of Ursula and Birkin in the latter part of the book remain the same blend of assertion and resistance heard earlier, so that while the union may escape the confining responsibilities of society, it remains bound to the conditions of tension in human relationship itself. For example, in the chapter "A Chair" their first move toward the domesticity of buying some furniture turns first to quarrel and then to the precarious compromise—still not quite an accord—of giving away their just-purchased chair to the working-class couple also buying furniture at the market. Although Ursula and Birkin both like the chair, they cannot agree on how to talk about its attractiveness, and this dissension ruins their very desire to have the chair. Birkin characteristically goes on to elaborate an entire theoretical stand against the power of possessions: "You have to be like Rodin, Michael Angelo, and leave a piece of raw rock unfinished to your figure. You must leave your surroundings sketchy, unfinished, so that you are never contained, never confined, never dominated from the outside" (p. 349). Ursula characteristically listens, "contemplating," and then protests against Birkin's high-flown generalizations with her commonsense intelligence and directness. In a new mood of conciliation, however, she invents the charming solution of a gift to the other couple—an idea Birkin accepts, but only reluctantly, and without entirely yielding his stand.

> "And we are never to have a complete place of our own—never a home?" she said.
> "Pray God, in this world, no," he answered.
> "But there's only this world," she objected.
> He spread out his hand with a gesture of indifference.
> "Meanwhile, then, we'll avoid having things of our own," he said.
> "But you've just bought a chair," she said.
> "I can tell the man I don't want it," he replied.
> She pondered again. Then a queer little movement twitched her face.
> "No," she said, "we don't want it. I'm sick of old things."
> "New ones as well," he said . . .
> "Let us give it to *them*," whispered Ursula. "Look they are getting a home together."
> "*I* won't aid and abet them in it," he said petulantly, instantly sympathising with the aloof, furtive youth against the active, procreant female.
> "Oh yes," cried Ursula. "It's right for them—there's nothing else for them."
> "Very well," said Birkin, "you offer it to them. I'll watch." (p. 349)

Lawrence can make the rub of strong personalities against each other humorous and attractive as well as ugly. Disagreements about chairs, or even about words—"old" things and "new," "this world" and others—in a sense constitute the "something else" that Ursula and Birkin have, beyond the elemental male / female antagonism of the inarticulate working-class couple. We have the sense that their life will never be dull; even such a routine act as the purchase (or nonpurchase) of a chair sets off the delicate springs of character so that their union remains, with or without furniture, always unfinished, never fully contained in any scheme, even of their own devising.

The idea of further release from this tiring as well as invigorating tension of relationship obviously appeals to Lawrence, as well as to Birkin. But just as Ursula does not remain in the still position of a "star" for more than a night, the sounds of living speech intruding upon Lawrence's imagination thwart (or protect) him in relation to his own visionary metaphysic. There is more strain, more undissolved threat of divisive opposition in the continuing disagreements between Ursula and Birkin than the visionary ideal of "star-equilibrium" implies. Yet it is through this strain that the characters construct and reconstruct both their individual characters and their relation to each other. If their tension does not, at the end of the novel, seem doomed to rupture the union altogether, that is perhaps mainly because Lawrence matches the forces of these personalities so evenly in strength—an equality we understand only by following the shifting, inconclusive play of power between them and comparing it, say, to the unbalanced matches of strength between Gerald and Birkin. It is true that Lawrence also unites Ursula and Birkin in their knowledge that this tense union is what they need, or at least what they cannot do without. They know their need at some level deeper than consciousness—each has an intuitive recognition that a living future exists for them only in relation to the other—but they also pursue the relationship deliberately, through all that back and forth insistence which Lawrence makes so exhausting and yet so alive, to the very last page of the book.

The gestures of speech, then, in the Ursula / Birkin relationship, can be neither disregarded nor deciphered into some more primary force of life, for it is in the sound and texture of the speech itself that the precarious kicking and cleaving of the relationship exist. The contrast, both striking and subtle, with Gerald and Gudrun again calls for close attention to the nuances of spoken experience. Although Gerald and Gudrun are in one sense doomed, so the narrator insists, by the deep destructiveness of their impulses, the poignancy of their failure depends on the detailed wrongness of what also seem to be their choices in the social situations of their relationship.

One conversation that seems significant for its strange combination of the portentous and the plain occurs when, at Gerald's urging, Gudrun stays for dinner at Shortlands and he tells her, against the hush of the sickroom upstairs, of his feelings of fear and helplessness.

"I don't know what the effect actually *is* on one," he said, and again looked down at her. Her eyes were dark and stricken with knowledge, looking into his. He saw her submerged, and he turned aside his face. "But I absolutely am not the same. There's nothing left, if you understand what I mean. You seem to be clutching at the void—and at the same time you are void yourself. And so you don't know what to *do.*"

"No," she murmured. A heavy thrill ran down her nerves, heavy, almost pleasure, almost pain. "What can be done?" she added.

He turned and flipped the ash from his cigarette on to the great marble hearth-stones, that lay bare in the room, without fender or bar.

"I don't know, I'm sure," he replied. "But I do think you've got to find some way of resolving the situation—not because you want to, but because you've *got* to, otherwise you're done. The whole of everything, and yourself included, is just on the point of caving in, and you are just holding it up with your hands. Well, it's a situation that obviously can't continue. You can't stand holding the roof up with your hands forever. You know that sooner or later you'll *have* to let go. Do you understand what I mean? And so something's got to be done, or there's a universal collapse—as far as you yourself are concerned."

He shifted slightly on the hearth, crunching a cinder under his heel. He looked down at it. Gudrun was aware of the beautiful old marble panels of the fireplace, swelling softly carved, round him and above him. She felt as if she were caught at last by fate, imprisoned in some horrible and fatal trap.

"But what *can* be done?" she murmured humbly. "You must use me if I can be of any help at all—but how can I? I don't see how *I* can help you."

He looked down at her critically.

"I don't want you to *help,*" he said, slightly irritated, "because there's nothing to be *done.* I only want sympathy, do you see: I want somebody I can talk to sympathetically. That eases the strain. And there *is* nobody to talk to sympathetically. That's the curious thing. There *is* nobody. There's Rupert Birkin. But then he *isn't* sympathetic, he wants to *dictate.* And that is no use whatsoever."

She was caught in a strange snare. She looked down at her hands. (pp. 317–18)

The touching distress of this scene comes from the fact that, despite the loud foreboding of the narrative directions, it takes more than a moment to locate exactly what makes Gerald's talk so wrong, as well as what makes Gudrun's response to him so dismally unhelpful, even destructive. And it takes further time to decide, if one can do so at all, whether any alternative gestures between them are within their power to choose.

Gerald is speaking with remarkable frankness, but a strange impoverishment of vocabulary shows in his repeated emphasis of the most commonplace, inexpressive words. Gudrun, moreover, accurately makes out, through the constrained speech, the real enormity of Gerald's need and of his demand—and it is this recognition that makes her feel both trapped and thrilled. Yet it is hard to fault her for keeping these feelings to herself. By any conventional standard of civilized talk, her replies, however weak, are surely less sinister than Ursula's telling Birkin that he looks repellently ill!

But of course it is the standard of Ursula's speech that allows us to measure the emptiness of Gudrun's responses. The problem is not that Gudrun is simply hypocritical or selfish or even that her impulses are sinister, worse than Ursula's. More subtly, Lawrence makes us feel the void that Gudrun makes of herself by her failure to create any vital expressive form out of her confused emotion. Although she feels trapped, her speech makes no gesture of resistance, really no gesture of individuality at all. She merely dissolves herself into conventional formulae of decency—in Lawrence's terms, one of the most fatal dissolutions of all. Lawrence had already shown Gudrun perform another, almost heroic version of decency at the sickbed of the father, where the conventional forms of social speech were good enough to sustain the dying man a bit longer. Gerald, however, is not yet irrevocably dead; he seeks the reality, not merely the illusion of life. Although Gerald is awkward in his appeal, he is also touching in his effort to "catch into connection with the living world" through contact with Gudrun in speech. Neither one, however, can use speech to make such a contact occur.

Gudrun is in a way accurate in responding so impersonally to Gerald's words, in that he seems hardly to be speaking to her individually, and barely to be speaking as an individual himself. He imagines, conventionally, that he wants sympathy, "to ease the strain." But his voice sounds more dissociated from feeling than strained. Lawrence has a good ear for how English personal pronouns can shift around to hollow out personal presence from cultivated spoken language. Gerald's pronouns keep changing reference: "I don't know what the effect actually *is* on one"; "You know that sooner or later, you'll *have* to let go." Gerald avoids the accusative and accusatory forms of speech so pointed in the talk between Birkin and Ursula, and even between himself and Birkin. Those forms of speech in Lawrence's dialogue disconcertingly identify potential intimacy with socially objectionable tones of bullying, taunt, and quarrel. Gerald's talk with Gudrun is more decorous, yet by that very fact, also empty of any promise of real contact. With Gudrun, Gerald neither asserts himself as subject nor clearly locates Gudrun as object of his statements. And her constructions are correspondingly empty of clear personal reference: "But what *can* be done?" By reducing her own self to a merely passive anonymous vessel of sympathy, Gudrun avoid Birkin's irritating manner of "dictating" but fails to create the resistant force which Lawrence would persuade us is the only hope for Gerald's own revival.[24]

Gerald's image of holding a roof up over a void evokes the terror of a consciousness aware of its own lost connection to any natural structures of support. The image, however, in itself shapes Gerald's destiny as much as it represents it, for the narrative has presented a view of Gerald's depths that shows less a void than a maelstrom of conflicting desires and fears, not so different from the depths of the other characters. That is why Gerald is more interesting than Skrebensky, the more truly hollow version of Gerald's type that Lawrence presents in *The Rainbow*. In *Women in Love* the image of a void is at least in part Gerald's own despairing construction (or deconstruction) of a character and a condition that could be interpreted differently, just as Birkin's many and even contradictory versions of his own character and condition are constructions, interpretations made by his consciousness. Birkin's final post mortem charge against Gerald as "the denier" addresses that refusal (or inability) of self-construction in Gerald which is as much a failure of character as of impulse; or rather, Gerald's conviction of his own void is a failure in the power of consciousness to make a living character out of the confusion of the depth.

Ursula at the end, however, calls Birkin's idea of Gerald's failure "an obstinacy, a theory, a perversity" (p. 472). She objects specifically to Birkin's continuing provocative insistence that he wants, in addition to marriage, "eternal union with a man," and that such a union would have saved Gerald. Ursula not surprisingly objects to this intimation of her insufficiency, but she is also repeating her earlier acute perception of how so many of Birkin's statements and ideas are obstinate perversities in the sense that they willfully twist the evidence of what can be discerned as true even by simple examination of one's own experience. As in *The Golden Bowl,* where the reader has narrative evidence that resists Maggie's theory of betrayal, the reader at the end of *Women in*

Love has even more evidence than Ursula to assess the perversity of Birkin's theorizing about Gerald. The novel has earlier presented a considerably more ambiguous pattern of mutual approach and withdrawal between the men than Birkin acknowledges in his plaintive and blaming last comment: "He should have loved me . . . I offered him." In the wedding scene the narrator made both men equally determined to deny "heartburning." And even in the wrestling scene, Birkin's awkward unresponsiveness to Gerald's quite open profession of love raises the question of what, exactly, Birkin "offered." It was Birkin, more clearly than Gerald, who withdrew from intimacy on that occasion, when he turned ("reverted") in thought and then in speech away from Gerald and back to Ursula and his marriage proposal. Without deliberately lying in his later reconstruction of the friendship, Birkin (like Maggie in *The Golden Bowl*) characteristically turns away from disinterested probing of the depths in favor of more self-protective theorizing.

In his famous affirmation of "the struggle for verbal consciousness" in the Foreword to *Women in Love,* Lawrence seems, like Birkin at later points, to envision a kind of "utterance" that would bear direct expressive relationship to the "deep, passional soul" (p. viii). The novel itself, however, dramatizes a more ambiguous relationship of all utterance to the deep self. Lawrence brings Birkin closest to recognizing that ambiguity when he has him wonder for a moment whether his insistence with Ursula on a new kind of love was "only an idea, or was it the interpretation of a profound yearning" (p. 245). The key word "interpretation" in a sense answers the question that Birkin's alternatives do not fully articulate. Through Birkin, and indeed through the novel as a whole, Lawrence shows how the vitality of ideas (and finally of all verbal expression) comes from the way in which they are interpretations of profound yearnings—which is also to say that the language made by characters is never directly expressive of impulse, but always a construction, sometimes even a perversity.

Although Bersani is thus right to perceive that language in *Women in Love* is shown to be a "mediating and distorting vehicle," Lawrence goes further to affirm the value of language as medium, especially in the form of social speech where individual interpretations of yearnings encounter the responses and the counterpressures of other personalities. Maggie Verver, like James himself, seeks to rise above the ugliness of such open human struggle; she acts on her theories but keeps them mainly to herself. For Lawrence, however, the sounds of struggle in talk are crucial signs of life. The worst aspect of Gerald's frozen

corpse is its "terrible look of cold, mute Matter." Death is mute in
Women in Love, and failures of speech freeze character in deadly
isolation. Gerald's reluctance (or inability) to turn his deepest impulses
into any but conventional verbal forms dooms him in Lawrence's world
as fully as any destructive qualities in the impulses themselves. Birkin
recovers from the blow of Gerald's death in the same way that he
recovers himself at earlier points: he turns—in a way, turns aside—
from the confusing depths of feeling to speech. His precarious success,
like that of Lawrence in the novel itself, depends on neither the whole-
someness nor the coherence of his deep yearnings, but on the untiring
inventiveness with which he can move from depth to surface, and from
private yearning to spoken encounter, thus forever constructing supports for the "roof" of character, however shaky the foundations.

5

Near and Far Things in Lawrence's Writing of the Twenties

The Spectacle of Reality:
Australia, the Sea, and Sardinia

In the twenties the give and take of conversation diminishes in Lawrence's writing, along with the hope of personal relationship that conversation served in *Women in Love*. "Speech is like a volley of dead leaves and dust, stifling the air," the hero of *Kangaroo* complains. "Human beings should learn to make weird, wordless cries, like the animals, and cast off the clutter of words" (pp. 391–92).[1] In *Kangaroo* marital dialogue has become a nightmarish caricature of the conversations between Ursula and Birkin: the wife, Harriet, rants at her husband in long, shockingly brutal tirades of ridicule; he closes his ears against her abuse, except insofar as her sarcasm becomes one of the tones in his own soliloquies of self-contempt. In the best moments of Lawrence's prose of the twenties, however, the interplay of speech that in *Women in Love* identified the possibility of human sanity still occurs—often more wittily and vigorously than before. Only now, the drama of assertion and rebuttal arises from the single source which we recognize as the voice of Lawrence himself. Whether or not he is literally by himself, even when he gives volleys of speech to other characters, Lawrence most often seems to be alone, wandering the world—somewhere, nowhere—while speaking to a distant reader or arguing with himself.

Both the exhilaration and the horror of this solitude show in the uneven success of the art, even within single books. Lawrence's style in the twenties—I am talking about the criticism, letters, and travel writing as well as the fiction—becomes more often dazzling in its wit, its rapid shifts of reference, its verbal play and freedom. And it also more often collapses for long stretches into self-indulgent rant and tirade. Eruptions of rage, disgust, and prophetic soliloquizing are horrible in the way they flow uncontrollably over everything, without the discriminations enforced by the "but," "still," or "after all" of social interchange. At the same time, the striking solitude of utterance makes the energy and quirky sociability all the more striking when they appear. There is exhilaration from the conviction that freedom—of expression as well as of feeling—does not depend on what Birkin calls a "perfected" human intimacy any more than on a stable, geographical home. To be free, to speak freely, may indeed require considerable distance from intimacies with both people and places. Instead of pointing to the "free" place in which to be free with one or a few other people, in Birkin's terms, travel for Lawrence in this period comes to promise the fuller freedom of getting apart from people altogether, "out of this loathsome complication of living humanly with humans," as he puts it in one of the essays on Melville (p. 132).[2]

Thus the exuberant lyricism of the departure by boat in the travel memoir *Sea and Sardinia*:

> It is the motion of freedom. To feel her coming up—then slide slowly forward, with the sound of the smashing of waters, is like . . . the magic gallop of elemental space. That long, slow, waveringly rhythmic rise and fall of the ship, with waters snorting as it were from her nostrils, oh, God, what a joy it is to the wild innermost soul. One is free at last—and lilting in a slow flight of the elements, winging outwards. Oh, God, to be free of all the hemmed-in life—the horror of human tension, the absolute insanity of a life among tense, resistant people on land. And then to feel the long, slow lift and drop of this almost empty ship, as she took the waters. Ah, God, liberty, liberty, elemental liberty. (p. 35)[3]

Hence the vivid imaginative engagement with other solitary artist-adventurers, especially Americans like Melville, who conjure a tougher, bolder freedom than anything in the more sentimental English tradition.

The greatest seer and poet of the sea for me is Melville. His vision is more real than Swinburne's, because he doesn't personify the sea, and far sounder than Joseph Conrad's, because Melville doesn't sentimentalize the ocean and the sea's unfortunates . . . never was a man so passionately filled with the sense of vastness and mystery of life which is non-human. He was mad to look over our horizons. Anywhere, anywhere out of *our* world. To get away. To get away, out! (pp. 131, 134)

The vitality of this writing comes from the way Lawrence takes his own reckless and passionate liberty with the decorum of prose. As a literary critic he is slangy, lyrical, confessional, prejudiced—just as he pleases and all at once, in the same paragraph or even sentence or sentence fragment. Literary allusions (as to Baudelaire's prose poem "Anywhere Out of the World") are tossed off casually, like colloquial exclamation. The syntax is loose, often broken, but the rhythm is alive and the texture of the language dense with interesting words and images, surprising turns of phrase and tone, in the manner of exceptionally brilliant conversation: "Perhaps Melville is at his best, his happiest, in *Omoo*. For once he is really reckless. For once he takes life as it comes. For once he is the gallant rascally epicurean, eating the world like a snipe, dirt and all baked into one *bonne bouche*. . . Good as an experience. But a man who will not abandon himself to despair or indifference cannot keep it up" (p. 140).

Lawrence enacts in his own style the reckless energy that now so often becomes an explicit object of his admiration. Yet beyond and along with the recklessness is the deflating insight into its limits, its impossibility finally as an experience that a human being can or should keep up. It is not necessary for Lawrence to give the voice of deflation the name of another character in a fictional dialogue; Lawrence in the twenties can perform his own deflations, in tones of witty and sometimes despairing aside. An acerbic voice of judgment assesses what happens when gallant recklessness goes awry in himself and other writers, like Melville with his false profundities in *Moby Dick*: "One wearies of the *grand sérieux*. There's something false about it. And that's Melville. Oh dear, when the solemn ass brays! brays! brays!" (p. 146).

Lawrence sees that without the constraining tension of living humanly with humans, gallant recklessness is always on the verge of puffing out into the *grand sérieux* or breaking down into hell-rage. In the novel *Kangaroo,* bombast and breakdown are closely allied in the rhetorical eruptions of the hero, Richard Lovatt Somers, whose desperate instability finally breaks apart the novel as a whole. For although Lawrence and Somers himself (the two are not very distinct in the novel) can vividly diagnose the pathology of the condition, insight does not generate control.

> He cared for nothing now, but to let loose the hell-rage that was in him. Get rid of it by letting it out. For there was no digesting it. He had been . . . trying to soothe himself with the sops of travel and new experience and scenery. He knew now the worth of all sops.—Once that disruption has taken place in a man's soul . . . something has broken in his tissue and the liquid fire has run out loose into his blood, then no sops will be of any avail. (p. 308)

Some of Lawrence's writing in *Kangaroo* is compelling by its diagnostic brilliance, but hell-rage in the form of social tirade and messianic vision too often turns the language of diagnosis itself into yet another symptom of disease. The very harshness that both character and narrator turn on various forms of what the book calls "blather," draws even self-criticism into the circle of frenzy.

> So behold the poor dear on his pinnacle lifting his hands. "God is God and man is man; and every man by himself. Every man by himself, alone with his own soul. Alone as if he were dead. Dead to himself. He is dead and alone. He is dead; alone. His soul is alone. Alone with God, with the dark God. God is God."
> But if he likes to shout muezzins, instead of hawking fried fish or newspapers or lottery tickets, let him.
> Poor dear, it was rather an anomalous call: "Listen to me, and be alone." Yet he felt called upon to call it. (p. 331)

"Shouting muezzins," the Mohammedan call to prayer, is one derisive image for the political-mystical-sexual "call" so loud in *Kangaroo,* as in other of Lawrence's writings of the twenties. Even in the form of self-parody, a little of this "hawking" goes a long way. The problem in *Kangaroo* is not an insufficiency of self-criticism, but outbursts of uncontrolled vituperation directed everywhere, including against the self. Somers has no normal place to speak from: he is either up on a pinnacle or under a volcano. He has come to Australia uncertain whether he is a tourist, a potential settler, or (the possibility emerges in the novel) a providential leader for this still new-frontier continent. By the middle of the novel all these alternatives have collapsed and Somers sees himself "at the end of his tether." Nor does any new direction for recovery hold shape: his farfetched fantasies of political leadership disintegrate, along with the uneasy male friendship with which they were entangled. To settle into domesticity in Australia with his wife, Harriet, would reduce him to "a fly in the ointment"—"embalmed in balm." At the end of the novel Somers and his wife set out rather aimlessly for America. The sea is only a passageway between lands; departure is not a joyful flight of the wild innermost soul, but only a half-sorry, half-desperate further rending of fragile human ties, like the breaking of the colored paper streamers which briefly connect departing passengers to their friends on the dock: "One by one the streamers broke and fluttered loose and fell bright and dead on the water . . . the crowd stood alone at the end of the wharf, the side of the vessel was fluttering with bright, broken ends" (p. 421).

Scattered through the sick darkness of *Kangaroo,* however, there are intermittent flashes of another, brighter (if also broken) kind of color. As Lawrence said about Melville in *Omoo,* Somers (Lawrence) is perhaps "at his best, his happiest" in interludes where, for not altogether accountable reasons, he for a while seems able to take life as it comes, dirt and all. The key chapter for this writing in the book is called, significantly, "Bits": fragments—broken bits—of Australian life come to Somers in this chapter, not laden with the melancholy of the broken streamers at the end, but with a freer and more gallant humor.

Most literally, the bits in question come from the correspondence columns of a newspaper, the Sidney *Bulletin,* where anonymous or rather pseudonymous figures—"Cellu Lloyd," "K. Sped"—exchange bits of observation and advice: how to cure mange in horses, how a "fluke" made a tiger snake double back and bite the leg of a motorcyclist who had just run over it. Lawrence gives several pages to these newspaper bits. There are some openly racist items about "Binghi" (slang insult for aborigine) and some not-very-funny jokes about the skills of survival in this crude country. In Lawrence's rendering, the throwaway journalism has an entirely different significance from comparable items in either Joyce or more Laurentian writers like Doris Lessing. Emphasizing neither squalor nor pathos, Lawrence lets the newspaper bits speak simply for the rawness of life as handled by some quite raw people. Somers likes the newspaper; for a while, at least, it soothes him, restores his sense of proportion: "He liked its straightforwardness and the kick in some of its tantrums. It beat no solemn drums. It had no deadly earnestness. It was just stoical and spitefully humorous" (p. 316). Like Australia itself, the newspaper bits have virtually no esthetic or moral pretension. Yet Lawrence lets their very vulgarity represent an attractive kind of strength: "Bits, bits, bits. Yet Richard Lovatt read on. It was not mere anecdotage. It was the momentaneous life of the continent. There was no consecutive thread. Only the laconic courage of experience" (p. 319).

As if to show his character refreshed by this stoical sanity, Lawrence goes on in the chapter to report in detail an unextraordinary walk taken by Somers and Harriet down Main Street in the coastal town Wolloona. Lawrence's language for the episode is more resourceful than the prose of the newspaper as quoted, but the spirit is similar—no deadly earnestness, just stoic and spiteful humor, and laconic respect for the sheer life of this continent, so distinctively Australian and yet so very like the mangy corners of common life anywhere.

> "I like it," said Harriet. "It doesn't feel *finished.*"
> "Not even begun," he laughed.
> But he liked it too: even the slummyness of some of the bungalows inside their wooden palings, drab-wood, decrepit houses, old tins, broken pots, a greeny-white pony reminding one of a mildewed old shoe, two half-naked babies sitting like bits of live refuse in the dirt, but with bonny healthy bare legs: the awful place called "The Travellers Rest—Mrs. Coddy's Boarding Home"—a sort of blind squalid corner-building made of wood and tin, with flat pieces of old lace-curtain nailed inside the windows, and the green blinds hermetically drawn. What must it have been like inside? (pp. 320–21)

This narrative voice belongs to the Lawrence we know from the letters and the travel writing. He can give such bits of "momentaneous life" in Australia or anywhere. The location is far from home, but the vantage point is close up and at ground level, staying off heights that might expose the upsetting insides of houses (or souls). The writing is interesting, lively, fun, though one must wonder what art beyond a letter (or a newspaper article) could be constructed out of such fragments. Somers, who is officially a journalist, cannot shape a life (or a writing career) out of mere bits of observation. He cannot even sustain his good mood to the end of the day. Although he likes the "really nice" Australians on the bus ride home, rising hell-rage can be discerned already in his dangerously edged repetitions of praise: "They were really awfully nice"; "So nice, so nice, so gentle." By the time Somers reaches home he is back on his volcanic pinnacle, still thinking about the newspaper bits, but unable now to resist a symbolizing inflation of them. The most emblematic one is about a herd of bullocks in Gippsland that drowned in a hole after following one after the other in a line over a path edge. Somers shouts "muezzins" for the rest of the chapter.

> That, thought Richard at the close of the day, is a sufficient comment on herd-unity, equality, domestication, and civilisation. He felt he would have liked to climb down into that hole in which the bullocks were drowning and beat them all hard before they expired, for being such mechanical logs of life.
> Telepathy! Think of the marvellous vivid communication of the huge sperm whales. Huge, grand phallic beasts! Bullocks! Geldings! Men!— R.L. wished he could take to the sea and be a whale, a great surge of living blood: away from these all-too-white people, who ought *all* to be called Cellu Lloyd, not only the horse-mange man. (p. 327)

The stoic, humorous observer gives way to the prophet and visionary. Evangelical political leadership and private romantic escape merge into a single rhetorical rejection of "taking life as it comes." By the close of day, travel has lost its association with the activity of detailed human observation so enjoyable on the streets of Wolloona, and instead becomes an emblem of imagined flight away from the human altogether, as in Lawrence's reading of Melville, where the sea is identified not only with freedom but also with abstraction and rhetorical extravagance: "Human life won't do. He turns back to the elements . . . The sea-born people, who can meet and mingle no longer: who turn away from life, to the abstract, to the elements" (p. 132). Instead of walking amid fragments of human reality—broken pots, dirty babies, pieces of lace curtain—there is imaginative flight to the glamour of "huge, grand phallic beasts!" From Lawrence's point of view, the fact that Somers—like Melville—soon has had enough of Cellu Lloyd and Co. is to his credit, for "a man who will not abandon himself to despair or indifference" cannot keep up an appetite for the dirt of the world. The problem is that the alternate movements of flight—up, down, or simply away—lead to no better outcome. Lawrence pictures Somers, the would-be savior, shouting himself down into a ditch to beat the proverbial dead horse!

To beat dead horses (or bullocks) not only wastes energy, it may be deceptive in the seeming intensity of energy displayed. In *Kangaroo* hell-rage is the style of fatigue, of a man "at the end of his tether." There is a factitiousness to the vitality of tirade elsewhere in Lawrence's writing of the twenties that similarly signifies more the loss than the release of energy. Although bits of observation continued to come easily to Lawrence in these years, the tough yet amused spirit of his best late style was not at all easy for him to sustain. By comparison, the rhetoric of "shouting muezzins" was simpler, almost a mechanical trade, like hawking fish or lottery tickets. In *Kangaroo* the sheer hawking repetitiveness of Lawrence's visionary rhetoric finally breaks down the novel itself, leaving it interesting to read only in "bits," in isolated passages and chapters. At the same time, the terms of the human and stylistic predicament in the novel as a whole give an excellent guide to Lawrence's remakably sustained achievements in the two short masterpieces of the decade: *Sea and Sardinia* (which comes before, in 1921) and *St. Mawr* (which comes after, in 1924). In both the travel memoir and the novella, questions of where to go in the world and how to take it, spiritually and rhetorically, are investigated by Lawrence with a poise and vigor that hardly flag.

In *Sea and Sardinia* the twin extremes of naive rapture and disillusioned rage loom only just large enough to add interest to the scene, like the volcanoes Etna and Eryx, which are among the menacing influences Lawrence leaves Sicily to escape. The slim travel record of this week-long holiday in 1921 tantalizes by the apparent ease of its happiness—in a sense, the book resembles the island of Sardinia itself: a "somewhere" just beyond reach of Europe, much closer than Australia, yet unaccountably more different in the experience offered than its proximity would suggest.

Yet Sardinia is not a place where Lawrence would choose to live, nor were holiday trips a mode of life that he could, on a large scale, approve (or afford). In a letter dated one week after the trip, Lawrence wrote: "We made a dash to Sardinia—liked the island very much—but it isn't a place to live in. No point in living there. A stray corner of Italy, rather difficult materially to live in."[4] Lawrence's delight as a traveler in Sardinia, as a tourist really, is so special, so unstable, and perhaps necessarily so transitory, that it ends by narrowly demarcating as well as exemplifying the ideal of freedom longed for as a permanent condition by every wandering Laurentian hero.

Finally, of course, it is the writing in *Sea and Sardinia* that makes the high spirits of the trip impressive, specifically as the achievement of a man who is remarkable as much for his power of language as for his energy in travel. While the figure of Lawrence in Sardinia may, from one point of view, seem that of a man on holiday from any or no occupation, Lawrence's style in the book, his evident delight in language and his absorption in the esthetic as a distinct mode of experience, indirectly identifies the travel memoir as the work of a writer, of an artist whose imaginative and expressive resources differentiate him from fictional characters who are mere travelers or would-be settlers. Although no explicit allusions to literary ambitions or projects evoke Lawrence's artistic career, such clues matter less than the pervasive impression of a sensibility which makes, and remakes, experience through brilliant forms of language. Neither Birkin, nor the journalist Somers, nor Lou Witt in *St. Mawr* has this great talent, which appears so effortless in Lawrence's nonfictional prose that perhaps only the comparison of Lawrence to his less gifted fictional characters makes his difference from them vivid.

The artistic identity first asserted by Lawrence's language at the start of *Sea and Sardinia* sounds positively defiant in its unregenerate romanticism, especially set against the very different exertions of his most famous world-wandering contemporaries. The tone of the travel memoir at the start is impulsive: a colloquial prose version of the inspired spontaneity at the start of a Romantic lyric. "Andiamo," "Let us go then," he announces boldly, inviting the reader into the excitement of an immediate adventure. It seems uncanny that, in 1921, Lawrence can still strike sparks out of the old romantic call to departure, as if "Prufrock" had not dampened that heroic phrasing for generations to come: "Let us go then, you and I, / When the evening is spread out against the sky / Like a patient etherised upon a table." Although already mortally ill in 1921 (and perhaps for that very reason), Lawrence wants nothing to do with being "like a patient" of any sort. He shows himself full of energy, up and ready to go at dawn, equipped with his little "kitchenino," his knapsack, his canteens of hot tea, and Frieda ("q-b" for queen bee).

Nor does it matter to him that parts of Joyce's *Ulysses* have appeared, and that the boat to Sardinia stops first at Trapani, the port which Samuel Butler had pronounced the true location of all the original Odyssean wanderings. Hugh Kenner makes of Trapani a rich emblem of what the new map of the ancient literary world made available to the modernist imagination during "the Pound era." Kenner likes to guess that Joyce related the Homeric world to one city after Butler's model, "for what had been built out of the town of Trapani could be concentrated once more into the town of Dublin: like Trapani, a seaport on an island."[5]

Lawrence, however, was not seeking to build new relationships to the Homeric world, nor was he after any of the dense, intricate, ironic connections between modernity and the past so absorbing to such contemporary literary travelers as Eliot, Pound, and Joyce. On the contrary, Lawrence chose Sardinia in 1921 precisely because it seemed to promise freedom from all offerings of past as well as present connections: "Where then? . . . Sardinia, which is like nowhere. Sardinia, which has no history, no date, no race, no offering. Let it be Sardinia . . . It lies outside, outside the circuit of civilization" (p. 11).

Although the literary associations of Lawrence's primitivism are to romantic rather than to ancient or modernist images of travel, there is also sharp acknowledgement that 1921 is a late date for romantic escape and that the world is, or has become, quite small, as Ursula had already pointed out to Birkin: "After all, there *is* only the world, and none of it is very distant" (p. 307). Italy, for example, the goal of so many earlier romantic voyages (including those of Lawrence himself), looks now like just another outpost of European gloom and corruption: "Romantic, poetic, cypress-and-orange-tree Italy is gone. Remains an Italy smothered in the filthy smother of innumerable lira notes: ragged, unsavoury paper money so thick upon the air that one breathes it like some greasy fog" (p. 37).

Given the penetrating capacities of the Laurentian eye, *Sea and Sardinia* seems set up to present the predictable *échec* of the romantic traveler, high as a balloon over the sea, deflated by every close look into what seems so beautiful in imagination or from the outside, from the sea. The conventional pattern indeed does appear at Trapani, for while unredeemed by Homeric reverberations, that Sicilian port is civilized enough to resemble the seamier parts of any town: "One should never enter into these southern towns that look so nice, so lovely, from the outside . . . we crossed the avenue which looks so beautiful from the sea, and which when you get into it, is a cross between an outside place where you throw rubbish and a humpy unmade road in a raw suburb, with a few iron seats, and litter of old straw and rag" (p. 45). If this irascible observer is not going to control squalor within a Joycean structure of irony, it seems hard to envision how he shall do other than lapse into the hell-rage that does in fact break down the language in *Kangaroo*.

The details in *Sea and Sardinia* call out quite loudly for either irony or open disgust even before the boat has fully cleared the harbor of Palermo, for the loathed civilization turns out to be on the boat itself, fully in evidence when the surly crew produces the first wretched meal.

> Bash comes a huge plate of thick oily cabbage soup, very full, swilkering over the sides. We do what we can with it . . . In the doorway hovers a little cloud of alpaca jackets grinning faintly with malignant anticipation of food, hoping, like blowflies, we shall be too ill to eat. Away goes the soup and appears a massive yellow omelette, like some log of bilious

wood. It is hard and heavy, and cooked in the usual rank-tasting olive oil. The young woman doesn't have much truck with it: neither do we. To the triumph of the blowflies, who see the yellow monster borne to their alter. After which a long slab of the inevitable meat cut into innumerable slices, tasting of dead nothingness and having a thick sauce of brown neutrality: sufficient for twelve people at least. This, with masses of strong-tasting greenish cauliflower liberally weighted with oil, on a ship that was already heaving its heart out, made up the dinner. Accumulating malevolent triumph among the blowflies in the passage. So on to a dessert of oranges, pears with wooden hearts and thick yellowish wash-leather flesh, and apples. Then coffee.

And we had sat through it, which is something. The alpaca bluebottles buzzed over the masses of food that went back on the dishes to the tin altar. Surely it had been made deliberately so that we should not eat it! (pp. 39–40)

So much, it might seem, for romantic joy, the "magic gallop of elemental space" celebrated only four pages earlier. Instead of "winging outwards" to liberty, the dingy steamer altogether replicates the hemmed-in, oily, corrupt (and expensive) civilization supposedly left behind. One waits for Lawrence's hell-rage to erupt.

But there is, amazingly, no hell-rage in *Sea and Sardinia*. It is not that Lawrence strains to hold his temper in check, any more than he orders sordid detail through irony. More remarkably, his imaginative gusto simply breaks right through the logic and the conventional patterns of romantic and postromantic disillusion. For the Lawrence of *Sea and Sardinia,* even the squalid crew of "alpaca bluebottles" is enlivening to watch in action. His spirit, at least the spirit of his writing after the event, positively thrives on every oily detail of cabbage and crew. Lawrence is full of curiosity on the boat. Peeping around passages, into the kitchen, through cabin windows, he does not miss a single malevolent gesture of the crew or any sign of folly and pretension in the other passengers. And it is all registered in the same entertaining style of exact detail transformed and animated by joyfully insolent response.

The clear impossibility of performing any role other than that of passenger and spectator seems to release Lawrence to enjoy the wretched society of the boat almost as a comically melodramatic stage performance. Or perhaps it is his own stamina which delights him as he sees the other passengers collapse, felled one after another by the heaving sea, the bad wine, or simply by deficiencies of imagination. While other passengers are shown to succumb to "faint wails" and general misery, Lawrence presents himself as undauntable: "The most downtrodden, frayed, ancient rag of a man goes discreetly with basins, trying not to let out glimpses of the awful within. I climb up to look at the vivid, drenching stars, to breathe the cold wind, to see the dark sea sliding. Then I too go to the cabin, and watch the sea run past the porthole for a minute, and insert myself like the meat in a sandwich into the tight lower bunk" (p. 53). In Lawrence's strong voice, discomfort and even indignation are carried aloft by the comic and celebratory verve of the language. Delight is the dominant tone, a delight which can include squalid detail because it depends not on the beauty of objects, but on Lawrence's own indefatigable alertness to every ragged bit of life as it goes by.

Before Lawrence ever gets to Sardinia, his description of the boat trip prepares for a more elusive relationship between the imagination and reality than anticipated by the romantic desire for escape at the start. The squalid reality of the boat exerts peculiarly little power over his initial heroic vision of the sea voyage. Oppressive, even sickening details coexist with symbols of joy and freedom, however incongruously. Though it is true that he has to sleep in a "match box" cabin, he can easily climb up to the open space of the deck. And anyway, for all his claustrophobia in "hemmed-in" Europe, on the boat Lawrence did not mind sleeping like "meat in a sandwich." As long as the motion of travel continues, as long as the spirit is cut loose from the tense entanglements of home, hardly any actual awfulness along the way is so bad as to spoil the fun . On the contrary, the frayed and downtrodden details of the scene may be more engaging to the imagination than the blank emptiness of the sea.

It needs to be noticed, however, that (at first glance, at least) many details of Sardinia do fit romantic expectation—almost too neatly. Lawrence is not quite accurate in saying that Sardinia appealed because it was "like nowhere," for he did have an elaborated vision of a place that conformed to symbols both familiar from other romantic literature and developed further by himself in reaction against the bloodless and bloody Europe he knew. "Indomitable" Sardinia obviously belongs with the many other wild and primitive images through which Lawrence had already tried to envision alternatives to a society enfeebled, as he saw it, by money, mind, and will. In his writing before 1921, only the Cornwall of some of the stories offered geographical location for his visionary images of phallic beauty and blood consciousness. In the major novels these ideals appear primarily as either nostalgic or prophetic imaginings: in the mythic history at the start of

The Rainbow, for example, or in the theories of Birkin, whose fantasies are rather poor in geographical specification. Sardinia, like the Australian bush or Mexico or the New Mexican mountains, is one of those actual, reachable places which Lawrence sought after the war for their anticipated correspondence to long-standing imaginative desires. And Sardinia does offer in plenty at least visual embodiments of key Laurentian social and psychological ideals.

The Sardinian peasants in beautiful costume, for example, seem dressed up as if to illustrate a Laurentian diatribe against the "proletarian homogeneity and khaki all-alikeness" (p. 103) of postwar Europe. The very first costume encountered appears like an image in a Laurentian dream come true: "I seem to have known it before: to have worn it even; to have dreamed it."

> On his head he has the long black stocking-cap, hanging down behind. How handsome he is, and so beautifully male! He walks with his hands loose behind his back, slowly, upright, and aloof. The lovely unapproachableness, indomitable. And the flash of the black and white, the slow stride of the full white drawers, the black gaiters and black cuirass with the bolero, then the great white sleeves and white breast again, and once more the black cap—what marvellous massing of the contrast, marvellous, and superb, as on a magpie.—How beautiful maleness is, if it finds its right expression.—And how perfectly ridiculous it is made in modern clothes. (p. 71)

With the same exactitude that he elsewhere brings to the description of flowers or birds, Lawrence gives the cut and texture and design of Sardinian costume in such loving detail that it becomes an interesting, beautiful object and also an inspiriting symbol.

Yet Lawrence's rapid leap from description to social, political, and sexual reverie also threatens to land him in the kind of shallow rhetorical ditch that even sympathetic critics find disturbing as well as naive in other of his writings from the twenties.[6] There is only a short step for Lawrence between enthusiasm for Sardinian stocking caps and revulsion against the whole modern "tide of enlightenment," what he too blithely disdains as "cosmopolitanism and internationalism" (p. 102). The description of Sardinian costume soon does all but erupt into the notorious Laurentian mixture of rapture and vituperation, as Lawrence rushes with characteristic zeal into making a sign out of the picturesque: "Coarse, vigorous, determined, they will stick to their own coarse dark stupidity and let the big world find its way to its own enlightened hell. Their hell is their own hell, they prefer it unenlightened . . . I love my indomitable coarse men from mountain Sardinia, for their stocking-caps and their splendid, animal-bright stupidity. If only the last wave of all-alikeness won't wash those superb crests, those caps, away" (pp. 102–3).

In 1921 facile celebration of "stupidity" cannot be taken as harmless imaginative play, especially not in writing as explicitly engaged with social and political judgment as *Sea and Sardinia* is from the start. Here, imaginative exuberance has its least attractive face: a blotchy mixture of sexual and political fantasy covered over by excessive trust in the picturesque. It is some version of this mixture that lures Somers into protofascist political involvement in Australia and that makes the Mexico of *The Plumed Serpent* the least convincing of Lawrence's favored locations. *Sea and Sardinia,* however, is saved from the crass symbolic equivalences of *The Plumed Serpent* and even from the confused impulse toward political action in *Kangaroo* by the very modesty of its lighthearted tone and anecdotal design. On this holiday occasion Lawrence was relatively content to stay in his spectator's role and, more important, he was able to dramatize the impediments to political judgment and even to imaginative love consequent upon his circumstances as traveler. The emphatically visual character of the descriptive language for the costumes, for example, makes it clear that Lawrence as a tourist could hardly know more of these peasants than of exotic birds with superb crests and marvelous designs of color. In the travel memoir Lawrence never blurs the fact that he has only the tourist's minimal experiences to go on and a spectator's glimpse, mainly through windows, of a foreign life passing by as in a parade.

The diarylike simplicity of the travel memoir allows Lawrence to show how the special conditions of tourism not only free the imagination but also check its symbol-making propensities. In contrast to Wordsworth, the poet-traveler who leaves his picturesque leech gatherer or solitary reaper before any prosaic needs interfere with his imaginative love, Lawrence has just enough involvement with Sardinians to break apart his dreamlike visions. The splendid peasant, for example, does not sustain his heroic aura for very long in *Sea and Sardinia.* When even Lawrence's great resilience as a traveler is pressed past a certain point, imaginative love gives way to thorough bad temper. Lawrence is not reluctant to display the sudden unraveling of the romantic voyager into a tired, hungry English tourist, marooned among dirty and indifferent strangers.

One crisis occurs the same day, and only a few pages after the hymn to the stocking caps. In the "magic little town of Sorgono" there is only one squalid inn and only one available room, with "a large bed, thin and flat with a grey-white counterpane, like a large, poor, marble-slabbed tomb in the room's sordid emptiness" (p. 106). Worse yet, no milk, no food, no fire, perhaps not for hours, perhaps never. Lawrence and Frieda take a walk and land in a stinking lane, the thick of the outdoor public lavatory. By the time they get back to the inn, Lawrence has reached a towering rage, not to be soothed by "q-b" 's more philosophic equanimity: "Why don't you take it as it comes? It's all life." "But no, my rage is black, black, black . . . I cursed them all, and the q-b for an interfering female" (p. 110).

Lawrence's eruption of temper in Sorgono, however, becomes more comic than despairing through the deliberately melodramatic emphases of the style. The self-abuse so disturbing in *Kangaroo* is entirely absent. In this writing, black rage becomes itself colorful. Lawrence presents his own cursing self as a rather amusing spectacle. Moreover, black rage yields, in hardly more than a page, to new wonder at a "brilliant flamy, rich fire" of oak root that suddenly manifests itself in a deserted room of the hotel where an old bearded man appears to roast a kid with elaborate ritual. Lawrence's symbol-making imagination can revive instantly in the warmth of such a fire: "It was evident he was the born roaster. He held the candle and looked for a long time at the sizzling side of the meat, as if he would read portents. Then he held his spit to the fire again. And it was as if time immemorial were toasting itself another meal" (p. 113). The lyric potentialities of this new symbol are held within the tone of witty touristic anecdote. Lawrence goes on to describe how the roasted kid disappears. More hours go by. All they ever see of the kid again are five pieces of cold roast: "Mine was a sort of large comb of ribs with a thin web of meat: perhaps an ounce" (p. 125). The kid of Sorgono then turns into a different symbol, this time (with a tourist's version of almost Miltonic severity) an emblem of modern hunger: "Simply one is not *fed* nowadays. In the good hotels and in the bad, one is given paltry portions of unnourishing food, and one goes unfed." The ounce of cold roast kid expands into a general instance of the disappointment awaiting those who wander the world in search of who knows what kind of nourishment. Yet this disillusion is also in turn soon diverted by the animated sound of a bus driver's sarcastic analysis of the Sardinian labor situation. Although Lawrence scorns the man's smug socialism, he also catches with amused precison the lively intonations of his political invective.

To accompany Lawrence in Sardinia is to experience through his rapidly shifting tones his sometimes irate, mainly humorous, always intense activity of response. Although he undoes symbols as fast as he makes them, his deconstructive activity has no systematic insistence; it beats no solemn drums. The visible doing and undoing of symbols recalls the performances of imaginative activity in certain English Romantic lyrics: Wordsworth's "To a Butterfly," for example, or Coleridge's conversation poems. Yet the mixture of the sublime and the tawdry in the detail and the reckless acrobatics of Lawrence's responses give a new, less solemn edge to this modern version of English creative imagination. The very intemperateness of his responses and his capacity, his need even, to respond to everything with equal energy, all become part of the amusing travel story. Every object encountered makes its vivid mark and at the same time is caught up in tireless but finally lighthearted interpretation. The rapid pace and colloquial informality of the writing make the acts of interpretation seem remarkably spontaneous; to see signs and portents everywhere is for Lawrence only a slight extension of the act of observation itself. But he discards the symbols almost as quickly as he makes them, and then he revives and transforms them yet again. What remains constant are not the symbols themselves so much as the imagination that encounters the squalid as well as the glamorous items of an alien world with unflagging curiosity and zest.

Lawrence's response to the Sardinian landscape follows the same unstable pattern as his reactions to the people. Visually, Sardinia is "harder, barer, starker" than even Cornwall and appeals, as anticipated, for its very lack of those knowable depths finally tiresome in Italy, where "it is all worked out. It is all known: *connu, connu!*" (p. 133). Sardinia is the *inconnu* of romantic desire, thrilling for its very resistance to human penetration: "that strange feeling as if the *depths* were barren, which comes in the south and the east, sun-stricken. Sun-stricken, and the heart eaten out by the dryness" (p. 96). Lawrence's descriptive language assimilates Sardinia to his long-standing fascination with the unhumanized and the impenetrable in nature as well as in people.

Yet the natural symbolism quickly reaches the same limit as the human symbols in *Sea and Sardinia*. Lawrence hardly relinquishes for a paragraph his own altogether human performance of a consciousness reacting against as well as yearning toward the inhumanly primitive. The figure of "q-b" taking nothing morally to heart is played off against Lawrence's probing intensity: "I like it! I like it!" cries the "q-b" about the barren, sun-stricken scene (as Somers's wife, Harriet, also says about Wolloona). Lawrence's voice makes tougher distinctions: " 'But could you live here?' She would like to say yes, but daren't" (p. 96). Without losing his balance like Somers, Lawrence keeps visible a vivid sense of the limits of his own daring, and of the crucial difference between liking and living in symbolic landscapes. We shall see that such distinctions become urgent in the brilliant finale of *St. Mawr,* specifically in the interpolated story of the New England woman who has learned painfully the difference between loving a beautiful landscape and living in relation to it as an "immediate object." In *Sea and Sardinia* the reality of such everyday living appears not through an extended narration but, more offhandedly, through the colloquial intonations, the tawdry details, the questions and self-corrections of Lawrence's voice, set skeptically against his own capacity to live through the eyes and into the distance.

The contrast between distant vision and immediate experience recedes as a problem in *Sea and Sardinia* partly because Lawrence is on holiday, and perhaps for that reason in a mood to delight in the immediate human scene of Sardinia as well as in the distant picture. On the bus ride to Terranova, for example, while the "high humanless hills" roll by, Lawrence has at least one eager eye on the human spectacle within the bus. There is, first, the driver, "wrapped in his gloom like a young bus-driving Hamlet," and the bus driver's mate: "He smoked his cigarette bounderishly: but at the same time with peculiar gentleness, he handed one to the ginger Hamlet. Hamlet accepted it, and his mate held him a light as the bus swung on. They were like man and wife. The mate was the alert and wide-eyed Jane Eyre whom the ginger Mr. Rochester was not going to spoil in a hurry" (p. 161).

In the enclosed world of the bus, and from his passenger's seat close behind, Lawrence freely invents dramas out of the gestures of these unknown people, renaming them as he likes, enjoying the incongruity as much as the fit of his identifications and plots. Although the literary allusions in these perceptions bear some superficial resemblance to modernist mock-heroic devices, Lawrence's playfulness creates a really quite different effect from the ironic correspondences between the commonplace and the literary in T. S. Eliot or Joyce. For what amuses Lawrence is the perception of a genuinely theatrical if not heroic flair to the spectacle of Sardinian reality. Lawrence's wit, in other words, takes the real bus driver more dramatically, and the literary Hamlet or Rochester less seriously, than comparable yokings of the actual and the literary in modernist irony. Reality, at least in Sardinia, offers to Lawrence genuine examples of theatrical types, suited to the plots of novel or stage.

Trivial incidents in Sardinia assume the color of high or at least operatic drama. Sometimes a fully formed plot offers itself in the most mundane circumstances: for example, in a quarrel over pigs on the same bus ride to Terranova.

> There is an altercation because a man wants to get into the bus with two little black pigs, each of which is wrapped in a little sack, with its face and ears appearing like a flower from a wrapped bouquet. He is told that he must pay the fare for each pig as if it were a Christian. *Cristo del mondo!* A pig, a little pig, and paid for as if it were a Christian. He dangles the pig-bouquets, one from each hand, and the little pigs open their black mouths and squeal with self-conscious appreciation of the excitement they are causing. *Dio benedetto!* it is a chorus. But the bus-mate is inexorable. Every animal, even if it were a mouse, must be paid for and have a ticket as if it were a Christian. The pig-master recoils stupefied with indignation, a pig-bouquet under each arm. "How much do you charge for the fleas you carry?" asks a sarcastic youth. (p. 163)

Lawrence's language intensifies the dramatic expressiveness of commonplace exclamation and vulgar objects. Every emotion is pitched to extremity: the bus mate "inexorable," the pig-master "stupefied with indignation," even the pigs joining in with delight as a chorus. As on the boat, however, Lawrence's pleasure in such dramas seems proportionate to his nonparticipation, even as a chorus. Perhaps his slight but fixed distance as a foreigner, with even a different language, is what allows the bus ride in Sardinia to remain so much less unnerving than its Australian counterpart in *Kangaroo*. Or perhaps the difference comes from the character of the Sardinians themselves. The "very, very nice" Australians infuriated Somers, while the cursing Sardinians soothe and relax Lawrence.

A sense of paradox remains, however, in the fact that the events most enthusiastically described by Lawrence in Sardinia conform exactly to the patterns of modern social life rather than embodying alternatives to them. Fruitless quarrel with the "conductors" of a ticketed, timetable world is the very image of being caught in that insane "machine persistence" which Lawrence hoped to escape. Yet as enacted on the bus to Terranova or on the boat, even bureaucratic struggles become inspiriting, like battles on the popular stage where everyone overacts and the audience delights in every new turn of the catastrophe. The fat man whose wife gets left behind on the godforsaken train station of Mandas suffers, and so does his wife, but they, and the righteous guard, too, seem positively transfigured into something more like gaiety by the sheer style with which they perform their emotions.

> Now behold her with hands thrown to heaven, and hear the wild shriek "Madonna!" through all the hubbub . . . The train inexorably pursues its course. Prancing, she reaches one end of the platform as we leave the other end. Then she realises it is not going to stop for her. And then, oh horror, her long arms thrown out in wild supplication after the retreating train: then flung aloft to God: then brought down in absolute despair on her head. And this is the last sight we have of her, clutching her poor head in agony and doubling forward. She is left—she is abandoned . . .
>
> So, his face all bright, his eyes round and bright as two stars, absolutely transfigured by dismay, chagrin, anger and distress, he comes and sits in his seat, ablaze, stiff, speechless. His face is almost beautiful in its blaze of conflicting emotions. For some time he is as if unconscious in the midst of his feelings. Then anger and resentment crop out of his consternation. He turns with a flash to the long-nosed, insidious, Phoenician-looking guard. Why couldn't they stop the train for her! And immediately as if someone had set fire to him, off flares the guard. Heh!—the train can't stop for every person's convenience! The train is a train—the time-table is a time-table. What did the old woman want to take her trips down the line for. Heh! . . .
>
> So they bounced and jerked and argued at one another to their hearts' content. (pp. 84–85)

In Sardinia Lawrence sees ordinary human misadventure played out with flourishes that liberate the spirit rather than stifling it, as in the "tense, resistant" life of the mainland. Although a sentimental woman or two may, like the "q-b" at Mandas, "shed a few tears," for Lawrence (as for the majority of Sardinians) the very stylization of suffering brightens the human figures and lifts them beyond common sorrows. Lawrence's writing catches hold of this stylization and underlines it. The fat man becomes "almost beautiful," his wife is transfigured into the very symbol of abandoned womanhood. The guard is a virtual allegory of Inexorable Officialdom.

Lawrence was not, of course, the first Northern traveler to enjoy the theatricality of the Mediterranean character. In *Italian Hours* Henry James suggests that to travel anywhere, but especially to Italy, is, "as it were, to go to the play." James's metaphor of theater, however, sets up a much greater distance between spectacle and spectator than does Lawrence's style. Lawrence's seat is right up front, if not actually on the side of the stage, while for James the foreign scene preserves its theatrical aspect only from a middle row of the opera house, or through the long vista of a painterly landscape. Thus when James describes a *contadini* who slowly comes toward him up the winding path of an ancient hill town singing "like a cavalier in an opera," he quickly goes on to correct the fancy by reporting that brief conversation with the man revealed him to be "a brooding young radical and communist, raging with discontent and crude political passion."[7] James gives up his operatic image with mild self-mockery: "This made it very absurd of me to have looked at him simply as a graceful ornament to the prospect, an harmonious little figure in the middle distance." To James, the theatrical charm of foreign life is an illusion of "the middle distance," while it is Lawrence's originality to see greater rather than less intensity of flourish the nearer and closer his attention moves. Lawrence is less conventionally bound than James to the established operatic cast of smiling and singing *contadine,* and less bound than is commonly realized to even his own cast of stocking-capped peasants. He may dislike the politics of brooding young radicals as much as James did, but even from close up he sees them (as well as bus drivers and plain husbands and wives) performing the opera of everyday life with as many flourishes as any cavalier on the regular stage.

The most striking official pageant which Lawrence sees in Sardinia thus becomes the emblem rather than the exception to the everyday spectacle of reality. In this pageant, a masquerade carnival, young boys and men dressed up in makeshift women's costumes mimic every type of female behavior, from the drooping grief of a widow to the officious humility of an old housewife sweeping everything in sight, including the spectators. Lawrence hugely enjoys the insolent extravagance of the masqueraders. Yet there is oddly little difference between their wild improvisations and the "real" dramas of bus or train station. All of Sardinia has the quality of a masquerade carnival to Lawrence, not mainly because some Sardinians still wear the old stocking caps, but because Lawrence perceives in all the Sardinians a love of performance perhaps even more congenial to him than their supposed "animal-bright stupidity."

James is nevertheless right in seeing that it is the privilege and presumption of the tourist to take in the human misadventures of a foreign scene with the indifferent frivolity of a playgoer. For all his closeness of observation, Lawrence may appear no better than the stereotyped American or English or German enthusiast of charming

Southern emotionality. Although he allows his figures to come forward out of the middle distance, the impression of drama still depends on his slight reduction of objects to something less than full size. The trains and buses are all "little"; fat husbands, Hamlet-like bus drivers, and little pig-bouquets all have an almost toylike animation, and their passion never quite surpasses the entertaining unreality of a stage show.

The redeeming consequence of this touristic condescension, at least as enacted by Lawrence, is that the traveler too may be liberated to reduce the dimensions of his own self and his own passions. Lawrence's black, black rage at Sorgono has the same stylized excess as the indignation of the fat husband or the pig-keeper. Sardinia is congenial to Lawrence—travel is finally congenial—not so much because flight effaces the fever and the fret of human society, but because that fret itself changes color and scale in the holiday atmosphere of a trip. In travel, and then in the zestful written record of travel, Lawrence could achieve the magically right distance from reality for his imagination to work most happily—near enough for exact observation of the human scene, but just far enough to keep the figures (including himself) slightly less than life-size. The freedom Lawrence finds in Sardinia is a freedom not from familiar human predicaments, only from the tight and tense spirit which ordinarily pervades those predicaments at home.

The essentially esthetic character of this freedom becomes most explicit when Lawrence chooses for the last episode of the book a marionette show which he and the "q-b" attend on their return to Sicily. The show is a bewildering but splendid legend cycle about the paladins of France, performed on three successive nights before an audience mainly of rapt Sicilian urchins. Handsomely costumed puppet knights flourish weapons and pronounce brave words: "So then, the glittering knights are ready. Are they ready? Rinaldo flourishes his sword with the wonderful cry 'Andiamo!' Let us go—and the others respond: 'Andiamo.' Splendid word" (p. 211).

With the splendid *Andiamo,* Lawrence returns to the spirited cry of his own initial departure for Sardinia. Now it is an actual stage show that carries him, along with the rest of the audience, into a magical and heroic space. Lawrence enjoys the fearsome battles of the old legend-plays. But what he also relishes is the manifest make-believe of the marionette figures, examples of how the very artifice of esthetic form can liberate human passion. He wishes that all drama in the theater maintained the same esthetic freedom: "For in fact drama is enacted by symbolic creatures formed out of human consciousness; puppets, if you like: but not human *individuals*. Our stage is all wrong, so boring in its personality" (p. 211).

During the marionette show the distinction between the drama on the stage and the consciousness of the spectator blurs, as Lawrence appropriates the marionettes for the favorite symbolic creatures of his own consciousness. The very word *Andiamo*, for example, becomes the most splendid emblem yet of "massive, brilliant, outflinging reck-lessness in the male soul." And there is a ghastly old witch, to Lawrence the perfect embodiment of female evil: "With just a touch, she would be a tall benevolent old lady. But listen to her. Hear her horrible female voice with its scraping yell of evil lustfulness" (p. 212). The witch is marvelously burnt to bits, though Lawrence notes that only little boys take the victory for real: "Men merely smile at the trick. They know well enough the white image endures" (p. 213). The trick is not only the stage-burning of the puppet witch, but the thrilling special freedom of the entire show: so profoundly satisfying in its projections of elemental human desires and fears, so profoundly liber-ating in the obvious make-believe of its puppets and their actions.

Placed at the end of *Sea and Sardinia,* the marionette show offers an implicit commentary on the real and imaginative pleasures of the en-tire holiday, for even though it takes place back in Sicily, the show is in the spirit of the whole Sardinian trip. In paradoxical reversal of the famous Laurentian demand that art be as earnest as real life, in *Sea and Sardinia* the drama of real life becomes exhilarating just at the point where it assumes some of the unreality of art—a certain edge of play, a pleasure in the bravura of style and in the almost ritualistic performance of elemental human type and role.[8] For the boys cos-tumed as women in the carnival, the boringness of individual personal-ity was transcended by exaggerated imitation of conventional roles and parts. The same self-transcendence occurs for the fat husband or the Hamlet bus driver or, more important, for Lawrence himself. As he sees the Sardinians enact, indeed overact, the passions of their person-alities and predicaments, he adds the bravura of his own style to their performances, so that actors and writer alike play "to their hearts' content" an imitation of passion which preserves their essential spirit free, intact, almost untouched.

Yet there is a further Laurentian standard which perceives connec-tions between this essentially esthetic play and other, more sinister imitations of life. A glimpse of the ignoble company to which Law-rence's touristic estheticism may lead appears near the end of *Sea and*

Sardinia in the sketch of a brief reunion with artistic English friends in the Rome station. Thrilled by exotic adventures in the Sahara and elsewhere, they are ready now for Sardinia. Only Lawrence's sardonic withdrawal (and the sudden departure of the train) saves him from being absorbed into a mockable troop of itinerant social parasites, protected from reality by each other and by the sop of taking the world as only a sequence of scenic displays.

> In my ears murmurs he of the monocle about the Sahara—he is back from the Sahara a week ago: the winter sun in the Sahara! He with the smears of paint on his elegant trousers is giving the q-b a sketchy outline of his now *grande passion*. Click goes the exchange, and he of the monocle is detailing to the q-b his trip to Japan, on which he will start in six weeks' time, while he of the paint-smears is expatiating on the thrills of the etching needle, and concocting a plan for a month in Sardinia in May, with me doing the scribbles and he the pictures. What sort of pictures? Out flies the name of Goya. And well now, a general rush into oneness, and won't they come down to Sicily to us for the almond blossom: in about ten days' time. Yes, they will—wire when the almond blossom is just stepping on the stage and making its grand bow, and they will come next day. (pp. 191–92)

Although the capacity to perceive the world—landscape and character— as on a kind of stage effectively sustained Lawrence's own exuberance in Sardinia, the connection between this attitude and the communal thrills of a trivial and idle social group fills Lawrence with disdain. Dashing down to view the annual debut of the almond blossom becomes emblematic of an effete estheticism, even though these artists are Lawrence's friends and the "scribbles" he has just produced declare no more earnest relation than their proposal to either human or natural spectacle.

Lawrence's distaste for the type of the "drifting artist" has contributed to the merely secondary status of his own performance in the role of artistic traveler and traveling artist.[9] Lawrence himself often seems to urge us past his informal "scribbles" about places and incidents, so that we can engage with the perennial would-be settler carrying the same rather heavy rhetorical baggage all over the world. I have given such full attention to *Sea and Sardinia* because it is a special achievement within Lawrence's work. For almost the whole space of the memoir, he allows the pleasures of the traveler to exemplify a more than trivial conception of imaginative freedom, a conception which still adheres to Romantic belief in creative perception, while going forward to a sharper, tougher, more modern definition of the right esthetic spirit in which to take reality: neither the sublime spirit of high Romanticism nor the hell-rage of modern alienation, but the more playful, rude, indecorous spirit of carnival, parade, and melodrama. The art of *Sea and Sardinia* celebrates imaginative travel not into elemental liberty but into an esthetic gaiety where even inexorable officials and pig-bouquets become wonderfully engaging objects. In Sardinia the spectacle of reality awakens Lawrence's creative powers to a performance of the freedom still available to his imagination, wherever he might be. Yet this freedom is so precarious, so contingent on just the right coming together of spirit and place, that its gaiety seems less a matter of principle than of luck. Lawrence's "scribbles" about Sardinia have the enduring brightness of art, but of an irreverent, consciously playful art, without illusions about the "trick" of style which can only temporarily defeat the wicked witches of consciousness, as in the puppet show.

St. Mawr: Spectacle and Symbol

Lou Witt, at the start of *St. Mawr,* is in no holiday mood: "Lou Witt had had her own way so long that by the age of twenty-five she didn't know where she was. Having one's own way landed one completely at sea" (p. 3).[10] In the charged colloquial style of *St. Mawr,* idioms like "landed one . . . at sea" are wittily played for verbal paradox and also for figurative connotations relatively dead in ordinary speech. Lawrence lightly registers the absence of any concept of elemental or other kinds of freedom in social speech by playing on the limited colloquial meaning of being "at sea."[11] While resembling other Laurentian "world-lost" characters—"a sort of gypsy, who is at home anywhere and nowhere"—Lou has no more consciousness of freedom than others in her society; at the start, she has barely any consciousness at all, only a kind of nerve-worn bewilderment.

The narrator in *St. Mawr* is sympathetic with Lou's vague and socially limited point of view at the outset, but his voice has a liveliness quite different from her numbed fatigue. In contrast to the merging of hero and narrator in *Kangaroo,* Lawrence in the novella does establish a measurable distance from his main character. He places Lou, along with her "drifting artist" husband, Rico, and her democratically snobbish and scornful mother, with a comic energy beyond Lou's own powers. There is a nasty bite here to Lawrence's mimicry of the postwar London "show" not heard in his accounts of Sardinian and even Australian goings-on; still, the tone of comic observation links this narrator to the gallant and reckless reporter heard elsewhere in Lawrence's travel writing of the period. Although his gossipy malice and dismissive psychological summary claim an inside knowledge of these people unavailable to the mere tourist, their inward life seems so obvious that to grasp it takes hardly more than an act of astute seeing. In skill and assurance of observation, the narrator is closer to sharp-eyed Mrs. Witt at the start than to Lou: "Mrs. Witt kept track of everything, watching, as it were, from outside the fence, like a potent well-dressed demon, full of uncanny energy and a shattering sort of sense" (pp. 6–7).

Mrs. Witt is an outsider and a snob, and so is the narrator. Both despise the nicely named world of Rotten Row, but at the beginning that does not seem to mean that they cannot join in the show as satirical spectators and even performers: "So, to the great misgiving of Rico, behold Mrs. Witt in splendidly tailored habit and perfect boots, a smart black hat on her smart grey hair, riding a grey gelding as smart as she was, and looking down her conceited, inquisitive, scornful, aristocratic-democratic Louisiana nose at the people in Piccadilly, as she crossed to the Row, followed by the taciturn shadow of Pheonix, who sat on a chestnut with three white feet as if he had grown there" (p. 8). Though undoubtedly less colorful than a carnival pageant, or even a bus ride in Sardinia, the "regatta-canal" of English social life seems amusing enough as a spectacle, without being so intrusive as to threaten seriously the poised alertness of types like Mrs. Witt or the narrator. By comparison Lou, in her vagueness, her ineffectual spoiled willfulness, and her "odd spasms" of irony, seems pathetically unfit to be effective even as an outsider.

Of course, from the very beginning of the novella Lawrence also deftly separates himself from Mrs. Witt. His comic energy has a free, exuberant lilt missing from her menacing scorn. Perhaps even more important, Lawrence's flexible range of tones can take in even Mrs. Witt's habit of satire as an object of comic (and more than comic) disapproval. Narrative rebuke of Mrs. Witt's satiric stance challenges her conceit right from the start: "Mrs. Witt came and sardonically established herself in a suite in a quiet but good-class hotel not far off. Being on the spot. And her terrible grey eyes with the touch of a leer looked on at the hollow mockery of things. As if *she* knew of anything better!" (p. 6). A sense of something rather sinister in Mrs. Witt's merely negative spectatorship, as well as the insinuation that one ought to know of something better than sardonic leering, distances the narrative voice in *St. Mawr* from social satire in general, as well as from

Mrs. Witt in particular. The very strength of Lawrence's comic writing makes his pressure for knowledge of something better than satire command a respect in the novella not quite earned by the fevered disorder of *Kangaroo*. One feels that Lawrence could, if he chose, go on in comic high spirits indefinitely in *St. Mawr,* doing up not only the London social scene but also the English country-house world and then the New World, too: Havana, Texas, New Mexico. Just enough of those other settings is, in fact, deftly sketched later in the novella, to keep us in touch with satiric comedy as one way of settling with social reality, as Lawrence did more thoroughly in some of the late short stories—"Two Bluebirds," for example, or "Mother and Daughter."

St. Mawr, however, achieves an entirely different dimension from those stories as well as from the more feverish novels of the twenties because in it Lawrence, while at the very peak of his comic form, also deliberately presses beyond wit for a language in which to articulate that human demand for something better that is such an urgent force in his entire career. In *Sea and Sardinia* that demand is recognized but kept at bay by the conditions of holiday; in *Kangaroo* it is out of control, raging through the hero and the book itself like a disease. In *St. Mawr* Lawrence succeeds by his own stylistic virtuosity in making us believe that movement beyond even the best kinds of social wit to more speculative and visionary forms of language is a choice of strength and healthy judgment. In a holiday place like Sardinia, the amusing spectacle of reality has just the right degree of make-believe to free the spirit, at least for a week. But the social show of English life is at heart more mechanical than a marionette show, and to live in it is to be either wound up tight like a doll (or time bomb) or else hollowed out like mere cardboard. The acts of will required to animate what is only a mechanical or cardboard facsimile of life may finally surpass what even the most energetic observer can—or should—keep up. In the plot of *St. Mawr* it is Mrs. Witt's eventual loss of vitality that most explicitly dramatizes the judgments made in a freer spirit by Lawrence's own range and shifts of style.

Lou's mother still has the capacity to be an amused tourist-participant when the household moves from London to the country: "Mrs. Witt had now a new pantomime to amuse her: the Georgian house, her own pew in church—it went with the old house: a village of thatched cottages—some of them with corrugated iron over the thatch: the cottage people, farm labourers and their families, with a few, very few, outsiders: the wicked little group of cottages down at Mile End, famous for ill living" (p. 29). But after she has expended some sarcasm on the Dean, arranged for a barrel of beer per week for the laborers, and completed the entertaining job of clipping the hair of the Welsh groom, Lewis, the pantomime begins to pall. On the riding excursion which ends so badly in St. Mawr's throwing of Rico, Mrs. Witt already gives signs of a more desperate recklessness. To the nameless "fair young man" who has hovered around her throughout the ride, she takes sarcasm past the boundary of entertainment: " ' I should like *so* much to know,' she said suavely, looking into his eyes with a demonish straight look, 'what makes you so certain that you exist' " (p. 65). The full sense that the game has run out for Mrs. Witt does not occur, however, until the condolence call made by the country friends after Rico's accident. Mrs. Witt's masterfully sarcastic mimicry of English social ritual in serving tea to Dean and Mrs. Vyner is her greatest triumph and also her last performance in the English *belle-mère* mode. Her success in dumbfounding the Dean and his wife through her witheringly bland defense of the horse is as good as if she had followed her first impulse to pour the tea into Mrs. Vyner's crumpled cup-and-saucer-looking hat. Even Lou is roused to a "complete grin."

Afterward, however, mother and daughter are equally depressed. There is a sense of overkill in Mrs. Witt's attack on these insignificant English neighbors, and consequently a cheapening of Mrs. Witt herself for having spent so much energy of sarcasm on them. Mrs. Witt suggests this feeling of disproportion even before the tea visit, in her grim scorn for the climate: "I don't think the English climate agrees with me. I need something to stand up against, no matter whether it's great heat or great cold. This climate, like the food and the people, is almost always lukewarm or tepid, one or the other. And the tepid and the lukewarm are really not my line" (p. 81). Like the very, very nice Australians who drive Somers back to shouting muezzins, the tepid and the lukewarm in English social life eventually turn restless Laurentian personalities more desperate than serious forms of adversity or even evil. After the tea party, when Mrs. Witt is reduced to staring out the window at a funeral, thinking almost wistfully of the possibly stimulating reality of death, Lawrence has brought this vigorous traveler to a curious impasse. There is perhaps something newly attractive and almost youthful in Mrs. Witt's subdued state, as she lapses into Lou's kind of bewilderment: "I should *really* like, before I do come to be buried in a box, to know where I am" (p. 85). Yet Lou is right to be frightened by the new vagueness in her mother, for it is both too late and too out of Mrs. Witt's characteristic range for anything good to come of bewilderment for her. The running down of the mother's

energy for satiric pleasure indirectly endorses Lou's yearning responsiveness to any glimmers of something better outside the social show;
Mrs. Witt herself eventually can do no more than give herself up to
stony silence.

Mrs. Witt's collapse is precisely traceable, as a plot sequence, yet
Lawrence also leaves an irreducible mystery to her failure of energy.
After the tea party she still has the mischief to plan to remove St.
Mawr, with Lewis, out of enemy reach, and she sets out adventurously
enough in the rain, impressive in her large waterproof cape. But the
ride is depressing, full of the desire and dread of death. Her proposal
of marriage to Lewis, whom she had earlier admired but so thoroughly
"placed" as her social and intellectual inferior, seems an uncharacteristically self-demeaning gesture. And after the ocean voyage she can
respond to Havana and then to Santa Fe only with "grim silence":
"There was no getting a word out of Mrs. Witt, these days" (p. 132).
When, after these lapses and withdrawals, the mother does break her
silence at the end, to question Lou's obscure passion for the New
Mexican ranch, her voice still has a residue of "shattering sense," but
somehow without its earlier authority. At the least, her wit has lost
power to "keep track" of Lou's adventure. The book ends with Mrs.
Witt's cryptic quip about the "cheapness" of the ranch, but her last
word fails to close the subject decisively if only because her meaning,
her attempt to play off the name of the ranch ("Las Chivas": the
goats), is so uncharacteristically obscure. Although the decline of Mrs.
Witt's formidable social, personal, and verbal energies does not convert her to Lou's vision, it does limit her power to dismiss the spirit in
Lou that her vision of the ranch gropes to express. "As if *she* knew of
anything better!"

The first hint in the novella of powers not contained within the
"cardboard let's-be-happy world," and not containable within a style
of social satire, comes from the stallion St. Mawr. At the end, the
ranch becomes the symbol of the "something else" that Lou envisions.
How to interpret and evaluate these key symbols—and Lawrence's
language of symbolic evocation—has proven more difficult, however,
than merely recognizing that the novella relies on symbols to carry the
heroine (and the book's style) out of social confinement.

It is perhaps Lawrence's special combination of social narrative and
symbolism that causes confusion, for the impulse of critics is always to
push Lawrence decisively in one direction or the other. Thus one of
the more sympathetic early reviewers, Stuart P. Sherman, rather
crudely explains that *St. Mawr* is "a piece of symbolism."[12] That is to

say, it "is not a contribution to contemporary 'realism,' and should not be so approached." Sherman does not fully explain his distinction between realism and symbolism, but he proceeds as if the labeling first of all eliminated the necessity of getting the narrative line straight. "The immediate upshot of the affair," he blithely summarizes, "is that mother and daughter fall in love with the horse and with the grooms and carry them off to America." Sherman continues to approach the "upshot" of the plot as if turns of affection carried the same weight as in a "realistic" love story, but because it is "symbolism" he gives himself license to handle the narrative details loosely. Like so many later readers of Lawrence, Sherman underrates the realistic intelligence continually active in Lawrence's best writing, even when it becomes insistently symbolical. Indeed, there is no better example of this intelligence at work in Lawrence than his exact working out of the horse's status as an object of love in *St. Mawr*.

While Lou and her mother do take the horse and grooms to America, the issue of falling in love with them, an explicit point of contention between Lou and her mother all along, has been quite finished off before they embark. In one conversation with her mother, Lou is at pains to explain that she is not in love with the horse nor does she want to be one. Somers, in *Kangaroo,* had moods when he longed to be a great sperm whale, but even he could at other times see this rhetorical fantasy as "blather." In *St. Mawr* Lawrence gives a more powerfully sustained critical intelligence to his heroine. Her longings and disgusts may not be entirely clear intellectually, even to her, but they include enough distinctions to show that she is eager not to be misunderstood:

> —And don't misunderstand me, mother. I don't want to be an animal like a horse or a cat or a lioness, though they all fascinate me, the way they get their life *straight,* not from a lot of old tanks, as we do. I don't admire the cave-man, and that sort of thing. But think, mother, if we could get our lives straight from the source, as the animals do, and still be ourselves. (pp. 49–50)

It is because Lou sees her mother flirting with a primitivism less discriminating than her own, that she is later so disheartened by Mrs. Witt's reckless proposal of marriage to Lewis. But that degrading and farcical experiment is over by the end of the horseback ride to Merriton, as Lou assures Lewis in urging him to come on the trip to America. Lou, meanwhile, is herself quite adamant about *not* falling in love with the half-breed Phoenix, however conventionally suspicious Mrs. Witt may be. Phoenix too has some conventional vulgar fantasies. But

Lou, we feel, can handle Phoenix as well as her mother. By the time of the trip to America, Lou (and her mother, too) have become peculiarly uninvolved with the horse, even though the ostensible motive of the trip is to carry St. Mawr to safety. Many readers of *St. Mawr* pass over Lawrence's bold move of making St. Mawr, the horse of the title, virtually disappear as an important figure in the action. While Lou goes on to find her ranch in New Mexico, the horse, we are told, settles down in a strangely comfortable new home in Texas with a suitable mare, and with ranch hands who appreciate his "stuff" without going in for any symbolical fuss.

> The ranch-man mounted him—just threw a soft skin over his back, jumped on, and away down the red trail, raising the dust among the tall wild yellow of sunflowers, in the hot wild sun. Then back again in a fume, and the man slipped off.
> "He's got the stuff in him, he sure has," said the man. And the horse seemed pleased with this rough handling. Lewis looked on in wonder, and a little envy . . .
> Lewis was silent, and rather piqued. St. Mawr had already made advances to the boss' long-legged, arched-necked, glossy-maned Texan mare. And the boss was pleased.
> What a world! (p. 130)

If Lawrence were more of an ironist, the demystifying influence of the Texas ranch might be taken as a device to deflate the overblown European imagination, including the "folk" imagination of the Welsh groom, Lewis. There is nice ironic potential in the evident relief of this horse relaxing into natural horsiness after all the symbolic burdens he was made to carry in the "old" world. And Lawrence does, I think, want to underline a separation between the natural horse and the symbolic one that Lou, especially, had been handling so preciously in her imagination. Lawrence also wants to make a point about Texas— an ambiguous point, for he at once admires and disdains the queer natural ease of the place, attractive and yet shallow in its immunity to any fevers of imagination: "No consciousness below the surface, no meaning in anything save the obvious, the blatantly obvious" (p. 130).

Yet since Lawrence is never (and known never to be) entirely ironic, his dismissal of the symbolic horse in Texas has been mainly confusing to critics. Leavis notices the point but goes by it quickly without comment.[13] Others are positively embarrassed on Lawrence's behalf, as for example Monroe Engel: "Lewis and St. Mawr—who has finally found his mate in a long-legged Texas mare: a touch that surely fails to add to the seriousness of the story—drop out before the end and

Phoenix, too, is in effect disposed of."[14] If the fate of the horse is as clumsy a touch as Engel implies, the success of a story in which this horse figures so centrally must be judged rather more precarious than Engel, a mainly appreciative reader, concedes.

It is, however, the exact but unstable relationship between the comic and the serious and between the real and the visionary that distinguishes Lawrence's most successful art in the twenties, an achievement which his defenders have not always been more helpful in explaining than his detractors. It is not helpful, for example, when Engel instructs us that "part of the real creative accomplishment of the story is that it can make ideas and notions that we might find absurd out of context convincing and moving in context."[15] Lawrence, we have seen in Chapter 4, is very interested in the dramatic and psychological context of ideas and notions, but he does not use the refuge of context to excuse the foolishness of ideas. Somers's breakdown in *Kangaroo* gives psychological context for his political "blather," but it does not thereby render it more convincing (as Somers himself recognizes in his cooler moods). In a sense, the emphatic discarding of the horse in *St. Mawr* has the very opposite effect from what Engel suggests, for in addition to suggesting the horse's sanity, as it were, and also Lou's, it testifies to Lawrence's own readiness to meet any standards of the serious and sane that one might care to bring to his story. Indeed, from the beginning Lawrence's comedy sets up a rigorous critical light in which absurd ideas and notions have no hiding place. Even F. R. Leavis, for all his great appreciation of both the comedy and the serious scope of *St. Mawr,* is so eager to celebrate Lawrence's "creative triumph" in the writing about the horse that he draws back from acknowledging the skeptical as well as affirming force of the book's variety of styles. While Leavis does describe, with exactitude, how it is *Lou's* quest for the "real" that makes the horse matter to the reader, he also wants to endow the horse itself with more stable positive symbolic import than the movement of the story justifies: the stallion, in Leavis's view, "represents deep impulsions of life that are thwarted in the modern world"; "St. Mawr, the stallion, *is* that life."[16] By equating the spontaneous life symbolized by the horse in the first half of the book with the "creative intelligence" enacted by Lawrence in the book as a whole, Leavis underrates the skeptical daring that is so important a part of Lawrence's approach to the human activity of making and unmaking symbols.

It is true that the horse is crucial in stimulating Lou to envision something else beyond the world she inhabits. And Lawrence writes about the horse in powerfully evocative descriptive language to suggest the vitality that Lou so vividly feels and sees in it. At first she seems really to need direct contact with the beautiful beast to keep her new vision alive. But after Rico's accident her earlier image of St. Mawr's noble beauty is almost displaced by her horrifying visual impression of the frenzied horse thrown backward onto the impotent rider who still holds the reins. It is not just that Lou comes to see the wicked under-side of the beauty and power she loves, though a vicious wildness in the look of the overturned horse does make her wonder about its possibly evil spirit. More important, however, than the ambiguity about the horse's moral nature is the change in its symbolic meaning to Lou. No longer flashing hints of another, more vital world, it comes to embody the very essence of the distorted, thwarted human world that the earlier vision of the horse had led her to see beyond: "Mankind, like a horse, ridden by a stranger, smooth-faced, evil rider. Evil him-self, smooth-faced and pseudo-handsome, riding mankind past the dead snake, to the last break" (p. 70).

To my mind, the pages of Lou's vision of evil are the only real failure of writing in the book, not because the ideas are absurd (they are not), but because Lawrence cannot resist elaborating this vision of evil into a digressive essay written in a language of the *grand sérieux* that is boring by comparison to the other styles in the book. The idea that the horse changes its symbolic import for Lou comes to life more interestingly once the narrative resumes. In her last significant en-counter with the horse, just before Mrs. Witt's tea party, Lou's de-pressed and subdued mood comes to focus in a new sadness she per-ceives emanating from the horse, too. What had been, right after the accident, a pressing question of good or evil in the horse's ferocity evaporates, as Lou no longer perceives the horse primarily as a figure of wild spirit. By this point in the story Lou's conception of wild, brave nobility has in a sense become detached from any symbol. She has reached a state of consciousness in which no real objects can even symbolically represent the values she cherishes. In this state of newly fierce isolation, Lou herself becomes nastier, her alienation showing in the new kick and bite of her own sardonic wit.

"The horse," Lou sadly observes, "is superannuated" as a means of transport for modern man, and the horse becomes superannuated, too, as a symbol for Lou at this stage of her consciousness. The fading away of the horse is thus as significant as its earlier dominance to Lawrence's seriousness in the novella. A lesser writer, or Lawrence in a lesser work, might give us a piece of symbolism in which the last embers of spontaneous vitality glow from the eyes of a black stallion. But it is Lawrence's distinction in *St. Mawr,* as it was in a more lighthearted way in *Sea and Sardinia,* to reach a more sophisticated recognition of symbol-making as a dynamic but unstable activity of modern consciousness, limited by specifically modern possibilities of belief, experience, and language. The question of what the horse may or may not represent matters less to Lawrence than the pressing question for Lou of where she is to live and with whom. It is the rousing of Lou's courage to break out of her cardboard box that is the most important image of vitality in the story, and it is significant that, just past the middle of the book, Lawrence so conspicuously dramatizes this movement through a renewed version of social narrative in Lou's voice: namely, the remarkable series of scathing letters to her mother about Rico's convalescence.

Lou's letters make only sardonic reference to myths or folktales or symbols of any kind. In her irreverent mood she ridicules as "prosaically romantic" the figure cut by her mother, riding off in a cape with St. Mawr and Lewis: "Hope the roads were not very slippery, and that you had a good time, *à la Mademoiselle de Maupin.* Do remember, dear, not to devour little Lewis before you have got half-way— (p. 110). Lou also mocks Flora Manby as "the goddess of flowers" and Rico as Priapus, painting "lifelike apples on the trees": *"Why, Sir Prippy, what stunningly naughty apples!"* (p. 111). Finally, she even ridicules Phoenix's fantasy of a rebirth in horse worship: "Phoenix wants us to go and have a ranch in Arizona, and raise horses, with St. Mawr, if willing, for Father Abraham" (p. 112). In these letters, as in the conversation of Mrs. Witt at the country-house party, Lawrence shows his skill in representing the reckless wit of social voices near the end of their tether. Lou's vision of how she might be healed is much less formed than anything to be found in the classical dictionary of Flora and Rico or in any of the other versions of old myth and fairy tale attractive to the other characters. She wants only to be alone and somehow, vaguely, "to remove her own self into another world, another realm of existence."

Lou's eventual indifference to the horse as guide to a new world is connected to the sense of history that Lawrence grants her. St. Mawr had initially had such liberating force for Lou's perception of the contemporary social world because she saw its aura as coming from an older historical time: "A battle between two worlds. She realized that

St. Mawr drew his hot breaths in another world from Rico's, from our world. Perhaps the old Greek horses had lived in St. Mawr's world. And the old Greek heroes, even Hippolytus, had known it"(p. 19).

Lawrence shares the anthropological recognition of his generation that symbols have their power from sources deeper and older than the individual imagination. And he even shares the official symbolist faith in the phoenixlike power of old symbols to come to life again in modern consciousness. But Lawrence is distinctive among postromantic symbolists by the strength of his view of history as progressive and not cyclical or repetitive in pattern. His preoccupation with this linear conception of history, together with his insistence that the imagination serve rather than shelter the spirit in its actual modern life, keep Lawrence closer to Wordsworth than to modern symbolists. The pastness of old symbols—both mythological and religious—endows them with power and yet also limits their value, because they refer to no contemporary realities. As Lou is given dimly to understand, the imagination must be responsible to history if it is to lead actual life anywhere other than into nostalgia or fairy tale.

In his introduction to a book called *The Dragon of the Apocalypse* by Frederick Carter (the friend who was the original of the artist Cartwright in *St. Mawr*), Lawrence uses the complex historical and religious status of pagan astrological symbolism as an opportunity to reflect upon the nature of symbols more generally. Distinguishing the power of symbols from any translatable allegorical meaning (for example, the Christian allegorizing of astrological symbolism in Revelation), Lawrence emphasizes the more undifferentiated liberating action which symbols can perform: "All one cares about is the lead, the lead that the symbolic figures give us, and their dramatic movement: the lead, and where it will lead us to. If it leads to a release of the imagination into some new sort of world, then let us be thankful, for that is what we want."[17]

For most of this essay, Lawrence is as vague as Lou in the early part of *St. Mawr* about the mysterious process of old symbols leading to "some new sort of world." At times Lawrence seems unable to say where such imaginative release may indeed lead modern consciousness, except to heightened disgust with the wasteland of modern "thought-forms." At the same time he is finally impatient with such self-consciousness. His quest is for a new mythic sense of life that will still be responsible to an acute consciousness of contemporary reality: "Our state of mind is becoming unbearable. We shall have to change it. And when we have changed it, we shall change our description of the universe entirely. We shall not call the moon Artemis, but the new name will be nearer to Artemis than to a dead lump or an extinct globe. We shall not get back the Chaldean vision of the living heavens. But the heavens will come to life again for us, and the vision will express also the new men that we are."[18]

In Lawrence, nostalgia for the living universe of outworn creeds struggles against clarity of historical perception and also against a quite personal restlessness with any theological (or otherwise established) form of symbolizing the universe. What is necessary is not the revival of old symbolism, Christian or pagan. Attractive or not, the universe so described cannot command belief. It is no longer our real space. Thus the horse St. Mawr is a dated symbol belonging to "another world," not "our world," and after it has served its function of awakening Lou's consciousness, it can and should be discarded. Lou needs to discover new symbols, indeed, a whole new universe for her new sense of being. The ideal Laurentian sequence is outlined (albeit not very clearly) in the introduction to *The Dragon of the Apocalypse*: "And so the value of these studies in the Apocalypse. They wake the imagination and give us at moments a new universe to live in. We may think it is the old cosmos of the Babylonians, but it isn't. We can never recover an old vision, once it has been supplanted. But what we can do is to discover a new vision in harmony with the memories of old, far-off, far, far-off experience that lie within us. So long as we are not deadened or drossy, memories of Chaldean experience still live within us, at great depths, and can vivify our impulses in a new direction, once we can awaken them."[19]

Lawrence's somewhat loose association between memory and discovery, the "deep" and the "far-off," suggests how literal travel to new worlds might become for him the best and perhaps the only way of finding new direction for the modern imagination intent on staying in the region of the real. Thus Lawrence has Lou Witt embark for America, a real place. It is literally her old home, but potentially a new world both because her American identity has been lost within her, and even more because America is a country new enough so that its old, living natural form has not yet been entirely obliterated by civilization. The New Mexican ranch becomes the most compelling object for Lou's imaginative vision and for Lawrence's, too, precisely because one need not think of it merely as a symbol but as a real place, just as the Chaldeans took their universe as real.

At the ranch Lou goes further in a new direction of experience than any character in Lawrence's writing of the twenties. Yet the discrepancy between Lawrence's theory of imaginative renewal and his dramatic realism also movingly shows the limit of her achievement. Lou's image of herself as vestal virgin in some new temple of Apollo (p. 140), for example, recalls the classical dictionary that Flora brought up to entertain Rico in his convalescence. It is true that Lou's image has an earnestness missing from the English playacting of heroes and gods that Lou mocked so nastily in her letters to her mother. The performances of Flora and Rico were cardboard imitations of sacrifice and worship, while Lou really means to enact a withdrawal from social to solitary religious experience in nature. But the role (as Lou herself has to call it) of vestal virgin itself belongs to a symbolism that can be ridiculed as superannuated or else merely fashionable, as Mrs. Witt insinuates when she mentions the convent retreats which were in style in her generation. The difficulty of breaking through into genuinely new thought-forms is further and more ominously suggested by Lou's continuing vocabulary of love in relation to her New Mexican universe. Her vision of a spirit in the landscape that "loves me and wants me" shows the Laurentian hero (or heroine) in a characteristic predicament—just on the verge of a breakthrough into a new experience of feeling, yet still caught in the vocabulary of old thought-forms. Lawrence's almost obsessive preaching against modern idolatry of love makes us feel that he could not unambiguously endorse Lou's version of her new faith. But Lawrence's equally emphatic admiration for the struggle toward any new imaginative experience invites an attitude more like expectant sympathy than ironic disdain for Lou's experiment.

This sympathy gains force from the impression that Lawrence, as the artist "placing" Lou in the new world of America, has attained a further stage of imaginative freedom than she has, yet still without having arrived in a new universe where he (or anyone) can actually live. His freedom shows in the powerful and splendid yet exactly detailed landscape description embedded in the report of the New England woman who formerly inhabited the ranch. Lawrence does thrillingly present a universe that is alive like the living space of the old Chaldean heavens, yet remarkably free of borrowings from the classical or any other mythological dictionary. He describes a genuinely living universe, visible as vision to the New England woman, too.

From her doorway, from her porch, she could watch the vast, eagle-like wheeling of the daylight, that turned as the eagles which lived in the near rocks turned overhead in the blue, turning their luminous, dark-edged-patterned bellies and under-wings upon the pure air, like winged orbs. So the daylight made the vast turn upon the desert, brushing the farthest outwatching mountains. And sometimes the vast strand of the desert would float with curious undulations and exhalations amid the blue fragility of mountains, whose upper edges were harder than the floating bases. And sometimes she would see the little brown adobe houses of the village Mexicans, twenty miles away, like little cube crystals of insect-houses dotting upon the desert, very distinct, with a cottonwood-tree or two rising near. And sometimes she would see the far-off rocks, thirty miles away, where the canyon made a gateway between the mountains. Quite clear, like an open gateway out of a vast yard, she would see the cut-out bit of the canyon-passage. And on the desert itself, curious puckered folds of mesa-sides. And a blackish crack which in places revealed the otherwise invisible canyon of the Rio Grande. And beyond everything, the mountains like icebergs showing up from an outer sea. Then later, the sun would go down blazing above the shallow cauldron of simmering darkness, and the round mountain of Colorado would lump up into uncanny significance, northwards. That was always rather frightening. But morning came again, with the sun peeping over the mountain slopes and lighting the desert away in the distance long, long before it lighted on her yard. And then she would see another valley, like magic and very lovely, with green fields and long tufts of cottonwood-trees, and a few long-cubical adobe houses, lying floating in shallow light below, like a vision. (p. 147)

In his visionary descriptive language Lawrence is less tied than Lou to the vocabulary of love. The universe as seen from the New Mexican ranch is sumptuous and bristling with its own life, yet it is not loving but indifferent and even hostile to the human life whose signs of life it reduces to "insect-houses." To the artistic observer, to the eye of even the New England woman, the animosity of the place is in a way more thrilling than oppressive. In New Mexico as in Sardinia, the beauty of inhuman landscapes can thrill the imaginative eye of the artist-traveler with a yearning for the sublime. In *St. Mawr,* however, Lawrence places his splendid landscape description in the story not of artists or tourists but of would-be settlers, first the trader and his New England wife and then Lou Witt. The New England woman had, in great measure, the eye and imagination of an artist, which is why Lawrence gives his important description of the scene from her point of view. But living, Lawrence is at pains to insist, can never be merely a matter of artistic vision.

And if it had been a question simply of living through the eyes, into the *distance,* then this would have been Paradise, and the little New

England woman on her ranch would have found what she was always looking for, the earthly paradise of the spirit.

But even a woman cannot live only into the distance, the beyond. Willy-nilly she finds herself juxtaposed to the near things, the thing in itself. And willy-nilly she is caught up into the fight with the immediate object. (p. 148)

The colloquial "willy-nilly" marks the shift from distant vision back to daily experience, living as a matter of doing and making do with near things as they are, immediately and in themselves. And from this point of view, the story of the New England woman's debilitating struggle with an inhospitable natural environment is a story of heroic but painful defeat.

Lou too comes to the ranch as a settler of sorts, rather than as tourist or artist. Though she has no evident need or intention of raising chickens or making goat cheese, it is not at all clear what other relation to the near things of this world is imaginable for her on the ranch. Lou's fantasy of a loving spirit in the landscape may represent, then, not only the residue of old thought-forms, but also the sentimentality of a symbolist esthetic disconnected from human struggle with the near things of daily experience. The question of vision rigorously posed at the end of *St. Mawr* is left unresolved, however. Settling for neither a mere "piece of symbolism" nor a mere "contribution to realism," Lawrence's brilliant shifts of style press for a more practical relationship between vision and the willy-nilly of daily life than even he can successfully imagine.

The introduction to *The Dragon of the Apocalypse,* like other examples of Lawrence's didactic prose, draws back from the counterpressures which the fiction tolerates more fully as unresolved drama. In the essay the question of how to live, how to plan or predict a life, is contemptuously placed historically as the beginning of man's fall from true vision to mere "horoscopy": "Man always deteriorates. And when he deteriorates he always becomes inordinately concerned about his 'fortune' and his fate. While life itself is fascinating, fortune is completely uninteresting, and the idea of fate does not enter. When men become poor in life then they become anxious about their fortune and frightened about their fate."[20] Yet horoscopy is not a bad image for the preoccupation of the novelist with reading the signs of fortune and misfortune in the lives of his human characters. Lawrence is even more horoscopic than other novelists, in that he so often gives us characters in their most radical actions of choosing or changing their fortunes, reading or misreading the signs of their fate. Moreover, Lawrence is committed in principle to the proposition that novels represent characters in their daily human activity of living: that is "Why the Novel Matters," to cite the title of his most famous critical essay.

Lawrence's manipulation of the slippery words "life" and "living" both illuminates and blurs his struggle to reconcile the visionary and the practical in his writing of the twenties. "Life" may have esthetic reference, as in "Morality and the Novel." It is what Van Gogh gives in his painting of the sunflower—a dazzling record of a living moment in the artist's relation to the flower: "And this perfected relation between man and his circumambient universe is life itself, for mankind."[21] The achieved relation to the circumambient universe is what Lawrence himself gives in his vision of the New Mexican mountains, but the New England woman could not live through the eyes alone, into the visionary distance. Nor did Lawrence wish to live in Sardinia. "I like it! I like it!" cried the "q-b" about the beautiful mountain scene there. "But could you *live* here?" Lawrence's own practical voice on that occasion demanded.

Lawrence stands out among modern novelists for his acute awareness of what is exacted by living juxtaposed to the near things of particular places and in time. Although his story of the heroic but doomed New England woman has some of the quality of a legend, it is also as sensitive to the willy-nilly of day-after-day life on an isolated ranch as were the accounts of the colliery world in the early stories. In *St. Mawr* Lawrence's detailed social narrative gives forceful presence to this reality of human living, while his other, equally vivid imagination of life as vision also achieves extraordinary dignity through the power of symbolically suggestive description. The tension, however, between the life of vision and the life experienced in actual time and place remains. It is not clear at the end of *St. Mawr* in what way Lou could live on the ranch from day to day, and it is equally unclear how any character can live, in the real world of any time and place, in a landscape hospitable only to vision from the distance. Artists—and tourists—alone have the freedom to come and go through a universe experienced as a succession of living moments. Lawrence in the twenties wrote out of his own special, adventurous experience of such a life, but also out of his intermittent revulsion from it. Traveling through the circumambient universe as either tourist or artist could seem to him no more than a "sop," to be kept up only by people given over to either indifference or despair.

This unresolved tension about travel brings into focus much of the vitality and also the confusion of Lawrence's writing in the twenties.

"Life," Lawrence argues in "Why the Novel Matters," comes from the free embrace of flow and change.[22] But freedom, another Laurentian voice insists, has nothing to do with such straying and breaking away. "Men are free when they belong to a living, organic, *believing* community . . . Not when they are escaping to some wild west."[23] Lawrence's art, in its struggle within the coils of this paradox, records the restlessness of his imagination, separated not only from any actual community in his homeland, but also from the esthetic community of what he saw as "drifting artists," readier than he to make art itself their only reality in an indifferent world.

6

Postures and Impostures
of English in *Ulysses*

Dramatic Language: "Every word is so deep"

The vexed question of what makes for life in language has been a crux in *Ulysses* commentary from the start. The astonishing verbal inventiveness of the book is its most conspicuous quality, and also the most difficult to evaluate. For one thing, it is virtually impossible for the reader to come into total possession of the book's language and, as Joyce himself so frequently makes vivid, an insecure sense of possession heightens anxiety about the value of both language in itself and one's relationship to it. While Joyce in *Ulysses* gives the reader a full experience of such anxiety, most (though not all) readers also feel that he gives something further—something more alive and thereby more liberating and profound. To identify such freedom and depth matters enormously in any account of literature, but especially with *Ulysses*: Joyce began his own career probing the bitter sorrow of not being in clear possession of language. *Ulysses* marks a liberation for him as much as for any reader.

Everybody knows the episode from *A Portrait of the Artist as a*

Young Man where Stephen is angered and humiliated by the way the college dean of studies (an English Jesuit convert) patronizes him for using what the dean takes to be the quaint Irishism "tundish" instead of "funnel." The exchange provokes Stephen to elaborate inner formulation of how the very language of English in which he is conversing with the dean is an alien language, not really belonging to him, Stephen, an Irishman: "The language in which we are speaking is his before it is mine . . . His language, so familiar and so foreign, will always be for me an acquired speech. I have not made or accepted its words. My voice holds them at bay. My soul frets in the shadow of his language" (p. 189).[1] In the diary at the end of the novel, Stephen records his discovery that "tundish" is, after all, an English word, "English and good old blunt English too" (p. 251), but his confirmed sense of superiority does not fundamentally change his alienation from a language that the Englishman still owns, however incompetently he manages it: "What did he come here for to teach us his own language or to learn it from us. Damn him one way or the other!"

Incidents to feed an appetite for alienation occur all the time in Joyce's accounts of Stephen. Earlier in the same conversation at the college, the hapless dean had fallen into the confusion of mistaking for a direct bit of conversational courtesy an *exempla* made by Stephen as part of a demonstration about language.

> —One difficulty, said Stephen, in esthetic discussion is to know whether words are being used according to the literary tradition or according to the tradition of the marketplace. I remember a sentence of Newman's, in which he says of the Blessed Virgin that she was detained in the full company of the saints. The use of the word in the marketplace is quite different. *I hope I am not detaining you.*
> —Not in the least, said the dean politely.
> —No, no, said Stephen, smiling. I mean . . .
> —Yes, yes: I see, said the dean quickly, I quite catch the point: *detain.*
> He thrust forward his under jaw and uttered a dry short cough. (p. 188)

Although Stephen first formulates his difficulty in terms of two separate but equal traditions of language, the marketplace is really for him (and for Joyce at this point) a deleterious influence, producing mediocrities like the dean of studies who trade in words emptied of their earlier dignity. Revulsion from the cheapening of words as they descend from the literary tradition to the marketplace appears even more explicitly in *Stephen Hero*, where, as already noted in Chapter 1, the boy precociously chooses to value only those words which he can steal back, as it were, for the private treasure house of his mind. In *Ulysses* the traditional hierarchy of styles loses the authority it had earlier for Joyce, as the literary tradition becomes less distinct from the market-place, and even "esthetic discussion" becomes a commodity that everybody trades in but nobody, least of all Stephen, can afford. Yet the sharper irony toward literary language does not simply transfer value to commonplace speech. In *Ulysses,* as in Joyce's earlier books, it is rare for anyone to *say* anything of value at all.

In both *A Portrait of the Artist* and *Ulysses,* Stephen hardly facilitates significant communication through speech, since virtually everything he says comes bracketed within some posture or impersonation—he per-forms, often quite sarcastically, gestures of verbal self-expression, while keeping himself apart from the language he uses, even the very plainest configurations of words. For example, his response to the dean's clichés of reassurance hides contempt beneath a surface of modest-sounding simplicity.

> — . . . First you must take your degree. Set that before you as your first aim. Then little by little, you will see your way. I mean in every sense, your way in life and in thinking. It may be uphill pedalling at first. Take Mr Moonan. He was a long time before he got to the top. But he got there.
>
> —I may not have his talent, said Stephen quietly.
>
> —You never know, said the dean brightly. We never can say what is in us. I most certainly should not be despondent. *Per aspera ad astra.* (p. 190)

Although Stephen does feel despondent in this conversation, it is not because he doubts his talent compared to any Mr. Moonan! At the same time, the dean's cliché about not being able to "say what is in us" indirectly makes an important point about Stephen. Inchoate desires and shame and feelings of superiority (and inferiority) are indeed in Stephen, and so are words and phrases, some from the marketplace and others, more precious to him, from the literary tradition. Yet while emotions and sensations become attached to words in his consciousness, gaining color and music from the association, the same fretful distance between feeling and word appears in his mind as in his talk. Even worse in his judgment, he cannot even trust the treasure house of language in his mind. When he catches himself misremembering Thomas Nashe's line, "Brightness falls from the air" as "Darkness falls from the air," he is disgusted by the false images of feeling he had attached to the misquotation, what he had wrongly taken to be "the verse with its black vowels and its opening sound, rich and lutelike" (p. 233). In "Brightness falls from the air," the opening not only makes a different sound but names a different light, making a mockery of his high appreciation for the perfect union of sound and image and mood in a famous line of poetry, and a mockery as well of his more private pleasure in attaching his own moods to rich phrases from the literary tradition: "He had not even remembered rightly Nash's [sic] line. All the images it had awakened were false. His mind bred vermin. His thoughts were lice born of the sweat of sloth" (p. 234).[2]

Stephen's tough-sounding self-reproach here may at last have the ring of authentic self-address. Making an image out of the real lice which he had just caught on his neck a few sentences earlier seems to signal a breakthrough into a truer form of self-expression, a language of his own, if only to express self-loathing. Yet even such breakthroughs are never without ambiguity in Joyce's prose. Duffy, in "A Painful Case," had a habit of making short sentences in his mind about himself in the third person, and this habit arguably contaminates even his epiphany of loneliness at the story's end: "He felt that he had been outcast from life's feast."[3] The phrasing (repeated later in the paragraph) seems too perfectly poised for the feeling, the image of "feast" too bounteous for the meagerness of life in the story's world. The indirect narration leaves ambiguity about the value and even the ownership of such a sentence; between the upset feeling of being outcast and the high rhetoric of the sentence falls the shadow of a literary posture.

Similar shadows attend all the verbal formulations of Stephen's shame in *A Portrait of the Artist*. He also has a habit of making sentences about himself in the third person and of filtering even his grossest feelings and sensations through phrases from books. Before formulating his harsh self-rebuke for the mistake about Nashe, his mind moved from the lice on his neck to "a curious phrase from Cornelius a Lapide which said that the lice born of human sweat were not created by God with the other animals on the sixth day" (pp. 233–34). Even the most concrete monosyllabic particulars—"lice," "sweat"— come to Stephen not directly from reality but "acquire" their significance by passing through remembered quotation. The oxymoron "sweat of sloth" connects with lice only by passing through the cryptic fragment from Cornelius a Lapide. Quite involuntarily, Joyce suggests, there are always circulating in Stephen's mind a variety of curious quotations; they mingle with his own sensations and fantasies, enriching their suggestiveness, to be sure, but also cutting a space between words and whatever else is in him, that individual and personal self which contemporary literary theory has accustomed us to call the self as "Subject," the longed-for but never fully attained origin of speech in romantic ideology since Rousseau.

As a characteristic of the fictional Stephen Dedalus, in both *A Portrait of the Artist* and *Ulysses,* alienation from a language at once sought obsessively and held at bay belongs to the particular predicament of Stephen's adolescent precocity, pride, and isolation. As a characteristic of Joyce's own mature writing, continual display of language whose meaning is acquired from suspect or at least alien traditions constitutes the method of Joyce's famous irony, that perpetual crossing of the circuits in all ostensibly expressive gestures of language which seems to join him to writers like Flaubert and to other ironists, especially in France.

New assertions of this affiliation, now influenced by French literary theory, have the goal of re-claiming Joyce from the English culture which, it is suggested, eventually assimilated (part of) his work only by domesticating its ironies.[4] By any international laws of literary ownership, of course, it is not only predictable but even somewhat just, that Paris should now undertake the reclamation of Joyce. For even though Joyce stopped short of Beckett's transposition of himself into a French writer, it was in Paris that Joyce was sheltered and lauded and, most important, published for the stretch of more than fifteen years when postal, customs, and other public authorities in the English-speaking world were making fools of themselves by condemning works they had barely read, much less understood.[5]

There is a danger, however, of sentimentalizing the story of Joyce's exile into "a melancholy tale for English cultural historians," as one of a new generation of commentators is satisfied to say.[6] In its most reductive form the story joins in unholy alliance the philistine official censorship, the snobbery of Bloomsbury, and the chauvinistic English exclusiveness of Leavisite Cambridge against the brave and radical independence of Joyce, the Irish exile in Paris, supported by a handful of other expatriate artists and farseeing Frenchmen. The picture needs, however, to accommodate such complicating details as the young Leavis's daring to teach Joyce (as well as Lawrence) to Cambridge undergraduates in the mid-twenties, a bit of independence that did much to initiate Leavis's own trouble with Cambridge officialdom, specifically when he was caught trying to secure a copy of *Ulysses* through legal channels for teaching purposes.[7] Leavis's defense was that undergraduates were in any case all reading the book (easily procured through barely clandestine "illegal" means). *Ulysses* was already an important book in advanced and even undergraduate English-speaking literary circles by the mid-twenties; its banned status only increased its glamour.

Leavis's early conviction that Joyce (along with Lawrence) was among the very few contemporary prose writers who could reward the kind of close stylistic analysis he was already bent on introducing into English studies should help to refine the significance of his later, more famous criticisms of Joyce. The 1933 essay in *Scrutiny* (already mentioned in Chapter 1) emphatically rejects the experiments of *Work in Progress* but reaffirms, as a matter of significant critical import, the major accomplishment of *Ulysses*.[8]

While for Leavis, as for many later Anglo-American readers, setting a boundary between *Ulysses* and *Finnegans Wake* is one of those crucial acts of critical discrimination central to the establishing of intelligent standards in literary judgment, French-style critics regard resistance to *Finnegans Wake* as reprehensible failure to accept the true Joycean challenge to English linguistic and cultural prejudice. Both sides in this dispute recognize that it is the Joyce of *Finnegans Wake* who most thoroughly belongs to Paris. Thus this last book of Joyce's presides in spirit over such endeavors as the recent anthology of critical essays entitled *Poststructuralist Joyce: Essays from the French.* Four of the eight essays in this collection largely concern *Finnegans Wake;* all eight read back from this last book to *Ulysses, A Portrait of the Artist,* and even *Dubliners.* Of course orientation toward the final curve of the Joycean career equally serves the purpose of assimilating Joyce's work to already established cultural categories. And as with the contrary judgments, interpretive principles partially derived from Joyce's own writing are fleshed out by theories brought from elsewhere—in this case from Paris, where such luminaries of the new French criticism as Derrida, Lacan, Kristeva, Cixous, and others discovered (in the 1960s and 1970s) that Joyce's work, especially *Finnegans Wake,* had remarkable affinity with their own developing ideas of the "indeterminate Text" and the "fragmented Subject."[9] The unifying principle now, paradoxically, becomes the idea of nonunity, "an infinitization of fictions," as Stephen Heath calls it, or a vast unstable configuration of "strategic intertextual nexuses," according to André Topia.[10]

A half-century of Anglo-American annotation and explication, however, lands current endeavors to "defamiliarize" Joyce in the awkward predicament that the terms for defamiliarization are themselves entirely familiar from within the existing body of commentary. Indeterminacy, fragmentation, and the ironic effect of intertextual cross-references have hardly gone unnoticed in Anglo-American studies of *Ulysses,* to say nothing of *Finnegans Wake.* The editors of *Poststructuralist Joyce* report how one established Joycean reacted to a lecture by Derrida "with a mixture of disappointment and relief": "but this is not so different from what we . . . have been doing for years."[11] A certain nervous ambivalence may be noticed among Anglo-American critics who recognize the not-new in current French-style Joyce studies. Its counterpart on the other side is an equally awkward vacillation between aggression and humility: along with the battle cry to liberate Joyce from his Anglo-American prison of "readability," there is acknowledgment that the effort to "read" Joyce (in practice) joins a great variety of past and present interpretive procedures. Thus the editors of *Poststructuralist Joyce* concede: "The power of the Joycean text is such that it tends to lead its perceptive and unprejudiced readers, whatever their theoretical backgrounds, to similar procedures of reading."[12] Perceptive readers have long recognized that Joyce's uses of language in *Ulysses* undermine closure about certain kinds of significance, at the same time that Joyce's distinctiveness tends to direct critical attention to a shorter list of recurrent questions and choices than many other kinds of writing provoke. Thus the continuing centrality, even in poststructuralist Joyce criticism, of the questions with which I began: what gives or takes away life in language? What difference does it make whether the words belong to the character, to the author, to alien traditions, or to everyone or no one in particular?

It is, to be sure, the weighting of judgment in relation to these questions that can vary significantly. While recognizing the characteristics of "word-book" and "word-tale" in *Ulysses,* Anglo-American critics have tended to object to the book—or to those parts of the book— where Joyce seems bent on no more than systematic and mechanical experimentation with "intertextuality." Even wholehearted supporters of Joyce, like Edmund Wilson and Hugh Kenner, have thus sought ways of defining a further subject, a motive, an action, a set of values to account for power that no mere "word-book," from their point of view, could have.[13] For the poststructuralist, it is precisely this search for a locus of value in *Ulysses* beyond the "mechanisms of its infinite productivity" that is judged disabling and that makes those more hostile early critics (who saw *Ulysses* only as an antihuman word-book) closer to the mark: "their negative charge switched to positive."[14] Such mechanical inversion of literary valuation dismisses with the flick of a switch the long, disputatious Anglo-American brooding about how *Ulysses* gains its extraordinary hold on the reader's imagination. From the poststructuralist perspective, it is no more than the machinery of words—"the intertextual matrix," the "discontinuous conglomerate," the tension between the "strategic intertextual nexuses" and the "typographic continuum"—which compels our attention, even in the so-called interior monologues.[15]

By the standard of this rigorous limitation of possible significance in *Ulysses,* the eloquent equivocations of a Hugh Kenner look like flight into an entirely wrong kind of indeterminacy. Here is Kenner at the start of *Dublin's Joyce,* equivocally feeling out the distinction between Flaubert and Joyce, a distinction as important in English studies as that between *Ulysses* and *Finnegans Wake.*

> No Dubliner acts from his nature; no Dubliner knows what his nature is; he acts on the promptings of *idées reçues* and talks in words that have for too long been respoken. Yet the words and actions can partake of a passion it would be difficult to call factitious; human spirits are imprisoned in these husks. Cadence and image crackle with continual racy unexpectedness, though phrase and action are drearily conventional . . . By the time Flaubert had gotten to *Bouvard et Pécuchet* he was concerned to prove a general thesis about the limits of human knowledge . . . But when Joyce makes Bloom suddenly ask, "Do fish ever get seasick?" we are in the presence not of an exercise in nineteenth-century pessimism but of a tribute to the unpredictable leaps of the human soul.[16]

In *Dublin's Joyce* (as in his later books), Kenner goes on to shift the emphasis from living spirits to "husks," as he denies Bloom and also Stephen any access to knowledge of reality because of the way their spirits are indeed imprisoned in the "too long respoken." True knowledge for Kenner (and, as he proposes, for Joyce) requires an intellectual discipline hardly known in western culture since before Locke. So although "racy unexpectedness" and "creative leaps" are striking to Kenner in the language of *Ulysses,* their definable positive value in his interpretations of the book as a whole has a way of disappearing. Kenner's evasive approach to the vitality of Joyce's language makes trouble for many Anglo-American critics in precisely the same way as his insistence on Joyce's difference from Flaubert disconcerts the French. For the Anglo-American reader what makes for the crackle of vitality separating *Ulysses* from *Bouvard et Pécuchet* is a matter of life and death, yet Kenner always backs away from the issue just at the crucial points.

The alternate Leavisite approach offers the advantage of more flexible assumptions about language, but it encounters similar problems for different reasons. Allowing a much more various ("intelligent" rather than "intellectual") view of what might legitimately pass for knowledge in writing or speech, Leavis nevertheless proceeds on the conviction that the language of literature is open to direct evaluative judgment by standards rooted in life itself. This conviction takes Leavis part of the way toward his distinction between a merely mechanical verbal ingenuity in *Finnegans Wake* and something more richly and urgently expressive in *Ulysses*. But it does not answer the question of how, exactly, Joyce made an expressive medium in *Ulysses* out of a language so conspicuously shot through with clichés and *idées reçues*. If poststructuralist scorn for the entire Anglo-American commitment to expressiveness in language can hardly resolve this problem, it does have the use of underlining just where Joyce most teasingly foils Leavisite principles of explanation, if not the actual procedures of reading that follow (sometimes loosely) from them.

We have encountered the key tenets of the Leavisite position already in the early *Scrutiny* essay on Joyce and elsewhere. The standard, as earlier noted in Leavis's criticism generally, is Shakespeare. Since Eugene Jolas, the editor of *transition,* had himself invoked the Shakespearean comparison in his tribute to *Work in Progress,* there is more than one reason for Leavis to bring to his own assessment of Joyce the touchstone most significant to him.[17] The study of a play by Shakespeare, Leavis concedes and even insists, "must start with the words," but (and this is the crucial qualification) words alone were not where Shakespeare started or, by implication, where the reading of Shakespeare ends: "the words matter because they lead down to what they came from."[18]

The rub here is how to identify this depth. Leavis does not want to specify an ideological or sociological or even psychological source or origin for the language of literature. His whole vocation is to show how such specifications displace direct experience of literature by inert categories. Leavis does not believe in a separate, namable region of idea or feeling underneath the language of literature. Yet he cannot do without the word "depth" for the sense of a pressure exerted from somewhere on the language of great literature and giving that language its value as an expressive medium. The nature of this pressure cannot be demonstrated through nonliterary evidence. Yet it can be known, as a matter of perception and experience, according to the basic procedures of "intelligent" knowing. It is "plain," Leavis asserts (meaning that it is perceptible to him and, he hopes, to other perceptive readers), that the language of Shakespeare's plays shows "a pressure of something to be conveyed," a "burden" to be delivered, while in *Work in Progress* "the interest in words and their possibilities comes first."[19] Similarly S. L. Goldberg, setting out to account for his "keen and deep" enjoyment of *Ulysses,* distinguishes that response from his lesser interest in *Finnegans Wake,* which "certainly opens up possibilities in the use of language," but without meeting the "deeper" obligations of art.[20]

Such discriminations between *Finnegans Wake* and *Ulysses* at once evade and call attention to the difficulty of identifying the "depth" so often cited in tribute to *Ulysses.* Precisely because so much of the book is made from cliché, quotation, and stylistic parody, it becomes not at all plain how the words may be said to lead "down," in Leavis's word, to anything but half-baked or embalmed fragments of other verbal forms. The pressure behind or underneath Shakespeare's language, Leavis explains, come not only from his individual apprehensions of life, but from the richness of the verbal medium shared by playwright and audience. It is important to Leavis to see continuity between modern literature and that earlier richness of English. But he draws back from fully confronting what happens to the very conception of expressive language in the art of a modern writer preternaturally sensitive to the derivative, alien, and artificial elements of English and every other language passed down through the machinery of both book and marketplace. In *A Portrait of the Artist,* I began by noting, a pressure of self-loathing seems perceptible in the sentence of Stephen's mind: "His thoughts were lice born of the sweat of sloth." But the words only partially lead down to that moral and psychological depth; in another sense they stop short and are deflected off the mind's surface to a remembered page from a book by Cornelius a Lapide. A source of words that is deep, in the sense of "arcane," may directly interfere with the sense of depth in the immediate, human, experiential way that Leavis means.

In *Ulysses* the problem of thinking about depth in literature is compounded by the general marketplace currency of the topic for the characters themselves. Everybody, from the Dublin literati who gather for esthetic discussion in the library to Bloom entertaining himself alone in the street, has ideas about how literature is "deep."

Most of these ideas reflect the influence of turn-of-the-century symbolist theorizing, directly represented in *Ulysses* by the voice of Yeats's friend A.E.: "The supreme question about a work of art is out of how deep a life does it spring. The painting of Gustave Moreau is the painting of ideas. The deepest poetry of Shelley, the words of Hamlet bring our minds into contact with the eternal wisdom, Plato's world of ideas" (9.50–53 / 185). The deep—and high—vagueness of the Yeatsian circle is caught in the voice of A.E. In his 1900 essay about Shelley, Yeats obscurely suggests how "profound symbols" can float up into the mind, producing a sublime dizziness: "the sudden conviction that our little memories are but a part of some great Memory that renews the world and men's thoughts age after age, and that our thoughts are not, as we suppose, the deep, but a little foam upon the deep."[21] In Joyce's version of symbolist esthetics, the rhetorical foam has thickened, the very word "deep" serving mainly as a cover for intellectual incoherence. Over the rhythmic surface of A.E.'s intoning, the unthinking mind can glide from the source of art to its effect, from painting to poetry to words of a character in a play and then to eternal wisdom, without pause or distinction. Such foamy rhetoric about deep art was fashionable in Dublin in 1904, and in America, too, as Stephen notes in his mental jeering at A.E. in the library: "A.E. has been telling some yankee interviewer. Wall, tarnation strike me!" (9.54–55 / 185). In the international literary marketplace the idea of depth in art seems no more than the debased coin of that second-rate journalistic criticism for which Stephen, like Joyce, has nothing but disdain.

Yet it is not so absolutely clear that Stephen has entirely outgrown the vague spirituality that came to be one of the main offenses to Joyce of the foggy Irish twilight of romanticism. Stephen jeers in the library partly because he has been left out of a literary party. It is true that he can turn an equally sharp wit against his own former spiritual conceit— during his walk on the beach in "Proteus," for example: "Remember your epiphanies written on green oval leaves, deeply deep, copies to be sent if you died to all the great libraries of the world, including Alexandria" (3.141–43 / 40). Joyce must mean Stephen to be thinking of the words written upon leaves that Yeats admires in Shelley's *Prometheus Unbound*.[22] Insofar as Stephen mocks his own earlier "deeply deep" literary pretensions, he seems ready to pass beyond the Shelleyan phase of his own adolescent romanticism to become a more modern, that is, a more skeptical and even ironic poet. Yet the actual poem about the pale vampire that Stephen stops a few minutes later on the beach to jot on a scrap of Deasy's letter confuses the evidence. We get to hear the stanza composed on the beach some pages later, in "Aeolus," when the paper of Deasy's letter is produced in the newspaper office:

> *On swift sail flaming*
> *From storm and south*
> *He comes, pale vampire,*
> *Mouth to my mouth.* (7.522–25 / 132)

Outside the context of *Ulysses,* it is hard to know what standard to bring to bear on the judgment of this poetic fragment. How does it compare to Joyce's own earlier poems in *Chamber Music,* for example, or to the single line from Blake which Yeats quotes admiringly in his 1900 essay, "The Symbolism of Poetry": "The gay fishes on the wave when the moon sucks up the dew."[23] Within *Ulysses* Joyce's network of parallels, cross-references, and deflating detail has a mainly ironic effect. Pale vampires, gay fishes, waves, wings, sails, some hungry sucking mouth: these are made to seem the common repertory of "deep" poetic symbols in Dublin in 1904. So that the couplet composed by Bloom during the day is not clearly less deep than others:

> *The hungry famished gull*
> *Flaps o'er the waters dull.* (8.62–63 / 152)

If one tries to measure the comparative depth of these poetic fragments, contrasting conceptions of art's deep "spring" immediately come into play. In giving Stephen's mental processes during his poetic composition, Joyce arranges glimpses of connection between the ghoulish sexuality of the vampire image and Stephen's morbid obsession with his mother's death from cancer. But Bloom's stream of consciousness, flapping around the subjects of hunger, suicide, and the death of Reuben J's son, also suggests a spring of personal depth to his image, even though one might not know it from the couplet itself. It is not evident that Stephen is significantly more effective than Bloom in communicating the particular, personal spring of feeling in his image, or even that he cares about such a personalized sense of depth. Yeats is not talking about personal springs of poetry in 1900, but about "spiritual essences" and the "great Memory." Joyce's glimpses of personal depth here have the effect of showing what is absent from the poetic fragments of both Bloom and Stephen as much as what has come into them through association. As with his poem "To E-C" in *A Portrait of the Artist,* Stephen has left out any elements of the "common and insignificant" that might identify his imagery with a concrete personal experience. From the symbolist perspective, that would seem to be the way to affiliate oneself with the "great Memory." Stephen, however, more immediately relies on quite particular memories of other literary models: Pater's vampire, for example, from his description of the Mona Lisa, later anthologized (in the form of vers libre) as Yeats's first selection in his *Oxford Book of Modern Verse*.[24] Stephen is more skillful than Bloom in devising a poetic sound for language, but he is hardly distinctive in his infatuation with the idea of harmonious sound, and he is not yet working in vers libre. Joyce shows us Stephen savoring his rhymes: "mouth south: tomb womb"; Bloom does the same thing: "gull dull."

There is nothing, of course, inevitably ridiculous or even narrowly symbolistic about the identification of poetic depth with single images drawn from the literary tradition and organized in patterns of sound. In *The Pound Era* Hugh Kenner describes how the symbolist idea of deeply evocative verbal configurations became modernized through new archaeological interest in the fragment or "scrap." By breaking and framing the verbal fragment in new ways, Pound and other early modernists sought release from vague late-Romantic solemnities.[25] But the isolated verbal fragment (whether excavated from buried texts or designed anew) is still granted talismanic power in this early modernism. I shall say more later about how Joyce's way of breaking and organizing verbal fragments both follows and moves apart from this early modernist revision of symbolist technique. Here, my point is simply to notice that Joyce's new effects stand out against a background of ironic parallel between Stephen and Bloom: "pale vampire" does not go much deeper than "hungry, famished gull"; "mouth south" does not bring the mind into contact with eternal wisdom any more powerfully than "gull dull."

Bloom, as an object of humor, links the high and low in poetic commonplace and shows the weakness they have in common. Like Stephen, A.E., and so many other Dubliners, Bloom takes Shakespeare as his touchstone: "That is how poets write, the similar sounds. But then Shakespeare has no rhyme: blank verse. The flow of the language it is. The thoughts. Solemn. *Hamlet, I am thy father's spirit / Doomed for a certain time to walk the earth*" (8.67–68 / 152). It is hard to know what thoughts Bloom finds in his (slightly misquoted) Shakespearean fragment; as for A.E., it seems mainly the "flow of language" that creates a literary aura of solemn thought for Bloom. And even though Bloom sometimes thinks irreverently about literary people, his readiness to scoff at "dreamy, cloudy, symbolistic" esthetes does not prevent him from submitting to their influence in poetic matters. When A.E. (and a young woman with droopy stockings) cross Bloom's path, shortly after he has composed his couplet, the sight inspires him to revise his lines about the gull, incorporating the very words "dreamy" and "cloudy" that had come into his mind first with derision. His revised couplet is moving closer to Yeatsian "foam upon the deep":

> *The dreamy cloudy gull*
> *Waves o'er the water dull.* (8.549–50 / 166)

Bloom's not altogether approving, but not altogether critical sense of the affinity between musical flow and poetic wisdom leads him to share in what may be called a "quotational" idea of literary profundity, an idea Joyce shows to pervade high and low culture alike. Bloom's version appears again in relation to Shakespeare when he reconsiders the postscript to his letter to Martha Clifford, composed to background music at the Ormond bar: "Too poetical that about the sad. Music did that. Music hath charms. Shakespeare said. Quotations every day in the year. To be or not to be. Wisdom while you wait" (11.904–6 / 280).

While the distinctive movement of Bloom's inner voice here (as elsewhere) cuts across conventional Dublin rhythms, he also echoes received opinion in especially audible form. The appeal of euphonious quotation as an easily portable commodity emerges from Bloom's only half-joking play on the language of advertising slogan: "Wisdom while you wait." The quick movability of a quotation is one of its its attractive qualities: that is why it can be transferred to so many situations as to seem no less than eternally and universally true. The kinship is apparent between literary quotation, thus understood, and cliché. Of course in cliché all consciousness of earlier usage has been lost, and it is the delusion of originality that increases the effect of stupidity.[26] Colloquial idiom, as I have earlier distinguished it from cliché, in a sense behaves more like literary quotation, the origin of the idiom located not in a particular writer but in the language of the community as handed down through speech. In idiomatic language, fixed phrases, also released from original or specific contexts, carry the authority of common experience and wisdom. In literary quotation it is *uncommon* wisdom that seems to become magically manifest through a set combination of words, even through the mere tag of a phrase, "To be or not to be." Bloom's inner speech, I have earlier observed, often breaks up the smooth flow of cliché and quotation with colloquial phrases and rhythms that give his voice the strength of common sense against pretensions to uncommon wisdom. But Bloom, like other Dubliners, also has considerable respect for quotational wisdom. Bloom's jokelike colloquial adaptations of epigram and commercial slogan in the Ormond

Bar, like Stephen's intensities of scorn and self-scorn, represent only very partial freedom from common Dublin esthetic opinion. Neither of Joyce's main characters conceptualizes or enacts in his own language an alternative conception of verbal depth.

Leavisite readings of *Ulysses,* as performed for example so impressively by S. L. Goldberg, stake too much on the direct enactment of positive values by the language of Joyce's characters. Thus Goldberg overstates the depth of Bloom's apprehensions of the world and exaggerates what he calls the "critical responsiveness" of both Bloom and Stephen in the interior monologues. This bias also turns Goldberg against the parodic chapters which seem so aggressively to degrade the heroes.[27] Yet even in the most recognizably dramatic portions of the interior monologues, Joyce makes constant mischief with all conventional ideas of how a character's language becomes a deep medium of expression. While it is true and important that *Ulysses* does give both Bloom and Stephen a large degree of expressiveness in the first half of the book, Joyce's unique version of novelistic depth is accomplished even there through all his many adjustments of our distance from the characters' own language. In the interior monologues Joyce devises language to bring us extraordinarily close to particular events of consciousness; at the same time, we are made to see how consciousness itself positively relies on language to avoid deep apprehensions of both world and self.

A good example of Joycean depth achieved through tension with the language of the Bloomian monologue is the passage from "Lotus-eaters," where Bloom glances at a notice for *Leah the Forsaken,* a play he remembers his father talking about, which is to be performed that night in Dublin.

Hello. *Leah* tonight. Mrs Bandmann Palmer. Like to see her again in that. Hamlet she played last night. Male impersonator. Perhaps he was a woman. Why Ophelia committed suicide. Poor papa! How he used to talk of Kate Bateman in that. Outside the Adelphi in London waited all the afternoon to get in. Year before I was born that was: sixtyfive. And Ristori in Vienna. What is this the right name is? By Mosenthal it is. *Rachel,* is it? No. The scene he was always talking about where the old blind Abraham recognises the voice and puts his fingers on his face.

Nathan's voice! His son's voice! I hear the voice of Nathan who left his father to die of grief and misery in my arms, who left the house of his father and left the God of his father.

Every word is so deep, Leopold.

Poor papa! Poor man! I'm glad I didn't go into the room to look at his face. That day! O, dear! O, dear! Ffoo! Well, perhaps it was best for him. (5.194–209 / 76)

Paternal grief and filial guilt are deep themes evoked by this passage, but the inner language of Bloom at once opens and blocks access to them. Not only is Bloom's most intense feeling wordless ("Ffoo!"), but his entire flow of associations follows a zigzag path around the edges of the abyss glimpsed through the passage as a whole. In contrast to the memory of his father's response to *Leah*—"Every word is so deep"—Bloom's own language seems the very opposite of deep, taken by either word or phrase. That is not to say that his voice is dull or unevocative. The speechlike rhythms, syntax, and colloquial phrasing noted as characteristic of Bloom's interior monologues in Chapter 1 have here their usual enlivening effect. There is an entertaining sociability in this style—not only in the "Hello" at the start, but also in the characteristically lively pattern of rapid self-addressed questions, answers, and shifting of topic. As in conversation among friends, such a rhythm can accommodate a great deal of only partial knowledge and even ludicrous surmise (Hamlet: "Perhaps he was a woman. Why Ophelia committed suicide"). Not only foolish but also poignantly evocative images intermittently rise off the surface of the language, even when it is not especially quotable: "Poor papa! How he used to talk of Kate Bateman in that. Outside the Adelphi in London waited all the afternoon to get in." Despite a phrasing utterly devoid of verbal distinction, Bloom's prosaic fragment of memory calls up some fullness of life in the father who later committed suicide: there is a fleeting glimpse of a young Virag in London adoring an English actress, and then another hint of full life in the father's pleasure in reminiscing to his son. But this living sense of Virag flits as quickly as possible through Bloom's stream of consciousness. As readers, we are in a position to linger over the pathos of the memories more than Bloom does. But we are also more critically detached than Bloom from the whole sequence, for he is unaware of the ironies embedded in his inward articulation of memory and feeling.

It is ironic, for example, that in a situation where the admonition was to attend to "every word," what Bloom remembers his father quoting has no authority even as quotation. Bloom's version of the lines from *Leah the Forsaken* is juicier, more rhythmic and emotional, than the original or, to be more precise, the established English translation of the "original" German (itself indebted to earlier theatrical conventions of melodrama). As popularly performed on the stage in London and Dublin, the English version is unquotably flat by comparison: "He left his father to die in poverty and misery since he had forsworn his faith, and the house of his kindred."[28] Moreover, whether the "improved" quotation belongs to Virag or to Bloom or to somebody else, it gets its "deep" flow from the same Biblical intonations that we hear as cliché in all Dublin oratory—for example, when Professor MacHugh recites John F. Taylor on Ireland, Moses, and the "house of bondage." The difference between the translated German melodrama and Irish oratory is mainly in the tone of the clichés: in the play, Old Testament echoes are used for pathos rather than prophecy. In addition the actual play *Leah,* in whatever language, trusted much less to words than Bloom (or Virag) suggests; the dramatic climax in the play's big scene of recognition introduces thunder, lightning, and the onstage strangling of the old Abraham by the villainous apostate Nathan. There is a typical Joycean nest of rather obscure jokes here that the reader, once armed with annotation, might well find to overwhelm any simple poignancy in the dramatic image of Bloom remembering his father's quotation.

The larger irony of the passage, however, is clear without annotation, for it is evident that in no version of the melodrama *Leah the Forsaken* is the language likely to seem deep to a serious literary taste. Even more important, Bloom himself shows little interest in probing more deeply any of the themes touched on so rapidly in his memory of the quotation. The play *Leah* comes to mind only because of the signboard; an associative zigzag then connects Mrs. Bandmann Palmer to Hamlet to images of suicide in literature and then closer to home. For this most private and disturbing familial image, Bloom has in his mind no deep words. Indeed, he has hardly any words at all, only a sighing exclamation that eventually issues in a cliché: "O, dear! O, dear! Ffoo! Well, perhaps it was best for him." Finally Bloom puts the whole disturbing train of association aside as quickly as possible, blaming it on his unpleasant meeting with M'Coy and distracting himself by turning the corner and fixing attention on the sight of feeding horses: "Mr Bloom went round the corner and passed the drooping nags of the hazard. No use thinking of it any more. Nosebag time. Wish I hadn't met that M'Coy fellow" (5.210–12 / 76). The spectacle of horses feeding allows Bloom to get back into his more comfortable stream of inner speech: "Poor jugginses! Damn all they know or care about anything with their long noses stuck in nosebags. Too full for words. Still they get their feed all right and their doss. Gelded too: a stump of black guttapercha wagging limp between their haunches. Might be happy all the same that way. Good poor brutes they look. Still their neigh can be very irritating" (5.215–20 / 77).

To be too full for words, in Bloom's judgment, is a condition of bestial unconcern, although to the reader Bloom's own momentary failure of inner language seemed to signify fullness of painful feeling and not satisfied appetite. Still (to use Bloom's favorite connective), it is Bloom's human addiction to language that holds most of our attention both before and after he turns the corner, rather than either the silence of full feeding or the silence of pain. The language of the interior monologue gives us enough glimpse of depth to surmise the feelings that Bloom is turning away from. We do not, however, know more about his emotion (or his father's) than he puts into words to himself. His main impressiveness in the passage comes from the very deftness by which he skirts obscure depths, and the rich repertory of common verbal devices he has for evasion.

Once safely around the corner, the texture of Bloom's inner language thickens as his mind catches onto new material for observation and musing: "Gelded too: a stump of black guttapercha wagging limp between their haunches." There is no reason to follow Kenner's stingy impulse to transfer the most impressive language in Bloom's monologues to some other source.[29] Wedged as it is between the two fragments of looser colloquialism, the dense description of the gelded horses belongs to Bloom, being one of those moments that show his capacity to put together words in interesting ways. Curiously, however, the most interesting verbal events in the Bloomian monologue often bear only the most oblique relationship to the glimpsed depths of feeling. Bloom's most expressive language paradoxically tends to belong to his deliberate activity of self-distraction, after his mind has dismissed direct contemplation of painful subjects: "No use thinking of it anymore." The very appeal of Bloom's entertaining stream of inner language, along with its continual forward movement, carries us quickly past whatever depths of sorrow, anxiety, or guilt may for an instant have crystallized in his glimpse of old Virag and himself in the age-old roles of fatherless son and sonless father.

Joyce's movement of language in this as in so many other passages of Bloomian monologue thus works against the impulse to descend on a straight vertical axis through the stream of consciousness down to deeper spiritual or psychic structures.[30] It is true that a psychoanalytic interpreter might well see in those gelded horses around the corner the projected image of a sexual punishment Bloom may feel himself to deserve for the patricide that a father's suicide is often taken to signify in the unconscious as presented in psychoanalytic theory.[31] Joyce was aware of psychoanalytic theories of projection and transposition; we shall see that the phantasmagoria of "Circe" display them with a (ludicrous) vengeance. "The doctor can tell us what those words mean," says Steadfast John in the library (9.739 / 204). But in the interior monologues there is little motive for insisting on unconscious determinants of meaning. The image of the gelded horses, like all the other images, moves rapidly along in the stream of verbal consciousness. The images are appealingly idiosyncratic, but they show none of the pressure of dreams or of waking obsessions into which unconscious conflict has been projected. In contrast to Lawrence, for example, whose narrative language points to the unspeakable intensities of projected feeling in such climactic moments, say, as Gudrun's watching Gerald master the horse, Joyce shows in Bloom a consciousness adept at maintaining balance amid the rise and fall of psychic stress. It is noticeable, of course, how frequently this consciousness catches onto one or another image of sexual impotence—monks, eunuchs, gelded horses—but Bloom's curiously mild integration of these images into his quotidian inner speech diminishes the quality of obsession even while hinting at it. The momentum of the monologue encourages us to follow Bloom's turn of attention to the horses in the same spirit that he consciously performs it, as a voluntary distraction from upset, a soothing absorption in the not intensely significant surface of the visible and speakable world. The fact that language fails him here for the duration of a "Ffoo!" indicates a stress—all the fault of "that M'Coy fellow"—but Bloom recovers his verbal equilibrium in a moment.

In Bloom, Joyce creates the wonderfully engaging presence of a personality skillful at negotiating the corners of his experience in the strong if unsteady vehicle of his inner speech. Balance is maintained by continuing movement forward rather than down. And this effect also exerts a kind of centripetal force against fragmenting ironies. Poststructuralist comparison of Bloom's stream of consciousness to a "radio band" or an "electronic network crisscrossed by multiple circuits" falsely equates the shallowness of intellectual or psychological penetration with the absence of individual personality as a presence alive in language.[32] Although Bloom does not have the degree of apprehension that Goldberg often wants to claim for him in the interior monologues, neither is he a merely passive (and wrongly wired) piece of machinery.

Nor is the universality of Bloom's unarticulated pain as much at the center of our interest as the mythic emphases of critics like Joseph Frank suggest.[33] Joyce does exploit the mythic suggestiveness which can be retained by discredited pieces of language: even the melodrama *Leah* can evoke eternal patterns of family betrayal and suffering. Yet emphasis on the eternal structures of experience abstractable from particular instances of language too readily discounts the vivid representation of a particular character in his temporal activity of life that makes for so much of Joyce's success in the interior monologue. Frank compares the emphasis on mythic prototype in *Ulysses* to the abandoning of perspective and foreground in nonnaturalistic painting. But Bloom's distinctive inner speech keeps him very much in the foreground of his monologues: his mythic counterparts remain in the background, as flat as the signboards which announce their various theatrical incarnations. Bloom, enacting his distinctive personality through the temporal movement of his inner speech, is a modeled figure given a generous allowance of time and space to make his weight felt. The mythic pattern to which his individual experience belongs is sketched so that it aids rather than collapses the three-dimensionality of the impression: the eternal pattern of fathers and sons makes a structure that gives significance to Bloom's individual situation without obliterating his distinctiveness. To take a further step, it is precisely through the particular bumpy progress of this undistinguished but distinctive figure that Joyce gives new meaning to the idea of a mythic prototype. For it is not mainly the static condition of father or son that he allows us to know, but the living movement of human consciousness, maneuvering around and past the pain of elemental human conditions by dint of every resource of language available. This human movement away from anxiety, sorrow, and guilt is finally a key part of Joyce's deep rendering of Bloom's (and our) human life in language. No single, brief configuration of words can express this kind of depth, because the effect is in the larger movement. Clichés, skewed quotations, trivial or distracting or witty observations, colloquial scraps of question and answer—all contribute to this arhythmic flow; the prosaic human depth of the situation is *in* the motley life of verbal consciousness enacted by the character, as he uses language to lead himself away from rather than down to deeper depths.

The interior monologue, in its very fidelity to verbal consciousness, is probably less suited to the plumbing of psychological depth than other narrative techniques, as Dorritt Cohn has observed.[34] In the Joycean interior monologue a powerful sense of interiority is accompanied by an equally powerful sense of how consciousness resists the chaos and dissolution of the deepest psychic depths. Shakespearean analogy is, after all, pertinent here, especially analogy to the Shakespearean use of soliloquy in *Hamlet,* the great, infinitely ambiguous drama of soliloquies so fascinating to everyone in Joyce's Dublin.

In *Ulysses,* Shakespeare's *Hamlet* becomes most suggestive in relation to Stephen, partly because of Stephen's reputation as a *Hamlet* expert. Joyce gives further dramatic relevance to *Hamlet* by pointed echoes of Shakespearean detail in the initial Stephen scenes: the setting of the tower, Stephen's silent accusation of Mulligan as "Usurper," even his conjuring of a reproachful parental ghost. Most important, Joyce follows the model of *Hamlet* by dramatizing the need of his character for a protected interior space of language. Although Mulligan is no king, there is enough bullying power in his taunting speech to justify strategies of self-protection. A whiff of moral rot comes off Mulligan's plausible common sense about "beastly" death that reminds us of Claudius's sophistries about the "natural" loss of fathers. Mulligan's talk is equally callous to individual realities of feeling, and equally energetic in using the rhetoric of common sense to press for his own personal power.

At the same time, without Shakespeare's initial objectifying scene on the ramparts, Joyce allows more taint of exaggeration to attach to Stephen's "moody brooding" at the start. Narrative passages which attend to Stephen in a tone different from Mulligan's speech only ambiguously counter this impression. The narrative creates a different style of language for Stephen to be set against the vigorous social idiom of Mulligan's "wellfed" voice, but it is not entirely clear how we are to react to this registering of what Stephen will not "cough up" on demand from his companion: "Pain, that was not yet the pain of love, fretted his heart. Silently, in a dream she had come to him after her death, her wasted body within its loose brown graveclothes giving off an odour of wax and rosewood, her breath, that had bent upon him, mute, reproachful, a faint odour of wetted ashes" (1.102–05 / 5).

As in *A Portrait of the Artist* the very elegance of the style devised for Stephen's inner life calls into question the relationship of his private words and images to his feeling. All the disorder of deep emotion, at least of the sort that breaks out in spontaneous associations of present and past, dream and sensation, has here already been refined into perfectly poised verbal formulation. The literary elegance of words like "fretted," and even the distribution of the pauses marked by commas, has the unnerving effect of distracting attention away from the substance of the inner life to the verbal dignity that can be given to its articulation.

Similar interference with intimate engagement in Stephen's pain occurs when almost the exact wording of the dream image is repeated a
few pages later, this time in the midst of a passage that moves from
narrative into interior monologue, and then out and in again:

A cloud began to cover the sun slowly, wholly, shadowing the bay
in deeper green. It lay beneath him, a bowl of bitter waters. Fergus'
song: I sang it alone in the house, holding down the long dark chords.
Her door was open: she wanted to hear my music. Silent with awe and
pity I went to her bedside. She was crying in her wretched bed. For
those words, Stephen: love's bitter mystery.
    Where now?
Her secrets: old featherfans, tasselled dancecards, powdered with
musk, a gaud of amber beads in her locked drawer. A birdcage hung in
the sunny window of her house when she was a girl. She heard old
Royce sing in the pantomime of *Turko the Terrible* and laughed with
others when he sang:

> *I am the boy*
> *That can enjoy*
> *Invisibility.*

Phantasmal mirth, folded away: muskperfumed.

> *And no more turn aside and brood.*

Folded away in the memory of nature with her toys. Memories
beset his brooding brain. Her glass of water from the kitchen tap when
she had approached the sacrament. A cored apple, filled with brown
sugar, roasting for her at the hob on a dark autumn evening. Her
shapely fingernails reddened by the blood of squashed lice from the
children's shirts.
    In a dream, silently, she had come to him, her wasted body within
its loose graveclothes giving off an odour of wax and rosewood, her
breath, bent over him with mute secret words, a faint odour of wetted
ashes.
    Her glazing eyes, staring out of death, to shake and bend my soul.
On me alone. The ghostcandle to light her agony. Ghostly light on the
tortured face. Her hoarse loud breath rattling in horror, while all prayed
on their knees. Her eyes on me to strike me down. *Liliata rutilantium te
confessorum turma circumdet: iubilantium te virginum chorus excipiat.*
    Ghoul! Chewer of corpses!
    No, mother! Let me be and let me live.
—Kinch ahoy!
    Buck Mulligan's voice sang from within the tower. (1.248–80 / 9–10)

This famous passage is theatrical in obvious ways, and also charged with more particularized dramatic pressure: it reveals the hidden sin and horror that will oppress Stephen all through the day and night. Yet the somewhat gratuitous repetition of the dream image from a few pages earlier oddly interrupts the dramatic intensity by shifting attention from Stephen's intense emotional reverie to the verbal event of the repetition, whether it be ascribed to the narrator or to Stephen. Most likely, we integrate the dream image into the surrounding interior monologue and take the repetition as a kind of self-quotation by Stephen's own consciousness: but what depth of feeling can be associated with a voice so absorbed in the activity of making (and then repeating with slight revision) deep-sounding configurations of words? In withdrawing from social speech, Stephen in *Ulysses,* as in *A Portrait of the Artist,* may seem only to substitute one kind of verbal performance for another.

The advance of *Ulysses* over the earlier novel, however, appears in the wonderful variety and range of the styles and particular details given to Stephen's inner language. Stephen here may not be as dazzling as Hamlet in his first soliloquy, but he is impressive enough. Inside what Mulligan dismisses as "moody brooding," Joyce shows a world of remarkably varied and suggestive images: a line of poetry from Yeats, connected here to a particular memory of his mother, and then other poignant images and a remembered quotation passed on from his mother's own memory of her youthful pleasures: "She heard old Royce sing in the pantomime of *Turko the Terrible* and laughed with others when he sang." Like Bloom's images of his father waiting outside a London theater, these images of remembered life neither state feelings nor work as symbols of emotion in the sense that Yeats meant, when he described symbols which "because of their preordained energies or because of long association . . . call down among us certain disembodied powers, whose footsteps over our hearts we call emotions."[35] Stephen's particular images are too mundane, too personal in reference to call down "disembodied powers" of universal emotion; they are evocative, moreover, precisely because they call up the individual *bodily* reality of his own mother's life and death. The very particularity of such images in *Ulysses* gives them a haunting power beyond the more conventional ghostliness of dream. At the same time, the emotions suggested by even the concrete and mundane imagery seem strangely suspended as more potential than actual for Stephen. If his diffuse pain were indeed to reach "the pain of love," it would be through the release of emotions bound up in *Turko the Terrible* and the plain glass of water by the deathbed. In the interior monologue, however, pain is being controlled and distanced by Stephen's verbal activity all along, in the perfect economy of wording (even for *Turko*) and, especially, in the writerly phrases of summary and comment: "Phastasmal mirth, folded away: muskperfumed." A subtle curtain of "wavewhite wedded words" never fully opens, although the pressure of what might tear through is perceptible.

The ghost's appearance at the end of act 1 in *Hamlet* comes as so much of a relief, especially to Hamlet himself, because the ghost legitimizes his emotions while freeing him, if only temporarily, from the need for private formulation of them. In "Telemachus" no actual ghost appears to command or relieve Stephen. Joyce shows his young brooder verbally conjuring his own ghosts and creating his own heroic encounters with them, as if psychic forces from within lead him to the same simplifying theatrical organization of emotion that the external ghost provides in *Hamlet*. It is in part this more exclusively self-invented (as well as derivative) quality of Stephen's dramatic posture that keeps him from winning anything close to the urgent attention we give to Hamlet. In Shakespeare too, however, theatrical self-formulation pervades Hamlet's soliloquies. Joyce has the same gift as Shakespeare for creating a character who interests us partly because his private verbal self-presentations are so brilliant, and partly because we (and intermittently even he) recognize that through words he is wasting his life as much as saving it.

The action of language, as powerful usurper and also as powerful preserver of life, is much more centrally the theme of *Ulysses* than of *Hamlet*, where, after all, a public action of usurpation and murder has to be worked out. Details of very late revisions of *Ulysses* show Joyce's continuing preoccupation with this internal drama of language for Stephen, even after he had discarded the technique of interior monologue in the second half of the novel. The recurrence of Stephen's phrase "Agenbite of inwit" provides a rich example. The phrase initially appeared only once, in the library scene, as a fragment of spoken language in Stephen's fantastical theory of Ann Hathaway's religious old age: "Venus has twisted her lips in prayer. Agenbite of inwit: remorse of conscience. It is an age of exhausted whoredom groping for its god" (9.809–10 / 206).[36] Only in the 1921 revisions did Joyce additionally punctuate Stephen's earlier thoughts with the phrase, making "Agenbite of inwit" a key signature of Stephen's internal verbal life.

The phrase "Agenbite of inwit" quotes the title of a medieval manual of virtues and vices, designed to remind the layman of the hierarchy of sins and the distinctions among them.[37] The phrase is well-suited to Stephen, for both its archaic glamour and its aura of moral and religious solemnity. Michael Groden argues that the added repetitions of "Agenbite of inwit" make it a "leitmotif of Stephen's guilt," lessening the impression of erudite affectation made by the single context of the phrase in the library scene: "as one occurrence of a repeated motif, it functions as Stephen's natural and less arrogant verbalization of a phrase that has been in his mind all day."[38] Yet while the revisions unquestionably do internalize the phrase, something rather less than an effect of the natural attaches to all its appearances, and even its connection to a feeling of guilt *in* Stephen is ambiguous from the start.

In "Telemachus" Joyce made the initial appearance of "Agenbite of inwit" occur in a passage where Stephen is less accusing of himself than of others. While holding himself sullenly aloof from Mulligan's goading of him to perform a bardic role before the Englishman Haines, he allows himself more inward "sayings" than he will utter, including "Agenbite of inwit":

> Then he [Mulligan] said to Haines:
> —The unclean bard makes a point of washing once a month.
> —All Ireland is washed by the gulfstream, Stephen said as he let honey trickle over a slice of the loaf.
> Haines from the corner where he was knotting easily a scarf about the loose collar of his tennis shirt spoke:
> —I intend to make a collection of your sayings if you will let me.
> Speaking to me. They wash and tub and scrub. Agenbite of inwit. Conscience. Yet here's a spot.
> —That one about the cracked lookingglass of a servant being the symbol of Irish art is deuced good.
> Buck Mulligan kicked Stephen's foot under the table and said with warmth of tone:
> —Wait till you hear him on Hamlet, Haines. (1.474–87 / 15–16)

Stephen may perhaps be understood as remorseful here for his helpless complicity in Mulligan's games; while ostensibly refusing to play, Stephen cooperates in his assigned role of bardic speaker, even through the cryptic epigram of his rebuff. But in the explicit context of a response to what "they" are saying, the phrase "Agenbite of inwit" makes more sense as Stephen's inward accusation against his companions, calculated to put them at a moral remove more decisively than he is willing to do in actual speech. The moral charge first touches

Haines, whose bland geniality strikes Stephen as a shallow cleansing gesture for English crimes against the Irish. And it touches Mulligan, too, whose hypocritical conviviality with Haines offends Stephen even more than Haines does himself. It is a bit hard to be absolutely sure of Stephen's target, partly because the moral judgments he is leveling, the moral sources he is quoting, seem so out of proportion to the social occasion. It is likely, however, that we are not to take either "Agenbite of inwit" or the allusion to Lady Macbeth so very solemnly. There is something more idle, even frivolous in Stephen's impulse to decorate his sense of injury with portentous inner sayings. The content of the allusions may matter less than the characteristic gesture of his retreat from both sociability and open conflict into a self-protective savoring of quotation and cryptic allusion.

This posturing in the phrase acquires more intense dramatic significance later, when it becomes more urgent to assess how much Stephen's inner language retains any real bite for self-examination or expression. At another moment in the library, for example, Stephen's witty inner dialogue about the money he owes A.E. only parodies the examination of conscience originally designated in a manual like the medieval "Agenbite of inwit."

> How now, sirrah, that pound he lent you when you were hungry?
> Marry, I wanted it.
> Take thou this noble.
> Go to! You spent most of it in Georgina Johnson's bed, clergyman's daughter. Agenbite of inwit.
> Do you intend to pay it back?
> O, yes.
> When? Now?
> Well . . . No.
> When, then?
> I paid my way. I paid my way.
> Steady on. He's from beyant Boyne water. The northeast corner. You owe it.
> Wait. Five months. Molecules all change. I am other I now. Other I got pound. (9.192–206 / 189)

Stephen's own Mulliganesque talent for blasphemy and parody appears here both amusing and depressing, for now there seems virtually no language available to Stephen's inner voice except quotation susceptible to parody, including language Stephen earlier seemed serious about. The fragments of internal dialogue certainly convey the tension of Stephen's mood—he is intensely uneasy with himself as with the others. But that unease takes the form of an unrelenting parody of introspection and of the language of conscience. Hamlet's apology to Laertes in the final act of *Hamlet,* for example, is burlesqued here by witty sophistry about ducking a debt of money: "I am other I now. Other I got pound." Even the vowels of the alphabet turn into material for witty manipulation: "A.E.I.O.U." Hamlet shows a similarly ingenious but almost desperate wit in his "mad" scenes, but Shakespeare significantly distinguishes those performances from Hamlet's sustained effort of introspection in the soliloquies. In the library scene, "Agenbite of inwit" seems to belong to an inner voice imprisoned in verbal wit, hardly capable of any natural expression of guilt, whether for the venial sins of bedding a clergyman's daughter and squandering borrowed money, or for the more serious sin of squandering language and life itself in this desperate play. To be sure, Stephen's verbal posturing in the entire library scene also serves the purpose of protecting him against the very palpable assaults of the others in the form of both insult and belittling platitude. Whether or not his "deep" language can operate only as weapon or shield, and the psychological and intellectual cost of being so armed, are questions about Stephen raised by all his appearances in the book.

"Agenbite of inwit" figures again in one of the most moving of such episodes, the scene in "Wandering Rocks" where Stephen unexpectedly runs into his sister Dilly at the secondhand book cart. He sees the pathos of her lank hair and nervous laugh as she holds out for his approval the coverless French primer which she has just bought for a penny. And even more sharply, he sees his own nervous fear of being dragged down by her mute family claim on him for rescue. Finally, he sees that he rejects the claim, a choice he judges morally by the repetition and variation of "Agenbite of inwit."

> She is drowning. Agenbite. Save her. Agenbite. All against us. She will drown me with her, eyes and hair. Lank coils of seaweed around me, my heart, my soul. Saltgreen death.
> We.
> Agenbite of inwit. Inwit's agenbite.
> Misery! Misery! (10.875–80 / 243)

Large consequences follow from the difficult choices to be made about how to take Stephen's words here. The simple, even clichéd "All against us," and then the isolated "We," recall the interrupted verbal flow under stress of painful feeling in Bloom's monologues, intensified here by the separation of the verbal fragments on the page.

But whereas Bloom only gets back into the current of his characteristic language when he safely rounds some corner, Stephen's by now familiar "Agenbite" appears three times in the very midst of his greatest strain. If his use of the phrase retains bite enough to signify the actual expression of remorse, then this episode shows in Stephen a strong capacity for moral self-recognition. In that reading the exclamation "Misery! Misery!" leads *down,* in Leavis's sense, to complex emotion and insight, carrying the burden of Stephen's sense of his and Dilly's shared helplessness, their common struggle not to sink under the weight of their moral and material impoverishment, and finally Stephen's own guilt and remorse for refusing to risk helping her. But "Misery" is a contaminated word for suffering in *Ulysses,* cheapened by the melodramatic clichés of plays like *Leah the Forsaken.* And if "Agenbite of inwit" has become, through Stephen's own usage, only a more rarified theatrical cliché, then his whole experience of painful self-recognition becomes indistinguishable from a stage posture of guilt and remorse, the deep words of feeling being quoted as it were, in a verbal counterpart to the very refusal of emotional engagement that they ostensibly condemn.

Joyce's careful placements of "Agenbite of inwit" sustain ambiguity, while tipping the balance of judgment toward distrust. Not only have earlier dramatic contexts accustomed us to hear "Agenbite of inwit" as a self-distancing gesture of Stephen's language, but the repetitions even within the meeting with Dilly have a further denaturalizing effect. The phrase seems to have become for Stephen a kind of magical incantation, like one of the "charms or invocations" that he had just been browsing over in the esoteric books on the stall.

> Thumbed pages: read and read. Who has passed here before me? How to soften chapped hands. Recipe for white wine vinegar. How to win a woman's love. For me this. Say the following talisman three times with hands folded:
> —*Se el yilo nebrakada femininum! Amor me solo! Sanktus! Amen.*
> (10.845–49 / 242)

"Agenbite of inwit" seems another exotic recipe, this one for warding off claims which threaten to drown the spirit in unfathomable moral and emotional depths.

Joyce's dramatization of Stephen's movements of consciousness thus connects him to Bloom in the same domestic drama of menacing anxiety and guilt, warded off by self-saving gestures of verbal defense. The forms of assault and defense are significantly different for the two characters—that is why neither one seems a mere emblem or proto-type—but the impression of depth to the individual dramas also draws on the layering effect of the parallels. Too-often-respoken words like "Misery" even gain new expressive meaning because Joyce's structure expands and shifts their reference. The powerful misery dramatized in Stephen's monologue has to do not only with his situation of familial poverty and abandonment, but also with the more universal human need to grasp onto language as a magical protection against over-whelming assaults of feeling. For Joyce's characters, more unambi-guously than for Lawrence's, depth is dangerous; true to the Homeric analogy, shipwreck and drowning are to be feared and avoided. To be "in the same boat" with others, to use one of Bloom's idioms, may name a troubled situation, but still one directed toward survival. One crucial difference between Stephen and Bloom, however, is Stephen's arrogant refusal to recognize this common aspect of his condition. He has less awareness of his own self-preserving strategies than Bloom does, nor is it obvious that he himself does not mistake his verbal evasions of depth for the thing itself.

Stephen's encounter with Dilly appears in "Wandering Rocks," the tenth chapter of *Ulysses*. Only a few of the items in this section (just past the mid-point of Joyce's epic scheme) continue the stream-of-consciousness technique, largely put aside between the library scene (Chapter 9) and Molly's finale. Joyce's radical change of technique mid-way through *Ulysses* is partially covered over by such intermit-tent revivals of interior monologue. Yet Joyce meant the shift to be remarked and it has been, if not with universal enthusiasm. S. L. Goldberg has serious objections to virtually all the later episodes except "Circe" and "Ithaca."[39] Even Pound, in the correspondence which accompanied Joyce's episodic publication of the novel as it was being written, began to complain with "Sirens" that Joyce was per-haps overdoing ingenuity with his systematic invention of "a new style per chapter."[40]

Without going over again all that has been said for and against Joyce's formal decisions for the second half of *Ulysses,* it is possible to understand further how the fundamental shift away from interior monologue is not just a technical repudiation of the dramatic, but a formal means of enacting what the early style eventually makes us feel as nothing less than a dramatic necessity. Joyce remarked to Frank Budgen, at about the time of Pound's letter, that Stephen no longer interested him much, because he was fixed, unchanging.[41] His reduction of Stephen's interior monologue to desperate self-parody in the library scene suggests this impasse by displaying internal postures so rigid that they are hardly distinguishable from social behavior. In spite of his theories about Shakespeare's openness to experience, Stephen himself seems even more stuck in himself than before. Since Bloom's stature was less tied from the start to that sense of potential so important to our regard for Stephen, his repetition of the same motions in the interior monologues jeopardizes his interest as a character less. But even for Bloom, the stream of consciousness eventually reaches an impasse. The very power of the technique to dramatize the self-protective strategies of consciousness marks its limit as an instrument of representation. The surface details might continue to vary, and the density of interconnection might continue to increase. But since, beneath that surface variety, Bloom and Stephen essentially keep reenacting the same kinds of mental sequences, there comes a point after which no deeper knowledge of their characters— and especially of the value of their characters—can emerge.

That point comes for Bloom at the end of "Lestrygonians" (Chapter 8). In one of the most expressive episodes of Bloomian interior monologue, Joyce demonstrates what the technique can do and why it can do no more. The crucial sequence begins with Bloom's sight of the blind stripling and ends with Bloom's hasty retreat into the museum away from the sight of Blazes Boylan. In brilliantly condensed form, with mannerisms exaggerated almost to the point of parody, Joyce re-presents, in remarkably fresh form, all the signatures of Bloom's inner voice. His detailed speculations about blindness contain his usual mixture of pseudoscientific conjecture and empathic platitude, rescued from mere confusion or sentimentality by the final characteristic jump to a candid gesture of personal taste (and distaste).

> Poor fellow! Quite a boy. Terrible. Really terrible. What dreams would he have, not seeing? Life a dream for him. Where is the justice being born that way? All those women and children excursion beanfeast burned and drowned in New York. Holocaust. Karma they call that transmigration for sins you did in a past life the reincarnation met him pike hoses. Dear, dear, dear. Pity, of course: but somehow you can't cotton on to them someway. (8.1144–50 / 182)

Bloom moves from stereotyped pity for the blind to a hodgepodge listing of other famous sufferings and famous talismanic words of religious explanation and consolation. A slight lyrical rise at the start ("What dreams would he have, not seeing? Life a dream for him") lifts the reverie a bit above the flat commonplace of the opening, but it is the final colloquial expression of a distaste that pity cannot overcome which is the strongest signature of Bloom's individual vision in the passage—what distinguishes him from his more conventional "one-eyed" fellow-citizens.

The next moment, however, when Boylan blazes across his visual path, the entire significance of blindness changes for Bloom.

> Straw hat in sunlight. Tan shoes. Turnedup trousers. It is. It is.
> His heart quopped softly. To the right. Museum. Goddesses. He swerved to the right.
> Is it? Almost certain. Won't look. Wine in my face. Why did I? Too heady. Yes, it is. The walk. Not see. Get on.
> Making for the museum gate with long windy steps he lifted his eyes. Handsome building. Sir Thomas Deane designed. Not following me?
> Didn't see me perhaps. Light in his eyes.
> The flutter of his breath came forth in short sighs. Quick. Cold statues: quiet there. Safe in a minute.
> No. Didn't see me. After two. Just at the gate.
> My heart!
> His eyes beating looked steadfastly at cream curves of stone. Sir Thomas Deane was the Greek architecture.
> Look for something I.
> His hasty hand went quick into a pocket, took out, read unfolded Agendath Netaim. Where did I?
> Busy looking.
> He thrust back quick Agendath.
> Afternoon she said.
> I am looking for that. Yes, that. Try all pockets. Handker. *Free-man.* Where did I? Ah, yes. Trousers. Potato. Purse. Where?
> Hurry. Walk quietly. Moment more. My heart.
> His hand looking for the where did I put found in his hip pocket soap lotion have to call tepid paper stuck. Ah soap there I yes. Gate.
> Safe! (8.1168–93 / 183)

Interior monologue here contracts to the irregular staccato of an agitation close to panic. Bloom hurries first his eyes and then his mind as rapidly as possible away from the overwhelming sight of his wife's lover, Blazes Boylan. Although he had just remarked on the pitiable life of the blind, hardly real, like a dream, Bloom urgently tries to will his own consciousness away from a reality too upsetting to contemplate. To be forced to see Boylan, and even to be seen by him, gives a reality to his cuckoldry as intolerable as was that other dread sight, the hotel room where his father killed himself. As in the earlier episode where Bloom recalls and then turns away from the scene in memory, Joyce registers Bloom's experience of danger by breaking up the verbal flow. The breakup, however, goes very much further here, the language hardly able to establish any rhythm other than the beat of an agitated pulse. It is not the experience of repression that Joyce is showing here. Bloom knows what he wishes not to see; he both sees it and knows that he cannot stand the sight.[42] The interior monologue powerfully dramatizes a moment of acute, recognized danger. In the earlier scene of lesser menace, safety was gained "round the corner" in the visual and mental observation of the horses; here Bloom more awkwardly and frantically negotiates his rescue by rushing into the museum and into the act of "steadfastly" fixing eye and mind on "cream curves of stone." The statues, plus the ad for Agendath and the talismanic potato, all become part of his equipment for survival, though it is really only the soap that he has bought for Molly with husbandly solicitude that restores his calm, returning him, as it were, to the dream of marital peace that he chooses to live within.

Modern depth psychology, like earlier doctrines centered on the virtue of true vision, makes severe judgments on the cost of safety through this degree of willed self-blinding. Whether or not Joyce encourages equal severity—psychological or moral—remains one of the disputed issues of interpretation posed by *Ulysses* as a whole. The significant point at the end of "Lestrygonians," however, is the limited use of the interior monologue as an instrument for exploring such questions of value. Bloom's habit of retreat to his talismanic objects and distractions at the moments of greatest crisis, like Stephen's retreat to talismanic sayings, gives insufficient basis for judgment. No single configuration of their words can serve as a recipe for wisdom, because all the verbal expressions in the interior monologues are implicated in the human action necessary to judge. Deeper insight into the worth and cost of differing forms of survival must be gained through verbal techniques less bound by the limitations of what the characters themselves are able or willing to "see."

The Comedy of Psychic Depth:
"You ought to see yourself"

As the chapter of *Ulysses* conspicuously devoted to psychic depth, "Circe" has been earnestly probed by many commentators, even though everyone also notices that the episode offers the most extravagant comedy in the book. Taken earnestly, Joyce's vast phantasmagoria of shame, guilt, and perverse fantasy seems to correspond to what modern depth psychology has uncovered as the "real" underworld of human character. The psychic ordeal of entering and surviving this form of underworld can seem the very emblem of modern heroism in *Ulysses*. Thus Kenner sees Bloom undergoing a form of "purgation" in "Circe," through which he cleanses himself first of one deep guilt, then another, until the sequence can be seen as a "nearly accidental psychoanalysis, wholly lacking an analyst."[43]

Whatever problems the idea of accidental psychoanalysis without an analyst might pose for professional analysts, there is the more immediate literary problem that a serious psychological story can be extracted from "Circe" only by running the psychology alongside but distinct from the comedy. Joyce himself noted this trap for the psychologists in *Ulysses* as a whole, when he lightly dismissed Jung's acknowledged troubles with what Jung called Joyce's "exceedingly hard nut": "He seems to have read *Ulysses* from first to last without one smile. The only thing to do in such a case is to change one's drink."[44]

Analogy to drink is especially apt for "Circe," where Joyce's language produces such intoxicated dizziness: fascinated by the psychological drama, we are not quite able to keep it in stable focus. Alertness to the tantalizing double action of the language is very hard to sustain: here is a story about psychic depth, but also a burlesque of that story and of other pious contemporary stories about the virtue of getting "psoakoonaloosed," in the word of *Finnegans Wake*.

In the Dublin Christmas pantomimes often cited among Joyce's models for "Circe," the story is usually a simple fairy tale in burlesque dramatic form, dispersed through an entertainment with many other acts as well.[45] The frequent interruptions and distractions matter little because everyone knows the plot already. In "Circe" Joyce entertains (and baffles) us with what was rapidly becoming the most popular, if still shocking, fairy tale of modern times, the mystery-magic thriller of how the beasts and demons of the unconscious must somehow be confronted before a hero, or any man, can accomplish a deed of valor. This story, so intricate in detail yet so relatively simple in underlying structure, runs through the phantasmagoria of Nighttown. Yet the picture of Bloom's psychopathology is so overdone, the stage effects of his dramatized fantasies are so excessive in detail, sometimes portentous but sometimes absurd, that the whole drama of psychic assault and survival comes to seem as much parody as probing of psychoanalytic conceptions of depth.

As in the whole second half of *Ulysses,* Joyce in "Circe" plays with the desire he has himself created for deeper revelations about his characters. His experimental techniques tease the modern appetite for more and more material of knowledge by reformulating in many different terms what we essentially already know. Rather than giving us secret information to settle the matter of judgment, Joyce makes us realize that judgment rests on styles of knowing, that is, on the categories of judgment that different forms of language and thought impose. Psychological categories have no more authority than others, though a ludicrously confident air of authority marks this (like other) dogma.

The temptation to psychological reductiveness matters more for the reader than for the characters in "Circe," since neither Bloom nor Stephen is present as an observing consciousness in the scene. The jokes in "Circe" about how to "see" Bloom have charge mainly for the reader who is busy making interpretations and judgments: "Mrs Breen (*screams gaily*) O, you ruck! You ought to see yourself!" (15.431 / 444). Like so many of the calls to vision in the episode, Mrs. Breen's line pulls in contrary directions at the same time. On one side, she repeats the exhortation to self-confrontation that Bloom's ordeal is ostensibly about. On the other side, Joyce through her language mocks the decline of an ancient wisdom: from the Socratic "Know thyself" to the grotesquerie of this psychological cliché, presented here as both scolding and flirtatious, and coming from a woman who has herself declined into quite a sight—from "prettiest deb in Dublin" to bedraggled wife of a man also "not all there," to her final Circean posture, roguishly baring "*all her herbivorous buckteeth*" (15.388 / 442). Like the pithy profundities of every sort parodied throughout *Ulysses,* remarks like Mrs. Breen's summons to self-vision at once exude an air of traditional authority and, in their local absurdity, disqualify whole schools of wisdom from any serious claim to authority at all.

Joyce's comedy subverts conventional pieties about psychic pain and psychic ordeal by turning both the action and the material of disclosure into laughable matters. In psychoanalytic theory, as well as in our experience outside *Ulysses,* psychopathology is never freely laughable because it so conspicuously carries the mark of pain. The accusing apparitions in "Circe" are determined to intensify this pain, mainly through outrageous verbal attack. Virtually everyone joins in some declaration of Bloom's pathology: "You're too beastly awfully weird for words!" (15.833 / 459) exclaims the apparition of the newspaper author, Beaufoy. Yet the humorous dilation of colloquial, childlike insult in the wording of such charges makes figures like Beaufoy comically weird themselves, especially because the wild mudslinging never produces any serious image of suffering in the shifting forms of Bloom himself. It is not only that Bloom, by some masochistic transformation of aggression, enjoys beng abused; nor does he possess extraordinary strength to withstand brutality. The reason why there is so little suffering in "Circe" is that Joyce has cast the entire episode not in the form of nightmare but in a sweeter dream of comic play where pain does not hurt the way it does in "real life," or even in the more naturalistic parts of Joyce's own book. In contrast to "Hades," for example, where Bloom was palpably hurt by the innuendos of his companions on the way to Dignam's funeral, in "Circe" all the fantasized characters throw *"soft pantomime stones"* at Bloom, and pantomime versions of Bloom weep only soft pantomime tears or die soft and temporary pantomime deaths. Joyce, of course, in contriving the stupendous degradation of his hero, is the primary source of all the aggression in the scene. Yet the absence of any deep evocation of suffering has the effect of allowing an extraordinary freedom of aggressive energy to be let loose in the episode as a whole, without danger to its benign and playful spirit.

Joyce's key aggressive move in "Circe" is to take away from Bloom his characteristic resources of self-distraction. In the interior monologues Bloom was most often able to quiet anxiety by taking note of other things: "With a quiet keep quiet relief his eyes took note this is the street here middle of the day of Bob Doran's bottle shoulders" (8.594–95 / 167). In Nighttown the spectacle of things offers no relief because everything enacts the same degrading reminders. Bloom has been shown as a man unusually deft at making use of the world's otherness to maintain a freedom from obsession, even if it is his underlying psychic stresses which lead him to note some things rather than others. In "Circe" it is as if the things of the world will no longer cooperate in this activity of distraction and displacement. Virtually all Bloom's former objects of attention reappear, even Bob Doran, but now they pop out insistently to poke at those sorest areas of feeling for which they were earlier an alternative or balm.

This puppetlike animation of things (and even words) makes for much of the comedy of "Circe," in the classic Bergsonian sense of substituting a mechanical quality for what we expect to be human—that is, in Bergson's terms, natural and free.[46] In Nighttown, what psychoanalytic theory technically calls the "mechanisms of defense" run amok; the pieces of Bloom's psychic machinery fly apart in a way that no form of Bloom can control or even direct, as consciousness seemed to do in the interior monologues. The explosion of this machinery, however, discloses not only Bloom's ignominy, but also the comedy implicit in the entire concept of psychic mechanisms. Freudian theory, in its mechanical model of the conversions and exchanges between unconscious and conscious mental life, takes no account of Bergson's famous dictum that any resemblance to automatism in human life produces laughter. Bergson, because of this formulation, excludes from comedy the laying bare of the "secret portion" of the self, which he calls the "tragic element in our character."[47] In Bergson's romantic imagery, "volcanic eruptions" from the depths of passion resemble upheavals of nature and not mutinous machinery. Lawrence's movement out of comic modes respects this distinction, even when the volcanic eruptions of a character (Somers, say, in *Kangaroo*) are being judged by other than romantic standards. Freud, on the other hand, appears to perceive no intrinsic contradiction between a tragic view of human experience and a mechanistic model of the psyche. Joyce follows Freud in showing psychological dysfunction to resemble the breakup of an intricate machinery rather than a natural cataclysm. But Joyce also follows (or at least enacts) Bergson's association of the mechanical with laughter. Psychic depth, in this conjunction, thus ceases to elude the reach of comedy; indeed, comedy becomes the exactly appropriate mode of deep psychological representation.

Comedy, however, conventionally relies for laughter on obvious forms of exaggeration. The comic excesses of "Circe," taken in relation to Joyce's presentation of Bloom earlier, create a basis for resisting as well as submitting to the authority of Nighttown's psychological picture. So many extravagant insults are heaped upon Bloom in Nighttown that our judgment is comically repelled as well as seduced by the reductions of judgment stated within the scene. Bloom as "lame duck" and "stick in the mud" is the verbal construction of the apparitions *within* "Circe." Such phrases of insult punningly disclose the latent psychic charge held by the half-dead metaphors of colloquial idiom, but the very familiarity of the phrasing also turns such disturbing realities as sexual impotence into a kind of harmless verbal joke. The Bloom known from the interior monologues, moreover, was less pathetic than the images imply, taken either colloquially or figuratively. Kenner calls him "guiltridden" before Nighttown, and glimpses of guilt and shame are, we have seen, visible at key moments. Yet in his secret correspondence, or in his habits of ogling women or enjoying the feel of his bowels or belly, Bloom is, by the standard of the culture, remarkably *un*ridden by guilt. His secretiveness about a number of his private pleasures is not the same as guilt, and it is significantly different, too, from what psychoanalytic theory calls repression. The major scandal of *Ulysses* came, after all, from the pleasures of Bloom openly reported in the detailed language of his consciousness. His enjoyment of his own bodily functions—on the toilet, in the bath, even farting on the street—differentiates him not only from tight and dry Stephen Dedalus, but also from most characters in literature since Rabelais, and perhaps from most "real" characters in the social world Joyce knew.

In "Circe," therefore, when an outraged servant girl followed by a procession of Honourable Ladies appears to accuse Bloom of assorted perverse liberties, these hallucinatory figures do not exactly arise from buried psychic depths. They are the familiars of Bloom's habitual and conscious fantasy life. For example, in "Lotuseaters" Bloom keeps up his end of a conversation with the annoying M'Coy, while at the same time pursuing in mind the legs of a handsome woman mounting a carriage across the street. He freely associates the tempting sight of these legs with other memorable female attractions: "Like that haughty creature at the polo match" (5.103 / 73). He reminds himself of his taste for the "classy" and powerful in women, and also amuses himself with witty insinuations about the sexual realities behind haughty appearances: "Women all for caste till you touch the spot. Handsome is and handsome does. Reserved about to yield. The honourable Mrs and Brutus is an honourable man. Possess her once take the starch out of her." He puts no restraint on his excited pleasure at a glimpse of this particular honorable woman's legs, and when a tramcar suddenly puts an end to the adventure, he consoles himself for his interrupted voyeurism with a resignation that is more humorously fatalistic than guilty: "Always happening like that. The very moment. Girl in Eustace street hallway. Monday was it settling her garter. Her friend covering the display of. *Esprit de corps.* Well, what are you gaping at?" (5.104–6 / 73).

The difference in "Circe" is that Bloom's previously fleeting mental images now expand and recombine into more than life-size dramatic forms. The device of hallucination, among its other advantages, frees Joyce to create a whole new population of dramatic figures whose own follies and vices become targets for some of the comedy's aggressive energy. The accusations of Bloom by the hallucinatory figures are laughable for what they show in the speakers (and even in the discrete elements of their speech) as much as for what they show in Bloom, so that the critical force of the comedy becomes diffused and in part deflected from the main story line of Bloom's descent into psychic depth. Thus the Honourable Mrs. Mervyn Talboys, created by enlarging and combining earlier Bloomian fantasy, is a marvelous comic figure in her own right:

> (*in amazon costume, hard hat, jackboots cockspurred, vermilion waistcoat, fawn musketeer gauntlets with braided drums, long train held up and hunting crop with which she strikes her welt constantly*) Also me. Because he saw me on the polo ground of the Phoenix park at the match All Ireland versus the Rest of Ireland. My eyes, I know, shone divinely as I watched Captain Slogger Dennehy of the Inniskillings win the final chukkar on his darling cob *Centaur*. This plebeian Don Juan observed me from behind a hackney car and sent me in double envelopes an obscene photograph, such as are sold after dark on Paris boulevards, insulting to any lady. I have it still. It represents a partially nude señorita, frail and lovely (his wife as he solemnly assured me, taken by him from nature), practising illicit intercourse with a muscular torero, evidently a blackguard. He urged me to do likewise, to misbehave, to sin with officers of the garrison. He implored me to soil his letter in an unspeakable manner, to chastise him as he richly deserves, to bestride and ride him, to give him a most vicious horsewhipping. (15.1058–73 / 467)

The comic force of Mrs. Mervyn Talboys depends on the way her language—a brilliant piecework of high-toned social euphemism, obscene innuendo, and clichés of female scolding—directs laughter in many directions at once. While extravagantly compounding the evidence of Bloom's perversions, Mrs. Mervyn Talboys also stands forth as one of the many caricatures of Outraged Female Decency in "Circe," figures through whom Joyce makes fun of the female penchant for mixing righteousness with crude vanity, protests of violated purity with little giveaway signs of lascivious excitement. Ellmann suggests that Joyce may have been taking a bit of comic revenge against his patroness (and noted horsewoman) Mrs. McCormick, who had wanted to send him off to Jung for treatment in 1919.[48] Whatever Joyce's private jokes (there are others in the passage), the caricature also in part belongs to Bloom's own satiric perception of haughty women and other social pretenders in the interior monologues, a perception which he uses defensively, if you will, but with a humor that joins him in spirit to Joyce, his creator.

Joyce's new dramatic characters come together in "Circe" as comic indictments of the culture that has surrounded Bloom in so many configurations from the beginning. At some points, Joyce seems to be dramatizing how a culture exists internalized (and then projected) by the individual psyche: Bloom encounters, in the forms of his individual shame, versions of what the culture as a whole pronounces shameful. But Bloom's oddly ill-fitting place all along, just at the edge of social convention, gives Joyce comic opportunities for suddenly reversing the processes of exposure and judgment in "Circe." Honourable Women, and also clichés of hypocritical respectability, are as much the target of Joyce's wit in the Mrs. Mervyn Talboys sketch as Bloom's secret obscenities. Moreover, since the social code of decency according to which Bloom is being charged in "Circe" holds sway most rigidly *outside* his mind, this code is subjected to comic exposure according to a conception of the humanly natural partially embodied in Bloom himself.[49]

In his daytime experience Bloom copes with pressures toward shame largely by a deflating skeptical humor. Goldberg's view of Bloom's positive enactment of critical values is pertinent here, though still only up to a point. While Bloom has been the quickest of any character in *Ulysses* to inspect all appearances of the human for cracks—even the classical statues in the museum—Bloom cannot exert real force against the repressiveness of the culture. His insights are too undiscriminating and transient, while his allegiance to the natural shows itself only in mild jokes and little acts that he believes to be secret. In "Circe" Bloom is at first more defenseless than usual against the shaming forces in the culture and in himself, and then, after his button snaps, more fantastically self-assertive. His bold challenges to the Nymph who embodies all the many forms of repressive prudery in the culture succeeds in cracking her plaster form with a decisiveness as implausible as any event in Nighttown. Meanwhile Joyce uses the plot of Bloom's encounter with his shames as a mold within which to recast—and more effectively shatter—the plaster idols of culture that Bloom will continue to cope with in his resourceful but compromising way.

While thus partially reaffirming Bloom's humor as a value, Joyce enacts through comedy a freedom so much more active than Bloom's that it seems different in kind as well as degree. According to Freud, humor is distinguishable from comedy by its inclusion of more consciousness of distress: humor is "a means of obtaining pleasure in spite of the distressing affects that interfere with it."[50] In the comic, Freud suggests, the pleasure is more primitive; an object conspicuously unlike ourselves reevokes the helplessness of infancy, especially the infant's incomplete control of bodily functions and his lack of any just sense of proportion. Comedy is thus pleasurable because it allows us to enjoy a distance from infantile helplessness, even while we recognize ourselves in it with secret pleasure as well as shame. While Freud values the psychological satisfaction of all forms of humor and comedy, he ranks humor as a higher achievement of psychological organization because it allows more presence to the feelings that it dispels.

In the comedy of Nighttown, Joyce not only reaches above Bloom's intellectual range for witty allusion, wordplay, and plot device, but also goes below Bloom's characteristic humor to a mode of comedy at once more primitive and more radically liberating. In the interior monologues Bloom shows no taste for comic extravagance; his humor is all in the same leveling, deflating key. It has the power to offer him passing relief and moderate entertainment in the course of his solitary wanderings, but not the great release of energy that Joyce's inflations and distortions make possible. In Nighttown, Bloom himself becomes a comic figure in Freud's sense—like a baby, he is the helpless object of female scolding and an infinitely malleable physical creature. But he is in no position to enjoy the comedy. Laughter belongs to Bloom's experience in this episode only as the projected form of his shame, turned back against the self in degrading ridicule. The nasty laughter of the apparitions punctuates the episode's sequences of accusation, trial, and punishment; it loudly enacts the reproachful malice that Bergson detects in all comic pleasure, but which Joyce objectifies, as if to free us as spectators from the rigid mechanisms of ridicule that enclose the figures within the phantasmagoria as within the actual social world.

The whores and Lynch, for example, laugh raucously at the climax of Bloom's degradation as cuckold when, by Boylan's invitation, he witnesses the noisy and acrobatic copulation of Molly and her lover: "Ho ho! Ha ha! Hee hee! . . . Hu hu hu hu hu!" (15.3819–20 / 567). We too laugh at the ludicrous copulation scene, and we also laugh at the laughing whores. The reader may experience a moment of tension in the need to differentiate his amusement from the malicious "Ho ho" of the apparitions; but the generous laughter induced by the whole of the episode does make this differentiation possible. Meanwhile there is no uncertainty about Bloom's exclusion from any form of comic response. His pathos itself becomes mildly comic as he speaks up in somewhat tattered dignity: "BLOOM (*smiles yellowly at the three whores*) When will I hear the joke?" (15.3831 / 568).

None of the forms of Bloom in "Circe" hears any of the jokes, nor would Bloom—either before or after Nighttown—be likely to enjoy them if he did. Bloom's humor is a resource for survival and even for pleasure amid oppressive realities, but Joyce invites the reader to a fuller, more active freedom than Bloom can attain. The meaning of this freedom peculiarly overflows the internal design of *Ulysses* from the fact that, at the very time of composition, earlier portions of the book were being attacked in real courts by real prosecutors in much the same terms as Bloom is attacked by the upholders of public decency within the scene. Ellmann's report of the fiasco of one witness who attempted "tortuously" to defend "Nausicaa" in terms of Freud suggests, however, one joke that Joyce enjoyed even at the expense of his own supporters—the joke of how the distinction between accusation and defense vanishes in the murky area of up-to-date psychological theory.[51]

In the courtrooms of "Circe," the prosecution of character mixes moral and psychological language in a way that effaces the distinction between sin and psychopathology. Thus Alexander J. Dowie, Scotch-Australian-American evangelist, charges Bloom with "infantile debauchery, recalling the cities of the plain" (15.1756 / 492). And later, Bello enacts a ludicrous part combining theatrical impresario, hanging judge, and diagnostician. After calling forth the chorus of Bloom's "SINS OF THE PAST," Bello anounces, with officious psychological authority, that Bloom's worst sin of all is his perverse desire for all his trials and punishments: "What you longed for has come to pass" (15.2964 / 535). Then she hands Bloom his "punishment frock." Thus at the same time that the permutations of Bloom's masochistic psychology become a vivid spectacle, Joyce ridicules the punitive theatricality of psychopathological interpretation itself.

Joyce goes further to dramatize, as a related joke, that ostensible defense of character in psychological terms is as damaging as any prosecution. In one courtroom scene a call *"from the presstable"* echoes Buck Mulligan's first crude demand in "Telemachus" that Stephen "cough up" his hidden troubles. In "Circe" Professor MacHugh calls out to Bloom: "Cough it up, man. Get it out in bits" (15.928 / 462), suggesting some fundamentally emetic quality to psychological interrogation, at the same time that the colloquial phrase of bullying links social to new "professional" forms of intrusiveness. Amid uproars and catcalls, Bloom's defense is inaudible. He is then represented by J. J. O'Molloy, *"speaking with a voice of pained protest."* Like Dr. Malachi Mulligan later, what O'Molloy produces on behalf of his client is a hilariously damaging indictment under the guise of a defense. Mixed in with simultaneous denial and admission to the crime (or noncrime, "the trumped up misdemeanour"), there appears in O'Molloy's speech appeal to virtually every known psychological explanation for aberration: heredity, hallucination, cultural dislocation, atavism, physical wreckage (and also shipwreckage), somnambulism, and simple craziness—"Not all there, in fact." Bloom meekly supports his defense by promptly turning into a vaudeville version of a Mongolian idiot, *"apologetic toes turned in . . . and with a shrug of oriental obeisance."* The howls of the courtroom audience, along with the degradation of Bloom's posture and Chinese-nonsense speech, display the dubious solace to be gleaned from a defense to any charge on psychological grounds!

Psychological categories of diagnosis are shown in "Circe" to clothe the human figure in costumes that are just as humiliating (and just as ludicrous) as those of the psychic depths they supposedly illuminate. And if the howling courtroom audience is no better than a "pack of curs and laughing hyenas," the figure of Bloom in the role of being "not all there" shows equally bestial features, being *"pigeonbreasted"* with *"tiny mole's eyes."* Not the least of the temptations toward bestiality in "Circe" comes from the terms of the diagnoses proposed with equal nonsensical assurance by Bloom's defenders and accusers alike. Dr. Malachi Mulligan has discovered (in addition to symptoms like "chronic exhibitionism," latent "ambidexterity," a "family complex," and "metal teeth") an addiction in Bloom to self-abuse. But perhaps the worst self-abuse in "Circe" is one that the Bloom we have seen earlier does not practice, that is, the masochism of seeing the self as a "wreck." While building into the Bloomian spectacles of "Circe" a rich portrayal of a masochistic psychology, Joyce simultaneously converts the whole idea of such a psychopathology into another self-abasing fantasy. As an especially dehumanizing vision of the self, the language of psychological categorization is no more authoritative and rather more degrading than other vocabularies of vision and judgment.

The idea of Bloom's ordeal as a kind of psychoanalysis, accidental or otherwise, cannot really survive all this comic play. Even at the simplest level of narrative sequence, there is no necessity to see Bloom's eventual practical aid to Stephen as the consequence of psychic purgation. All Joyce shows is that, at the end of the episode and twice in the middle, Bloom reorganizes into a single personality so as to act with some poise and practical purpose. Bloom succeeds, as he did more than once earlier in the day, in turning his attention outward, to take note of something other than himself. In the brothel it is Stephen's mounting crisis that finally catches hold of his attention and restores his poise.

At the beginning of "Circe" a fantastical version of Bloom's immigrant father berates in broken English a dirty form of the young Bloom: "Nice spectacles for your poor mother!" (15.279 / 438). At the end, Bloom's dirty "spectacles" are displaced by the practical demands of Stephen's need. "Look," Bloom says, approaching Stephen as if to recall the younger man to common sense. And then, since he is ignored, he begins again, "I say, look." This "look" marks the turn away from psychological spectacles and back to the Bloomian idiom of colloquial sense and practical judgment. The gesture of helping requires no purgation of psychic demons on Bloom's part. What is brilliantly new is the radically different scale and proportion of a pattern already seen earlier in the book. The world of grandiose and menacing fantasy is here given a boundless stage, while outer objects have to become vastly more striking before they catch Bloom's attention. But most significantly, our judgment of this pattern changes through the action of Joyce's own comic spectacles. Liberated by the end from any further pressure to excavate Bloom's psychic depths, the reader can recognize that Bloom needs no heroic purgation to succeed in helping Stephen in Nighttown. Bloom survives as the decent, solicitous, relatively sane man he has been all day. At the same time, the confusion of motive and of understanding suggested by his misinterpretation of Stephen's speech and by his final grandiose vision of Rudy also marks the limits of his power and freedom. He remains, at the end of "Circe" as before, bound to see all his experience through the workable but cracked and not perfectly clean lens of his habitual "spectacles."

Stephen Dedalus also survives in Nighttown, even more unambiguously the same as he was, since he retains throughout the episode his daytime shape of character, only thrown off balance by the setting and by drink. In Stephen's case, however, the need for a purgation not easily achieved is made to seem pressing, consciously so to Stephen himself: "But in here it is I must kill the priest and the king" (15.4436 / 589). Biddy the Clap is impressed by the "marked refinement of phraseology" in Stephen's declaration, and Cunty Kate agrees: "Indeed, yes. And at the same time with such apposite trenchancy" (15.4445 / 590).

Stephen's grand sentence has impressed some of Joyce's commentators, too, as a trenchant statement of Joyce's own pacificistic valuing of mental over physical strife, and also of the faith in heroic feats of mental liberation dramatized in the episode of "Circe" as a whole.[52] Yet the fact that Stephen himself accomplishes no liberating action in Nighttown (his violent gesture crushes only the paper and the chimney of the brothel lamp) signifies that he is unready in more than one way for true liberating action of mind. Indeed, the comedy of Nighttown calls into question

Stephen's whole conception of a mental freedom to be achieved by means of aggressive rejection, a conception that has governed Stephen's mind as well as behavior from the novel's beginning.

Although Stephen shows himself in Nighttown to be the very opposite of the Bloomian hangdog masochist, his assertiveness is no more liberating than Bloom's meekness. In response to the hallucinated appearance of his mother's ghost, Stephen defiantly rejects her reproaches and her tenderness, too: *"Ah non, par exemple!* The intellectual imagination! With me all or not at all. *Non serviam!"* (15.4227–28 / 582). This polyglot self-assertion is in the character of Stephen's sayings of the whole day, and there is a certain intellectual grandeur to his defiance of the ghoulish apparition through the medium of heroic phrases from the literary tradition. Yet the self-quotation of his own futile earlier heroics against the ghost, in the opening tower scene, limits the impressiveness of his performance here. Even more explicitly than before, his high-toned defiance is shown not to be purgative; the stage directions of the Circean drama make clear how postures of heroic resistance threaten to freeze Stephen in a paralysis indistinguishable from that of his most contemptible and pathetic fellow citizens: "(*strangled with rage, his features drawn grey and old*) Shite!" (15.4222 / 582).

Stephen maintains an aggressive isolation through "Circe" that differs not only from Bloom's disorganized helplessness, but (even more significantly) from the masterful transformation of shame and aggression into comedy exemplified by Joyce's own art. While Joyce gives exuberant presence in Nighttown to every variety of vice and folly, Stephen is still caught in clever one-liners: "Will someone tell me where I am least likely to meet these necessary evils?" (15.4575 / 595) This is the same witty, arrogant spirit whose sayings impressed Haines in the morning. Joyce, to be sure, in part admires these sayings; they come from his wit as much as does Bloom's deflating, tolerant humor. But Joyce, in his capacity for so many kinds of wit, humor, and comedy, also exposes the self-imprisonment of a spirit armored rigidly, even when drunk, in tight, grim sayings of rejection.

None of the forces identified as oppressive in "Circe"—be it priest or king, nymph or mother, faithless wife or hangdog self—is killed by Joyce's comic action, but their tyrannical power is greatly diminished. Earlier, when Stephen had a rare moment of compassionate self-recognition with the shamed schoolboy Sargent, he saw the internal suffering inflicted by the tyrannical secret self: "Secrets, silent, stony sit in the dark palaces of both our hearts: secrets weary of their tyranny: tyrants, willing to be dethroned" (2.170–71 / 28). The comic art of "Circe" suggests that freedom and power to dethrone dark secrets come not through defiance, nor even through such sorrowing compassion as Stephen can momentarily feel for a Sargent (or for his mother or sister). The interior monologues build up our sense of the potential force of these reservoirs of feeling, but "Circe" radically shifts the ground of judgment by suggesting that liberation from dark tyrannical secrets comes most effectively from the action of a comedy that Stephen (like the culture around him) hardly knows how to appreciate. Stephen confirms the power of his secrets over him by the costumed weariness of his bitter melancholy. Bloom's humorous endurance of his own secrets seems less disabling, in the scales of judgment constructed by *Ulysses*. But Joyce's comedy opens up a freedom from both psychic and social tyrants beyond the reach of either character as portrayed within the book. Nor does Joyce give allegiance to the promises of freedom attached to old or new cults of wisdom, with their solemn ritualized probing of dark secrets. "You ought to see yourself" becomes in Nighttown a joke on all orthodox moral, religious, social, and even psychoanalytic injunctions to face the dirty depths. At the same time, Joyce characteristically gives discredited conventional language new vitality and meaning. The comic spectacle of psychic depth in Nighttown invites the reader, if not the characters, to see the human self freely through laughter rather than through any heroic or painful ordeal.

Interpretations of "Circe" that emphasize the "terrifying" nightmare world of guilts, egotisms, and sexual inclinations that Joyce encourages us to "face" and "endure," lose touch with the action of the comedy almost as much as do interpretations that deny any significant human value at all to Joyce's verbal extravaganza.[53] While Bloom and Stephen may be said merely to endure Nighttown, Joyce's comic energy goes beyond endurance, and the laughter he generates not so much faces as outfaces what might otherwise be terrifying, if it were not so deeply entangled with the harmless and the absurd. Thus Joyce in a sense tames the entire fearsome idea of psychic depth at the same time that he makes a story out of its exploration. While the hallucinatory drama of Nighttown exposes the bizarre substructure of character evaded by the surface movement of consciousness, Joyce refuses to make either palace or church in this hidden depth. His comedy not only dethrones old tyrants, but displays his irreverent freedom from even the most up-to-date new ones.

The Shelter from Fact in "Eumaeus"

Of the three final episodes in *Ulysses,* I pick "Eumaeus" to write about here. I think it is one of the funniest though least appreciated chapters in the book and its relative failure to please seems explicable in terms of the comic freedom—obvious and yet so disorienting—in "Circe," the chapter just before it. In one view of Joyce's design, "Eumaeus" belongs to the homeward movement of the book, completed by "Ithaca" and "Penelope." In another view, "Circe" and "Eumaeus" form a pair.[54] Bloom picks Stephen up from the gutter of Nighttown and takes him to the cabman's shelter for a resuscitating beverage; but there is nothing palatable to be had in the temperance parlor. After some desultory words with each other and some listening to the talk of the other run-down types also taking shelter there, Bloom decides they would do well to "clear out," and they leave for Bloom's house. The extravagant burlesque of psychic depth in Nighttown has given place to an extravagant travesty of social shelter from every kind of depth. "Circe" and "Eumaeus" together display the world of *Ulysses* in more-than-life-size degradation: there is not only a degraded Bloom and a dilapidated Stephen, but the the tawdriness of common life more generally—in its secret depths and on its public surface. Yet in both episodes Joyce not only exposes tawdriness but lifts us past conventional judgments by the comic vitality he gives to words and things that might otherwise be more simply repellent.

In contrast to the general acclaim for "Circe," however, response to "Eumaeus" has been remarkably half-hearted. Edmund Wilson calls it "an interminable letdown."[55] Arnold Goldman objects that it is "superficial": "and the manner of it only exposes its own inability to encompass the matter."[56] Even those who accept in principle Joyce's design in the later chapters to reformulate many times an essentially meager amount of matter, tend to take the style of "Eumaeus" as nothing more than tired and murky.[57] The running on of an ineffectual verbal machinery seems to correspond only too obviously to the anticlimactic fact that nothing interesting and important happens between Bloom and Stephen when they finally get together. The richer ambiguity of even this point in "Ithaca" adds to the impression of gratuitous excess in "Eumaeus." At one moment within the episode, Bloom rather wearily reflects upon "there being more languages to start with than were absolutely necessary" (16.352 / 622). To many, "Eumaeus" itself has seemed one of the least absolutely necessary chapters in Joyce's many-chaptered book. A sheer proliferation of contemptible commonplace seems to issue forth here, as if Joyce merely set out to show how much more language than necessary there is, even within the single vernacular of English, and even within the apparently closed field of common idiom and cliché. "He could spin those yarns for hours on end all night long and lie like old boots," Bloom remarks to Stephen about the sailor in the shelter (16.824 / 635). The same could be said about Bloom's own mental yarns of conjecture and fantasy in the scene, and even about Joyce's whole production of language in the chapter.

Much of the language in "Eumaeus" follows Bloom's ineffectual effort to interpret Stephen and also the sailor who audibly dominates the scene—Murphy, if that is his true name. The indeterminate quality of the evidence, together with the inadequacy of the language available for such interpretation, utterly defeats Bloom's enterprise: "And when all was said and done the lies a fellow told about himself couldn't probably hold a proverbial candle to the wholesale whoppers other fellows coined about him" (16.845–47 / 636). The skeptical thought is Bloom's, strung out in the wobbly procession of clichés that constitutes the chapter's style. But the tone of somewhat strained tolerance corresponds to the sentiments of many readers, too, near the end of a book where the distinction between fact and fabrication, precious truth and "wholesale whoppers," has become ever harder to establish, while still seeming to matter for the achievement of moral and intellectual balance. It is precisely this sense of language as at once indeterminate (in relation to truth) and fixed (in reproducible formulae) that draws French poststructuralists to *Ulysses* as a whole. Yet the same combination alienates many English-language readers from chapters like "Eumaeus," where the excessive demonstration of futility in language seems to be all the matter there is.

Both French fascination and English impatience with the verbal excess in "Eumaeus" tend to discount the equally crucial contrary effect of a certain few (mainly unappetising) facts, conspicuous even through the murkiness of such a place. The unmistakable impoverishment of things assumes in itself the status of intractable fact in the cabman's shelter: not only the poor quality of the undrinkable coffee and the uneatable roll, but the human dilapidation of the individual characters and of the collective society, too. Moreover, by this point in *Ulysses* certain more universal conditions of life—isolation, loss, disappointment—have also acquired, through their reappearance in so many verbal reformulations, the ineluctability of fact. If we think of a fact as a reality that cannot be denied, even though it may not be understood, the elemental shape of human life in general has in this book taken on the quality of fact, as will be reformulated again in yet other terms in "Ithaca": "the fact of vital growth, through convulsions of metamorphosis, from infancy through maturity to decay" (17.1005–6 / 697).

Although the facts of life in *Ulysses* may be impenetrable, as to deep cause or meaning, they are also as undissolvable as the sailor's spit plug of tobacco, the object in "Eumaeus" that Bloom identifies with most confidence. As in "Circe," where a few rather squalid psychic facts underlie all the spectacles, in "Eumaeus" a few hard and thick social facts both generate and show through the wholesale display of unnecessary language. There are not very many facts, but the ones there are constitute an even comically recalcitrant substratum of reality that language neither hides nor transcends. What language does—what Joyce makes even clichéd language do—is act in relation to fact. The action of language shapes and reshapes fact, like the sailor chewing over his plug of tobacco for a very long time, before finally spitting it out. To call the undrinkable coffee "a boiling swimming cup of a choice concoction labelled coffee," in no way dissolves the reality of this object, for which the word "coffee" is already a euphemism. There is nothing indeterminate about the awfulness of this "untastable apology for a cup of coffee," "the offending beverage," "what was temporarily supposed to be called coffee." Even Bloom spits out the repellent truth of the object when he finally concedes to Stephen, "You can't drink that stuff" (16.1646 / 658). Joyce's elaborate verbal play all along has in no way disguised the true quality of the "stuff" in the cabman's shelter; it is indeed its unnamable sordidness that the euphemisms and circumlocutions take as their starting point.

The comedy of "Eumaeus" is built upon an ambiguous parallel—at once analogy and contrast—between the squalid material stuff of the world and the stale if not also squalid stuff of language. The offending style of the chapter is also a choice concoction made out of miserable ingredients; it is not a satisfactory narrative style, only something that temporarily substitutes for a palatable style. But whereas the mug of nauseous liquid in the shelter can hardly be raised from the brown puddle it has leaked out on the table, the verbal stuff of "Eumaeus" turns uncannily bright, sharp, and mobile through the action of Joyce's comic art. The stuff of language, therefore, is at once a version of squalid fact and, in the medium of Joyce's art, a source of freedom and protection from it. As in "Circe," Joyce's verbal inventiveness works to display the base quality of many words as well as things, while refusing to grant mere "stuff" power to paralyze the spirit.

There is a moment in "Eumaeus" when Bloom, in deferential inquiry into Stephen's Catholicism, ventures to characterize "the soul" in terms that he, a non-Catholic, might accept: "the brainpower as such, as distinct from any outside object, the table, let us say, that cup" (16.749–50 / 633). Bloom cannot take the point further; it is loosely connected in his mind to admiration for the invention of X rays. In context, the whole point evaporates in the "mystical finesse" of Stephen's doctrinal doubletalk. For the reader, however, the point is pivotal: in "Eumaeus," brainpower operates very little like an X ray; the pleasure of the writing is instead posited on comic acceptance of a reality that no mental and verbal activity has power to penetrate. And in another sense, there is no need for X-ray vision in this place where the essential *quality* of things is only too apparent. Joyce thus irreverently sets aside most theories of language as an instrument of insight, including even his own earlier secularized idea of the "epiphany."[58] Instead of capturing a "sudden spiritual manifestation" of reality, as Joyce described the epiphany in *Stephen Hero,* language in "Eumaeus" registers only pseudorevelations or drawn-out, inconclusive conjecture. "Soul" or "brainpower" in language appears as an action of inventive construction on the surface of a reality that clearly fares better when viewed away from any sudden shafts of light. Joyce amuses us because his own inventiveness so freely accepts, as a basic condition of brainpower, the discrepancy between a shabby as well as opaque reality and the refreshing, if not exactly fresh, verbal forms that the human spirit can muster.

I am suggesting here a quality of comic affirmation that makes for continuing high spirit even amid the most meager things. The quality of this Joycean affirmation is very different, however, from the more easily understandable high (or low) spirits of D. H. Lawrence. At least to an English-language reader, Lawrence seems more recognizable in his verbal inventiveness, because he adheres to intelligent faith in "full contact" between himself as perceiver and the true nature of outside objects, whether persons or things. That faith underlies Lawrence's probing narrative explorations and also his hatreds and enthusiasms. In *Sea and Sardinia,* I have observed, Lawrence's pleasure rests on the conviction that his activity of language only half-creates the vitality of, say, a pig-carrier or an abandoned wife on a train platform. For Lawrence, bits of reality, even dingy babies on a dustheap in Australia, have their own momentaneous life, which in a sense tests the responsive capacities of the observer. It is the artist's power to re-create that life in his language; he translates it, so to speak—gives it language if it is not verbal (as is often the case), or gives it English expression if it is foreign. The reader is fully aware of Lawrence as the maker of the language—sometimes portentous, sometimes playful, as when he names the bus driver in Sardinia Hamlet or Rochester. But even such fantastical names are not dissociated in Lawrence from the fundamental action of intelligent perception. They purport to register some penetrable truth of moral and psychological reality in the object: the virginal remoteness of Artemis in the look of modern young women at the start of *Women in Love;* the glamour of a storybook hero discernible at the wheel of a Sardinian bus.

Joyce's play on proliferating names in "Eumaeus" proposes a very different relationship between verbal inventiveness and the reality of things. Take the sailor, for example, variously called Murphy, Shipahoy, Sinbad, globetrotter, and the Ancient Mariner. None of these more or less generic names for "sailor" is rooted in anyone's particular perception of this character, if such a drowsy, run-down specimen of a sailor can even be said to have a character. In contrast to Lawrence's imaginative perceptions of living forms, Joyce shows a verbal inventiveness that works in the face of virtually no cooperation from objects which in themselves are barely suggestive of distinctive life at all. The sum effect of Joyce's multiple naming of the sailor is to convince us that his true name matters very little. The figure is a dilapidated version of the genus sailor, a type diverting to contemplate partly because he has appeared under so many names and with so many entertaining variations in familiar life, in this book, and in the long history of human story, poem, and song.

The art of "Eumaeus," in Joyce's official schema, aptly labels the busy verbal movement over uninviting depths by the term "navigation." Epic and romantic associations to travel are undercut as well as evoked. The superficial exoticism of Murphy's stories does not disguise the stronger impression that the cabman's shelter offers in hardly new form even depressingly familiar realities. The colloquial metaphors of travel ("drift," "train of thought") point to the navigating motion of minds (especially Bloom's) wherever they are in Joyce's world. In the cabman's shelter Bloom's mind stays even closer than elsewhere to his central preoccupations, and Stephen's mind hardly budges at all. Stephen still carries, in his by now sparsely furnished brain, a harsh picture of his fatherless house, where the weak tea and oatmeal-water milk are about as unpalatable as the "socalled" roll and coffee of the shelter. When Bloom asks Stephen, "but why did you leave your father's house?" (in another quotation of the cliché from *Leah the Forsaken*), Stephen mentally "repictures" the "family hearth," where it is precisely the missing father that gives the final touch of meanness to the scene (16.267–70 / 620). For Stephen, the picture is nothing new: he has been handling it in his mind all day. Meanwhile Bloom eventually takes out a faded photo of Molly, "her fleshy charms on evidence in an open fashion" (16.1428 / 652). Murphy also has his pictures: a well-fingered postcard of naked savage women, the large tattoo on his chest, and his yarns. And the other strays and waifs eventually come round to yet another go at Ireland's favorite and familiar domestic pictures of woe and glory: the story of Parnell's fall, and the prophecy of England's certain ruin-to-come.

Since the only alternative to home offered by the shelter seems more degraded replications of already poor "originals," the mystery may be what keeps anyone hanging around in a public place of so little promise. Bloom, at least, has in his home a more comfortable social shelter than the squalid temperance parlor, but he is in no hurry to get there. From the beginning of the book, Bloom is as inveterate a frequenter of public places as any Dubliner. In "Eumaeus" he even imagines how the entire public transport system might be rearranged to encourage recreative travel for his fellow citizens, "instead of being always and ever cooped up since my old stick-in-the-mud took me for a wife" (16.542–44 / 627). The "stick-in-the-mud" echo of "Circe," together with other details, points toward some combination of sexual and social ineffectuality as the motivation for seeking public shelter. Thus the sailor Murphy—seven years gone from "his own true wife"—dawdles telling stories in the shelter, while the Keeper, "Skin-the-Goat, Fitzharris" (if that is who it is), appears to be hiding out because of his peripheral role as one of the "Invincibles" in the Phoenix Park murder.

Just as the psychic underworld produces variations on a few familiar patterns of fantasy, the lowest version of social refuge in *Ulysses* reflects in seamier form patterns of sought-for diversion already seen elsewhere in this world. Although one never gets far from the already known in *Ulysses*—neither far out nor in deep—the need for diversion is one of the clearest facts of the human condition portrayed. In the writing of the book, it is Joyce's brilliant capacity to play unending variations on the familiar which makes for so much of the reader's diversion. The colloquialism "stick in the mud," for example, was already comically surprising in "Circe" as a sexual pun; when the familiar phrase shows up again in "Eumaeus" as part of Bloom's fantasy of civic reform, not only the interpretable connections but also the unpredicted freshness of the new appearance makes for pleasure. In relation to language as well as experience, there seems no limit in Joyce to the number of new constructions that can be made out of pieces which offer very little new in themselves. And this combination of recurrence and fresh variation makes the entire idea of ineluctable reality into a kind of joke in *Ulysses*—a source of amusement rather than sorrow.

In "Eumaeus," as in "Circe," Bloom does not hear this or any other joke. If the reader is also left bewildered, perhaps that is because we are likely to start here from a position much closer than elsewhere to Bloom's hopes and disappointments, especially about what language ought to but does not accomplish. Bloom by and large accepts both the limitations and the unpredictability of reality—with prudent qualifications, such as his thought that public food (like public sex) ought to be medically inspected and subject to licensing. Similarly, he tolerates whoppers in the language of public talk. But he is too scrupulous, too practical, too decent, finally, to take pleasure in any of the debased variations on familiar things found in the rigmaroles of the shelter. While Bloom's own language, from the beginning of the book, can hardly sustain a very strict testing for original truth, we have seen that Bloom looks to language for the authoritative expression of some true wisdom or passion. "Being of a sceptical bias," he tends to deflate the pretensions in most of what he hears, while still reserving admiration for language he does not quite understand, like literary quotation or, in "Eumaeus," the Italian of the ice-cream vendors. Insofar as Bloom grasps Stephen's arrogant words in the shelter, he is troubled, dismayed, poignantly eager to see himself under some misapprehension. He can take no pleasure in the seemingly useless sayings produced by Stephen between yawns and vacant stares, as for example "Count me out" (in response to Bloom's advice about work) and "But I suspect . . . that Ireland must be important because it belongs to me" (as a rejection of Bloom's reassurance that thinkers as well as peasants belong to Ireland) (16.1148–65 / 644–45). Bloom is even more impatient with the "surplus steam" of the patriotic Irish whoppers. He does not value whoppers for sheer diversion. In the shelter he keeps trying to go through language to some truth that will be extenuating (for Stephen) or incriminating (for the others). He tolerates the prevalence of falsehood as an allowable human weakness, but hardly one to applaud (except, of course, on the legitimate and commercially successful stage).

Joyce, however, shows all the characters in "Eumaeus," including Bloom, going through their routines on whatever stage is at hand, however commercially unsuccessful. And if we follow Joyce's lead, our freedom will come from the slightly illegitimate fun generated by these unproductive productions. Bloom's commitment to the ascertaining of deeper truth in the episode becomes one of his endearing yet mockable virtues. All through "Eumaeus" Joyce shows Bloom "Sherlockholmesing" the human situation of the shelter. He has many more and less plausible hypotheses, opinions, analogies, and other constructions of what he wants to call "the facts." The only too apparent facts of squalor and dilapidation fail to satisfy his quest for further understanding, deeper interpretation. The only decisive insight he achieves appears in his answer to Stephen's query about the reason for chairs in pubs and restaurants being turned up on tables at night: "To which impromptu the neverfailing Bloom replied without a moment's hesitation, saying straight off:—To sweep the floor in the morning" (16.1711–13 / 660). As an emblem of what the mind can attain—drawing on logic, common sense, and experience—this Bloomian inspiration sets a rather sharp limit to human possibility. It is also a waste, for Stephen made the query only out of some confused desire "to be original on the spur of the moment," and there is no sign that he cares (or should care) about the answer.

One needs to tilt the proverbial candle a bit to see that in "Eumaeus" the comic appeal of "yarns," "genuine forgeries," and "wholesale whoppers" (even the juiciness of such phrases themselves) amounts to a Joycean reformulation of what language is worth, not only the grossly degraded language of the episode, but all language as used as a kind of public shelter against the silent buffetings of both cosmic and domestic fact. The mendacity of sailors, in this light, is not a vice peculiar to them; Murphy, the sailor, along with the rest of this "decidedly miscellaneous collection of waifs and strays and other nondescript specimens of the genus *homo*" (16.327–28 / 621), is squalid but still representative. Bloom's fantasy of writing up the place as "a miniature cameo of the world we live in" is not entirely wrongheaded. Bloom's trouble, or at least one of his incapacities compared to Joyce, comes from his (hardly idiosyncratic) reluctance to let go of the expectation that his account should directly represent the truth of the situation. Bloom here aspires to a journalistic version of truth in language, as seen in the title for the piece he imagines writing for a newspaper: "*My Experiences,* let us say, *in a Cabman's Shelter*" (16.1231 / 647). One joke of Bloom's literary fantasy hinges on Joyce's way of giving Bloom so little experience in this miserable place; a further, more significant joke turns on the futility of Bloom's decent but merely conventional understanding of what language can do to give an account of experience which amounts to so little. The paucity of experience in the cabman's shelter, like the mendacity of sailors and the absence of palatable food and drink, may be the very truth that needs telling. But an art beyond Bloom's is necessary to picture this sorely reduced reality in words.

Joyce invites us to a quite un-Bloomian engagement in the huge production of "genuine forgeries" which he, along with all the characters in the shelter, devises in the absence of more original truths. While Bloom never ceases to be preoccupied with the futile investigation of the boundary between fact and fabrication, truth and forgery, Joyce playfully embraces the common human resources of diversion through language. Various forms of euphemism nicely exemplify the kind of verbal fabrication that Bloom himself produces but cannot fully appreciate in Joycean terms. As a signature of Bloom's social character, the euphemisms both honor and mock his impulse to "put a good face on the matter" of his whole sojourn at the shelter, as he tends to do elsewhere regarding all his experience. It is not that Bloom is deluded, but, "faultfinding being a proverbially bad hat," he tries "not to put too fine a point" on a number of the realities he encounters. Bloom does not suffer from the paralysis of perception associated with euphemism in early Joycean figures like the "Sisters" in *Dubliners*. His avoidance of naming the worst and most manifest facts of experience is part of his general strategy for how best to navigate reality without sinking into one or another form of indecency or despair. In addition, Bloom can be seen straining for a decorum suitable to conversation with the refined young man he takes Stephen to be. Bloomian euphemism takes its place in quite another design, however, as Joyce displays the creative as well as cautious impulses that the device of euphemism can serve. The multiplication of euphemism in "Eumaeus" does not at all work to avoid finding fault, but rather to show the inexhaustible resources of human language for naming (or rather, not simply naming) even the most miserable things. Euphemism, in this context, becomes one of the rhetorical signs of human spirit, ingeniously refusing to yield itself to the simple tyranny of mere stuff.

Bloom adheres to a more perceptual conception of spirit, "brainpower" (what he also calls "intelligence") (16.749 / 633). Like other intelligent observers I have noted, he wants to use his brainpower for acts of penetrating insight, worthy of a species capable of inventing X rays. Thus he persists in the culturally respectable enterprise of examining the character of Murphy, the sailor, despite the fact that a notable absence of perceptible character is one of the main facts about this unprepossessing human specimen. Bloom's enterprise of perception fails by his own standard, but the activity is not a total flop from all points of view: Bloom is shown not only baffled but also stimulated by his endeavor. He patches his few visual impressions together with each other and with the evidence of the sailor's story of murder in Trieste, calling upon a huge repertory of formulaic language to construct the incongruous bits into a human figure—all of which results in an uncannily colorful if hardly profound verbal design.

> He had been meantime taking stock of the individual in front of him and Sherlockholmesing him up ever since he clapped eyes on him. Though a wellpreserved man of no little stamina, if a trifle prone to baldness, there was something spurious in the cut of his jib that suggested a jail delivery and it required no violent stretch of imagination to associate such a weirdlooking specimen with the oakum and treadmill fraternity. He might even have done for his man supposing it was his own case he told, as people often did about others, namely, that he killed him himself and had served his four or five goodlooking years in durance vile. (16.830–38 / 635–36)

It takes no violent stretch of the imagination to note the paltriness of evidence which Bloom has to work with for the construction of his man. The detail of baldness and the summary label, "weirdlooking," oddly echo the language used to construct Bloom's own character in "Circe": the echo partly suggests the meager sameness of the signs on which all constructions of character are made, and partly points to the projective activity which makes up so much of so-called perception (a point even Bloom knows about from popular psychology). Bloom may be identifying as attributes of the sailor details that belong to his own case. That is another of the jokes in "Eumaeus" that Bloom does not hear. The main joke, however, is that the simple, indisputable fact of the sailor's squalor hardly requires "Sherlockholmesing." It is only that Bloom, as a "student of the human soul," wants to see more. For us, the very impossibility of any further "flood of light" underlies the comedy. Without a chance of accomplishing any true detection, Bloom's activity of "taking stock" becomes the occasion for his producing a big verbal event full of energetic motions and a huge flow of words. The event is diverting precisely because it is superabundant, so far in excess of what the elementary and paltry facts require.

For many readers, this comedy of nonperception in "Eumaeus" is upsetting because it so conspicuously diminishes Bloom's earlier stature as a not inconsiderable observer of human character. It is this debasement that bothers S. L. Goldberg when he objects to how Joyce absorbs Bloom into the anonymous emptiness of cliché in "Eumaeus," as if "to deny more than has been *shown* to be there."[59] One needs to be less committed than Goldberg to the virtue of intelligent perception to allow that there may be gain as well as loss in Joyce's radical redesigning of elements presented earlier with admittedly different effect.

What has been lost is clear enough. In the interior monologues Bloom was allowed many small accomplishments of perception, almost to the point of exemplifying the virtue of sympathetic imagination. When he responds to Simon Dedalus on the ride to the cemetery, for example, Bloom's language shows how astute observation can be enlarged by projective identification—not in any great moral or intellectual feat, to be sure, but as part of the ongoing life of decent, intelligent consciousness: "Noisy selfwilled man. Full of his son. He is right. Something to hand on. If little Rudy had lived. See him grow up. Hear his voice in the house. Walking beside Molly in an Eaton suit. My son. Me in his eyes" (6.74–76/ 89). Colloquial idiom here ("Full of his son," "Something to hand on") belongs to a mind that recognizes the humanity others have in common with him, even those he does not especially like. It is, of course, only a short step between the reverie of Rudy in an Eton suit and the more full-blown whoppers of hallucination and fantasy in both "Circe" and "Eumaeus." At this and other key moments in the interior monologues, however, the punctuated brevity of colloquial idiom holds this excursive flow of mind and language in check. Rhythm and syntax enforce the impression of discrete though intimately related mental acts: observation, judgment, projection, personal reverie. Moreover, Bloom's generous perception gains stature from our own multiple perspectives: we have just heard the "noisy selfwilled" voice of Simon Dedalus for ourselves in the scene, as well as Stephen's earlier, more bitter renditions of it. Bloom's tolerance sets a contrasting, more mature standard of perceptive, intelligent response to human character. In "Eumaeus," however, Bloom's authority as perceiver collapses, while his impulse to projective or even more gratuitously inventive storytelling spreads without restraint, not even blocked by the conventional boundaries fixed in the rhythm and shape of common language. Strung out together without regard for either the sound or sense of common usage, Bloom's idioms in the act of "Sherlockholmesing" seem to run on their own bizarre tracks, making only the most minimal contact with the ostensible object of perception.

To define what is gained through this new activity of verbal construction requires a release from conventional judgement hardly less radical than what is needed for the comedy of "Circe." And yet the appeal of the comedy in both cases is also immediate, the very opposite of obscure. A good example appears in one of the passages where Bloom tries to take further stock of Stephen's evident dilapidated condition. Putting together the "facts"—Paris, the recent orgy in Nighttown, the look of father and sister in the eye, plus inferences from his baffling sentence about how Ireland "belongs" to him—Bloom comes up with an utterly banal, if not entirely untrue construction of Stephen's character. "Probably the homelife, to which Mr B attached the utmost importance had not been all that was needful or he hadn't been familiarized with the right sort of people" (16.1177—79 / 645). Slight dislocations of common usage (as in the odd placement of "familiarized") give some amusing distinctiveness to the string of clichés, but the comic vitality of Bloom's construction really comes a bit later, when a certain lack of satisfactory closure seems to propel the language further, to more fabulous images of other young men "nipped in the bud of premature decay," like "the case of O'Callaghan, for one, the half-crazy faddist . . . with his mad vagaries among whose other gay doings when rotto and making himself a nuisance to everybody all round he was in the habit of ostentatiously sporting in public a suit of brown paper (a fact)" (16.1185–89 / 645).

The case of O'Callaghan nicely exemplifies the special comic success of "Eumaeus," where entirely gratuitous images and figures suddenly come into half-crazy life. As he pops up fully formed in the midst of Bloom's search for illuminating analogy, he seems a wholesale whopper, incongruously put together out of cheap slang ("rotto"), respectable cliché ("making himself a nuisance"), and ludicrous detail (the suit of brown paper). The striking irrelevance of such a figure to Stephen's predicament makes his appearance seem a kind of mad vagary on Bloom's part, even while Bloom remains stuck with his reflexive gestures toward verification, as in the seemingly irrepressible final parenthesis "(a fact)." Turning the joke around, however, vivid figures like O'Callaghan in his brown paper suit do oddly take on an almost factual presence of their own in "Eumaeus." Whether or not he really existed, he acquires a sharp reality in the book's language. The sense of well-circulated gossip, enforced by the patchwork of cliché, frees the figure of O'Callaghan from any single creator; he does not have to bear even the burden of ambiguous attachment to Bloom's psyche, like the hallucinatory figures in "Circe." And however unnecessary O'Callaghan is to the plot of this episode, or to the ostensible activity of Bloom's effort to understand Stephen, he is a positive addition to the world of the book; fact or fabrication, he takes his place as one among many "rotto" nuisances, none of whom is absolutely necessary for any purpose, except the vital one of diverting the mind from the paltry facts of the present, actual scene.

Half-crazy specimens of common language, even apart from any distinct human figure, also become diverting living forms in "Eumaeus," however little light they contribute for other purposes. The vitality depends on the exact manipulative movements performed by Joyce on pieces of language connected to and yet set apart from the individual voices within the scene. Since Joyce himself has no voice apart from the used bits of public language that he arranges so brilliantly, his comic success discloses the latent sparkle in language valued too cheaply by the very population to which it belongs. The Joycean act of revaluation in a sense extends the heroic fantasy of the young artist in *Stephen Hero* in directions unimagined by him. Stephen dedicates himself only to redeeming the former dignity of language sullied by the marketplace. He could not envision an art where the best words might be picked right out of the street. But the value still does depend on the saving activity of the artist's arrangements. He has gone into the streets to get his material; then he constructs his saving designs at a distance, apart, in the forging-house of his own mind.

"Eumaeus" thus shows another version of the complex adjustment between intimacy and distance notable in all Joyce's formulations of the artist's relation to a language that does not naturally belong to him. The equipoise achieved in "Eumaeus," as elsewhere in *Ulysses,* has the paradoxical effect of giving back as a kind of gift to the community verbal resources that have become valuable only through the artist's bold appropriation of them. The manifest artifice of these constructions never lets us forget that an act of artistic appropriation precedes the renewal of verbal life here; yet Joyce's comedy also has the more generous effect of reinfusing life into what remain public, if publicly discredited, possessions: "a positive flow," as Raymond Williams has remarked, "of that wider human speech which had been screened and strained by the prevailing social conventions."[60] As with so many of the sayings that Stephen pronounces while hardly seeming to understand them, Joyce gives further significance to Stephen's point: in relation to language at least, the artist does make the larger community newly important, not because he belongs to it but because he has found a way to make it, at least temporarily, belong to him. In *Finnegans Wake,* as Raymond Williams among others observes, the reforging activity of the artist goes so far as to dissolve language into a universal and totally anonymous surrogate for the speech of any known language. The impostures of common English in "Eumaeus" create a more delicate if also precarious comic balance, one which crucially relies on the immediate recognizability of all the undissolved verbal elements. Their degradation remains intact, even while Joyce redeems them through the also entirely visible ingenuity of his own rigmaroles. This same double effect of ridicule and redemption extends to the human figures also. While each named figure in the chapter is only the nominal source of the common language, the style remains affiliated with their characters and their social worlds; the language belongs to them as much as it does to Joyce himself.

The Joycean combination of intimacy and distance in *Ulysses* differs from more conventional novelistic slumming in the back streets of language or character. Joyce does not glamorize dinginess or squalor. That is why Murphy, the yarn-spinning sailor, occupies such a delicate position: in part he enacts the storytelling impulse through which all specimens of the genus *homo* seek shelter from grim fact[61]; at the same time, he is and remains the most run-down imaginable version of a storyteller, and his art accomplishes its goal of diversion only through the manifest act of rescue that Joyce's own art performs.

—I seen a Chinese one time, related the doughty narrator, that had little pills like putty and he put them in the water and they opened and every pill was something different. One was a ship, another was a house, another was a flower. Cooks rats in your soup, he appetisingly added, the chinks does.

Possibly perceiving an expression of dubiosity on their faces the globetrotter went on, adhering to his adventures.

—And I seen a man killed in Trieste by an Italian chap. Knife in his back. Knife like that.

Whilst speaking he produced a dangerouslooking claspknife quite in keeping with his character and held it in the striking position.

—In a knockingshop it was count of a tryon between two smugglers. Fellow hid behind a door, come up behind him. Like that. *Prepare to meet your God,* says he. Chuk! It went into his back up to the butt.

His heavy glance drowsily roaming about kind of defied their further questions even should they by any chance want to.

—That's a good bit of steel, repeated he, examining his formidable *stiletto.*

After which harrowing *dénouement* sufficient to appal the stoutest he snapped the blade to and stowed the weapon in question away as before in his chamber of horrors, otherwise pocket. (16.570–88 / 628–29)

Murphy exemplifies the human impulse toward storytelling about as ineffectually as Bloom in "Eumaeus" exemplifies the impulse to take stock of character. A clear distinction is preserved here between Murphy's crude inexpressiveness and another verbal construction which gives life to his stories. In a sense, Murphy is no better than the inexpressive, unsavory figures in early Joyce, like the pervert in "An Encounter" or (moving up the social scale) Corly or Gallaher. In *Dubliners* these figures are scrupulously revealed in all their unredeemed squalor of spirit and speech; the absence of vitality in them is one of the chief disclosures of Joyce's ironic epiphanies. In "Eumaeus," by contrast, the art only begins with the fact of Murphy's squalor. This "eloquent" fact does not need scrupulous exposure. What is remarkable instead is how Joyce can change our relation to the fact, making Murphy's stories come ever more to life, the more it is apparent that Murphy himself, the ostensible "doughty narrator," remains inert, his glance "heavy," "drowsily roaming about."

Joyce contrives to keep the rigmarole going despite the character and his actual audience (who never get beyond mild "dubiosity"). There is no implication that Murphy especially relishes his own routine, certainly not the way the abandoned wife in *Sea and Sardinia* laments "to her heart's content." Joyce's sailor reports on Chinese rat soup with more insistence than gusto. It is only the intervention of another verbal force that sets off the details and animates the account, pulling the effect from mock-wondrous to mock-grisly, in somewhat the same way that Murphy can change the expression of his Antonio tattoo by pulling on it with his hands. The audience in the shelter seems more interested in such visual effects than in any elaborate forms of verbal manipulation. The verbal life of the story exists only between Joyce and the reader. "Cooks rats in your soup, he appetisingly added, the chinks does." "That's a good bit of steel, repeated he, examining his formidable *stiletto.*" Placed within Joyce's design, even the lumpish pieces of Murphy's language come alive, rather like the Chinese putty pills that he implausibly describes opening into wondrous shapes when placed in water. James Maddox has suggested a playful allusion here to the Proustian flowering of inert fact in consciousness, famously associated with the magical effect of the madeleine in the tea.[62] Joyce's magic works in a virtually opposite way to Proust's: what opens up is public rather than private, anecdotal rather than emotional, and in the end vulgar rather than precious or refined. In Joyce, details like the putty pills and the tattoo suggest how much human ingenuity goes into efforts to make something out of very little at every level of culture. In *Ulysses,* popular entertainments like *Leah the*

Forsaken and *Turko the Terrible* are associated with memories of pleasurable life. Joyce's art in "Eumaeus" affiliates itself with all kinds of
common human pleasure in diversion, even while he never allows us to
lose sight of the human and cultural facts that we would be diverted
from.

Stephen Dedalus in "Eumaeus" is no readier than Bloom to appreciate the complex balancing act of this comedy. "Sounds are impostures," Stephen pronounces (16.362 / 622), rudely deflating Bloom's
misguided enthusiasm for the Italian ice-cream vendors' melodious-
sounding haggle over money. All the jokes in "Eumaeus" confirm a
view of language as imposture, the masking in colorful sound of realities which would be intolerably oppressive left bare. What Stephen
may eventually but does not yet see is how an art could at the same
time render with strict accuracy the contemptible quality of things and
yet make the elements open up into rich and fresh new forms. In his
"Parable of the Plums," recited earlier on the way to lunch in "Aeolus," Stephen gave "a loud young laugh" at the scrupulous exactitude
with which he caught the meager reality of two poor Dublin women
who silently spit plum pits from the top of Nelson's pillar. Many
readers endorse Stephen's pleasure in the progress this little story
shows in his literary ideas: away from the dreamy, cloudy solemnities
of his "deeply deep" phase and toward the exact irony of Joyce's own
Dubliners. But the laughter released by "Eumaeus" is beyond the
reach of Joyce's irony in *Dubliners,* as it is even further beyond
Stephen's less developed wit.[63]

Whereas the Joyce of *Dubliners* had already filled his head (and his
stories) with the common speech of his city, Stephen gives his ironically named "vestal virgins" in the "Parable of the Plums" no speech
worth repeating. Stephen seeks his shelter from the grimness of fact in
a wit that strains to keep a firm distance from the degraded city to
which he has been forced to return. Joyce, perhaps for the very reason
that he literally removed himself from the factual proximity of his
material, manages an entirely different verbal flexibility in relation to
it. And yet, even in *Ulysses,* it is clear that this activity of verbal
re-construction for Joyce also amounts to an urgently desired protection from realities that, taken plain, are still too oppressive to endure.

"Eumaeus," we shall see further, looks forward more than any other
chapter of *Ulysses* to the extraordinary rigmaroles in the fiction of
Samuel Beckett.[64] Joyce's comic affirmation, however, avoids Beckett's intense metaphysical anguish in a situation where story inventions
of forged language constitute the only diversion for the isolated spirit.

In *Ulysses* Joyce draws back before reaching any such generalization. Bloom exaggerates, after all, in taking the shelter as a "miniature cameo" of the world he lives in, for *Ulysses* does not end in the cabman's shelter. Bloom does eventually go home, where he can rest and where we can hear the voice of Molly, telling a story of her life and Bloom's that presents a less degraded picture of reality than the stories heard in the temperance parlor. To what extent the quality of yet another wholesale whopper in Molly's monologue limits the comfort of her warmth is a measurement that the art of *Ulysses* does not press us to make. The solid existence of Molly, waiting at home on Eccles Street, is among the facts in *Ulysses* which seem incontrovertible, even while not open to deepest probing. Joyce's storytelling throughout *Ulysses* never penetrates very deeply into the mysteries of such a fact or of what would happen if its apparent solidity were truly shattered. The larger shelter of Joyce's story is fabricated on the model of Homer's *Odyssey* rather than Shakespeare's *King Lear*. Joyce's words do not, after all, lead down to the depth of questioning reached by mad Lear both out in the storm and in the hovel to which he is led for shelter. In that sense, Joyce breaks continuity with the English expectation that language is a natural medium through which to explore and express the deepest and even the most unnatural convulsions of public and personal life. The profundity of *Ulysses* comes from the almost contrary demonstration of a sanity that is possible, if both the given world and a given language are accepted as constituted on somewhat alien ground. The English language offers Joyce such rich materials for all kinds of protective shelters in *Ulysses* precisely because he can manipulate it as material not coextensive with his spirit, not even entirely belonging to him. What was the fretful shadow of an alien speech in *A Portrait of the Artist* expands into a free space in *Ulysses* where the human spirit can safely play with the meager facts of life.

7

Signs of Life and Death
in Beckett's Trilogy

Le bon sens **and Horse-Sense**

By writing in two languages (and even translating his own work from
one to the other), Samuel Beckett put himself in the position of directly living out modernist commonplaces about language as transposition if not actually forgery—all speech is "translation," the speaker in
The Unnamable declares. The desolating side of this position is the
sense of estrangement in language that pervades Beckett's trilogy, finally becoming the burden of the speaker's lament in the third volume.
The instruments of speech betray and distort, yet there are no other
instruments to manifest the true being of the self which presses for
expression. In *Madame Bovary* Flaubert registered this plight in his
image of the human soul condemned to beat out its sorrows and longings on a cracked pot. The often insistent monotone of Beckett's style,
in both English and French, is in line with Flaubert's image of the
cracked pot. But Beckett's remarkable variations (also in both languages) show that there are more ways to beat on a pot, and more
kinds of pots, than dreamed of in Flaubert's philosophy. Beckett offers

another exemplary case of a modernist writer whose various and rich verbal surfaces are in permanent tension with the declared emptiness of language that is one of his chief themes. With Beckett, moreover, the activity of self-translation provides a unique opportunity to identify forces within English and French that give this very tension a different character in the two languages, even for the "same" works by the "same" author.

Beckett's unique achievement of creating distinctive human voices in two languages was not his plan for the trilogy at the outset. When he embarked on *Molloy* (in French) after World War II, he began in a new spirit, born partly out of discouragement with the failure of his English novel, *Watt,* to find a publisher. He wanted, he said, to write an authentically French novel, not an English novel in the French language.[1] The project of an English translation of this French novel was still in the future.

By 1947, with every tradition of the novel scrambled for a generation and more, it cannot be absolutely clear what constituted Beckett's conception of a French novel. Perhaps the idea appealed most as permission to exclude: less of the elaboration that made *Watt* so hard to read; less rigmarole of plot and people in relation to each other; fewer things, and a less affectionate or even satiric engagement with them—unlike Joyce, who kept his huge inventory of Dublin and other things with him throughout the years in Paris. And again, in contrast to Joyce, fewer words. By composing in a foreign language, Beckett necessarily confined himself to a smaller lexicon, significantly emptied of all those familiar named things that encourage the proliferation of memories, whether bitter or nostalgic.

Moreover French novelists, even native speakers, were used to practicing such austerities. The distinguished tradition of the *conte* and *récit* in French might be taken to authorize a severe contraction of the novelist's plan without demeaning his ambition. Proust, it might seem, had gone the other way, but not in Beckett's view. Already in 1931 Beckett had written admiringly of how Proust's esthetic was "not expansive, but a contraction." Beckett emphasizes not the crowded canvas of Proust's novel, but his uncompromising negations: "The only fertile research is excavatory, immersive, a contraction of the spirit, a descent. The artist is active, but negatively, shrinking from the nullity of extracircumferential phenomena, drawn in to the core of the eddy."[2]

Yet Beckett did not expect his radical exclusionary art to appeal to public taste in France any more than in England or Ireland in the

postwar years. His skepticism and political detachment were too nihilistic; recognizable reality and recognizable consolations were too thoroughly swept away, for people seeking to bind their war wounds. No
French publisher would make a commitment to Beckett's French fiction for years, until the near-bankrupt editor of Minuit took a chance
with the whole trilogy in 1951.³

As a foreigner—*l'Irlandais*—Beckett also had to contend with
French distrust of his linguistic presumption. What was he up to, putting forward these Irish-named derelicts, with their streams of French
sentences, carefully correct, yet peculiarly wired to give unpredictable
shocks on every page? Beckett himself worried about the audacity of
writing prose in French. During the composition of *Molloy* he spent
hours daily, going over every sentence with a French friend.⁴ Beckett
wanted an absolutely impeccable French for his novel, with every colloquial intonation right and not a single grammatical error. Even after
his many years in France, he needed the assistance of a native speaker
to ensure the fluent ease that characterizes the surface movement of
style in *Molloy*. At the same time, it was no doubt his own foreign ear
that helped him to be so finely attuned to ordinary French idiom and
syntax as a distinctive music—not merely a natural form of expression,
but a composition, a construction which he could manipulate to show
definite and limited shapes, boundaries, hollows, and unexamined habits of both suppression and containment.

Beckett's characters, Molloy and eventually Moran, arrive through
hard wandering at a similar acuteness of hearing. Even before his
journey (and perhaps as a sign of his suitability for it), Moran had
moments of lucidity during which he could hear beyond what he calls "le
fausset de la raison" (p. 166).⁵ The "falsetto of reason" (p. 167) is a
good image for the norm of Beckett's French in *Molloy:* thin, fluent, but
steadily unnatural, even displaying its quality of artifice. Outbreaks of
rage, disgust, or transcendent indifference—a violent curse, the flinging
of the plate of charity, sudden disavowals of whole trains of thought—
disrupt this smooth surface. Like many small eruptions in a volcanic
zone, they remind us that the ground underneath is unstable. But on the
whole, the surface holds. Even murder does not deeply shake it. Both
Molloy and Moran choose to keep to this surface, even while recognizing its artificiality and their own imperfect control. The alternatives, as
Molloy names them, are only lying or silence. Like Moran later, Molloy
submits to the conventions of lying, partly because he is required by
mysterious outside authorities to make a report, and partly because
some obscure inner imperative keeps him at the task of shaping the

formless murmur of his life, if only in sentences as false as a pensum, the punishment assigned to dull-witted schoolchildren.

Beckett thus makes comedy and pathos out of the artificial correctness of language in *Molloy*. While granting his heroes the wit to protest their confinement in false language, Beckett also shows them resigned to their pensum, their punishment of words and sentences, "with a beginning, a middle, and an end as in the well-built phrase, and the long sonata of the dead" (p. 31). Their eruptions of language, like their occasional physical violence, gesture toward a more active freedom. But the gestures prove inconsequential and are themselves all but absorbed into the artificial orderliness of the whole. By initially choosing French for his novel, Beckett elected to transpose his voice into the structures of a language not natural to him. Moreover, the French language which he adopted is in itself more restrictive than English—more committed to the register of reason in both literary and colloquial usage. And in *Molly* Beckett chose to write a kind of French that embraced rather than defied restrictiveness, or rather showed defiance mainly through the cool exaggerations of the embrace.

In *Malone meurt* and *L'Innommable* Beckett's heroes become progressively more alienated, closer to physical death, and thereby less tightly enclosed in the dead structures of conventional language. Not accountable, like Molloy or Moran, to any external authority, they seem freer to disrupt, interrupt, and play every kind of mischief with the language of their discourse, even though they remain obscurely constrained to continue it. Perhaps because Beckett's own linguistic daring in French grew with each novel, the tonal variety of the later heroes increases, the syntax loosens more often, finally the very structure of sentences disappears. Yet at the same time, Beckett's conception of the falsetto quality of language correspondingly expands, so that even the rolling fantasies of *L'Innommable* do not escape categorization as denatured, as being still a pensum. Moreover, a remarkable clarity of verbal structure within the phrases survives even the loss of sentence boundaries, as if rational form inhered so deeply in the very motions of speech, in the very breath of the spoken phrase, that it could finally be evaded only through a silence at once longed for and still ever postponed.

The English translations of the trilogy that followed later also show progressively more daring disruptions of conventional prose norms: odd dilations of syntax and original, even outrageous mixtures of diction and metaphor.[6] But we shall see that the burden of the stylistic experiments was different in the English. Beckett had from the start a rich—if anything, too rich—repertory of models for his most extravagant rhetorical ventures in English. What was less at hand was a way to transpose the falsetto quality so crucial to his French voices into a language quite different in its own range as well as in its personal relation to him.

To speak rationally in French is to echo, however weakly, the language of Descartes, and the surest way to mock rationality in French is to play tricks with Descartes, either by sabotaging his famous method or by performing acrobatics with his stiff formulae. Thus, near the end of his monologue, Molloy turns on its head the Cartesian dictum about "clear and distinct ideas": "je le crois, oui, je crois que tout ce qui est faux se laisse davantage réduire, en notions claires et distinctes, distinctes de toutes les autres notions" (p. 125). However Molloy, we shall see further, is not primarily acrobatic: he keeps trying, in the face of enormous obstacles, to tell a straight story, just as within the story he tries, even with all his physical disabilities, to move toward the destination of his mother's residence. In *Malone meurt* the supine hero explicitly dedicates himself to play as his sole remaining vocation. In the second volume, therefore, the pretensions of reason are more directly made fun of, through the mischievous moves of Malone's own games. It is in *Malone meurt* that we can best hear Beckett's French game of reason and, in *Malone Dies,* what happens to that game in English translation.

In one marvelous passage, Malone characteristically works himself backward through the famous Cartesian routine of proving his existence. The play of thought begins after a wave of disgust and boredom arouses in him the idea of throwing himself out the window. However, the suicidal fantasy is idle, he notes even while indulging in it, since he does not have enough use of his body to get out of bed, much less to accomplish athletic jumps out the window. But in addition, he realizes, he does not know how high his room is off the ground, and this uncertainty at once vitiates the idea of the jump and becomes in itself a temporary raison d'être as his thought begins to play with the calculation of his position relative to the ground. The impossibility of suicide generates the activity of reasoning, almost as a *pis aller*. As an activity, moreover, reasoning itself becomes so absorbing an exercise that it quickly, if only temporarily, displaces the impulse to end it all.

Since Malone, lying in bed, has no sensory evidence which decisively establishes his location, his speculative mind moves freely through the conundrum of where he is. This movement takes him far: maybe he is underground, maybe he is in a kind of inverted apartment house. Maybe, after all, he is already dead! At this point, the clarifying voice of *le bon sens* makes its bid for the argument that he continues in some sense to exist:

> Mais le bon sens veut que je n'ai pas encore tout à fait cesser de haleter. Et il invoque, à l'appui de cette façon de voir, diverses considérations ayant trait par exemple au petit tas de mes possessions, à mon système de nutrition et d'élimination, au couple d'en face, aux changements du ciel, etc. (pp. 83–84)

> But my horse-sense tells me I have not yet quite ceased to gasp. And it summons in support of this view various considerations having to do for example with the little heap of my possessions, my system of nutrition and elimination, the couple across the way, the changing sky, and so on. (pp. 219–20)

In Beckett's translation *le bon sens* changes to "horse-sense," and that one striking transposition shifts the wit of the entire passage. For the wit of Beckett's French here depends on our glimpsing, through an absurdly incongruous list of *considérations,* the impoverished remains of the once great game of Cartesian rationalism. In the language of Descartes, *le bon sens* signifies nothing less than reason itself, specifically reason as the faculty of judgment, the anchor of reasoning as a process. Consequential reasoning in Descartes requires the power to distinguish truth from falsity: "La puissance de bien juger et distinguer le vrai d'avec le faux, qui est proprement ce qu'on nomme le bon sens ou la raison."[7]

Cartesian authority is not hard to locate for the phrase *le bon sens;* the *Discours sur la méthode* opens with reflections on how *le bon sens* ought to be understood, and Descartes's formulation illustrates the first definition of the term in every French dictionary, even though in modern usage earlier philosophic dignity has been eroded to the level of mere "common sense." But Malone is the very opposite of loose in his treatment of *le bon sens.* If he remains noncommittal, that is because his rational impartiality is stricter, not looser than Descartes's. Malone restores Cartesian status to *le bon sens,* but only to demolish the very concept of judgment by a more thorough skepticism than even Descartes would allow. It is Malone's very obedience to the rules of the reasoning game that reduces even *le bon sens* to the most provisional authority. Malone hears the argument of *le bon sens,* but he is in a space where the equal possibility of all hypotheses reduces the claim of judgment to no more than another set of prejudices, one of many possible points of view, a mere *façon de voir*.

Le bon sens cannot be an arbiter for Malone partly because he cannot help but notice that, as a mode of "seeing," so-called rational judgment depends more heavily on problematic sensory perception than its Cartesian authority would suggest. Or perhaps it is only that the view from his room is so peculiarly uncertain as to call into question conventional inferences from even the most basic sensory perception. Take the evidence of the changing light, what *le bon sens* already prejudicially terms the *changements du ciel* (a phrase suggesting supernatural as well as natural prejudices). Malone's light changes, but not in evident conformity with any natural, much less divine law of the sky or heavens. He has, for example, known the light in his room to brighten suddenly, as if for morning, only to be quickly followed by a long return of darkness, as if for night again. Moreover, even the words for "night" and "day" are problematic for his light, which never really achieves the clarity of daylight, but rather keeps to a shade he is inclined to call gray, if it is a color at all: "cette sorte d'incandescence grisâtre" (p. 85). And, to consider yet one step further, this grayishness seems as much emitted *by* him as received from outside. I omit (not to lose hold of my own rational discourse) a number of other equally compelling complications to Malone's consideration of his light as it may or may not be related to other lights. The point to emphasize is the sheer proliferation of complication, where every distinction generates further obscurity and the very obsession with precise definition leads paradoxically ever further away from any "clear and distinct" idea. The only end point of the reasoning is Malone's summary conviction of separation from the moral as well as physical experience of other men.

> Bref il semble y avoir la lumière du dehors, celle des hommes qui savent que le soleil émerge à telle heure et à telle autre plonge à nouveau derrière l'horizon, et qui y comptent, et que des nuages sont toujours à prévoir mais qu'ils finissent toujours par se dissiper tôt ou tard, et la mienne. (p. 86)

> In a word there seems to be the light of the outer world, of those who know the sun and moon emerge at such an hour and at such another plunge again below the surface, and who rely on this, and who know that clouds are always to be expected but sooner or later always pass away, and mine. (p. 221)

Malone can repeat by rote conventional perceptions of nature (and the conventional moral inferences from them), but those common-places do not pertain to him; they do not pertain to *his* light, as they do not compose a sentence whose syntax includes him, except as an ill-fitting tag at the end. Cut off from the conventional moorings of judgment, Malone remains irretrievably disoriented, at once obsessed with the rational process of defining his position, and helpless to fix any stable point of reference in either his own mind or the outer world.

In this endless flux Malone's comically precise yet inconclusive reasoning becomes not so much a power ("la puissance de bien juger" was Descartes's phrase) as the reflex scratching of a mental itch or perhaps a drive in that more ambiguous category that Malone had just a few pages before referred to by the technical term "conation," a name for those human actions which seem to be voluntary but probably are not.

Malone had briefly become interested in conation as a way of grasping the mysteries of sex, but for him the unceasing motions of reasoning are more habitual than is sexuality, or perhaps this solitary playing with himself is his form of sexuality, with its own kind of stimulation and even its moments of release. The prose identifies release by a change of rhythm and a different imagery of potency and movement. At the end of the passage I have been discussing, Malone suddenly lets go of the entire exercise of assessing the relation of his light to other lights, and with it the entire conundrum of whether or not he is alive. These questions suddenly cease to interest him as he rises to a vision of his desire for less rather than more of any kind of light. He does retain some potency, at least enough for the action of entering further into an obscurity that sounds like a kind of transcendence. His very bed floats in a darkness without boundary and beyond all understanding.

> Et si je ferme les yeux, les ferme vraiment, comme ne le peuvent les autres, mais comme moi je le peux, car il y a des limites à mon impuissance, alors quelquefois mon lit se soulève et vogue à travers les airs, au gré des remous, comme un fétu, et moi dedans. Ce n'est pas une question de paupières heureusement, c'est comme qui dirait l'âme qu'il faut aveugler, cette âme qu'on a beau nier, perçante, guetteuse, inquiète, tournant dans sa cage comme dans une lanterne dans la nuit sans ports ni bâteaux ni matière ni entendement. (p. 88)

> And if I close my eyes, close them really, as others cannot, but as I can, for there are limits to my impotence, then sometimes my bed is caught up into the air and tossed like a straw by the swirling eddies, and I in it.

> Fortunately it is not so much an affair of eyelids, but as it were the soul that must be veiled, that soul denied in vain, vigilant, anxious, turning in its cage as in a lantern, in the night without haven or craft or matter or understanding. (p. 222)

In the desolate lyricism of this passage, Malone lets his voice float like the bed he describes, beyond and outside the preceding idle exercise of reason. There is a strange beauty to the vision, as the very syntax of the sentences loosens, and the obscurely evocative imagery dissolves the tangle of inconclusive speculation in the pages before. The vision is unresolvably ambiguous: the cage afloat signifies a freedom that is yet an imprisonment, and the soul is still unquiet in the lantern-cage, more as in life than in death, yet the boundless darkness is not the night of the natural world. The tone of the vision is ambiguous, too—serene and yet mournfully restrained, as the sentences themselves float free, without really breaking out of grammatical confines. The condition envisioned is neither life nor death according to our conventional distinctions. And therein lies its power to interrupt the game of reason as a release—until the vision is itself interrupted by Malone's sudden deflating dismissal of this flight of language as nothing but distraction, another game: "Ah oui, j'ai mes petites distractions" (p. 88) / "Ah yes, I have my little pastimes" (p. 222). The deflating sentence, however, itself breaks off in the middle, before the visionary distraction can be decisively placed. Another version of Malone's voice reports that, in mid-sentence, his pencil had dropped and forty-eight hours had been required to recover it.

At no point in this sequence does a voice of judgment appear to stabilize the shifting points of view we have been following. Instead, the discourse begins a new game of disoriented reasoning, as Malone ponders the relative merit of soft versus hard lead pencils. (In addition to his dropped and recovered stub, he has lost another pencil somewhere in the bed. Which is to be preferred?) Then this new futile but absorbing exercise of the rational faculty is also numbered among his *petites distractions*. Malone's styles at first oppose visionary to rational expression, but then reduce both to mere exercises of a pencil which itself then becomes the subject of speculation. The content, the style, and even the instrument of writing are equally interesting but equally insignificant distractions. Malone plays with them *tour à tour,* as Molloy sucked his sucking-stones—until he lost or threw them all away.

In the English version the sequence of speculative reasoning, enigmatic vision, deflation, and new game of reasoning about pencils follows the French, except that it is horse-sense and not *le bon sens* which makes the case for Malone on behalf of life. "But my horse-sense tells me that I have not yet quite ceased to gasp" (p. 219). To bring the crude nineteenth-century American slang of "horse-sense" into this passage is a bit of daring no merely conscientious translator would attempt, especially since the perfectly respectable English "good sense" is available. But Beckett's ear must have heard how "good sense" in English simply falls flat, carrying hardly a vibration of any bygone philosophic dignity. The Cartesian echo was invariably going to be lost in the English translation; hardly any Cartesian echoes reverberate in a language that never submitted to rationalist authority enough for its repudiation to have much force of irony. Beckett's solution—and we shall see other examples in the same vein—was boldly to discard the weak English version of his French wit and to devise a quite different effect in English, one different both in local texture and in its connections to the language of the book elsewhere.

Horse-sense may derive from the shrewd judgment of horse dealers or perhaps from the self-preserving instincts of horses themselves, for example, in their intuitive knowing better than to catapult off the edge of cliffs. Either way, this crude practical sense lies below even common sense. Horse-sense is as far as sense can be from *le bon sens* of Descartes; the English phrase quite simply blots out the Cartesian echo. Instead, there is a simpler, comic incongruity in English between Malone's acquaintance with a language of tough practicality and his incompetence to establish even whether he is alive or dead, to say nothing of his impractical notion of jumping out the window. Malone's very impulse to verify his existence through reasoning, an activity altogether respectable in the Cartesian tradition, becomes simply absurd by the standard of horse-sense, although there is a certain charm, too, in Malone's having among his toys the slang of a tough, manly community to which he so little belongs.

The joke of Malone's horse-sense cuts another way also, especially in this passage which follows so soon upon the brutal stories of dying animals in the Lambert farm narrative. In addition to the pigs that the farmer Lambert so enjoys slaughtering, there is a sickly hen and, described in detail, the mule that the farmer had horse-sense enough to save from the slaughterhouse, only in order to "screw six months" more work out of it. There are also the rabbits who possibly die of fright before the farmer's wife applies the knife. And there is Malone's subsequent musing on all the other varied forms of animal dying. Far from exemplifying shrewd self-preservation, the animals in *Malone*

Dies are conspicuous as images of mysteriously helpless submission to brutal conditions of both living and dying. There is macabre irony, then, in Malone's invoking an animal sense for evidence of his continuing existence. The animals of Malone's imagination have virtually no sense at all. They have only sense enough sometimes to refuse to thrive, and sometimes to make themselves die before they are killed. Which is, to be sure, more sense than Malone himself can quite muster. Animals, however, do not engage in reasoning. Malone remembers that his friend Jackson tried but failed to teach his parrot beyond the three words *Nihil in intellectu.* Then Polly would go into a rage and retreat with her toys to a corner of her cage. When Malone, in English, abandons reasoning in favor of his dark, strange lantern-cage, the visionary turn of mind carries further the undercurrents of pathos in this earlier animal imagery.

Although the cross-pattern of images—from the soul's cage to the parrot and the farm animals—may come to mind in Beckett's French, too, the half-buried but conspicuous metaphor in the colloquial term "horse-sense" calls attention to animal imagery in a way that the abstract denominator *le bon sens* plainly does not. And other details of language strengthen this difference. Instead of the French *aveugler,* for example, a word whose figurative meaning in relation to mind and soul is so conventional as to have all but lost any sensory reference, the English has Malone contemplating his soul as "veiled," a word with a wider range of sensory connotation than "blinded" (easily available for a literal translation). A veiled soul in a lantern-cage is more mysterious, even perhaps carrying some undersense of how birds are soothed in their cages by being covered—an image that returns to mind later, in *The Unnamable,* where much is made of Mahood's pleasure in having his jar covered and darkened with a tarpaulin when it snows.

I linger over the metaphoric reverberations of Malone's horse-sense to suggest one kind of density in Beckett's English that compensates for the weakened game of French reason. The greater tendency of English idiom to be made of buried metaphor, as observed in Chapter 1, has the natural effect of underscoring images. Examples abound from all three novels of the trilogy. Staying only with animal evocations, there is Molloy's vividly crude image of the city's morning patrol, emphasizing the bestial appetites unleashed through ordinary social virtues: "They wake up, hale and hearty, their tongues hanging out for order, beauty, and justice, baying for their due" (p. 67). In contrast is the sardonic formality of the French Molloy's more abstract version of the same perception: "Les gens se réveillent, frais et dispos, assoiffés d'ordre, de beauté et de justice, exigeant la contrepartie" (p. 101). Or there is the transposition (as Moran contemplates the pleasures of total paralysis) of the correctly technical French phrase "une aphasie complète" (p. 217) into the colloquial simile "blind as a bat" (p. 192). Or there is the difference between the abstract expression "toujours pour le tout" in *L'Innommable* and its metaphoric English counterpart in *The Unnamable,* when the speaker describes himself as "always out for the whole hog."

There is no need for an exhaustive list of such contrasts; more will occur in other contexts as we go along. The question that arises, even from the few examples added to our starting point in "horse-sense," concerns the cumulative coloration given to the soliloquizing voices by the often crude metaphoric life of the English idioms. If a sort of "incandescence grisâtre" is the luminous colorlessness of Beckett's French speakers, what incongruities or even irrelevancies of color mark their English counterparts, even to the point of subtly altering the shading of their personalities and the total effect of their soliloquies? A greater liveliness has often been remarked in Beckett's English by comparison with his French, and this impression may arise from the more particolored texture of the English idiomatic language. The cost of that coloring has also to be assessed, in a way that attends to the special incandescence which Beckett in French knew how to give to shades of gray.[8]

Molloy: *l'unijambiste*

Molloy is the best text to measure the losses as well as the sheer differences incurred by Beckett's transposition of the trilogy into English, for *Molloy* depends more than the following volumes on the ironic simulation of rational style, the aspect of Beckett's French most difficult to preserve in translation. Moreover, if Beckett was only in the process of perfecting his French style in the first novel of the trilogy, it is the English translation which sometimes shows strains of a still imperfectly mastered art. It must be considered, of course, that *Molloy* is the one book of the trilogy that Beckett did not translate exclusively himself: he allowed Patrick Bowles to make a draft of the whole before he then went over it carefully with him.[9] But it matters less who is responsible for each phrase of the English, than what makes for the most difficulty in translation and the significance of the compromises and solutions devised.

First, a passage about testicles, since the physical incompetence of the Beckett hero puts the heaviest burden on the voice of reason when the sexual organs come into play, or, as is normally the case, when their utter nonfunctioning more or less gratuitously comes to mind. In the following passage Molloy wanders into reflections on the state of his testicles in the midst of what begins as a quick report of how he helped—or did not help—the woman Lousse bury the dog he had knocked down with his bicycle. Molloy explains that he could not help much because his stiff leg incapacitated him for digging. We are caught in what Leo Bersani has nicely termed Beckett's "carnal irony," where the physical blockages of experience disable the rational progress of the discourse, even while the voice of reason shows remarkable and even absurd adaptive power.[10] Thus Molloy reasonably explains the obstacles to ordinary motion created by his bad leg and muses how he would have been better off with his leg amputated. That notion leads (reasonably) into a digression on the advantages of castration, as if this most famous human trauma were, to him, just another step in the movement of rational thought. Finally, he circles back to reflect on his fond if pointless "attachment" to his nonfunctioning bodily parts, an attachment he regards as mildly irrational, one of his rare lapses into sentimentality. Later, when the narrative gets around to Molloy's semireluctant sexual adventures with Lousse, this musing about impotence and castration may acquire new point, but the initial impression of irrelevance makes part of the comedy first, as does the sheer duration of the reverie at a moment in the story when Molloy has just set himself to go quickly past the already somewhat irrelevant incident of burying Lousse's dog. We will come to the English version shortly; taken in French first, the passage is a marvelous display of Molloy's falsetto in its most bizarre brilliance.

Je ne disposais pour ainsi dire que d'une jambe, j'étais moralement unijambiste, et j'aurais été plus heureux, plus léger, amputé au niveau de l'aîne. Et ils m'auraient enlevé quelques testicules à la même occasion que je ne leur aurais rien dit. Car mes testicules à moi, ballotant à mi-cuisse au bout d'un maigre cordon, il n'y avait plus rien à en tirer, à telle enseigne que je n'avais plus envie d'en tirer quelque chose, mais j'avais plutôt envie de les voir disparaître, ces témoins à charge à décharge de ma longue mise en accusation. Car s'ils m'accusaient de les avoir couillonnés, ils m'en congratulaient aussi, du fond de leur sacoche crevée, le droit plus bas que le gauche, ou inversement, je ne sais plus, frères de cirque. Et chose encore plus grave, ils me gênaient pour marcher et pour m'asseoir, comme si ma jambe malade n'y suffisait pas, et quand j'allais à bicyclette ils se cognaient partout. J'avais donc intérêt à ce qu'ils disparaissent et je m'en serais chargé moi-même, avec un couteau ou un sécateur, n'était la peur où je grelottais de la douleur physique et des plaies infectées. Oui, toute ma vie j'ai vécu dans la terreur des plaies infectées, moi qui ne m'infectais jamais, tellement j'étais acide. Ma vie, ma vie, tantôt j'en parle comme d'une chose finie, tantôt comme d'une plaisanterie qui dure encore, et j'ai tort, car elle est finie et elle dure à la fois, mais par quel temps du verbe exprimer cela? Horloge qu'ayant remontée l'horloger enterre, avant de mourir, et dont les rouages tordus parleront un jour de Dieu, aux vers. Mais au fond je devais avoir de l'attachement pour ces couillons, y tenir comme d'autres à leurs cicatrices, à l'album de photos de grand'mère. Ce n'étaient pas eux de toute façon qui m'empêchaient de bêcher, mais ma jambe. Ce fut Lousse qui creusa le trou pendant que moi je tenais le chien dans mes bras. (pp. 52–53)

Beckett's French here is an extraordinary balancing act, as if to perform the voice of Molloy, *unijambiste,* were to imitate a somewhat freakish but really marvelous kind of circus show, an analogy directly suggested by Molloy's own half-woeful naming of his testicles, "frères de cirque." One might go to the circus to see the performance of the unicyclist. In this passage Beckett shows the feats of his hero, Molloy, "moralement unijambiste."

The skill of a unicyclist shows first in his ability to accomplish all the moves of a more ordinary machine—and then, unexpectedly, to add yet one and then another embellishment. There must be no pause, no toppling—though he may *almost* topple. There must be no falling with feet on the ground, so to speak, though if he can levitate even for a moment, that would be remarkable.[11]

Molloy as *unijambiste* similarly maintains his superb balance of language, even while moving through the fiery hoops of subjects like impotence and castration. There are no topplings of anxiety or anguish. Even the sentence breaks are all but suppressed by the casual-seeming forward momentum of the connectives: *Et, Car, Car, Et, J'avais donc, Oui, Mais au fond.* And this steadiness is further enforced by the repetition of words and the parallelism of a syntax firmly centered in logical pivots: "il n'y avait plus rien à en tirer, *à telle enseigne que* je n'avais plus envie d'en tirer quelque chose, *mais* j'avais *plutôt* envie de les voir disparaître." To move so slowly and steadily across such treacherous terrain seems absurdly wonderful, especially because Molly as speaker displays no self-consciousness, no awareness of his action as a performance. The *unijambiste* moves as he does not to entertain, but for his own obscure needs and because of his own incapacity, finally, to move otherwise.

In this language Molloy's peculiar accomplishment is inseparable from his disabilities, the impression of disability coming not only from the content but also from the exaggerated precision of the distinctions and elaborations: not just one generic instrument for castration, but two. Not just the annoyance of his swinging testicles to movement in general, but that movement parsed into three distinct forms, and the third delicately suspended until after an extended parenthetical aside: "Et chose plus grave, ils me gênaient pour marcher et pour m'asseoir, comme si ma jambe malade n'y suffisait pas, et quand j'allais à bicyclette ils se cognaient partout." The impulse toward indignant woe in the aside slightly shakes the balance of the sentence, as does the note of lament in the metaphor of his long experience as if on trial, "ma longue mise en accusation." But whether from disability or ability, Molloy does not delve into the metaphors of feeling. His poise does not collapse into self-pity any more than into obscenity, even while dipping perilously for a phrase or two of crude physical detail and a vulgar pun.

The most conspicuous move away from the moderate middle style of musing explanation comes in the rise to grandeur signaled by the invocation "Ma vie, ma vie" and in the heavily charged if rather banal imagery of the clockmaker God. The beauty (and comic limitation) of Molloy's French here is not so much in the "philosophic" lyricism itself as in the apparent ease with which Molly rises into it and descends back to his earlier measured rhythm in the next sentence: "Mais au fond je devais avoir de l'attachement . . ." The balance is so secure, the rational stability of the syntax so firm, that hardly a tremor is caused by the final outrageous comparison of his superannuated testicles to a grandmother's photograph album! After that detail there is no embellishment left to make; the voice simply dismisses the whole digression as beside the point, and the language returns matter-of-factly to the basic elements of the narrative. The dog is buried and Molloy goes on to recount what befell him in the house of Lousse and elsewhere.

It is evident that Molloy's English digression will not be quite the same performance as soon as we notice that the Latinate elegance which elevates *moralement unijambiste* to an honorific title is missing from the English phrase, "virtually onelegged." The English-speaking Molloy performs wonderful feats of language, too, but the strange verbal (and mental) balancing act of the French is gone.

I had so to speak only one leg at my disposal, I was virtually onelegged, and I would have been happier, livelier, amputated at the groin. And if they had removed a few testicles into the bargain I wouldn't have objected. For from such testicles as mine, dangling at mid-thigh at the end of a meagre cord, there was nothing more to be squeezed, not a drop. So that non che la speme il desiderio, and I longed to see them gone, from the old stand where they bore false witness, for and against, in the lifelong charge against me. For if they accused me of having made a balls of it, of me, of them, they thanked me for it too, from the depths of their rotten bag, the right lower than the left, or inversely, I forget, decaying circus clowns. And, worse still, they got in my way when I tried to walk, when I tried to sit down, as if my sick leg was not enough, and when I rode my bicycle they bounced up and down. So the best thing for me would have been for them to go, and I would have seen to it myself, with a knife or secateurs but for my terror of physical pain and festered wounds, so that I shook. Yes, all my life I have gone in terror of festered wounds, I who never festered, I was so acid. My life, my life, now I speak of it as of something over, now as of a joke which still goes on, and it is neither, for at the same time it is over and it goes on, and is there any tense for that? Watch wound and buried by the watchmaker, before he died, whose ruined works will one day speak of God, to the worms. But these cullions, I must be attached to them after all, cherish them as others do their scars, or the family album. In any case it wasn't their fault I couldn't dig, but my leg's. It was Lousse dug the hole while I held the dog in my arms. (pp. 35–36)

Although many of the effects noted earlier survive in the translation, some are weakened and others deliberately abandoned and replaced, to the point of shifting the center of wit in the entire passage. Instead of the almost freakishly rational poise of the French, the one-legged English speaker touches ground, so to speak, at will: "And if they had removed a few testicles into the bargain . . ." Descent into the street-wise slang of "into the bargain" simply abandons the evenness of diction and rhythm so remarkable in the French: "Et ils m'auraient enlevé quelques testicules à la même occasion que je ne leur aurais rien dit." Elsewhere too, the English voice takes support from earthier colloquialisms and more colorful diction: "squeezed" instead of *tirer,* and the added colloquial image "not a drop." Instead of the formal French, "Et chose encore plus grave . . .," there is the brisker "And, worse still . . ." A greater sprightliness is heard again in "So the best thing for me . . ." instead of the elaborately reasonable slowness of "J'avais donc intérêt à ce qu'ils disparaissent . . ."

The English colloquialisms give a different vitality to Molloy's reverie, mainly perhaps because they break the even rhythm of the French prose. At every point of choice, the translation goes for this rhythmic variety instead of for the preternatural steadiness of the French. And along with the abandoning of the French rhythm go logical connectives like *à telle enseigne que,* which help to sustain the even pace of the French. The most elaborately logical French sentence about impotence is replaced by the radically different wit of the English Molloy's odd skip into Italian: "So that no che la speme il desiderio, and I longed to see them gone." The Italian fragment comes from Leopardi and has to do with how loss of desire follows loss of hope. Beckett had already used the quotation in his early essay on Proust.[12] Given to Molloy, the Leopardi fragment makes the voice seem both more erudite and less singular than in French, for here Molloy reaches out to a fellow disabled spirit, even leaning additionally on the verbal wit of Leopardi's archaic *la speme* for hope.

The English Molloy thus has access to verbal resources beyond what Beckett had given his French original. Whereas the wonder of the French Molloy comes in the hardly wavering motion he maintains through one of the most upsetting subjects known to man, the appeal of the English Molloy depends on his significantly different capacity for energetic and witty inventiveness around this same subject. In French, the accomplishment and the disability of the style are perfect rhetorical equivalents for Molloy's peculiar combination of impotence and composure. But in English, Molloy has such a variety of tones and sentences and verbal devices for the subject of his decayed testicles, that we are almost distracted from the impotence he is reporting. Or rather, there seems a sharper division between the physical debility of the English Molloy and his verbal energy, which asserts a different order of strength, even of fertility. With the same obsessions, the same skewed displacements of emotion, Molloy ends by seeming less abnormal in English than in French, for the range of the English speech enacts an admirable but familiar capacity to accommodate even radical disability within witty and imaginative speech. Thus although the language of Molloy in English is more far-fetched—even venturing into Italian—its coloration remains less alien than the freakish neutrality of the French incandescent gray. There is nothing so deranged, for example, in the English as Molloy's deadpan comparison of testicles to the quintessential emblem of bourgeois sentiment, "l'album de photos de grand'mère." The surprise which makes the grandmother's appearance so funny in French depends on the weirdly even balance of rhythm and diction throughout the passage. The different wit of the

English has broken up that surface, which is perhaps why Beckett does not even try for the same pointed irony in the translation: instead of the grandmother's photo album, he settles for the vaguer, flatter "family album." The detail goes by pretty much unnoticed, for the color and humor of the English passage are elsewhere.

I observed in Chapter 1 how English idiomatic expressiveness was especially effective in quarrels because it lent an air of physical robustness to voices, and also because it backed individual assertiveness by a social tradition of irreverent resistance—if only resistance to the authority of correct standard language. In Molloy's English voice, as in the Bloomian interior monologues in a different way, lively rhythms and pungent colloquial idiom have some of the same effect. Although Molloy rarely speaks to anyone long enough to quarrel, there is a kind of tension if not struggle within the very texture of his style, one side pulling toward a correct, though enfeebled orderliness, the other side resisting with livelier, more directly assertive energy. This tension at its best makes for an appealing and reassuring comedy in the English, especially in passages about physical collapse, where the robust touches in Molloy's language invigorate his self-representation. The same doubleness, however, somewhat weakens the social irony of the novel, for the English Molloy remains unaccountably affiliated, through his idiomatic language, with a social community otherwise devoid of positive presence in the book and without valued status in Beckett's explicit social vision.

In his rendering of the social world, Beckett is as uncompromising as Flaubert in emptying all vitality from common social voices. No pungent familial speech enlivens *Molloy,* as Walter Morel's dialect enlivens *Sons and Lovers* or as Simon Dedalus's jokes and stories haunt the ear of memory in *A Portrait of the Artist as a Young Man* and *Ulysses.* Molloy has no basis for an even ambivalent relation to familial speech; his mother has long since ceased to speak, if she ever did. Molloy's attachment to her, like his system of knocking her on the head, is independent of speech, and so is his inarticulable motive in seeking to visit her. In the second part of the novel, the bourgeois Moran confines his communication with his son to principles and commands so hollow that even before the journey he hears his own voice as ridiculous. And Moran hears no better voices: neither his housekeeper, nor the priest, nor his old lady neighbors, nor Gaber (from whom he takes orders), nor the farmer encountered on the road shows a trace of that vitality in common language which creates intense ambivalence in so much English-language fiction about exile and alienation. The message that finally turns Moran homeward is from his mysterious, invisible superior Youdi, as transmitted through Gaber. In English, the message ironically includes a recall to the optimistic formulae of the poetic tradition. What Youdi had told Gaber was, "life is a thing of beauty, Gaber, and a joy forever" (p. 164). In French, Youdi's dictum lacks the density of the ironic poetic allusion; it is the utterly flat hyperbole of an *idée reçue,* ordinary, empty bourgeois cliché: "Il m'a dit, dit Gaber, qui'il m'a dit, la vie est une bien belle chose, Gaber, une chose inouïe (p. 255). Youdi's message has a different irony in the French, where the reality of life has elsewhere been intimated to be, literally, *une chose inouïe,* unheard of and unspoken by any of the voices heard in the social world, not now and not in any imagined or recorded past.

The social point of reference for the English Molloy's idiomatic language is much less thematically rich than in Joyce, for Beckett offers fewer social concessions in content than does the Joyce of *Ulysses.* Perhaps that is why Molloy's idiom in English sometimes has a slightly false ring of jauntiness; the falsity comes because the idioms are so unconnected to the rest of the novel's social vision. When, for example, Molloy punctuates his elaborate report of his sucking-stone system with curses of indifference and disgust, the English curses strike a slightly too sociable note of homeliness: "But deep down I didn't give a tinker's curse about being off my balance . . ." (p. 74); "But deep down I didn't give a fiddler's curse about being without . . ." (p. 74). These curses are amusing in the English, but to a reader coming from the starker French, their folksiness seems to weaken the radical meaning of "deep down" disgust in the novel. Homely expressions—"tiny tot" and "in the thick of the fray" are other examples—give Molloy an amiability in disgust that is out of character with his perception of sterile brutality in the social world and his radical isolation from every social community.

In the world of *Molloy,* in other words, there is no tavern—not the Shakespearean tavern where Hal could learn "to drink with every tinker in his own language," nor even the less nourishing Joycean tavern where men's voices pass on to each other the consoling jokes and curses of more colorful bygone days. There is no trace of any tinker or fiddler anywhere in *Molloy,* as there is no trace of a vital common speech to root individual cursing in the common soil of other men's experience. In French, Beckett makes no rhetorical concessions to social affiliation, and this consistency of extreme alienation seems right, the true note of the book. The French original of the "tinker's curse" is the imperturbably correct abstract sentence, "Mais au fond je

me moquais éperdument de me sentir en déséquilibre." The original of
the "fiddler's curse" is, on the other hand, the most common of
French curses, one which simply breaks up the flow of speech without
any friendly gestures toward tinkers, fiddlers, or anyone else: "Mais en
manquer au fond je m'en foutais aussi, quand je n'en aurais plus je
n'en aurais plus" (p. 113). When the French Molloy breaks up the
surface of his correct standard language, he does it through curses as
alienating (if in their own way as banal) as a violent physical gesture,
the throwing of a plate, the clubbing of a suspected enemy.

In contrast to the uncompromising alienation sustained by the
French style in *Molloy,* the cumulative effect of the many more and
less successful events of verbal resourcefulness in Molloy's English
language is a softening of Beckett's irony and a qualification of his
rejections. Although a certain gain in vitality sometimes comes from
such verbal events, they also slightly blur Beckett's evaluation of different spiritual and emotional as well as rhetorical possibilities. The
irony of the French keeps a firmer orientation, not only toward the
despised social world but also, and more importantly, toward the entire idea of expressive individual personality. For any lapses into directly expressive language—speech that sounds the claim of cutting
close to the bone of personality—compromises the starkness of Molloy's stated alternatives of lying or silence. Likewise the frightening
collapse of Moran's rigid bourgeois structure of cliché in the second
half of the novel becomes tamed, if we can hear the lost agent compen-
sated for his shattered platitudes by the finding of a more authentic
expressive voice.

I am not arguing that the English voices in *Molloy* go so far as to
represent a coherent image of such compensation. That would be to
revise fundamentally the very structure and meaning of the novel, and
such a recasting does not occur in the translation. What does seem to
happen, however, is more a subtle loosening of the firm, clear French
structure through the conciliatory and concessive verbal gestures that
enter the text through the English translation.

The sense of dilution in the English affects even those rare passages
which come closest to suspending the ironic falsetto of the voice in the
French. I mean those moments when Molloy comments on his own
action of speech, telling of his desire for radical silence or for dissolution in the cosmic murmur heard beneath and beyond the rattle of
human noise.

One curious effect in the English is that the greater variety of heard
language throughout the novel reduces the urgency of these climactic

passages. For if, as with the English Molloy, the individual, personal voice does intermittently enjoy something like free, direct expressiveness, the pressure for freedom through dissolution is subtly relieved. Dissolution may still represent the fullest, the only complete release, but the weight of that absolute is lightened by the intermediate possibilities of relative freedom. Moreover, since the language devised to evoke the image of radical dissolution has to compete with other evocative language in the English, there seems just the slightest extra push toward grandiloquence in the English lyricism, which weakens its status further.

There was a night in Lousse's garden, to take one of the most notable evocations of dissolution in *Molloy,* when the silence was profound enough to make audible the sound ordinarily overlaid by human noises: "le bruit lointain toujours le même que fait la terre" (p. 73) / "the far unchanging noise the earth makes" (p. 49). In both French and English, memory of this night leads Molloy into lyric evocation of a recurrent, if rare, state of being when the sealed jar (*boîte* in French) of the self gives way, so that both the small dead things of nature and the vast strange motions of the universe at once invade and absorb him and, not unlike Wordsworth's Lucy, he is rolled round in earth's diurnal course.[13] Beckett's lyricism is striking in both French and English: each version has its own strange music and an obscure beauty achieved by the near obliteration of the speaking subject in the very motions of the sentences. But the power of the French is greater, both because the poetic effects are more subdued and because the lesser rhetoric counts for more in relation to the language of the book as a whole.

Oui, il m'arrivait d'oublier non seulement qui j'étais, mais que j'étais, d'oublier d'être. Alors je n'étais plus cette boîte fermée à laquelle je devais de m'être si bien conservé, mais une cloison s'abattait et je me remplissais de racines et de tiges bien sages par exemple, de tuteurs depuis longtemps morts et que bientôt on brûlerait, du campos de la nuit et de l'attente du soleil, et puis du grincement de la planète qui avait bon dos, car elle roulait vers l'hiver, l'hiver la débarrasserait de ces croûtes dérisoires. Ou j'étais de cet hiver le calme précaire, la fonte des neiges qui ne changent rien et les horreurs du recommencement. Mais cela ne m'arrivait pas souvent, la plupart du temps je restais dans ma boîte qui ne connaissait ni saisons ni jardins. (p. 73)

Yes, there were times when I forgot not only who I was, but that I was, forgot to be. Then I was no longer that sealed jar to which I owed my being so well preserved, but a wall gave way and I filled with roots and tame stems for example, stakes long since dead and ready for burning,

the recess of night and the imminence of dawn, and then the labour of
the planet rolling eager into winter, winter would rid it of these contemptible scabs. Or of that winter I was the precarious calm, the thaw of
the snows which make no difference and all the horrors of it all all over
again. But that did not happen to me often, mostly I stayed in my jar
which knew neither seasons nor gardens. (p. 49)

In both French and English, Beckett releases Molloy's voice into
strange imaginings of dissolution by means of delicate displacements of
ordinary prose rhythms and word order: "Ou j'étais de cet hiver le
calme précaire" / "Or of that winter I was the precarious calm." He
also maintains in both languages some continuing sense of confinement
within the prosaic voice by odd dips into the colloquial: *par exemple* /
"for example"; *qui ne changent rien* / "which make no difference." Yet
despite the similarities, the English in this passage moves more showily
than the French into a poetic music. The repetition and play of vowels,
for example, in "and the horrors of it all all over again" offer a familiar late Romantic melody in place of the more static dignity of the
French: "et les horreurs du recommencement." The English grammar
also is odder, calling more attention to irregularity, as if to imitate the
almost unintelligible self-obliteration stated by the words. In the
French, while the mind of the voice, so to speak, also entertains bizarre self-conversions, the order of the sentence more simply remains.
The French reflexive verb *et je me remplissais de* contains strangeness
within a regular grammatical form, while the English makes more
obscurity by omitting the self-referential object and playing between
transitive and intransitive possibilities of the verb: "and I filled with
roots and stems." Finally, there is in the English the grandly poetic
phrasing, "the recess of night and the imminence of dawn"—the rhetorical climax of the passage because of the sublimity of the diction and
also the grammatical isolation of the phrase in the sentence. Out of the
jar of self, the English voice escapes the confines of sentence logic and
enters a poetic space of mysterious vacancy and imminence. In French,
the effect of mystery and mystification is held down by syntax. "Du
campos de la nuit et de l'attente du soleil" belongs to the catalogue of
what Molloy fills himself with when the structure of his box gives way.
The effect of a continuing list is fairly clearly sustained through the
repetition of the prepositions *de, de, de, du, et de.* The lack of necessity for such prepositions in English grammar allows for more ambiguous syntax, and Beckett in English follows the opportunity offered by
that looseness to let the sublime phrases float off on their own.

Molloy's French reverie of dissolution stops short of sublimity, staying more closely bound to a human pathos. There is not only the sorrow implicit in the very movement of desire toward nonbeing, but the sorrow of the earth, too, as Molloy imagines it not altogether unlike himself, impassively rolling ever onward with its burdens, both of debris and of delusive expectations. In the French imagery Beckett ironically shows Molloy humanizing even the vast universe which supposedly releases him from his exile in manhoood: "et puis du grincement de la planète qui avait bon dos, car elle roulait vers l'hiver." It is significant that the touchingly incongruous human detail of the planet's strong and willing back (*bon dos*) disappears in English, replaced by the more elevated "labour" and the rather thin "eager": "And then the labour of the planet rolling eager into winter." Instead of the possibility of some sublime transcendence of the human, the French stays with the poignancy of Molloy's imagining himself dissolved into an earth as stoical but as burdened as himself.

As the rhetorical equivalent of Molloy's spiritual predicament, the limitations of the French visionary language are fully explicable and are, in fact, explained by Molloy himself. Even though he can recall times when the box of self gave way, he is speaking under the never-ceasing hail of icy words, "les mots glacés." He is still confined to lying, even when he turns his language toward silence, so the pathetic fallacy of the planet with a strong back is entirely congruent with his own self-perception of verbal constraint. Except that Molloy does not hear the intensity of human pain that Beckett makes sound through the touchingly "false" images and even through the strained syntax. Molloy hears only the cold names and the cold sequences of his sentences. And Beckett in French also makes us hear this touch of frost, even in the most lyrical passages. Life is *une chose inouïe,* as Youdi told Gaber. Its reality, including its horror, is not ever fully conveyed in the well-built phrase, not even in a phrase which explicitly names horror, "les horreurs du recommencement." The reality of horror, like the reality of pathos, is always felt behind, under, and in between the words and sometimes in their odd collisions, since hail is not, after all, a solid structure of ice.

In English, the impression of unceasing linguistic frost remains more theoretical, more of a stated theme than the fully enacted performance of the book's language. I have noted elsewhere how the idea, what some call the myth, of a nonverbal reality of being that is frozen out of all actual forms of language has a more insistent history in French than in English literature, starting from Rousseau.[14] It is perhaps not surprising, therefore, to observe how the English Molloy sounds less consistently frostbound than his French counterpart. For no interpretable reason, except perhaps reasons in the history and structure of the language itself, English, even Beckett's English, has a way of refusing to stay cold. At times, this greater warmth makes for strength and freshness, as in Molloy's inventive wit about castration and impotence, or in the powerful image of social revulsion noted earlier among the animal metaphors: "their tongues hanging out for order . . . baying for their due" (p. 67). At certain other moments, however, the English results in a language that is thawed out of its French intensity, so that the translated text may seem to exchange cold but bright hail only for tepidness: the mild "tinker's curse," the banal sublimity of "imminence of dawn," the soft euphony of "the horrors of it all all over again."

Throes and Calm in *Malone meurt* / *Malone Dies*

In *Malone Dies* the relative heat of language belongs to a different structure of rhetorical and spiritual equivalences that supports bolder stylistic ventures in French as well as English. In contrast to Molloy, helplessly chilled by the hail of words, Malone begins by openly proposing to regulate the temperature of his dying discourse. He wants a calming tepidness—neither intense heat nor cold: "je ne serai plus ni froid ni chaud, je serai tiède, je mourrai tiède, sans enthousiasme" (p. 8) / "I shall be neither hot nor cold any more, I shall be tepid, I shall die tepid, without enthusiasm" (p. 179). Of course the very emphasis heard in the opening dedication to calm evokes at the start the sense of menace that will in fact come to disrupt Malone's willed equilibrium. In the story games, for example—Sapo, Louis / Lambert, Macmann—intensities of sorrow, horror, and grotesque comedy keep disturbing the neutrality of tone in which the stories begin. As the book progresses, the ruminative passages, too—the games of reasoning, the calculations, the provisional inventories—sustain the chosen calm ever more precariously. Passages of what in Malone's own terms must be called feverish language keep invading the style, so that onslaughts of uncontrollable heat rather than imprisonment in inescapable frost come to constitute the predicament of language in the second volume of the trilogy.

By the time of the Macmann story, the temperature of the whole discourse has risen, even dissolving the boundaries between story and rumination. It is not surprising to hear Malone interrupt himself midway through the novel to report his perception of a strange increase of heat all around him and within. Tepidness is restored, but never securely until the final picnic episode. Before then, Malone's repeated invocations for new calm, along with the audible disruptions of calm, create in this volume a drama of will and feeling enacted rhetorically through the shifts in style and narrative form. Malone temporarily abandons stories when they are invaded by heat, or he shifts his thought games toward new prospective sources of calm.

In making the invasion of heat integral to Malone's drama, Beckett opens his French style to more richly expressive, emotionally charged language than accorded with the thematic design of *Molloy*. And this new construction of the drama of speech also creates thematic place for the more expressive impulses in the English translation. The French and English texts draw closest together in the second volume, even though there remain, even here, notable differences of evaluation and emphasis.

In English, the threat to lukewarm calm is formulated by Malone at the start as the danger of "throes." "Throes are the only trouble, I must be on my guard against throes. But I am less given to them now, since coming here" (p. 179). The wit of the English is in Beckett's recharging of "throes" by separating it from clichés of extremity—death throes, throes of agony, throes of childbirth. Taken alone, the word "throes" becomes eccentric, newly charged with its original physicality, though also comically assimilated to more ordinary physical disturbances like fits or cramps. Beckett shows here his skill at renewing cliché by dislocations of ordinary phrasing and a defamiliarizing literalness. The accomplishment of the sentences about "throes" shows up in the skill of the final version compared to the weaker first attempt printed in a fragment of translation in *transition:* "The only trouble is the throes. But my throes are better since I came here."[15] Although Beckett already has the idea of what to do with "throes," his first try does not yet give the recuperated cliché full prominence. And it is only in the final version that Beckett exploits the ambiguous play between the literal and figurative connotations of the colloquial "given to." "Throes" are a disturbance that Malone is "given to"—the phrase hovers between the connotation of mere habit and the very opposite, figurative suggestion of self-abandon.

The important contrast, however, is less between the two English versions than between the English and the French, where disturbance is not formulated as "throes" at all, but as the altogether different physical trouble of *sursauts:* "Il importe seulement de faire attention aux sursauts. Du reste je sursaute moins depuis que je suis ici." *Sur-sauts* are sudden little jumps, what in English we might call "starts." Although there is certainly eccentricity in a dying man's complaisance in noting his own progressive immobility, the French *je sursaute moins* lacks the complex play of the English. The wit of the French is simpler, without the ambiguity of "given to" and without the double action of at once diminishing and recuperating the intensity of sensation in "throes." The word *sursauts* merely minimizes the importance of the threats to calm; *sursauts* is not a term habitually used for ultimate agonies. A fuller irony gathers around *sursauts* later in the French, as the word comes to seem grotesquely inadequate for the extremity of mystery, sorrow, and also macabre comedy that overtakes Malone's language when its calm disintegrates. "Throes" seems none too strong a designation for the painfulness of the narrative when describing the farmer's wife alone and awake in the night, for example. "Throes," with its conventional association to the pains of childbearing, seems even more literally appropriate to the imaginative spasm in which the narrator later envisions his birth as an old fetus out of the putrid womb of his dead mother. Through the merely diminishing connotations of *sursauts,* the French deprecates such later spasms of language in ad-vance. Those spasms, in French as well as English, eventually become strong enough to withstand the derision of the French text's initial labeling, but we are aware of a sharper impulse than in the English to withhold undue valuation from any fevers or spasms to come. As mere *sursauts,* they are not ultimate enactments of reality like dying or giving birth, but only little jumps, temporary disorders of the calm.

The English at the start thus goes further toward entitling the most turbulent language in *Malone Dies* to a higher claim, not as more natural but rather as supranatural, the language of that suffering of being which emerges in intervals between the reigns of habit, such as Beckett had described à propos of Proust in his essay of 1931.[16] In contrast to the inert narratives designed to preserve the habit of calm, the rhetoric of "throes" has the quality of that artistic endeavor which we have seen Beckett praise in Proust: the "fertile research" which negates the surface in order to become "excavatory, immersive . . . a descent . . . drawn into the core of the eddy."

Throes take over Malone's discourse, for example, following the crisis of the lost pencil. In his report of this crisis, Malone at first becomes a psychological narrator, commenting on the simultaneity of psychic experience. In retrospect he tells us how, at the same time that he was looking for his pencil and also inspecting the surfaces of his room (walls and floor), in his head everything was "streaming and emptying away as through a sluice" (p. 224). He was also the interested spectator of this process of his living and dying, "able to follow without difficulty the various phases of this deliverance." In contrast to Joyce, however, Beckett has very limited interest in the disorderly simultaneous events of consciousness. His fiction of a writing narrator can proceed only under the guidance of the retrieved pencil, an instrument of selective attention. Even when registering turbulence, Malone's writing acts as an organizing recorder, excluding and subordinating certain sensations or thoughts to others. Throes, therefore, have a delicate status in Malone's written soliloquy: in part they refer to intense physical sensations (for example, of life streaming away as through a sluice), but they pertain more exactly to the quality of attention, of verbal presence given to such sensations in the writing. The sensations, Malone tells us, are really always there; what varies is the degree to which he is given to allowing them rhetorical presence. Malone is less given to throes in this room. To give himself to throes is to allow the spasms of being to displace habits of language whose very purpose, in this light, is to keep them beneath the surface.

A drama of invasion is enacted in the very motions of Beckett's style, for Malone's throes tend to begin in mid-sentence or mid-paragraph, seizing hold of a discourse which has been proceeding as if securely governed by dull rhetorical habit: "And I must say that to me at least and for as long as I can remember the sensation is familiar. . . ." In the midst of this willfully banal rhetoric of memory, the strange intensity comes like an unsolicited revelation—or seduction or even rape: "And sometimes, when all is quiet, I feel it [a blind and tired hand] plunged in me up to the elbow, but gentle, and as though sleeping. But soon it stirs, wakes, fondles, clutches, ransacks, ravages, avenging its failure to scatter me with one sweep. I can understand" (p. 224).

At first mildly erotic but then increasingly aggressive, Malone's image of a mysterious hand reaching into the very core of his being gives a physical intensity to his sensation that overpowers all the book's other language about the physical life of paralyzed limbs and intricately maneuvered physical routines. The distinction between physical and mental or spiritual experience disappears in this language, as does the controlling calm of a rational faculty which sustains such distinctions between mind and body. Other distinctions also dissolve, as between sleep and waking, fondling and ravaging, indifference and vengefulness. The obsession with such distinctions, characteristic of

Malone's calming game of reason, gives way here to dense, evocative metaphoric language. The physical diction is not symbolic, in that it does not stand for some set of ideas about life or death or God. But it is, as Malone himself says, somehow "about" life and death; it *leads down* to those ultimate conditions of being, in the Shakespearean way that Lear's mad visions do, without inviting translation into clear and distinct ideas.

One thinks also, as an English reader, of the daring imaginative evocations of a poet like Donne, commanding his God to ransack his being in a similarly violent action of destructive love. What is in Donne, however, a boldly willful rhetorical performance, a daring setting forth to God of the paradoxical (but logical) terms in which he must be saved, has become in *Malone Dies* even disturbingly modest, unwillful to an extreme. Malone does not strike a posture and pronounce logically intricate paradoxes. In Beckett, the rhetorical throes of the discourse seem to happen *to* the speaker, rather than being worked up *by* him; his very readiness to discount both sensation and rhetoric as "baseless" contributes to the opposite impression of an uncontrolled sincerity. In a discourse where the will is bent upon sustaining an unnatural calm, any appearance of involuntary disruption acquires the authority of a deeper truth. But of course this authority depends, finally, less on the dramatic fiction of the discourse than on the actual expressive power of the metaphoric language itself. In the English of *Malone Dies,* Beckett avoids the somewhat flaccid Romantic sublimity of such phrases as "imminence of dawn" noted in *Molloy.* The disruption of the rational surface occurs in a denser, tougher idiom which mixes levels of diction and saturates the most ordinary words with new intensity—a style which in Beckett's English belongs to a distinguished tradition of expressive prose and poetry, with the backing of such great earlier masters as Shakespeare and Donne.

In the French text the rhetoric of Malone's *sursauts* may seem an even more remarkable feat, because no comparable literary precedents give stature to the disrupted rationalism. Malone's *sursauts* into a powerfully evocative irrational prose in French thus seem more idiosyncratic, more mystifying: "Mais bientôt elle tressaille, se réveille, me flatte, crispe, fouille et quelquefois saccage, comme pour se venger de ne pas pouvoir me balayer. Je la comprends" (p. 93). The French of this passage is very like the English, but the emphasis falls somewhat more on the final claim of the comprehensibility—surprising even to Malone himself—of this language so little obedient to the rules for intelligibility established by the norm of the French style elsewhere.

The image of the probing, caressing, avenging hand is only another *histoire,* but it is perhaps more rather than less directly understandable than the rationalistic story games which it interrupts.

Through the style of *sursauts* and "throes" a new kind of *histoire* enters the second volume of the trilogy: not precisely descriptive (as in the overexact inventories of possessions or physical ailments), not rationalistic (as in the games of reasoning), and not neutral and inert (as in the planned stories of the make-believe characters). Malone's French word *histoire,* to be sure, has the same effect as *sursauts* in shadowing this new metaphoric storytelling with skepticism, for *histoire* in French carries colloquial connotations of the fantastical, the made-up. Yet this new kind of *histoire* also seems the rhetorical equivalent of strange inward forms of excavation and self-immersion. The images are irrational and fantastical, but infused with the heat of something like what we are accustomed to call imagination.

Not ideas about life and death, but imaginings, *histoires* of living, dying, and even of being born. On the page immediately following the image of the ransacking hand is Malone's even more strangely heated fantasy of how, at last, he is being born out of a gangrenous mother. This is a story of "throes" in the old-fashioned sense of labor pains, though neither in French nor in English does the spasm of imagining last quite long enough for the birth fully to occur. There is a brief and violent spasm of imagining. Then a dismissal of the *histoire* as false, with Malone returning to his conviction that he will never truly be born and thus never truly die.

While the language of the ransacking hand is arguably a shade more powerful in its English version, the *histoire* of gangrenous birth in French is unsurpassable in its extraordinary fusing of the macabre and the comic, the sublime and the colloquial, the metaphysical and the obscene. But there is no need to quibble about relative merit; the grotesque fantasy of the self as a bald, impotent fetus is searing in both languages.

> Yes, an old foetus, that's what I am now, hoar and impotent, mother is done for, I've rotted her, she'll drop me with the help of gangrene, perhaps papa is at the party too, I'll land headforemost mewling in the charnel-house, not that I'll mewl, not worth it. (p. 225)

> Oui, voilà, je suis un vieux foetus à présent, chenu et impotent, ma mère n'en peut plus, je l'ai pourrie, elle est morte, elle va accoucher par voie de gangrène, papa aussi peut-être est de la fête, je déboucherai vagissant en plein ossuaire, d'ailleurs je ne vagirai point, pas la peine. (p. 94)

The outrageous blasphemies of this abbreviated extravaganza form what Malone appropriately goes on to call a kind of "legend," a myth, or more literally, a reading of the self as told by and to the self in the throes of imaginative fever. From one point of view, these intense flashes have no more claim to truth than any other stories. They are, in a sense, wholesale whoppers, which do not even combine as either images or ideas, for the ransacking hand and the impotent fetus cannot be arranged as linear or logical parts of a single *histoire*. Yet they are tonally congruent, as fevers of a single recognizable imagination or sensibility. Although they represent no stable self-interpretation, only different enactments, different spasms of self-manifestation, their very outrageousness gives the impression of a voice liberated from the conventional deadness of language as it moves closer to the sensation of actual death. There is an exhilarating sense of breaking through barriers in these passages where the language violates every kind of decorum as recklessly as Joyce does in the most phantasmagoric passages of Nighttown. The Joycean recklessness, however, breaks through decorum to comedy; here the exhilaration never loses the quality of an agony. There is no doubt as to why Malone wants to preserve calm and tepidness. The color of this feverish language, even with its wit, is the color of intense pain.

Both the intensity of pain and the impression of the spasmodic, so strong in the very word "throes," disqualify the self-excavatory flashes from becoming a narrative mode that could be sustained, even if one so desired. Malone in any case does not so desire, and the sudden appearance of the character Macmann comes as such a satisfying resource, just after these crises of heat, because it allows a necessary cooling off and stretching out of the discourse; it allows a movement back in the direction of calm associated with the game of storytelling at the start.

Beckett's brilliance in both the French and English versions of *Malone meurt / Malone Dies* shows, however, in his power to go beyond any merely mechanical alternation of hot and cold styles of language and feeling. In both versions the story of Macmann rhetorically enacts the more complex process of fiction-making as a movement back toward composure—a composure, however, which comes to include, in unmistakable if subdued form, the pains of self excavated in the more turbulent earlier imaginings.

Pain is muted in the Macmann story, even transformed at times by the storyteller's absorbed pleasure in the turns of his invention. By returning to a character—or more precisely, by experiencing in his mind the return of a character—Malone reconstitutes himself as the composed narrator of a representational story. The story represents a human figure, complete with coat and hat and located in a describable physical space, with weather (rain) and landscape (at least, a ground to lie down on in the rain). With these minimal furnishings, later supplemented by a few other characters (chiefly the woman Moll) and another place (the asylum), the story unfolds a sequence of fictional events very like the events of other novels: illusion, disillusion, and self-castigation (in relation to the rain), and a romance complete with sex and love letters. And at the same time that this elemental fictional structure builds, Beckett allows us to see the self-composing origins and purposes of this (and by implication all other) so-called representational stories.

Fragments of Malone's (and Beckett's own) obsessions pervade the story of Macmann, but the structure of the created character and his experiences contains the earlier pain, even if awkwardly and with a palpable registering of the nearby menace of breakdown. For example, in the midst of a calm inventory, so to speak, of Macmann's skills and limitations, the language almost dissolves into obscurely urgent rambling. Malone had been describing Macmann's ability to fix the wooden pegs of his coat, and his need for at least this elementary skill: "For he had to, he had to, if he wished to go on coming and going on the earth, which to tell the truth he did not, particularly, but he had to, for obscure reasons known who knows to God alone, though to tell the truth God does not seem to need reasons for doing what he does, and for omitting to do what he omits to do, to the same degree as his creatures, does he?" (p. 245). In the English, as in the French, such passages enact the near derailing of the story and the near unraveling of the rhetorical thread. The "obscure reasons known who knows to God alone" gesture toward the bewildering breakdown of not only Macmann's will to go on, but of the narrator's also. Yet the breakdown does not occur and the enclosing structure of the Macmann fiction quickly reassumes its protective containment. The sanity, or pseudosanity, of calm returns: "Such then seemed to be Macmann, seen from a certain angle" (p. 245).

The Macmann story both enacts and parodies all the angles by which fictional narrative can displace anxiety and upset. Thus Malone at times enjoys an even pleasurably tender condescension toward his character Macmann—toward his deep errors of judgment, for example, or his irrational penchant for self-castigation, his imperfect foresight, his romantic bewilderment. Whereas the spasmodic ruminative passages show pain with an intensity that cannot be sustained, the Macmann story calms by distancing earlier crazed feelings of self-disgust and loathing. In a fictional space which eventually becomes a literal asylum, craziness is localized, distributed, and even tonally transformed: physical self-repugnance reappears in the more benign comic grotesquerie of the romance between Macmann and Moll; the wildly self-assaultive energies of the earlier throes are displaced onto the aggressive figure of Lemuel, where the upsetting earlier sense of self-laceration diminishes. The calming conversions of fiction-making do not require a scene crowded with characters and incident. The most meager rudiments of a story suffice to absorb Malone's excess heat, so that the final dissolution of the voice does occur, as initially desired, in tepid calm rather than in either fever or chills.

In the very final portion of *Malone meurt* / *Malone Dies,* the menace lifts so much as to leave an almost disconcerting surface of drained intensity. In the low-key story of the picnic and the final floating away of Macmann, intensity of feeling seems utterly withdrawn from the narrative voice, or so totally displaced that it is barely identifiable. Lemuel, as the figure of aggression, becomes vague and remote, hard to keep in focus by comparison with the earlier intimate self-projections of the narrator in Macmann, or even in Sapo and the farmer's family.

The specific virtues of Beckett's French falsetto return at the end of the second novel to differentiate the two versions of the text and to make, in my judgment, the surface of aimless neutrality more effective in French than in English. In part, the difference comes from the elusive incandescence already noted in Beckett's grayish tones in French, an effect so hard to match in English. In addition there is, even before the very final episode, a more convincing movement toward self-erasure in the French that gives dramatic support to the neutral concluding style.

One key moment near the end comes when Malone tells of Macmann's wish to escape from the asylum into a more total desolation. First, a wonderfully ironic narrative voice describes the unreasonableness of Macmann's dissatisfaction in this "little Eden." Macmann's own expressions of want are limited to blind groping for some break in the asylum's wall and, as the verbal counterpart to that physical gesture, the gross commonplace exclamation "J'en ai assez" / "I have had enough." Malone as narrator, however, gives further language to his creature's unarticulated desire for some ultimate way out. And in the French, this language not only describes the desire for a desolation beyond all desire, but this time seems uncannily to approach that goal through the completeness of its own verbal negations.

> . . . cherchant une issue vers la désolation de n'avoir personne ni rien, vers la terre au pain rare, aux abris rares, des terrifiés, vers la noire joie de passer seul et vide, ne rien pouvant, ne rien voulant, à travers le savoir, la beauté, les amours. Ce qu'il exprimait en disant, J'en ai assez, car il etait simple. (p. 197)

This language has not attained pure self-negation, of course, but it is moving remarkably close to escape from any ordinary expression of desire. In French, escape comes, not through a hole such as Macmann seeks, but by the virtual disappearance of the speaking self into a wall of language whose very blankness approaches the black joy so perversely desired. Toward the end of *Malone meurt,* the very emptiness of an utterly simple style acquires new paradoxical intensity as the linguistic sign of the freedom associated with death. There is no effort here to assert individuality by breaking rhetorical decorum or wrenching new vitality out of cliché. Hence the extraordinary simplicity of common diction and syntax: "la désolation de n'avoir personne ni rien," "seul et vide," "ne rien pouvant, ne rien voulant"; the undistinguished synecdoche: "la terre au pain rare"; the standard series of grand substantives: "le savoir, la beauté, les amours." The sentence moves toward and even into the condition of desolation with a composure which would seem also to be a perfect dignity, if dignity did not connote the presence of personality, which is precisely what is being emptied out of this space of language. In the middle, the oddly ill-fitting interpolation of "des terrifiés" juts out as the sole sign of some remaining fever of feeling, since the term strangely populates the imagined empty space of desolation with other people, terrified people. The verbal presence of this terror, its self-exposing idiosyncrasy, indicates the degree to which Malone has not yet entered the blankness of absolute neutrality. But the single word is tightly enclosed in the surrounding wall of language. It is not canceled, not even assimilated syntactically, but held tightly in, restricted in its resonance to the full extent possible with such a powerful word.

Beckett's translation of this passage illustrates again how the very mobility of his English resists the negating impulse in the French, so that the "black joy" of desolation remains a more theoretical as well as more elusive goal. What we hear in the English is still the voice of desire, unable to lose itself in neutrality, even for the space of this sentence. In English, the search for a "way out into desolation" is paradoxically blocked by the absence of a blank and firm enough rhetorical wall into which the voice can disappear.

> . . . seeking a way out into the desolation of having nobody and nothing, the wilds of the hunted, the scant bread and the scant shelter and the black joy of the solitary way, in helplessness and will-lessness, through all the beauty, the knowing, and the loving. Which he stated by saying, for he was artless, I have had enough. (p. 278)

In English, Macmann is called "artless," instead of "simple," as in French, and this shift oddly acknowledges the degree to which the English Malone is not only more articulate than Macmann, but also more artful or even arty, in the sense of calling upon all sorts of rhetorical effects. The self-negating style of the French is, of course, also artful in the extraordinary control maintained. But the English is artful in more overt ways. Poetic phrasings like "the black joy of the solitary way" color the stronger simplicity of "la noire joie de passer seul et vide"; the conspicuously heavy substantives "helplessness and will-lessness" display a voice straining beyond ordinary English diction, instead of smoothly effacing itself, as in the French "ne rien pouvant, ne rien voulant." The impressiveness of the negation in the French depends on the further ease with which the voice can list the grand abstractions of "le savoir, la beauté, les amours" simply as objects to be passed by. In English, Beckett chooses not to use the available substantives. Perhaps "knowledge," "beauty," and "love" (or "loves") are somehow not banal enough for the voice to be able to pass by with indifference. Or perhaps, since the English sentence has already become committed to variety and a more fluid movement of desire, Beckett chooses to go further into the evocation of sorrowful pain: "all the beauty, the knowing and the loving."

As noted in other passages of the trilogy, once Beckett hears the loss of the special hum of his French, he often seems rightly to exploit rather than minimize differences of effect. The English gerunds "the knowing and the loving," even the intensifier "all," give the English version a greater hum of emotion, evoking the very engagement in life that is being rejected. But for that same reason, the English phrasing specifically does not enact the move past the verbal signatures of the living world with anything like the uncompromising refusal of feeling in the French. And since there is no rhetorical equivalent in the English for the desolation of wanting nothing, the terror of such a bleak exile is also dissipated. Not surprisingly, the one sharp jolt of the

French in "des terrifiés" disappears or rather dissolves into one among many artful images of deprivation: "the wilds of the hunted, the scant bread and the scant shelter."

The gradual dying of Malone's voice is a subtly modulated rhetorical drama in both French and English, with many lurches back into life and many premature announcements and imperfect rehearsals. The differences of detail that add up to a total difference of effect come from the repeatedly greater resistance of the English to every gesture of self-erasure. For a last example of this contrast, it is fitting to note the significant moment when Malone repudiates the first person pronoun. ("I" / *Je* does not appear again in the book.) In the midst of yet another turn at the game of verifying his existence, Malone comes back to the conviction that he is still alive by means of certainty that he is now really dying: "Indéniablement mourant, un point c'est tout" (p. 207) / "Indubitably going, that's all that matters" (p. 283). Again, the sensation of dying appears as an *histoire* of death as an action of birth. This time, however, the grotesque earlier fantasy of an old fetus coming out of a gangrenous womb, that abortive spasm of imagination discussed earlier, moves further toward completion, and in a strikingly different tone of calm, even lightheartedness. "Grandiose souffrance" / "Grandiose suffering," he remarks, the denigrating notation signifying his dissociation from any grandiose *sentences* about this condition. In the French, this style of quick, fragmented, quietly witty notation dominates the paragraph.

> Fenêtre. Je ne la verrai plus, me trouvant à regret dans l'impossibilité de tourner la tête. Lumière à nouveau saturnienne, bien tassée, traversée de remous, se creusant en entonnoirs profonds à fond clair, ou devrais-je dire l'air, lumière aspirante. Tout est prêt. Sauf moi. Je nais dans la mort, si j'ose dire. Telle est mon impression. Drôle de gestation. Les pieds sont sortis déjà, du grand con de l'existence. Présentation favorable j'espère. Ma tête mourra en dernier. Ramène tes mains. Je ne peux pas. La déchirante déchirée. Mon histoire arrêtée je vivrai encore. Décalage qui promet. C'est fini sur moi. Je ne dirai plus je. (p. 208)

Malone retires the *je* from his discourse in a final action of somber playfulness. Although the large, deep image of light in darkness opens in the middle of the passage to some obscurely profound illumination, this impulse toward grandeur is stopped short of grandiosity by the incompleteness of the sentence fragment and by the quite beautiful but elegantly casual phrasemaking, "ou devrais-je dire l'air, lumière aspirante." In its context, the rich visionary image is held within a seemingly easy rhetorical game of one kind of phrase played off against another, with no one formulation allowed too much reverberation. Instead of the spasmodic, gasping intensity of the earlier fantasy of birth into death, here all is subdued, calm—grandiose suffering reduced to casual wit. Even the intense paradox of birth into death is thrown off as a manner of speaking, uninsistently, accompanied by mildly self-deprecating asides: "Telle est mon impression. Drôle de gestation." The wit of the passage lacks the pressure and also the macabre blasphemy of the earlier spasm of imaginary birth. Emerging feet first into death, and thus inverting the normal presentation of the newborn, Malone lightly conflates a language of formal courtesy and the jargon of the delivery room: "Présentation favorable, j'espère." His head will die last, which is why he will continue past this conclusion of his own personal story; the remainder of the narration seems an utterance not of the whole person, but of the head alone.

Already in this passage of self-abdication, the inclusive physical, emotional, and spiritual turbulence of the earlier seizures has drained out. Malone's dry tone makes it seem easy now to play out the remainder. The content of the language may be wrenching and rending, but the tone, even the syntax, leaves little opening for pain. Whereas in other French passages of chill or tepidness, Beckett uses the firm shape of well-built phrases in sentences as the structure which contains and restricts feeling, here the tightly constructed phrase alone stands as an even more effective syntactic unit to shut out the immediacy of a suffering self: "La déchirante déchirée." The phrase has an epigrammatic finality that leaves no opening for spillovers of personality.

While presumably renouncing the "I" with equal finality in the translation, the texture of Malone's English once again allows more presence to Malone's unreadiness to die—which is, to be sure, acknowledged in passing in the French also. I am measuring, as Malone is measuring, relative but not absolute degrees of readiness for death. In English, while the feet may be dead, more of the body seems to remain alive, and more of the life of language remains entangled in the body of words.

> The window. I shall not see it again. Why? Because, to my grief, I cannot turn my head. Leaden light again, thick, eddying, riddled with little tunnels through to brightness, perhaps I should say air, sucking air. All is ready. Except me. I am being given, if I may venture the expression, birth to into death, such is my impression. The feet are clear already, of the great cunt of existence. Favourable presentation I trust.

My head will be the last to die. Haul in your hands. I can't. The render rent. My story ended I'll be living yet. Promising lag. That is the end of me. I shall say I no more. (p. 283)

Beckett's English style remains, even here, more thickly and even awkwardly "given to" the throes of both birth and death—as if obstacles not only of his will but in the very medium of the language itself were blocking the passage to his imagined deliverance. In the English, for example, there is no equivalent to the smooth ease of the French: "Je nais dans la mort, si j'ose dire." By comparison, the English version is all awkward and clogged: "I am being given, if I may venture the expression, birth to into death, such is my impression." The passive construction, the clumsy combination of prepositions, the stiff interruption of the idiom "give birth" by a wordier, more pompous interjection—all these details make the whole process of birth into death more peculiar in English. Beckett's exact touch in these matters shows in his simply dropping from the translation the light French aside, "Drôle de gestation." It is not so much that English lacks a corresponding idiom as that the entire English passage lacks the lightness encapsulated in the French phrase. Birth into death in the English has not been subdued to the French "drôle de gestation." The movement of the translation is opposite, toward greater intensity at every point: "à regret," becomes the stronger "to my grief," and "Ramène tes mains," the more strenuous and even slightly heroic "Haul in your hands." Most strikingly, the elegant epithet "lumière aspirante" acquires more concrete and more upsetting resonance, both in sound and association, as "air, sucking air."

In the English version of *Malone Dies,* "throes" in a sense remain a trouble right up to the point where the narrative fades into the blandness of the picnic story. In English, that final blandness therefore is simply anticlimactic, since the difficulty of eliminating "throes" is not only the trouble but also the strength of the English version. In French, the resistant language is also valuable, but with more qualification, first because the representation of calm has a more compelling style of its own in French, and second because the *sursauts* of personality have been allowed less dignity all along in the evaluative language of the book. The successful effacement of the *je* in favor of a casual impersonality achieves, in French, the condition necessary for bringing the book to closure. In English, not only Malone but the book itself goes dead when the speaking subject withdraws. Without the strong personal self-presence of the earlier styles, the conclusion of *Malone*

Dies in English becomes duller and colorless rather than incandescently gray.

Le type respiratoire / **The Respiratory Type:**
L'Innommable / *The Unnamable*

From the perspective of *L'Innommable / The Unnamable,* the closure of *Malone meurt / Malone Dies* becomes newly problematic in both French and English. For a speaking subject returns in the third volume to dismiss all its earlier rhetorical inventions as not just *histoires* but *mensonges* / "lies." Malone's neutral calm, which now seems to derive from an authorial voice behind Malone, was only a playing dead, as indeed all Malone's other styles were nothing but a playing live. The open and insistent dis-appropriation of all language as inauthentic in the third volume goes much further in skepticism than did the earlier voices, though negation itself becomes so vociferous that it generates its own drama of language and personality in both the French and English of the final volume.

It is a critical commonplace to regard *L'Innommable / The Unnamable* as the most abstract novel of the trilogy, and the reasons for this reputation are obvious in the book's refusal—beginning with the title— to accept any of the names by which language presumes to attach itself to reality.[17] The third volume is abstract in the specific ideological sense that it denies the referential value of language that we have inherited along with other cultural values. The voice in *L'Innommable / The Unnamable* accepts no inheritance, generates nothing to be inherited. He will not play the games of the culture, refusing from the start, for example, to adopt even the verbal counters of the Cartesian *cogito:* not the pronoun *je* and not the verb *penser.* He may say the words, but the saying refers to no-thing: "Dire je. Sans le penser . . . J'ai l'air de parler, ce n'est pas moi, de moi, ce n'est pas de moi" (pp. 7–8) / "I, say I. Unbelieving . . . I seem to speak, it is not I, about me, it is not about me" (p. 291).

Obsession with the illusory references of language (and with the contradiction of exposing this falsity in the discredited words) does not, however, in itself dictate what we ordinarily think of as an abstract style in prose; indeed the very reverse is more likely true, since an abstract style trusts more rather than less to the naming power of words: not only for persons and things, but also for ideas and values and general truths. Common confusion between abstraction as a preoccupation and abstraction as a quality of language has misled readers of Beckett's third volume to become more abstract than Beckett himself. For he uses every imaginable device of language to manifest his distrust of language and his fear of being duped by the solicitations of language masquerading as realities. The intense, often violent drama of this unnamable voice in conflict with words which press—like things—from without and from within, may even be said to turn *The Unnamable* into the least abstract novel of the trilogy. This voice does not merely contemplate with philosophic detachment, nor does it subscribe to an abstract vocabulary, even though words like "aporia" and "ephectic" are among the verbal presences soliciting its acquiescence. More often, however, the solicitations come in concrete terms as a conspiracy of characters—the old ones from Beckett's other writings and new ones, some with names like Mahood, and others ("they") no less palpable for being anonymous. Solicitation comes also in the language of concrete imagery: lures on a fishhook, photographs offering identities for the taking, a stack of putrid bodies, the menu of a restaurant near a slaughterhouse, rocks on which to be lashed, precipices to be leapt off.

All these characters and images are mere inventions, of course. We are not allowed to believe in the novel's concrete language as we believe in the minimal fictional facts of a character named Malone, lying on a bed in a room. Yet within the insistent structure of denial, Beckett gives us a voice full of what we conventionally call concrete language. This language is made to seem seductive, since otherwise the voice would not be in such danger of being duped. Repudiation is necessary over and over again only because the temptation to believe in the referentiality of language cannot be decisively eradicated. As long as the voice continues, and it seems unable to stop, it keeps biting at the lure of concrete language. Going for the lure, but then just avoiding the hook—that is one image for the drama of this voice. Recognition that a lure is false food, like the insistence that words and images do not correspond to reality, does not have the effect of purifying the prose. If the book becomes oppressive, and I agree that it does, that is not because of its abstractness, but because of the unrelenting repetition of its solicitations and negations. Even this repetition acquires interest, however, from the extraordinary variety of lures Beckett includes. Virtually every kind of language we ordinarily use, and even expressions of primitive fantasy usually censored from the language we speak or even think, solicit attention in this style before they are repudiated.

From one point of view, the distinction between French and English hardly matters in this style. Beckett's French seems even freer and more various than before, at the same time that the argument of the book is disclaiming all language as foreign, learned word by word as from lists in school. In *Molloy* the hero's sense of estrangement in language was represented in the falsetto of Beckett's French, as if he had elected the foreign language as a guarantee against lapsing into false naturalness. But by the time of *L'Innommable* / *The Unnamable,* Beckett can handle any appearances of naturalness. The more natural the impression, the more intense the drama; the more compelling the "signs of life" (p. 372)—as the speaker calls sounds—the more urgent the gesture of rejection.

The effect works brilliantly in both French and English, but this time the English style has special advantages. As we have seen all along, the signs of life in Beckett's English tend to be livelier than in his French. And Beckett allows himself even freer rein with his English style in this third volume. With the thematic structure of the book as a protection against the lure of vitality in English, Beckett becomes reckless with a certain kind of irresponsibility. He may have been fed this language from the moment of birth itself, but he has not digested it. His utterance is only a form of throwing up.

A vomit of language: Beckett's sense of language as dis-ease, represented in *Molloy* as chill and in *Malone Dies* as heat and throes, takes the form of a convulsive nausea in *The Unnamable,* and it is in the texture of this vomit, as well as in the governing metaphor of vomit, that the macabre comedy of the book appears in both languages. But in English with more substance: a thicker vomit, thrown up with more convulsive force.

> Not to be able to open my mouth without proclaiming them, and our fellowship, that's what they imagine they'll have me reduced to. It's a poor trick that consists in ramming a set of words down your gullet on the principle that you can't bring them up without being branded as belonging to their breed. But I'll fix their gibberish for them. I never understood a word of it in any case, not a word of the stories it spews, like gobbets in a vomit. My inability to absorb, my genius for forgetting, are more than they reckoned with. (pp. 324–25)

> Ne pouvoir ouvrir la bouche sans les proclamer, à titre de congénère, voilà ce à quoi ils croient m'avoir réduit. M'avoir collé un langage dont ils s'imaginent que je ne pourrai jamais me servir sans m'avouer de leur

tribu, la belle astuce. Je vais le leur arranger, leur charabia. Auquel je n'ai jamais rien compris du reste, pas plus qu'aux histoires qu'il charrie, comme des chiens crevés. Mon incapacité d'absorption, ma faculté d'oubli, ils les ont sous-estimées. (p. 76)

In both French and English, the crude force of Beckett's outburst paradoxically owes its vitality to the "gobbets" of common language that the voice is in the very act of rejecting. "Walled round with their vociferations," as he goes on to say, he can vociferously refuse the fellowship of the human tribe only by throwing up gobbets of a common language of protest and outrage. The lively voice is therefore comically indeterminate; it does and does not belong to the speaker. The gesture of protest, the action of throwing up, is his. But the verbal pieces which constitute the substance of the action are the very signs of life he refuses. In French, there is a thickness of slang beyond the fluent colloquialisms of the earlier volumes: "la belle astuce," "leur charabia." In English, the gobbets are even thicker, beginning with the word "gobbets" itself. Moreover, the gobbets of English idiom are not set off as appositives, as in the French, but are more thoroughly, more naturally incorporated into the syntax: "It's a poor trick . . . ramming down your gullet . . . But I'll fix their gibberish for them." The very overload of idiom in the passage is almost a caricature of a voice spewing out protest. There is another voice, he tells us, at least he has the idea, the intuition of another voice which has not been heard from yet. That voice, which still cannot be articulated except in the same imagery of vomit, will be empty of gobbets, pure of alien color and alien substance, like the dry heaves of a starveling: "And I'll be myself at last, as a starveling belches his odourless wind, before the bliss of coma" (p. 325) / "C'est moi alors que je vomirai enfin, dans des rots retentissants et inodores de famélique, s'achevant dans le coma, un long coma délicieux" (p. 77).

The imagery of vomit is rich for Beckett's purposes in *L'Innommable* / *The Unnamable*. Since the last odorless heaves cannot be achieved, the more ordinary human retching of the voice as it speaks can signify all the ambiguity and paradox of Beckett's final vision of expression in language. For the undigested substance of vomit is still partially transformed; even if whole pieces remain hardly changed, some action has begun which distinguishes vomit from mere spitting back of rejected food. Digestive juices—in saliva, the stomach, or wherever—right away start their action of assimilation, so that what is given back is virtually never identical to what has been taken in. And the different odor, the different color is that of the self, manifested in the very action of not digesting.

This curious mixture of half-digested, convulsively spewed-out fragments is exactly what we find in the language of the third volume. The impure utterance is not absolutely detached from self-expression, which is why the voice does not stabilize into simple dissociation from its language. If he were only a parrot, and sometimes he does imagine himself this way, he would merely repeat "their" language unchanged. But some other force is at work, forcing a deeper convulsion, less simple than the heartless rote returns of a parrot: "But God forbid, that would be too easy, my heart wouldn't be in it, I have to puke my heart out too, spew it up whole along with the rest of the vomit, it's then at last I'll look as if I mean what I'm saying, it won't be just idle words" (pp. 335–36) / "Allons donc! Ce serait trop facile, le coeur n'y serait pas, il faut que le coeur me sorte par la gueule aussi, entortillé dans un vomi de boniments, là alors j'aurai enfin l'air de me croire, ce ne sera plus des paroles en l'air" (p. 99). In both French and English, Beckett's play on "heart" restores ambiguous self-expressiveness to the idea of language in the book. He cannot heave his heart up whole, yet for reasons not clearly articulable, his heart is mixed in with the alien puke, vitalizing the monologue beyond the impression of idle words. In its peculiar hovering between deadness and vitality, fragments of cliché are strangely mixed, both with each other and with the "juices" of a radically eccentric sensibility. In puking up the signs of verbal life which do not signify the essential substance of his being, the speaker manifests a character strangely and painfully entangled (*entortillé*) in the verbal material of the life he discovers.

When Buck Mulligan, at the opening of *Ulysses*, bullies Stephen Dedalus to "cough up" the truth of his grievances, Joyce exposes the demand for deepest sincerity to be a form of social bullying. As observed in Chapter 6, the echo of that bullying, directed at Bloom by one of his accusers in Nighttown ("Cough it up. Get it out in bits"), satirizes internalized and projected versions of the demand for deep and total self-excavation. Joyce seems intent upon exorcising the ghosts of all authorities demanding such sincerity, whether social, esthetic, psychological, or religious. Stephen, Bloom, and Joyce himself evade the worst aggressiveness of both exterior and interior commands to throw up their hearts whole. We have seen Joyce's registration of how even the unspoken language of consciousness disguises heart pains in words of strange color and fragrance. The mannered art of Stephen's interior monologue, like the more commonplace idiom of

Bloom's, works to maintain a self-protective distance in consciousness from the reality of suffering.

Our sense of such distance depends, of course, on Joyce's also showing us his characters intermittently beset by fragments of reality that are not fully subdued by the ordering and calming devices of inner speech. There is a category of verbal notation in *Ulysses* which approximates the painful facts of the emotional life, like the almost wordless exclamation "Ffoo!" when Bloom remembers his father's suicide, or the sharp fragments of imagery that evoke the haunting presence in Stephen's preconsciousness of feelings about his mother's life and especially her dying. In such passages Joyce dramatizes the intermittent invasion of consciousness by emotionally charged signs of life and death, and then shows the rapid, self-protective movements by which verbal consciousness subdues, organizes, or simply turns the corner away from painful realities which can be neither plainly confronted nor thoroughly repressed. As in Beckett's trilogy, Joyce's characters in *Ulysses* do not cough up their hearts whole, even in their interior monologues. They are, in a sense, also entangled in false verbal self-representations. And again, as in Beckett, this falsity at once keeps Joyce's characters from either living fully or dying fully. However, it is the protection from death that comes to seem the more important value in Joyce's epic of survival.

In *Ulysses,* deep vomit (like drowning) is associated with horrible death, as in Stephen's memory of his mother: "A bowl of white china had stood beside her deathbed holding the green sluggish bile which she had torn up from her rotting liver by fits of loud groaning vomiting" (1.108–10 / 5). Like Stephen, and also Bloom, Joyce is unattracted by the romantic association of death with bliss. Nor is he obsessed by the rhetorical counterpart of death, which is a yearning past the entanglement in life-preserving speech. Even Joyce's ridicule of the self-deceiving imitations of life in his countrymen's speech does not extend to yearning for liberation into absolute truth through wholehearted self-excavation.

Beckett's image of the "vomit" of speech extends Joyce's skepticism toward interior as well as social language, but in a different tone of romantic yearning. In *L'Innommable* / *The Unnamable* the longing for total self-manifestation is a constant inner urgency, while the disappearance of any rhetorical equivalent to Joycean fact creates a kind of void under even the most absorbing verbal inventions. In the Mahood stories, for example, where the voice sometimes comes remarkably close to the self-cheering resourcefulness of a Bloomian interior monologue, the unrelenting reminders of inauthenticity maintain the under-feeling of futile labor, a pensum, even amid a flow of speech rich in signs of life.

Here, for example, is part of a Mahood story, taken from the moment where the speaker has just presented his character inside a jar and affixed to the edge by a collar attached just below the chin. The fiction dissolves quickly into the seemingly more personal anxiety of the speaker's own fantasy of asphyxiation. The passage is so good that it deserves quotation at length, especially since the extended meditation on breathing offers a more engaging version of the obsession with life processes seen in the imagery of vomit elsewhere.

> There is really only one thing that worries me, and that is the prospect of being throttled if I should ever happen to shorten further. Asphyxia! I who was always the respiratory type, witness this thorax still mine, together with the abdomen. I who murmured, each time I breathed in, Here comes more oxygen, and each time I breathed out, There go the impurities, the blood is bright red again. The blue face! The obscene protrusion of the tongue! The tumefaction of the penis! The penis, well now, that's a nice surprise, I'd forgotten I had one. What a pity I have no arms, there might still be something to be wrung from it. No, tis better thus. At my age, to start masturbating again, it would be indecent. And fruitless. And yet one can never tell. With a yo heave ho, concentrating with all my might on a horse's rump, at the moment when the tail rises, who knows, I might not go altogether emptyhanded away. Heaven, I almost felt it flutter! Does this mean they did not geld me? I could have sworn they had gelt me. But perhaps I am getting mixed up with other scrota. Not another stir out of it in any case. I'll concentrate again. A Clydesdale. A Suffolk stallion. Come come, a little cooperation please, finish dying, it's the least you might do, after all the trouble they've taken to bring you to life. The worst is over. You've been sufficiently assassinated, sufficiently suicided, to be able now to stand on your own feet, like a big boy. That's what I keep telling myself. (pp. 332–33)

> Au fond il n'y a qu'une seule chose qui me tracasse, c'est la perspective de me pendre, si jamais je venais à raccourcir davantage. L'asphyxie! Moi qui ai toujours été le type respiratoire. La preuve, cette cage thoracique qui m'est restée, avec l'abdomen. Moi qui murmurais, quand j'y pensais, à chaque inhalation, Voilà l'oxygène qui rentre, et, en expirant, Voilà les saletés qui s'en vont et le sang qui devient vermeil. Le teint bleu. L'obscène protrusion de la langue. La tuméfaction de la pine. Tiens, la pine, je n'y pensais plus. Quel dommage que je n'aie plus de bras, il y aurait peut-être quelque chose à en tirer. Non c'est mieux ainsi. A mon âge, me remettre à me masturber, ce serait indécent. Et puis ça

ne donnerait rien. Après tout, qu'est-ce que j'en sais? A force de tractions bien rhythmées, en pensant de toutes mes forces à un cul de cheval, au moment où la queue se soulève, qui sait, j'arriverais peut-être à
un petit quelque chose. Ciel, on dirait que ça remue! Est-ce à dire qu'on
ne m'a pas coupé? Pourtant il me semblait bien qu'on m'avait coupé. Je
confonds peut-être, avec d'autres bourses. Du reste ça ne bouge plus. Je
vais me concentrer à nouveau. Un percheron. Allons, allons, un bon
mouvement, voyons, finis de mourir, c'est la moindre des choses, après
tout le mal qu'ils se sont donné, pour te faire vivre. Le principal est fait.
Ils t'ont assez assassiné, assez suicidé, pour que tu puisses te débrouiller
tout seul, comme un grand garçon. Voilà ce que je me dis. (pp. 93–94)

The analogy to Bloomian interior monologue here comes partly
from the humorous self-sociability of the voice in relation to such a
conventionally indecent and private subject as masturbation. The sociable tone is created by the interjections of surprise and curiosity, the
private jokes, and the seemingly loose and free associations. There is
even a more particular shadow of Bloom in the odd sexual association
to horses' rumps. And the sheer continuity of the verbal stream also
recalls Bloom, even in its uneven jumpiness. This voice differs from
the French Molloy, *unijambiste,* whose musing on impotence and castration was distinctive for its strange balance, although it does recall
the jauntier English version of that voice. Beckett's speaker, however,
now lacking arms as well as both legs and equipped with only a thorax
and abdomen (and perhaps a penis), has no possibility of balance even
in French. The characterizing trait of the voice is its sheer inexhaust-
ibility, its ever surprising fresh inventiveness, as figured in the revivify-
ing action of breathing itself. He is "the respiratory type," *le type
respiratoire,* at once terrified of asphyxiation and obsessed with the
impossibility of taking the last breath.

As a metaphor of style, the image of breath stands as analogue to
vomit, but in a less repellent mode, just as the lighter wit of the passage
is a relief from the book's more convulsive style elsewhere. Breathing,
puking, speaking: the governing images give a range of tonalities to the
basic ambiguity of every life-sustaining process. For in breathing too it is
"the impurities" (*les saletés*) which are emitted, as if the red blood of the
unspeakable true life revived only during a process of eliminating poiso-
nous alien substances. Moreover, the distinctiveness of a respiratory
identity is itself paradoxical since all men, and even lower species, belong to *le type respiratoire.* For a moment at least, the voice becomes
comical by cherishing as a special trait the sign of membership in the
most fundamental community of living creatures.

In its actual texture, the mixture of commonplaces in the style of *le type respiratoire* displays the same ambiguous life as the gobbets in the passages about vomit. There is color, odor, and motion in this language; it has signs of life, but the signs only ambiguously refer back to the voice which disowns the attributes posited in the language almost as fast as he articulates them. The very incongruity of the physical images makes for a comedy of repudiated referentiality. Right after this passage the speaker talks of needing to take "the last step" off the precipice. Yet he evidently has no legs and is collared to a jar, not at the edge of a precipice at all, if he indeed is in a jar, which he later also denies! And who are "they," toward whom he is constrained to feel this confusing mixture of resentment, obligation, and gratitude? Is the "they" any more than another piece of verbiage, the mere pronoun "they" being as empty of reference as the pronoun "I"? Beckett gives us neither a named speaker nor a sustained character named Mahood to whom we can attach pronouns, places of residence, or a definite inventory of bodily parts, however ill-functioning. The physical references, phrases of address, self-address, and fantasy in *L'Innommable / The Unnamable* thus carry a much stronger label of falsity than similar forms of language in the two earlier volumes, themselves so much more thinly rooted in fictional fact than Joyce's *Ulysses*. Yet the convincing rhythm of speech, along with the special morbid flavor of the wit, does all but seduce us into believing in the life of this "I" voice, regardless of all disclaimers. Although made up of ill-fitting, even contradictory fragments like gobbets in vomit, the impurities expelled in breathlike speech carry the distinctive odor of a particular breather, but inextricably mixed with the unindividualized impurities which belong to all human exhalation.

As in the rhetoric of vomit, Beckett's style for "the respiratory type" shows the advantage of his denser, thicker English. There are, for example, not only the same colloquial clichés as in French, but extra fillips such as the Hamlet-like "No, tis better thus," instead of the merely colloquial "non, c'est mieux ainsi." Not only the parody of bourgeois respectability in the self-rebuke for the indecency of senile masturbation, but the additional exuberance of bawdy puns and jokes made out of the physical underpinnings of English idiom: "With a yo heave ho, concentrating with all my might on a horse's rump, at the moment when the tail rises, who knows, I might not go altogether emptyhanded away." Beckett shows signs of having learned, from "Eumaeus" as well as from the Bloomian monologues, the Joycean comic art of stringing multicolored verbal clichés from different orders of discourse along a loose sentence thread so that they sparkle and jingle in collision. The French original here is sedate and static by comparison: "A force de tractions bien rhythmées, en pensant de toutes mes forces à un cul de cheval, au moment où la queue se soulève, qui sait, j'arriverais peut-être à un petit quelque chose." The joke of the French goes only in one direction, as the sentence comically runs down from its initial imitation of high, technical formality ("A force de tractions bien rhythmées") to the meager anticlimax at the end ("peut-être à un petit quelque chose"). More different jokes go on in the English, where the tone dips and rises several times within the sentence, and where the wit of "emptyhanded" introduces a new surprise rather than an anticlimax at the end.

Practical and morally bracing idioms which invoke hands and feet constitute exactly the kind of gobbet this voice has been fed: "You've been sufficiently assassinated, sufficiently suicided, to be able now to stand on your own feet, like a big boy. That's what I keep telling myself." Parental clichés—the sickening formulae which parents in Beckett from Moran to Sapo's papa force-feed their offspring—return here with a new degree of absurdity as an internalized idiom of self-reproach. The French enacts the same gesture, but the moral commonplace in French is abstract in phrasing: "pour que tu puisses te débrouiller tout seul, comme un grand garçon." In English, by contrast, where moral commonplace so often relies on models of physical robustness, the estrangement of the bodiless voice from the moral as well as sexual performances of common life becomes more sharply focused. Without hands one cannot masturbate; without legs one cannot perform the actions that constitute moral responsibility, not even suicide. The kernel of the point is there, in French, in the phrase, *le dernier pas,* but the full comic entanglement in a moral idiom rooted in bodily parts and actions comes to much fuller life in English, where the moral meaning of the speaker's physical mutilations emerges from the actual texture of common language. To be without hands or feet, to be Mahood or, more radically, Worm, or to have no body at all, is to be removed from the reference of moral language, outside the community of moral life altogether.

Yet the language of the communal life survives bodily amputations. And as it contaminates the utterances of the voice, it also strangely animates it. This voice seems not only to parody but even, uncontrollably, to enter with pleasure into its own vigorous performances of speech: "I like this colourful language, these bold metaphors and apostrophes" (p. 333). The more than slightly absurd energy of common idiom comes out with the other impurities of *le type respiratoire* in both French and English. But the color is stronger in English, which makes both the comedy livelier and the violent actions of dis-appropriation more upsetting.

In the "Eumaeus" chapter of *Ulysses* the public temperance shelter, with its offering of undigestible rolls, coffee, and whoppers in the way of stories, satirically corresponds to the shelter of language itself—in particular, language in the commonplace forms of cliché, euphemism, and diverting fabrication. As observed in Chapter 6, the tawdriness of language in "Eumaeus" hardly disguises the material and spiritual squalor of the scene, but language does wrap meager human facts in protective layerings. Measured by the standard of a true language, a language in which either the self or others may be truly known, the style of "Eumaeus" is ludicrously inadequate, just as the shelter itself is inadequate as a substitute for a home. And although Bloom eventually takes Stephen to his home on Eccles Street for further nourishment in the form of cocoa, the style of neither "Ithaca" nor "Penelope" offers a linguistic equivalent to that concrete image of hospitality and communion. Bloom's home is very quiet in the early morning hours of June 17. The style of "Ithaca" elaborately emphasizes all that is *not* said and, indeed, is unsayable between Stephen and Bloom, and then between Bloom and Molly. The full reality of these relationships remains ambiguous, never expressly defined.

Yet the intimation of relationship is sustained by all the different language at the end of *Ulysses,* as is the impression of a reality solid enough to rest in, at least for Molly and Bloom. If Joyce shows Bloom's home to offer no more trustworthy language than the whoppers of the shelter, the estrangement from truth attendant upon all language in Joyce's novel does not eradicate the fact that Bloom has a home, however disordered, and that he and Molly too are content to rest there, however imperfect their mutual position. Nor does Joyce show—either in his characters or in the design of the novel as a whole—imperious longings for a language more purely transparent to the imperfect facts of human life. While exposing all systems of verbal invention to be one or another kind of shelter, *Ulysses* encourages us to recognize the human urge for shelter as a link between Bloom and his wife, and also between the commonplace consciousness of a Bloom and the self-evading artiness of a Stephen Dedalus, and finally between all these characters and the rich self-transforming art of a great writer like Shakespeare—or Joyce himself. If only from the safe distance of his exile, Joyce perceived that both sanity and art depend on delicate, never finally completed wanderings toward and away from home—wanderings never totally beyond reach of the truths of common experience and not denying estrangement either, yet also not longing for fuller and more total immersion, whether in a place or in a pure language.

Although Beckett's fiction affirms the same life-preserving quality of verbal inventiveness, Beckett presents the condition of estrangement in language with an altogether different restlessness. Near the end of *L'Innommable* / *The Unnamable* the speaker gropes to articulate why he wanted to be silent before entering the final silence of death, and in both French and English the expression of this desire at first occurs in a lyricism of abstraction, as if the sheer grammatical play between forms of the verb "to be" could finally register the essence of longing for that repose of pure being unsettled by every verbal action: "I can't say why I should have liked to be silent a little before being dead, so as in the end to be a little as I always was and never could be, without fear of worse to come peacefully in the place where I always was and could never rest in peace, no, I don't know" (p. 396) / "je ne peux pas dire pourquoi j'aurais voulu me taire avant d'être mort, pour être un peu enfin ce qu'ayant toujours été je n'ai jamais pu être, sans peur de pire encore tranquillement là où ayant toujours été je n'ai jamais pu reposer, non, je ne sais pas" (p. 225).

This is the style that gives Beckett's third volume its reputation for abstraction. In the flow of the discourse, however, the abstractions provide no more repose, are no more conclusive than the other styles. The voice continues past the abstractions to the possibility of simplification through another figure, this one of the exile's longing for the peace and security of home: "it's simpler than that, I wanted myself, in my own land for a brief space, I didn't want to die a stranger in the midst of strangers, a stranger in my own midst, surrounded by invaders, no, I don't know what I wanted" (p. 396) / "c'est plus simple, je me voulais moi, je voulais mon pays, je me voulais dans mon pays, un petit moment, je ne voulais pas mourir en étranger, parmi des étrangers, en étranger chez moi, au milieu d'envahisseurs, non, je ne sais pas ce que je voulais" (p. 225).

Although the groping search for words to name the desire beyond naming continues, this poignant imagery of homesickness arrests attention beyond what the voice allows. Some simpler truth—of Beckett as well as of his nameless surrogate—seems to sound through the image of the exile's longing for rest in a native land. Yet the onward, unceasing movement of the sentence undermines the pull toward such literal referentiality; the opposition between home and exile is reduced to yet another colored metaphor, a false image moreover, precisely because none of the places evoked in this discourse is allowed to sustain the referential weight of either *en étranger* or *chez moi.* The French phrases are wonderfully suggestive in their double meanings. Home is as unnamable as the speaker himself; it is but another word for self (*moi*); it has no separable form; it is located in no place. There is, in other words, no namable home, as there is in *Ulysses,* and the very distinction between living (or dying) *en étranger* or *chez moi* is fictitious because both terms belong to the language of that life which the voice insists upon as foreign in its entirety.

While the style of impure gobbets is stronger in the English of *The Unnamable,* the obstinacy of this insistent alienation at the end of the trilogy is more striking in French. As the play on *chez moi* suggests, Beckett ends with a French which declares total estrangement in a voice that sounds totally at home in its colloquial fluency. In English the effect of estrangement is subtly but significantly different. The phrase "a stranger in my own midst" sounds eccentric, much further removed from common usage than *en étranger chez moi.* In his native language of English Beckett signals his estrangement by awkward dislocations of idiom, even avoiding the colloquial ease available in the translation of *chez moi* as "at home." In his acquired language of French the estrangement becomes, in a sense, *inouïe,* a hollow beneath a surface even smoother than the one in *Molloy.*

There is no rhetorical exaggeration, however, in either the French or English style here to flaunt particular falsities of common language. Even more than with the experiments in abstract statement, we feel that we are hearing a simplified language, a style earnestly stripped down to the closest possible approximation to truth. And it is this very simplicity which creates the effect of an essential, sharply painful rejection of life itself as either home or even a temporarily tolerable substitute for home. In contrast to the compensatory shelters created by Joyce with such gusto at the end of *Ulysses,* the stripped-down expression of pain at the end of *L'Innommable / The Unnamable* denies the possibility of both home and shelter in any form of language or life. The only fact that survives the unceasing negations is the fact of estrangement itself, irremediable estrangement as an existential condition and as a continual source of pain. At the end, the voice remains alive, so to speak, but only to insist ever more emphatically on its hunger for a wholeness of being violated by every living act of speech.

Beckett's theme of human exile in language (and in life itself) belongs to a romantic tradition in Western literature, and the trilogy, in both languages (as well as in other translations), is rightly recognized as a great twentieth-century rendering in fiction of a sense of estrangement not confined to any single national imagination. Yet it is not surprising that Beckett's most thorough expression of fundamental estrangement should sound more "natural" in its French version. Uncompromising alienation from the signs of life in language has paradoxically constituted a native French tradition, even a community of spirits in French literature, since Rousseau. Beckett, *en étranger chez moi,* shows himself an adoptive member of that community in literature. When, on the other hand, the voice of the trilogy becomes most thickly entangled in the gobbets of impure speech, Beckett moves closer to those other ambivalent exiles and artificers whom I have grouped together in this book. What draws these separate and idiosyncratic novelists toward an English-language tradition is their demonstration of how strongly—for better and worse—the claims of common language resist and even mock impulses to negation. Gestures of disentanglement from the signs of life in English are accompanied by great awkwardness, strain, even violence, and familiar sounds still haunt and taunt. "Hohohohohome," mocks the phantasmagoric voice of The Horse at the end of Joyce's Nighttown.

In 1958, the same year he finished the English version of *The Unnamable,* Beckett wrote *Krapp's Last Tape* in English. He wrote the play, with its wonderful variations on a single voice, for the Irish actor Patrick Magee, whom he had heard performing his work on the radio in 1957. Magee's voice, he is reported as saying, was the one he heard in his head.[18] The play is about an old man who replays tapes of his own earlier voice, tapes which themselves include commentary on still earlier tapes, in what we understand to be a lifelong occupation of talking and listening to himself. Now he does nothing but eat bananas, drink, play pieces of his tapes, and make yet one more record of brooding, mocking self-commentary. Mechanically preserved on the tapes, and replayed in fragments, the most intimate crises of life— mourning, love, regret, resolve—become (to us and also to Krapp) half deadened by sheer repetition. Yet he listens to his favorite spools with indefatigable interest, even obsession. Krapp's way of remaining fascinated as well as repelled by the signs of life and death audible in his recorded voice dramatizes again the intense and unresolved ambivalence toward the language of speech that so remarkably pervades the trilogy, too—an ambivalence which comes to seem in Beckett inseparable from the impure breath of life itself.

NOTES

Introduction

1. "I Could Give All to Time," *The Poetry of Robert Frost,* ed. Edward Lathem (New York: Holt, Rinehart & Winston, 1969), p. 335.

2. Deirdre Bair, *Samuel Beckett: A Biography* (New York: Harcourt Brace Jovanovich, 1978), p. 275.

3. Richard Ellmann, *James Joyce* (New York: Oxford Univ. Press, 1959), p. 21.

4. See *D. H. Lawrence: The Critical Heritage,* ed. R. P. Draper (New York: Barnes & Noble, 1970), pp. 89–109.

5. Letter from William James, October 22, 1905, cited by Leon Edel in *Henry James: Letters* (Cambridge, Mass.: Harvard Univ. Press, 1984), IV, 384, n. 3.

6. Robert Kiely emphasizes "the impulse to strain against categories" in Joyce and Lawrence (and Woolf) in *Beyond Egotism: The Fiction of James Joyce, Virginia Woolf, and D. H. Lawrence* (Cambridge, Mass.: Harvard Univ. Press), pp. 3–13. Kiely wants to move past strain, however, into the "unifying" and "universal" values desired by the novelists, while I am urging sustained engagement with unresolved dramas of strain, both toward and against a variety of categories.

Chapter 1

1. Letter to Louise Colet, December 16, 1852, in *Correspondance,* ed. Jean Bruneau, Bibliothèque de la Pléiade (Paris: Gallimard, 1980), II, 208–9. Cited by Jacques Barzun, Introduction, *Flaubert's Dictionary of Accepted Ideas,* trans. Jacques Barzun (New York: New Directions, 1954), p. 3. The history of Flaubert's composition of the *Dictionnaire* is recounted by R. Dumesmil, *Oeuvres de Flaubert,* ed. A. Thibaudet and R. Dumesmil, Bibliothèque de la Pléiade (Paris: Gallimard, 1948), II, 654–66. Quotations from the *Dictionnaire des idées reçues* refer by page number to this edition. My translation.

2. Roland Barthes, *The Pleasure of the Text* (1973), trans. Richard Miller (New York: Farrar, Straus & Giroux, 1975), pp. 40–41. Barthes also invokes "the army of stereotypes which stalks 'the classic text' " in *S/Z* (1970), trans. Richard Miller (New York: Farrar, Straus & Giroux, 1974), p. 206.

3. Geoffrey Hartman, *Criticism in the Wilderness* (New Haven: Yale Univ. Press, 1980), pp. 244, 297.

4. Barthes, *The Pleasure of the Text,* p. 40.

5. Michael Riffaterre, *Essais de stylistique structurale* (Paris: Flammarion, 1971), pp. 161–73. My translation.

6. Ibid., p. 174.

7. Ibid., p. 176.

8. Ibid.

9. Norman Page, *Speech in the English Novel* (London: Longman, 1973), p. 11.

10. Ibid., pp. 51–53.

11. Raymond Williams, *The Country and the City* (New York: Oxford Univ. Press, 1973), pp. 169–70. See also Page, *Speech in the English Novel,* pp. 126–27.

12. William Wordsworth, Preface to *Lyrical Ballads, Poetical Works,* ed. E. De Selincourt, II (London: Oxford Univ. Press, 1944), 387, 394. Wordsworth's controversial idea of "real" language had more influence as a principle than as an example since, in his poetic practice, Wordsworth's "purified" common language has little coloring of dialect or spoken idiom. Coleridge disputed the poetic principle itself in *Biographia Literaria,* edited with his *Aesthetical Essays,* ed. J. Shawcross (Oxford: Clarendon Press, 1907), II, 28–34.

13. Page, *Speech in the English Novel,* pp. 56–58.

14. F. R. Leavis, "Joyce and 'the Revolution of the Word,' " *Scrutiny* 2 (1933), 193–201; rpt. in *For Continuity* (Cambridge, Eng.: Minority Press, 1933), pp. 207–19.

15. Logan Pearsall Smith, *Words and Idioms* (Boston: Houghton Mifflin, 1925), p. 269.

16. Ibid., p. 156.

17. Logan Pearsall Smith, *The Prospects of Literature* (London: Hogarth Press, 1927), pp. 8–9.

18. Williams, *The Country and the City,* pp. 2, 12, 36, and passim. A further example of this cultural nostalgia appears in the same volume of *Scrutiny* as Leavis's essay on Joyce: see Adrian Bell, "English Tradition and Idiom," *Scrutiny* 2 (1933), 45–50.

19. D. H. Lawrence, "Daughters of the Vicar," *Complete Short Stories* (London: Penguin, 1955), I, 145.

20. Smith, *Words and Idioms,* pp. 189–211.

21. Ibid., p. 254. For other commentary on phrasal verbs, see John Earle, *English Prose* (New York: G. P. Putnam, 1891), pp. 266–67, and John Hilton, "Calculated Spontaneity," in *The Oxford Book of English Talk,* ed. James Sutherland (Oxford: Clarendon Press, 1953), pp. 399–404.

22. Smith, *Words and Idioms,* p. 238.

23. Hugh Kenner, *Dublin's Joyce* (London: Chatto and Windus, 1955), p. 10.

24. Christopher Ricks, "Samuel Beckett" (Paper presented to faculty seminar in literature at M.I.T., Cambridge, Mass., November 1977).

25. F. R. Leavis, *Two Cultures? The Significance of C. P. Snow* (New York: Random House, 1963), p. 36.

26. Roland Barthes, "La Rochefoucauld," in *New Critical Essays* (1972), trans. Richard Howard (New York: Farrar, Straus & Giroux, 1980), p. 8.

27. Barthes, *The Pleasure of the Text,* pp. 49–50. See also "The Triumph and Break-up of Bourgeois Writing," in *Writing Degree Zero* (1953), trans. Annette Lavers and Colin Smith (New York: Farrar, Straus & Giroux, 1968), pp. 55–61.

28. A recent exception to the polarization of Lawrence and Joyce appears in Robert Kiely, *Beyond Egotism.*

29. *Stephen Hero,* ed. Theodore Spencer, with additional pages edited by John J. Slocum and Herbert Cahoon (New York: New Directions, 1955), p. 37.

30. Ibid., p. 26.

31. The ambiguous presence of a "community of speech" in *Ulysses* is described astutely by Williams in *The Country and the City,* pp. 244–45.

32. Quotations from *Ulysses* follow the corrected text prepared by Hans Walter Gabler and refer by episode and line number to the Garland edition, 3 vols. (New York and London: Garland, 1984). Page references to the 1961 edition (New York: Random House) are also included for convenience of reference.

33. Letter to Arthur McLeod, September 1912, in *The Letters of D. H. Lawrence,* ed. James T. Boulton, I (Cambridge, Eng.: Cambridge Univ. Press, 1979), 456.

34. Letter to Arthur McLeod, October 1912, in *Letters,* I, 459.

35. The appeal of Morel in *Sons and Lovers* has been discussed by Mark Schorer, "Technique as Discovery," excerpted in *Twentieth Century Interpretations of "Sons and Lovers,"* ed. Judith Farr (Eaglewood Cliffs, N. J.: Prentice-

Hall, 1970), p. 98, and by Marvin Mudrick, "Looking for Kellerman," in *The Man in the Machine* (New York: Horizon Press, 1977), p. 27.

36. *Sons and Lovers* (London and New York: Penguin, 1976), pp. 196–97.

37. Quotations refer by page number to *Women in Love* (London and New York: Penguin, 1976).

38. Richard Poirier, *Robert Frost: The Work of Knowing* (New York: Oxford Univ. Press, 1977) p. 20. The phrase "taken fresh from talk" comes from a Frost letter of 1914 cited by Poirier, p. 73.

39. Poirier, *Robert Frost,* p. 152.

40. Ibid., p. 158.

41. *A la recherche du temps perdu,* ed. Pierre Clarac and André Ferré, Bibliothèque de la Pléiade (Paris: Gallimard, 1954), I, 155. My translation.

42. *A la recherche du temps perdu,* III, 374–75.

43. Gabriel Josipovici, *The World and the Book* (Stanford, Calif.: Stanford Univ. Press, 1971), p. 17.

44. Smith, *Words and Idioms,* p. 262. See also John Austin, *How to Do Things with Words* (Cambridge, Mass.: Harvard Univ. Press, 1962).

45. Smith, *Words and Idioms,* p. 258.

46. Ibid., p. 187.

47. Earle, *English Prose,* p. 255.

Chapter 2

1. Marcel Proust, *Contre Sainte-Beuve,* ed. Pierre Clarac, Bibliothèque de la Pléiade (Paris: Gallimard, 1971), p. 211. My translation; the looser English translation by Sylvia Townsend Warner erases the distinctive French emphases of Proust's language pertinent to my argument. See Marcel Proust, *On Art and Literature,* trans. Sylvia Townsend Warner (New York: Meridian, 1958).

2. I am indebted to Katherine A. Geffcken, professor of Greek and Latin at Wellesley College, for consultation about Latin usage.

3. *The Boke Named the Gouernour* (1531), ed. H. H. S. Croft (London, 1883), II, 373–74.

4. *Encyclopédie, ou Dictionnaire raisonné des sciences, des arts, et des métiers,* ed. Diderot and d'Alembert (Geneva, 1757; rpt. New York: Reader Microprint Corp., 1969), II, 482. My translation.

5. Samuel Johnson, *A Dictionary of the English Language* (London, 1755).

6. Gilbert Ryle, *The Concept of Mind* (London: Hutchinson's Univ. Library, 1949), pp. 26–27.

7. F. R. Leavis, *D. H. Lawrence: Novelist* (New York: Knopf, 1955), pp. 10–17. Leavis already distinguishes "intelligence" from "intellectual analysis" and offers D. H. Lawrence as a touchstone of intelligence in his early essay "The Literary Mind" (1932), in *For Continuity,* pp. 46–67. Although Leavis in this essay also praises "the quality of intelligence" in T. S. Eliot's poetry (p. 62), criticism of Eliot's dismissive attitude toward Lawrence already

appears the same year in "D. H. Lawrence and Professor Irving Babbitt" (1932), in *For Continuity,* pp. 149–59. See also *The Great Tradition* (London: Chatto and Windus, 1950), pp. 25–26.

8. *D. H. Lawrence: Novelist,* p. 15. Leavis is agreeing with the criticism of *Madame Bovary* in Henry James's essay, "Gustave Flaubert" (1902). Other derogatory comments about Flaubert and (to a lesser extent) Proust are scattered throughout Leavis's work: see, for example, *The Great Tradition,* pp. 4, 8–12.

9. Matthew Arnold, "The Function of Criticism at the Present Time" (1864), *The Complete Prose Works,* ed. R. H. Super, III (Ann Arbor: Univ. of Michigan Press, 1962), 263.

10. Charles A. Sainte-Beuve, "Chateaubriand" (1862), in *Pages choisies des Grands Ecrivains: Sainte-Beuve,* ed. Henri Bernès (Paris: A. Colin, 1909), p. 78; quoted by Proust in *Contre Sainte-Beuve,* p. 221. My translation.

11. *Contre Sainte-Beuve,* pp. 220–21.

12. "Chateaubriand," p. 80. Sainte-Beuve compares literary criticism to botany in this essay, p. 67.

13. "Chateaubriand," p. 74. See also "Gautier" (1863) in *Pages choisies,* p. 86.

14. In his *Nouvelle Critique ou nouvelle imposture* (Paris: J. J. Pauvert, 1965), Picard attacked Barthes's *Sur Racine* (Paris: Editions du Seuil, 1963). Barthes comments on this dispute in *Critique et vérité* (Paris: Editions du Seuil, 1966), pp. 9–22. For Barthes's analysis of "Lansonism," see "What is Criticism?" in *Critical Essays* (1964), trans. Richard Howard (Evanston: Northwestern Univ. Press, 1972), pp. 256–57.

15. Gustave Lanson, "Leçon d'ouverture du cours d'éloquence française" (1904), in *Méthodes de l'histoire littéraire,* Association des "Etudes Françaises" (Paris: Société d'édition "Les Belles Lettres," 1925), p. 18. My translation.

16. "L'esprit scientifique et la méthode de l'histoire littéraire" (1909), in *Méthodes,* p. 35.

17. Ibid., p. 34.

18. Ibid., p. 29.

19. *S/Z,* p. 206.

20. *Critique et vérité,* p. 29. See also "The Triumph and Break-up of Bourgeois Writing" in *Writing Degree Zero,* pp. 55–61.

21. *Critique et vérité,* p. 78. My translation.

22. Ibid., p. 31.

23. Ibid., p. 30. See also *Writing Degree Zero,* p. 60.

24. "The Function of Criticism," p. 270. See also "The Literary Influence of Academies" (1864), in *Complete Prose,* III, 236–41.

25. "The Study of Poetry" (1880), in *Complete Prose,* IX, 171.

26. "The Literary Influence of Academies," p. 235.

27. Ibid., p. 237.

28. Preface to *The Portrait of a Lady* (1908), in *Henry James: Literary Criticism,* ed. Leon Edel (New York: Library of America, 1984), II, 1074.

29. Preface to *The Princess Casamassima* (1908), in *Literary Criticism,* II, 1088–89.

30. "Gustave Flaubert" (1902), in *Literary Criticism,* II, 326.

31. Preface to *The Portrait of a Lady,* p. 1075.

32. Preface to *The Princess Casamassima,* p. 1091.

33. R. P. Blackmur, Introduction to *The Art of the Novel: Critical Prefaces by Henry James* (New York: Scribner's, 1946), pp. xii, xv. Blackmur contrasts James to both Joyce and Proust in this essay (p. xii).

34. Blackmur, *Art of the Novel,* p. xiii.

35. *The Great Tradition,* pp. 165–68.

36. The point appears everywhere in Leavis. For an early polemical formulation, see "The Literary Mind" in *For Continuity,* pp. 47–67.

37. "Milton's Verse," in *Revaluation* (London, 1936; rpt. Westport, Conn.: Greenwood Press, 1975), pp. 51–55.

38. "The Literary Mind," pp. 58–59.

39. "Joyce and the 'Revolution of the Word,' " in *For Continuity,* p. 197.

40. Preface to *The Spoils of Poynton* (1908), in *Literary Criticism,* II, 1138–39, 1147–48.

41. S. L. Goldberg, *The Classical Temper: A Study of James Joyce's "Ulysses"* (New York: Barnes and Noble, 1961).

42. "Writing and Speech," in *Writing Degree Zero,* p. 225.

43. *Contre Sainte-Beuve,* p. 225.

44. Ibid., p. 224.

45. "Surgery for the Novel—or a Bomb" (1923), in *Phoenix: The Posthumous Papers of D. H. Lawrence,* ed. Edward D. McDonald (1936; rpt. Viking Press, 1968), pp. 517–18.

46. Ibid., p. 520.

47. "Looking for Kellerman," in *The Man in the Machine,* p. 13.

Chapter 3

1. Preface to *The Princess Casamassima,* p. 1093.

2. Quotations in the text refer to the New York edition of *The Golden Bowl* (New York: Scribner's, 1909), whose volumes XXIII and XXIV correspond to the novel's Volumes One and Two. I use the latter volume numbers; thus (II, 236) = Volume XXIV, p. 236.

3. Leo Bersani, *A Future for Astyanax: Character and Desire in Literature* (Boston: Little, Brown, 1976), pp. 154–55.

4. R. P. Blackmur, Introduction to *The Golden Bowl* (New York: Grove Press, 1952), p. xiii.

5. See R. P. Blackmur, "The Loose and Baggy Monsters of Henry James"

(1951), rpt. in *The Lion and the Honeycomb: Essays in Solicitude and Critique* (New York: Harcourt, Brace, 1955), pp. 276–79. The brutality of James's self-division in *The Golden Bowl* is forcefully criticized by Sallie Sears in *The Negative Imagination* (Ithaca: Cornell Univ. Press, 1968), pp. 155–222.

6. A subtle analysis of the self-affirming characteristics of Charlotte's speech is given by Ruth Yeazell, *Language and Knowledge in the Late Novels of Henry James* (Chicago: Univ. of Chicago Press, 1976), pp. 4–14.

7. Richard Poirier, *The Comic Sense of Henry James* (New York: Oxford Univ. Press, 1960), pp. 124–26.

8. Ibid., p. 124; Bersani, *A Future for Astyanax,* pp. 136–38.

9. Henry James, *Notes of a Son and Brother* (New York: Scribner's, 1914), pp. 77–78, 461–65. Jean Kimball cites these passages in her identification of Charlotte as a Jamesian American type in "Henry James's Last Portrait of a Lady: Charlotte Stant in *The Golden Bowl,*" *American Literature* 28 (January 1957), 450–52.

10. Bersani, *A Future for Astyanax,* p. 132.

11. Ibid., p. 148.

12. Leavis, *The Great Tradition,* p. 160.

13. Henry James, "The Lesson of Balzac" (1905), in *Literary Criticism,* II, 131.

14. Ibid., pp. 132–33.

15. D. H. Lawrence, "A Study of Thomas Hardy," in *Phoenix,* p. 420.

16. Ruth Yeazell, *Language and Knowledge,* pp. 103, 120. Dorothea Krook emphasizes Maggie's intelligence in *The Ordeal of Consciousness in Henry James* (Cambridge, Eng.: Cambridge Univ. Press, 1962), pp. 240–324.

17. The case for an emblematic reading of the bowl (and of the whole novel) is presented by Quentin Anderson, *The American Henry James* (New Brunswick, N. J.: Rutgers Univ. Press, 1957), pp. 302–7 and *passim.*

18. Philip Weinstein, *Henry James and the Requirements of the Imagination* (Cambridge, Mass.: Harvard Univ. Press, 1971), p. 175.

19. *The Portrait of a Lady,* New York edition (New York: Scribner's, 1908), IV, 189. James praises Isabel's night vigil in the Preface to *The Portrait of a Lady, Literary Criticism,* II, 1084.

20. James develops his critical term "appreciation" in several of the prefaces. See for example the Preface to *The Princess Casamassima,* p. 1091, and the Preface to *The Spoils of Poynton,* pp. 1146–47. Yeazell (*Language and Knowledge,* pp. 111–14) also perceives, in somewhat different terms, the contrast between Maggie's "appreciation" of Charlotte and the activity of sympathetic imagination as proposed by George Eliot.

21. Preface to *The Spoils of Poynton,* p. 1139.

22. *The Portrait of a Lady,* pp. 413–14.

23. Ibid., p. 415.

24. Ibid.

25. See Laurence Holland, *The Expense of Vision* (Princeton, N.J.: Princeton Univ. Press, 1964), pp. 377–407.

Chapter 4

1. Current critical interpretation of character as ideological prejudice is summarized by Jonathan Culler, *Structuralist Poetics* (Ithaca: Cornell Univ. Press, 1975), p. 230.

2. Bersani, *A Future for Astyanax,* p. 165. Lawrence's frequently cited letter to Edward Garnett (June 5, 1914) appears in *The Letters of D. H. Lawrence,* II (1981), 182.

3. James Douglas, in *Star,* October 22, 1915; rpt. in *D. H. Lawrence: The Critical Heritage,* p. 93.

4. Ibid., p. 93.

5. Ibid., p. 94; J. C. Squire, "Books in General," *New Statesman,* November 20, 1915; rpt. in *Critical Heritage,* p. 106.

6. Helena Maria Swanwick, in *The Manchester Guardian,* October 28, 1915; rpt. in *Critical Heritage,* p. 98.

7. Bersani, *A Future for Astyanax,* p. 164.

8. Culler, *Structuralist Poetics,* p. 190.

9. Colin Clarke, *River of Dissolution* (New York: Barnes & Noble, 1969).

10. Julian Moynahan in a panel discussion, "Character as a Lost Cause," moderated by Mark Spilka, *Novel,* 11 (1978), 206. For Moynahan's emphasis on the "essential being" of Lawrence's characters in *The Rainbow,* see *The Deed of Life* (Princeton: Princeton Univ. Press, 1963), pp. 48–49.

11. Letter to Edward Garnett, January 29, 1914, in *The Letters of D. H. Lawrence,* II, 142.

12. Wilhelm Reich, *Character-Analysis* (1933), trans. Theodore P. Wolfe (New York: Farrar, Straus & Giroux, 1949), pp. 145–49.

13. Ibid., pp. 174–79. See also Anna Freud, *The Ego and the Mechanisms of Defense,* trans. Cecil Baines (New York: International Univ. Press, 1946), pp. 9, 51, 190–92.

14. T. S. Eliot's famous attack on Lawrence's incapacity for self-criticism appears in *After Strange Gods* (London: Faber and Faber, 1934), p. 539.

15. Daniel A. Weiss describes in psychoanalytic terms the pattern of neurotic anxiety manifest in Birkin's revulsion; see *Oedipus in Nottingham: D. H. Lawrence* (Seattle: Univ. of Washington Press, 1963), pp. 100–101; rpt. in *Twentieth Century Interpretations of "Women in Love,"* ed. Stephen J. Miko (Englewood, N.J.: Prentice-Hall, 1969), pp. 111–12.

16. The initial formulation of the "defensive" motive of Lawrence's theorizing in *Women in Love* was made by Middleton Murry, *Son of Woman: The Story of D. H. Lawrence* (New York: J. Cape and H. Smith, 1931), pp. 100–101.

17. "A Study of Thomas Hardy," in *Phoenix*, p. 479.

18. Lawrence's skepticism is suggestively linked to Nietzsche's by Michael Ragussis, *The Subterfuge of Art* (Baltimore: Johns Hopkins Univ. Press, 1978), pp. 2–5.

19. See Introduction to *The Dragon of the Apocalypse*, in *Phoenix*, p. 294.

20. "A Study of Thomas Hardy," in *Phoenix*, p. 479. See also "Why the Novel Matters," in *Phoenix*, pp. 535–36.

21. *Fantasia of the Unconscious* and *Psychoanalysis and the Unconscious*, ed. Philip Rieff (New York: Penguin, 1960), p. 23. F. R. Leavis observes the pertinence of *Psychoanalysis and the Unconscious* to *Women in Love* in *D. H. Lawrence: Novelist*, pp. 180–81, 189–90.

22. *Psychoanalysis and the Unconscious*, p. 40.

23. *D. H. Lawrence: Novelist*, p. 179.

24. Ragussis (*The Subterfuge of Art*, pp. 214–18) analyzes in detail the failures of speech between Gudrun and Gerald. His discussion of *Women in Love* on pp. 172–225 follows a different route to many of my own conclusions about the alliance of speech and life in the novel.

Chapter 5

1. Quotations refer by page number to *Kangaroo* (New York: Thomas Seltzer, 1923).

2. Quotations from Melville essays refer by page number to *Studies in Classic American Literature* (New York: Viking Press, 1968).

3. Quotations refer by page number to *Sea and Sardinia* and *Selections from Twilight in Italy* (New York: Doubleday, 1954).

4. Letter to Eleanor Farjeon, quoted in *D. H. Lawrence: A Composite Biography*, ed. Edward Nehls (Madison: Univ. of Wisconsin Press, 1957–59), II, 55.

5. Hugh Kenner, *The Pound Era* (Berkeley: Univ. of California Press, 1971), p. 48.

6. See F. R. Leavis, *D. H. Lawrence: Novelist*, pp. 66–74, and Julian Moynahan, *The Deed of Life*, pp. 104–14.

7. Henry James, *Italian Hours* (Boston: Houghton Mifflin, 1909), pp. 165–66.

8. Paul Fussell, although appreciating the comic exuberance of *Sea and Sardinia*, simplifies the esthetic character of its freedom when he describes the book as a celebration of "sheer kinesis." See *Abroad: Literary Traveling between the Wars* (New York: Oxford Univ. Press, 1980), p. 158.

9. F. R. Leavis discusses Lawrence's contemptuous image of "being an artist" in *D. H. Lawrence: Novelist*, pp. 373–81.

10. Quotations refer by page number to *St. Mawr* and *The Man Who Died* (New York: Vintage Books, 1953).

11. Lawrence plays on the same colloquial idiom in the title to Chapter 9 in *Kangaroo*: "Harriet and Lovatt at Sea in Marriage."

12. Stuart P. Sherman in *New York Herald Tribune Books,* June 14, 1925; rpt. in *D. H. Lawrence: The Critical Heritage,* p. 256.

13. F. R. Leavis, *D. H. Lawrence: Novelist,* p. 305.

14. Monroe Engel, "The Continuity of Lawrence's Short Novels," rpt. in *D. H. Lawrence: A Collection of Critical Essays,* ed. Mark Spilka (Englewood, N.J.: Prentice-Hall, 1963), p. 99.

15. Ibid., p. 98.

16. Leavis, *D. H. Lawrence: Novelist,* pp. 238, 231.

17. Introduction to *The Dragon of the Apocalypse,* in *Phoenix,* p. 297.

18. Ibid., p. 301.

19. Ibid.

20. Ibid., p. 299.

21. "Morality and the Novel," in *Phoenix,* p. 527.

22. "Why the Novel Matters," in *Phoenix,* p. 536.

23. "The Spirit of Place," in *Studies in Classic American Literature,* p. 6.

Chapter 6

1. Quotations refer by page number to *A Portrait of the Artist as a Young Man* (New York: Penguin Books, 1976).

2. The same line (and the two following) from Nashe's "A Litany in Time of Plague" are quoted by Yeats to exemplify "an emotion which cannot be evoked by any other arrangement of colours and sounds and forms." See W. B. Yeats, "The Symbolism of Poetry" (1900), in *Essays and Introductions* (New York: Macmillan, 1961), p. 156.

3. *Dubliners* (New York: Viking Press, 1962), p. 117.

4. See Preface, *James Joyce: New Perspectives,* ed. Colin McCabe (Bloomington: Indiana Univ. Press, 1982), pp. xi–xii and, in this collection, Patrick Parrinder, "The Strange Necessity: James Joyce's Rejection in England (1914–30)," pp. 151–67. Parrinder distinguishes English from less culture-bound American reactions. Objections to the entire Anglo-American assimilation of Joyce motivates the collection *Poststructuralist Joyce: Essays from the French,* ed. Derek Attridge and Daniel Ferrer (Cambridge, Eng.: Cambridge Univ. Press, 1984).

5. See Richard Ellmann, *James Joyce,* pp. 434–57, 511–23, 655, 678.

6. Parrinder, "The Strange Necessity," p. 165.

7. Ronald Hayman, *Leavis* (London: Heinemann, 1976), p. 8.

8. Leavis's later, harsher judgment of Joyce must be understood in the context of his public battle on behalf of D. H. Lawrence, especially after T. S. Eliot's scorning of Joyce as "the most ethically orthodox of our eminent writers" in *After Strange Gods,* p. 41. Leavis recapitulates his whole quarrel with Eliot over Lawrence and Joyce in *D. H. Lawrence: Novelist,* pp. 4–8, 382–93.

9. Preface, *Poststructuralist Joyce,* p. ix; "Introduction: Highly continental evenements," p. 10.

10. Stephen Heath, "Ambiviolences: Notes for Reading Joyce," in *Poststructuralist Joyce*, p. 39; André Topia, "The Matrix and the Echo: Intertextuality in *Ulysses*," in *Poststructuralist Joyce*, p. 116.

11. "Introduction," *Poststructuralist Joyce*, p. 11.

12. Ibid.

13. Edmund Wilson, *Axel's Castle* (New York: Scribner's, 1931), pp. 191–225. Hugh Kenner's definitions of the values affirmed in *Ulysses* have shifted in his successive books, but he has consistently sought to define values. See his *Dublin's Joyce* (1955); *The Stoic Comedians: Flaubert, Joyce, and Beckett* (Boston: Beacon Press, 1962); *Joyce's Voices* (Berkeley: Univ. of California Press, 1978); *Ulysses*, Unwin Critical Library (London: Allen and Unwin, 1980).

14. "Introduction," *Poststructuralist Joyce*, pp. 5, 10.

15. Topia, "Intertextuality in *Ulysses*," pp. 107, 116.

16. *Dublin's Joyce*, p. 10.

17. Eugene Jolas, "The Revolution of Language and James Joyce," in *Our exagmination round his factification for incamination of Work in progress* (Paris: Shakespeare and Co., 1929), pp. 77–92. Jolas's comparisons of Joyce to Shakespeare are cited by Leavis in "Joyce and 'The Revolution of the Word,' " in *For Continuity*, pp. 207–19.

18. Leavis, "Joyce and 'The Revolution of the Word,' " p. 208.

19. Ibid., p. 209.

20. *The Classical Temper*, pp. 16–17.

21. "The Philosophy of Shelley's Poetry," in *Essays and Introductions*, p. 79.

22. Ibid., p. 75. The allusion is to *Prometheus Unbound*, II.ii.139.

23. "The Symbolism of Poetry," p. 156.

24. *Oxford Book of Modern Verse: 1892–1935*, ed. W. B. Yeats (Oxford: Clarendon Press, 1936). In his introduction (p. viii) Yeats explains that he begins with the Pater fragment because it "was a passage which dominated a generation." Kenner comments on Pater's "vampire" in relation to both Yeats and Pound in *The Pound Era*, p. 28.

25. Kenner, *The Pound Era*, pp. 51, 85–91, 126.

26. The connection between literary quotation and cliché is suggestively noted by Jennifer Schiffer Levine, "Originality and Repetition in *Finnegans Wake* and *Ulysses*," *PMLA* 94 (1979), 114.

27. S. L. Goldberg, *The Classical Temper*, pp. 30, 279; *Joyce* (Edinburgh and London: Oliver and Boyd, 1962), p. 89.

28. *Notes for Joyce: An Annotation of James Joyce's Ulysses*, ed. Don Gifford with Robert J. Seidman (New York: E. P. Dutton, 1974), pp. 67–68.

29. *Joyce's Voices*, pp. 28–33.

30. The psychological depth supposedly revealed in the stream of consciousness dominated many Joyce studies in the 1940s and 1950s. See Frederick J.

Hoffman, "Infroyce," in *Freudianism and the Literary Mind* (1945), rpt. in *James Joyce: Two Decades of Criticism,* ed. Seon Givens (New York: Vanguard Press, 1948); Robert Humphrey, *Stream of Consciousness in the Modern Novel* (Berkeley: Univ. of California Press, 1954); Melvin Friedman, *Stream of Consciousness: A Study in Literary Method* (New Haven: Yale Univ. Press, 1955); Leon Edel, *The Modern Psychological Novel* (New York: Grosset and Dunlap, 1955).

31. Freudian theory is used by Sheldon Brivic to reconstruct unconscious patterns of projection in relation to father figures in Joyce. See "James Joyce: from Stephen to Bloom," in *Psychoanalysis and Literary Process* (Cambridge: Harvard Univ. Press, 1970), pp. 118–62.

32. Topia, "Intertextuality in *Ulysses,*" p. 112.

33. Joseph Frank, *The Widening Gyre: Crisis and Mastery in Modern Literature* (New Brunswick, N.J.: Rutgers Univ. Press, 1963), pp. 16, 51–60.

34. Dorritt Cohn, *Transparent Minds* (Princeton, N.J.: Princeton Univ. Press, 1978), pp. 56, 76–88.

35. "The Symbolism of Poetry," pp. 156–57.

36. Michael Groden, *"Ulysses" in Progress* (Princeton: Princeton Univ. Press, 1977), pp. 26–27.

37. *Notes for Joyce,* ed. Gifford and Seidman, p. 13.

38. Groden, *"Ulysses" in Progress,* p. 199.

39. *The Classical Temper,* pp. 138–42, 281–90.

40. Letter of June 10, 1919, in *Pound / Joyce: The Letters of Ezra Pound to James Joyce,* ed. Forrest Read (New York: New Directions, 1967), p. 157; cited by Ellmann, *James Joyce,* p. 473.

41. Frank Budgen, *James Joyce and the Making of "Ulysses"* (New York: Smith and Haas, 1934), p. 105; cited by Ellmann, *James Joyce,* p. 473.

42. Freud develops the concept of repression in many key papers, beginning with "Studies in Hysteria" (1893–95). See especially "Repression" (1915) in *Complete Psychological Works,* ed. James Strachey, XIV (London: Hogarth Press, 1957), 143–48. The distinction between repression and other psychological defenses is elaborated by Freud in "Inhibitions, Symptoms, and Anxiety" (1926), and the meaning of the distinction is extended in ways especially pertinent to the interior monologues in *Ulysses* by Anna Freud, *The Ego and the Mechanism of Defense.*

43. Hugh Kenner, "Circe," in *James Joyce's "Ulysses,"* ed. Clive Hart and David Hayman (Berkeley: Univ. of California Press, 1974), pp. 356, 360. Bloom's "purgation" is stressed also by Ellmann, *James Joyce,* p. 381, and by Goldberg, *The Classical Temper,* pp. 166, 180.

44. Ellmann, *James Joyce,* p. 641.

45. The Christmas pantomimes and other popular comic models for Joyce are suggestively presented by David Hayman, "Forms of Folly in Joyce: A Case Study of Clowning in *Ulysses,*" *ELH,* 34 (1967), 260–83.

46. Henri Bergson, *Laughter: An Essay on the Meaning of the Comic,* trans. Cloudesley Brereton and Fred Rothwell (London: Macmillan, 1911), pp. 18, 29, 57.

47. Ibid., p. 160.

48. Ellmann, *James Joyce,* pp. 480–83.

49. Joyce's conversion of Bloom's "secrets" into a device for social satire is astutely analyzed by Marilyn French in *The Book as World* (Cambridge, Mass.: Harvard Univ. Press, 1976), pp. 185–206.

50. Freud, "Jokes and Their Relation to the Unconscious," *Complete Psychological Works,* VIII, 222.

51. Ellmann, *James Joyce,* p. 518.

52. Ibid., p. 381; Goldberg, *The Classical Temper,* p. 128.

53. While discarding the idea of Bloom's "purgation," Marilyn French still attributes a heroic ordeal of psychological self-confrontation to the reader in *The Book as World,* pp. 205–06.

54. Joyce wrote "Eumaeus" while "Circe" was being typed. The paired quality of the two chapters is noted by A. Walton Litz, *The Art of James Joyce* (London: Oxford Univ. Press, 1961), p. 4, and by Groden, *"Ulysses" in Progress,* pp. 52–53.

55. *Axel's Castle,* p. 26.

56. Arnold Goldman, *The Joyce Paradox* (Evanston, Ill.: Northwestern Univ. Press, 1966), p. 104.

57. See Litz, *The Art of James Joyce,* pp. 20, 45; Goldberg, *The Classical Temper,* p. 291; Robert Adams, *James Joyce: Common Sense and Beyond* (New York: Random House, 1966), p. 162; Gerald Bruns, "Eumaeus," in *James Joyce's "Ulysses,"* ed. Hart and Hayman, pp. 363–83; Marilyn French, *The Book as World,* pp. 212–18; Karen Lawrence, *The Odyssey of Style in "Ulysses"* (Princeton, N.J.: Princeton Univ. Press, 1981), pp. 168–79. Hugh Kenner stands against general opinion when he praises the "energy" and "exquisite absurdity" of the chapter's style in *Dublin's Joyce,* p. 260.

58. *Stephen Hero,* p. 211.

59. *The Classical Temper,* p. 291.

60. *The Country and the City,* p. 245. See also Kenner, *Dublin's Joyce,* p. 135.

61. Murphy is identified as archetypal storyteller by James Maddox, *Joyce's "Ulysses" and the Assault upon Character* (New Brunswick, N.J.: Rutgers Univ. Press, 1978), p. 160.

62. Ibid., pp. 158–59.

63. The different tone and import of the social irony in *Dubliners* and *Ulysses* is finely articulated by Anthony Cronin, "The Advent of Bloom" (1966), in *Joyce: A Collection of Critical Essays,* ed. William M. Chace, Twentieth-century Views (Englewood Cliffs, N.J.: Prentice-Hall, 1974), pp. 90–94, 99–101.

64. Anticipation of Beckett in the style of "Eumaeus" is noted by Maddox, *Joyce's "Ulysses,"* p. 156.

Chapter 7

1. Deirdre Bair, *Samuel Beckett,* p. 368.

2. Samuel Beckett, *Proust* (New York: Grove Press, 1931), pp. 47–48.

3. For a description of Beckett's negotiations with French publishers during this period, see Bair, *Samuel Beckett,* pp. 358–64, 406–9.

4. Bair, p. 368. The friend was Marie Péron.

4. Page references to the French versions of *Molloy, Malone meurt,* and *L'Innommable* refer to the volumes published by Editions de Minuit (Paris, 1951, 1952, 1953). Page references to the English translations of the trilogy refer to *Molloy,* trans. Patrick Bowles in collaboration with Samuel Beckett, and *Malone Dies* and *The Unnamable,* trans. Samuel Beckett, in *Three Novels* (New York: Grove Press, 1958).

6. Dates of composition and translation: *Molloy:* French, 1948; English, 1953. *Malone meurt / Malone Dies:* French, 1948; English, 1956. *L'Innommable / The Unnamable:* French, 1950; English, 1958.

7. René Descartes, *Discours sur la méthode,* in *Oeuvres philosophiques,* ed. Ferdinand Alquié, Classiques Garnier (Paris: Garnier, 1963), I, 568. The passage from Descartes is cited, for example, in the dictionaries edited by E. Littré (1882) and Paul Robert (1964). The importance of Descartes to Beckett's trilogy is emphasized by Hugh Kenner, *Samuel Beckett: A Critical Study* (London: John Calder, 1961), pp. 17, 80–83, 117–21, and passim.

8. Hugh Kenner writes astutely about the losses of Beckett's translation of *Fin de partie* into the English of *Endgame* in *Samuel Beckett,* pp. 94–96. Earlier in this book Kenner oddly understates the distinctions between the French and English of the trilogy: "the English translations, mostly the author's own, are very close. The comedy . . . is prior to action and more fundamental than language" (p. 16).

9. See Bair, *Samuel Beckett,* pp. 438–39.

10. Leo Bersani, "Theory and Violence," *Raritan Quarterly* (Summer 1983), p. 56.

11. I am indebted to Hugh Kenner's suggestive and witty comments on Beckett's interest in bicycles and other machines, *Beckett,* pp. 117–28.

12. *Proust,* p. 7. I am grateful to Rachel Jacoff for help with Leopardi's Italian here, and to Leo Bersani for conversation about the French and English versions of this whole passage.

13. The Wordsworthian echoes in *Molloy* are noted by Kenner, *Beckett,* pp. 178–81.

14. Margery Sabin, *English Romanticism and the French Tradition* (Cambridge, Mass.: Harvard Univ. Press, 1976), pp. 18–19, 105, 258–59.

15. "Two Fragments" of self-translation by Beckett—a passage from *Molloy* and the opening paragraph of *Malone meurt*—appeared in *transition*, no. 6 (1950), pp. 103–6.

16. *Proust*, p. 8.

17. Ruby Cohn, for example, refers to the "forest of abstraction" in *The Unnamable* in *Back to Beckett* (Princeton, N.J.: Princeton Univ. Press, 1973), p. 109.

18. Bair, *Samuel Beckett*, p. 491.

Index